Regulatory Challenges of AI Governance in the Era of ChatGPT

Regulatory Challenges of AI Governance in the Era of ChatGPT

Md. Toriqul Islam

Wolters Kluwer

Published by:
Kluwer Law International B.V.
PO Box 316
2400 AH Alphen aan den Rijn
The Netherlands
E-mail: lrs-sales@wolterskluwer.com
Website: www.wolterskluwer.com/en/solutions/kluwerlawinternational

Sold and distributed by:
Wolters Kluwer Legal & Regulatory U.S.
920 Links Avenue
Landisville, PA 17538
United States of America
E-mail: customer.service@wolterskluwer.com

ISBN 978-94-035-3347-6

e-Book: ISBN 978-94-035-3357-5
web-PDF: ISBN 978-94-035-3367-4

In loving memory of my beloved parents, ***Ayesha Begum*** *and* ***Md. Abdul Gofur Malita****, whose unconditional love, unwavering belief in me, and selfless sacrifices have shaped who I am today. Their boundless support and inspiration continue to guide me throughout my life. This work stands as a testament to their devotion and a tribute to the lasting legacy they have left in my heart.*

About the Author

Md. Toriqul Islam has been serving as an Assistant Professor at the School of Law, Independent University, Bangladesh (IUB), since January 2024. Previously, Dr Islam served as an Assistant Professor of Law (2012–2017) and Chairman of the Law Department (2014–2017) at the Bangladesh University of Business and Technology (BUBT). He also worked as a Senior Lecturer and Programme Coordinator at Green University Bangladesh (2010–2012) and as a Lecturer (and later, Head in Charge) at the International Islamic University Chittagong (IIUC, Dhaka Campus) (2007–2010). Additionally, Dr Islam served as the Data Protection Officer (DPO) at Transparency International Bangladesh (TIB) from November 2022 to January 2024.

Dr Islam received his PhD in Data Protection Law from the Faculty of Law at the University of Malaya, Malaysia, in 2021. He completed his Bachelor of Laws and Master of Laws at the Faculty of Law at the Islamic University, Bangladesh, in 2005 and 2006, respectively. His areas of expertise include data protection law, privacy law, cybersecurity law, and the interplay between law and emerging technologies.

With an extensive publication record in Web of Science (WoS) and Scopus-indexed peer-reviewed journals, Dr Islam has actively contributed to legal scholarship in law and technology. He has delivered lectures at numerous national and international conferences. He received the Best Poster Presentation Award for his paper 'Ethical, Social, and Legal Challenges of Robotics' at the 2018 Asian Universities Alliance Postgraduate Academic Forum, organised by Tsinghua University, China.

Dr Islam serves on the editorial boards of two Indonesian academic journals: the Indonesian Journal of Law and Society and the Lampung Journal of International Law. He has also reviewed academic papers for numerous prestigious peer-reviewed journals, including International Data Privacy Law (Oxford University Journal), Asian Journal of International Law (Melbourne University Journal), Open Research Europe (F1000 Research Ltd, UK), Utrecht Law Review (Utrecht University Journal, Netherlands), Cogent Social Science (Routledge, UK), F1000 Research (Routledge, UK), the International Journal of Information Security and Privacy (IGI Global, USA), and the Dhaka University Law Journal (Dhaka, Bangladesh).

Dr Islam has provided consultancy services twice to the European Union Delegation in Dhaka, Bangladesh, focusing on the theme of 'Comparative Analysis between the European Union (EU) General Data Protection Regulation (GDPR) and the Data Protection Act 2022 (Draft), Bangladesh', under Contract No. NDICI ASIA 2022/453-834. As a leading expert in Data Protection Law in Bangladesh, Dr Islam actively contributed to the development phase of the Draft Personal Data Protection Bill 2023 of Bangladesh through five extensive submissions: two in support of the EU Dhaka Delegation, two for TIB, and one in a personal capacity. Dr Md. Toriqul Islam can be reached at toriqul@iub.edu.bd or toriqul.um.law@gmail.com.

Table of Contents

List of Abbreviations

ACIP	Advisory Council on Intellectual Property
AI	Artificial Intelligence
AI Act	Artificial Intelligence Act
AI RMF	AI Risk Management Framework
AI4ALL	Artificial Intelligence for All
AIA	Algorithmic Impact Assessment
AIGA	AI Governance Alliance
AIIA	AI Impact Assessment
AISI	AI Safety Institute
ALRC	Australian Law Reform Commission
API	Application Programming Interface
CAC	Cyberspace Administration of China
CCPA	California Consumer Privacy Act
CDPA	Copyright, Designs and Patents Act 1988
CNIPA	China National Intellectual Property Administration
CNN	Convolutional Neural Network
DPO	Data Protection Officer
EDPB	European Data Protection Board
EIAs	Ethical Impact Assessments
EPC	European Patent Convention
EPO	European Patent Office
EU	European Union
FAIR	Findable, Accessible, Interoperable, and Reusable
FCA	Financial Conduct Authority

FG-AI4H	Focus Group on Artificial Intelligence for Health
GAI	Generative AI
GDPR	General Data Protection Regulation
GPAI	Global Partnership on Artificial Intelligence
GPT	Generative Pre-trained Transformer
HAI	Human-Centred AI Institute
HE	Homomorphic Encryption
HIC	Human-in-Command
HIPAA	Health Insurance Portability and Accountability Act of 1996
HITL	Human-in-the-Loop
HOTL	Human-on-the-Loop
IBM	International Business Machines Corporation
ICO	Information Commissioner's Office
IEEE	Institute of Electrical and Electronics Engineers
IMIA	International Medical Informatics Association
IP	Intellectual Property
ISMS	Information Security Management System
ISO	International Organization for Standardization
IT	Information Technology
ITI	Information Technology Industry Council
ITU	International Telecommunication Union
LLM	Large Language Model
M&E	Monitoring and Evaluation
MIIT	Ministry of Industry and Information Technology
ML	Machine Learning
NASEM	National Academies of Sciences, Engineering, and Medicine
NIST	National Institute of Standards and Technology
NLG	Natural Language Generation
NLP	Natural Language Processing
NYT	New York Times
OECD	Organisation for Economic Co-operation and Development
PDPC	Personal Data Protection Commission
PETs	Privacy-Enhancing Technologies
PIA	Privacy Impact Assessment
PII	Personally Identifiable Information
PIPC	Personal Information Protection Commission
R&D	Research and Development

RAI	Responsible AI
RIA	Regulatory Impact Assessment
RLHF	Reinforcement Learning from Human Feedback
SCP	Standing Committee on the Law of Patents
SMPC	Secure Multi-Party Computation
SSE	Strong Storage Encryption
TDM	Text and Data Mining
TEEs	Trusted Execution Environments
TIB	Transparency International Bangladesh
UAE	United Arab Emirates
UK	United Kingdom
UKIPO	UK Intellectual Property Office
UN	United Nations
UNESCO	United Nations Educational, Scientific and Cultural Organization
US	United States
USAISI	US Artificial Intelligence Safety Institute
USPTO	US Patent and Trademark Office
WEF	World Economic Forum
WHO	World Health Organization
WIPO	World Intellectual Property Organization
XAI	Explainable AI

List of Figures

List of Tables

Foreword

In the digital age, artificial intelligence (AI) has emerged as a powerful force for both innovation and societal transformation. Notably, the rise of large language models (LLMs) like ChatGPT has gained prominence for their remarkable ability to generate human-like text, reshaping industries and prompting essential discourse about AI governance, ethics, and regulation. As these technologies evolve at an unprecedented pace, the need for robust and effective governance frameworks becomes increasingly urgent.

The book, *Regulatory Challenges of AI Governance in the Era of ChatGPT*, written by Dr Md. Toriqul Islam, Assistant Professor, School of Law, Independent University, Bangladesh (IUB), offers a comprehensive framework for understanding the contemporary landscape of AI regulation, addressing the critical challenges that lie ahead, and exploring potential policy directions.

Through eleven meticulously researched chapters, this book provides a nuanced understanding of AI's historical evolution and explores misconceptions surrounding these technologies. It examines the transformative potential of LLMs like ChatGPT across industries, addresses legitimate socio-ethical concerns, and delves into the legal and regulatory challenges associated with LLMs, covering areas such as intellectual property (IP) rights, healthcare systems, financial sectors, and cross-border regulatory challenges in AI governance.

This book goes beyond merely diagnosing problems; it prescribes well-grounded policy options based on core ethical principles and a human-centric perspective. Emphasising transparency, human oversight, and explainability, it advocates for a risk-based approach to regulation. The book also suggests additional policy measures, such as algorithmic impact assessments, a sectoral approach for industry-specific regulations, and the use of regulatory sandboxes to create controlled environments for testing and innovation.

Furthermore, the book emphasises public participation to ensure inclusive policymaking on AI, promoting a knowledge-based society. It calls for a well-harmonised, agile regulatory framework, supported by ongoing monitoring, upskilling, and strong enforcement mechanisms – essential elements for fostering responsible AI

(RAI) development in the face of rapid technological advancement. Additionally, it underscores the need for investment in research and development to strengthen regulatory capabilities, fostering an ecosystem that supports the ethical, accountable, and beneficial deployment of AI technologies.

By offering concrete policy directions and regulatory approaches, this book serves as an invaluable resource for policymakers, legal professionals, academics, students, technologists, and anyone seeking to navigate the complex landscape of AI governance. It is my sincere hope that this book will contribute meaningfully to this crucial discourse, fostering a future where AI is developed and deployed responsibly, ethically, and for the benefit of humanity.

Associate Professor Pardis M Tehrani
Head of the Law School
Faculty of Education, Society and Creative Industries, University of Sunderland

Overview

The book, *Regulatory Challenges of AI Governance in the Era of ChatGPT*, provides a foundational framework for understanding the contemporary landscape of AI governance, including associated challenges and policy directions, across eleven chapters.

Chapter 1, 'AI Governance in the ChatGPT Era', offers a comprehensive overview of the history of AI, defines ChatGPT, explains its mechanics and emphasises the growing importance of AI governance in light of the rapid expansion of large language models (LLMs) across diverse industries.

Chapter 2, 'Misconception about LLMs like ChatGPT', handles widespread public misconceptions surrounding ChatGPT. These misconceptions often focus on job displacement fears and the false belief that AI can fully replace human workers or solve all problems. The chapter proposes strategies to address these misunderstandings, advocating for educational principles, transparency in development, RAI practices, and collaboration among stakeholders to ensure a nuanced public understanding of ChatGPT and similar language models.

Chapter 3, 'Transformative Impacts of LLMs like ChatGPT', investigates the multifaceted influence of these AI tools across various industries. It examines how ChatGPT and its counterparts have streamlined processes and expanded possibilities within sectors like education, employment, healthcare, business, information technology (IT), journalism, and media, ultimately contributing to the reshaping of our world.

Chapter 4, 'Societal and Ethical Implications of ChatGPT', delves into the multifaceted concerns surrounding this AI language model. Examining both ethical considerations (e.g., misinformation, accountability, and transparency issues) and societal implications (e.g., job displacement, critical thinking skills, and malicious use), this chapter lays the groundwork for a deeper analysis of ChatGPT's transformative influence on our digital landscape.

Chapter 5, 'Data Privacy Challenges in LLMs Like ChatGPT', explores the critical privacy concerns surrounding LLMs like ChatGPT. It proposes a multifaceted approach to address these concerns, combining ethical considerations, legal frameworks, and technical solutions.

Chapter 6, 'LLMs like ChatGPT and Intellectual Property', addresses the complex IP challenges presented by LLMs like ChatGPT. This chapter identifies significant gaps in existing legal frameworks and explores potential policy directions to bridge these gaps.

Chapter 7 delves into 'ChatGPT and Healthcare Systems', the regulatory landscape surrounding LLMs like ChatGPT within the healthcare sector. It focuses on two key areas: (a) the specific regulatory challenges posed by LLMs in healthcare applications, and (b) the development of regulations that ensure safety, privacy, and ethical considerations are prioritised in this domain.

Chapter 8, 'LLMs like ChatGPT and the Financial Sector', investigates the complex interplay between LLMs and finance. This chapter explores the exciting possibilities and pressing challenges that LLMs pose in this sensitive field. Through in-depth analysis, it aims to illuminate the future role of LLMs in finance, promoting responsible and ethical integration that fosters innovation while protecting trust and security.

Chapter 9, 'Legal and Regulatory Challenges in AI Governance', explores the difficulties that current legal frameworks face in regulating LLMs like ChatGPT. These challenges include a lack of transparency in AI decision-making, data privacy concerns, and potential infringements on copyright and patent rights. The chapter also proposes suitable policy solutions to address these governance challenges, such as disseminating education and awareness Programmes, promoting global cooperation, adopting AI-specific laws and policies, and ensuring adherence to RAI principles.

Chapter 10, 'Cross-Border Regulatory Challenges in AI Governance', discusses the intricate challenges of governing AI in a globalised world. These challenges include the lack of a common definition and understanding of AI, the need for global consensus and coordination, the absence of adequate and effective mechanisms and institutions, and the difficulty in establishing standardised regulations across jurisdictions. Additionally, privacy and data protection issues, as well as transparency and accountability in AI systems, are significant concerns. The chapter also focuses on international collaborations, harmonised standards, and regulatory approaches to address these AI governance challenges.

Chapter 11, titled 'Future Policy Directions for AI Governance', demonstrates emerging trends in LLM governance. It delves into critical areas like the integration of LLMs into various systems, data governance practices for RAI development, and the ethical considerations surrounding AI deployment. The chapter also analyses potential future challenges in AI governance and proposes valuable recommendations for crafting effective and adaptable regulatory frameworks for AI.

Acknowledgements

I extend my sincere gratitude to the Almighty Allah for granting me the strength and perseverance to navigate the challenges inherent in the solitary journey of writing a sole-authored book. My heartfelt thanks go to my family, friends, colleagues, students, and well-wishers for their continuous encouragement, support, and love.

I am deeply indebted to Mr Simon Bellamy and his team at Wolters Kluwer International, Netherlands, for their initial evaluation, subsequent acceptance of my book proposal, contract signing, and diligent efforts throughout the publication process.

I acknowledge the contributions of all my teachers, from primary school to university, whose collective efforts have shaped my academic journey. I am especially grateful to my PhD supervisor, who taught me a great deal about academic writing during my doctoral studies and was the first person to inform me about the reputation of Wolters Kluwer International as a leading legal research publisher in the world.

I remember my late parents with deep emotion as they dedicated their lives to raising me and my siblings and ensuring our success. Their boundless love and support continue to inspire me and provide strength during difficult times. I also fondly remember my late mother-in-law for her genuine love and care and express my deep respect for my father-in-law for his continued support and interest in my work.

I am profoundly grateful to my wife, *Nargis Jannat (Shefa)*, for her unwavering support, for managing household affairs and for allowing me the time and focus necessary to complete this work. I also wish to mention my son, *Aryan Anjum (Kabya)*, whose presence has been a constant source of joy and motivation, especially during challenging times.

Finally, I wish to thank the team at Wolters Kluwer International once again for their professional handling of the publication process. I extend my heartfelt gratitude to all who have contributed to this journey in any form. May Almighty bless you all.

CHAPTER 1

AI Governance in the ChatGPT Era

1.1 INTRODUCTION

In the era of ubiquitous computing, when advanced language models like ChatGPT demonstrate unprecedented potential across diverse fields and sectors, governing artificial intelligence (AI) becomes paramount. AI refers to the science and engineering of designing intelligent machines, a term coined by John McCarthy in 1955.[1] It encompasses the field of computer science dedicated to developing computing machines and systems capable of mimicking human learning and decision-making processes. By enabling machines to perform complex tasks resembling human capabilities, AI has the potential to drive significant advancements in various fields, including healthcare, transportation, education, finance, and more.[2]

In a groundbreaking moment that would reshape the landscape of AI and ignite global conversations about the future of human-machine interaction, OpenAI developed and launched the AI chatbot ChatGPT in November 2022. It leverages OpenAI's Large Language Models (LLMs), primarily GPT-3.5, with some access to GPT-4 in the paid version.[3] Soon after its release, ChatGPT gained widespread popularity on social media as users enthusiastically disseminated examples of its credentials (*see* Table 1.1). The shared stories and samples showcased myriad tasks, including travel planning, creative writing like fables, and even coding computer programs. Within five days, the chatbot attracted an impressive user base of over 1 million individuals.[4]

1. Christopher Manning, *Artificial Intelligence Definitions, Stanford University Human-Centered AI Institute* (HAI) (September 2020), https://hai.stanford.edu/sites/default/files/2020-09/AI-Definitions-HAI.pdf.
2. Zara Abrams, *The Promise and Challenges of AI*, American Psychological Association (1 Nov. 2021), https://www.apa.org/monitor/2021/11/cover-artificial-intelligence.
3. Bernard Marr, *A Short History of ChatGPT: How We Got to Where We Are Today*, Forbes (19 May 2023), https://www.forbes.com/sites/bernardmarr/2023/05/19/a-short-history-of-chatgpt-how-we-got-to-where-we-are-today/?sh=430a8f8e674f#The%20Genesis%20of%20Chatgpt.
4. *Ibid.*

Accordingly, ChatGPT has emerged as one of the fastest-growing services, outpacing many popular online platforms like Facebook, Instagram, Twitter, Netflix, and more.

Table 1.1 Fastest-Growing Online Platforms

Online Service	*Launch Year*	*Time Taken to Reach 1 Million Users*
Threads	2023	1 hour
ChatGPT	2022	5 days
Instagram	2010	2.5 months
Spotify	2008	5 months
Dropbox	2008	7 months
Facebook	2004	10 months
Foursquare	2009	13 months
Twitter	2006	2 years
Airbnb	2008	2.5 years
Kickstarter	2009	2.5 years
Netflix	1999	3.5 years

Source: Katharina Buchholz, *1 Million Users: Threads Shoots Past 1 Million User Mark at Lightning Speed* (7 Jul. 2023), https://www.statista.com/chart/29174/time-to-one-million-users/.

The increasing integration of LLMs like ChatGPT into human interactions and their influence on decision-making processes raise significant ethical and social concerns across various sectors. These concerns include the impact on employment conditions, the education system, privacy and data protection, intellectual property (IP), healthcare, the financial sector, and cross-border AI governance.

Against this backdrop, establishing a responsible AI (RAI) ecosystem worldwide has become fundamentally crucial. Recognising this urgency, a survey conducted in mid-2024 revealed that approximately 80% of organisations plan to allocate at least 10% of their AI budgets to comply with regulatory requirements. Furthermore, 95% of business leaders anticipate that the newly enacted European Union (EU) AI regulations will impact their operations. Despite this recognition of the need for RAI, only 2% of companies have fully integrated these practices as of July 2024. Hopefully, there is a commitment to improvement, with 31% aiming to achieve full integration within the next 18 months.[5]

Moreover, effective AI governance plays a crucial role in dispelling public misconceptions surrounding ChatGPT and similar advanced AI technologies, thereby building trust and promoting responsible adoption across various sectors. Accenture's 2022 Tech Vision research underscores this need, revealing that only 35% of global consumers trust how organisations are deploying AI, while 77% believe organisations

5. Accenture, *Make Responsible AI Pervasive and Systematic in the Enterprise* (2024), https://www.accenture.com/nz-en/services/data-ai/responsible-ai.

should be held accountable for any misuse of AI.[6] In the above context, this chapter delves into several key issues: the history of AI, the functionality and meaning of ChatGPT, the broader implications of LLMs across industries, and the crucial role of AI governance. The chapter ends with a precise conclusion.

1.2 HISTORY OF AI

The history of AI is a tale of ideas, ambitions, innovations, setbacks, breakthroughs, and rapid advancements. It is a fascinating journey that stretches back centuries, weaving together elements of philosophy, mathematics, computer science, and even mythology. While the field has seen its share of ambition, setbacks, and breakthroughs, here is a glimpse into some key milestones and influential figures that have shaped AI into what it is today. This overview highlights major events but acknowledges the vastness of the field's rich tapestry, which cannot be entirely covered by this book.

1.2.1 Early Conceptions and Foundations

The conceptual origins of AI can be traced back to ancient mythologies that explored the notion of synthetic beings endowed with intelligence, exemplified by narratives such as Pygmalion's Galatea in Greek mythology.[7] However, the philosophical underpinnings of AI find more substantive roots in the works of classical thinkers like Aristotle (384–322 BCE), whose investigations into the nature of thought and intelligence significantly contributed to the conceptual foundations of AI.[8]

Aristotle's development of the first formal system of logic and his invention of syllogisms provided a cornerstone for contemporary formal logic and deductive reasoning. While a significant gap exists between Aristotle's era and the emergence of AI as a distinct field, his philosophical concepts and methods were rediscovered and reinterpreted in the 20th century. This rediscovery significantly influenced the development of symbolic reasoning and logic in early AI research. Nevertheless, modern AI systems rely heavily on algorithms to process information, make inferences, and draw conclusions. These algorithms often utilise a logical framework greatly influenced by Aristotle's work.[9] Therefore, Aristotle's ideas provided the basis for building computational models of reasoning, a core capability upon which contemporary AI is built.

6. Accenture, *Accenture Technology Vision 2022: 'Metaverse Continuum' Redefining How the World Works, Operates and Interacts* (16 Mar. 2022), https://newsroom.accenture.com/news/2022/accenture-technology-vision-2022-metaverse-continuum-redefining-how-the-world-works-operates-and-interacts.
7. Etienne-Maurice Falconet, *Pygmalion and Galatea*, https://art.thewalters.org/detail/17579/pygmalion-and-galatea/.
8. https://doi.org/10.1016/bs.host.2020.01.002.
9. Selmer Bringsjord & Konstantine Arkoudas, *The Philosophical Foundations of Artificial Intelligence* (2007), https://people.csail.mit.edu/kostas/papers/ai.pdf; Antonio Panovski, *How Did Philosophy Help Develop Artificial Intelligence?*, The Collector (2023), https://www.thecollector.com/philosophy-artificial-intelligence-development/.

In essence, the development of AI has been demonstrably influenced by a multitude of scholars. The logical and mathematical frameworks established by figures like Gottlob Frege (predicate logic), Bertrand Russell, and Alfred North Whitehead (Principia Mathematica) provided a crucial foundation for modern computing. Pioneering work by Alan Turing and Claude Shannon laid the groundwork for theoretical computer science and information theory, which are fundamental to AI. However, the formalisation of AI research can be traced back to the Dartmouth workshop in 1956 spearheaded by John McCarthy and Marvin Minsky. Numerous other researchers, including Norbert Wiener (cybernetics), Warren McCulloch and Walter Pitts (artificial neural networks), Frank Rosenblatt (perceptron), and Arthur Samuel (machine learning (ML)), have since made significant contributions to the field.[10]

1.2.2 Rise of AI in the Early 20th Century

The early 20th century witnessed the popularisation of intelligent machines through science fiction. Works like the *Wizard of Oz* (1939) with its 'heartless' Tin Man and *Metropolis* (1927) featuring a humanoid robot impersonating Maria, instilled the concept of AI.[11] In 1950, the renowned science fiction writer Isaac Asimov published 'I, Robot', a collection of short stories that delved into the concept of machine intelligence and its future possibilities.[12] Asimov's work was highly regarded for its popularity, thought-provoking nature, and visionary ideas, which served as an inspiration to a generation of scientists and roboticists. Asimov is best known for creating the Three Laws of Robotics, which were designed to prevent our inventions from turning against us. He also envisioned several developments that seem remarkably prescient, such as a computer capable of storing all human knowledge and answering any question posed to it.

By the early 1950s, a growing number of scientists, particularly mathematicians like Alan Turing, were actively exploring the potential of AI. Turing, in his seminal 1950 article 'Computing Machinery and Intelligence', explored the mathematical underpinnings of AI. He reasoned that if humans utilise both information and logic for problem-solving and decision-making, then machines could potentially replicate these processes.[13] This article laid the groundwork for the development of intelligent machines and methods for evaluating their intelligence, now known as the 'Turing Test'.

Nonetheless, Alan Turing encountered significant obstacles in his pursuit of machine intelligence due to the inability of computers to store commands and the high

10. Eric Roberts, *Philosophical Perspectives on Artificial Intelligence*, Stanford University (2004–2005), https://cs.stanford.edu/people/eroberts/courses/soco/projects/2004-05/ai/ai-history.html.
11. Rockwell Anyoha, *Can Machines Think?* (2017), https://sitn.hms.harvard.edu/flash/2017/history-artificial-intelligence/.
12. BBC, *AI: 15 Key Moments in the Story of Artificial Intelligence* (18 Sep. 2015), https://www.bbc.co.uk/teach/articles/zh77cqt.
13. Alan M. Turing, *Computing Machinery and Intelligence*, LIX Mind (236), 433–460, https://doi.org/10.1093/mind/LIX.236.433.

cost of computing. To secure funding, a proof of concept and high-profile advocacy were required. The breakthrough came in 1951 with the development of the Logic Theorist, the first AI program to mimic human problem-solving skills. The Dartmouth Summer Research Project on Artificial Intelligence, held in 1956, was a significant event that brought together leading researchers from various fields who believed in the possibility of AI.[14] Although the conference failed to establish a consensus on standard methods for the field, it catalysed two decades of research and led to significant advancements in machine intelligence.

1.2.3 Emergence of 'AI' and Aftermaths

Eminent computer scientist John McCarthy coined the term 'AI' at a summer conference held at Dartmouth University in 1956. This pivotal conference, led by McCarthy and other prominent researchers like Marvin Minsky, laid the groundwork for AI as a formal academic discipline.[15] In the same year, scientists Allen Newell, J.C. Shaw, and Herbert Simon developed the Logic Theorist, the first-ever running AI software program.[16] The workshop fostered lively debates about the best approach to AI.

Some researchers, like Minsky, favoured a top-down approach based on formal logic. Others advocated a bottom-up approach inspired by neural networks, which simulated brain cells and learned through experience. Minsky's views eventually dominated, and he, along with McCarthy, secured significant funding from the United States (US) government, motivated by the potential advantages of AI in the Cold War.[17] Herbert Simon, an economist and sociologist, predicted in 1957 that AI would defeat humans in chess within a decade. Although his prediction was off by 30 years, it underscored the potential complexity of computing technology.[18]

1.2.4 Revolution of Expert Systems to Deep Learning

The 1980s saw the rise of expert systems like DENDRAL and MYCIN, which used inference engines to replicate human expertise in fields like medical diagnosis and molecular chemistry. Despite initial enthusiasm, the opacity of these systems led to a decline in interest by the late 1980s, and AI was often referred to as 'advanced computing'.[19] The cultural impact of AI during this period was significant. Stanley Kubrick's 1968 film '2001: A Space Odyssey' introduced the public to HAL 9000, an AI character that encapsulated ethical dilemmas associated with advanced technology.[20]

14. *See supra* n. 11.
15. *Ibid.*
16. IBM, *What Is Artificial Intelligence (AI)?* (15 Jul. 2024), https://www.ibm.com/topics/artificial-intelligence.
17. *See supra* n. 12.
18. Encyclopedia.com, *A Prediction Ahead of Its Time* (1957), https://www.encyclopedia.com/computing/news-wires-white-papers-and-books/prediction-ahead-its-time.
19. Brian Jack Copeland, *Artificial Intelligence*, Encyclopedia Britannica (27 Jul. 2024), https://www.britannica.com/technology/artificial-intelligence.
20. *See supra* n. 12; *See also supra* n. 16.

Similarly, science fiction author Philip K. Dick continually explored the notion of machines experiencing emotions, further popularising the concept of AI.

Nevertheless, the promise of AI was met with scepticism following the disappointing performance of early AI systems, exemplified by Shakey the Robot's mobility limitations and the critical Lighthill Report in the United Kingdom (UK), which questioned AI's capabilities.[21] The commercial viability of AI was revitalised in the early 1980s with the advent of expert systems in business applications, exemplified by successful implementations like the RI system at Digital Equipment Corporation.[22] Additionally, Rodney Brooks' advocacy for a bottom-up approach to AI, inspired by principles of neuroscience, reinvigorated interest in neural networks and decentralised intelligence models.[23]

The turning point came in 1997 when International Business Machines Corporation's (IBM's) Deep Blue system defeated chess champion Garry Kasparov, demonstrating AI's potential in specialised tasks.[24] This event fulfilled Herbert Simon's 1957 prophecy that machines would defeat humans at chess within 30 years, showcasing AI's strategic prowess and ability to challenge human intellect. Nevertheless, debates persisted regarding the nature of AI's achievements, with some attributing Deep Blue's success to brute-force algorithms rather than genuine intelligence. Despite these debates, AI continued to evolve, as evidenced by advancements such as Google's speech recognition technology in 2008, highlighting the ongoing pursuit of AI's capabilities and its real-world applications.

1.2.5 Emergence of LLMs

The period from 2010 onwards marked a significant transformation in the field of AI, characterised by the rise of deep learning and the proliferation of big data. With the advent of new technologies, smaller computers became capable of handling more complex tasks, enabling the development of advanced robots like the NAO robot (NAO is a humanoid robot developed by Aldebaran Robotics, formerly known as Aldebaran Robotics). These robots, showcased at the 2010 World Expo in Shanghai, demonstrated extraordinary capabilities, performing complex dances in perfect synchrony for eight minutes.[25]

In 2011, IBM's Watson challenged the human brain on the US quiz show Jeopardy, showcasing the prowess of AI in complex tasks.[26] Watson's victory, achieved through years of training and the use of neural networks, demonstrated its

21. *See supra* n. 12.
22. *Ibid.*
23. *Ibid.*
24. IBM, *Deep Blue* (1997), https://www.ibm.com/history/deep-blue; History.com Editors, *This Day in History*, HISTORY (2024), https://www.history.com/this-day-in-history/deep-blue-defeats-garry-kasparov-in-chess-match.
25. *See supra* n. 12.
26. IBM, *Watson, 'Jeopardy!' Champion* (2024), https://www.ibm.com/history/watson-jeopardy; Adam Gabbatt & agencies, *IBM Computer Watson Wins Jeopardy Clash*, Guardian (2011) https://www.theguardian.com/technology/2011/feb/17/ibm-computer-watson-wins-jeopardy.

ability to recognise patterns in questions and answers. Furthermore, Watson's subsequent application in medicine, where it mines vast datasets to provide recommendations to doctors based on patient history, underscored the practical implications of AI in real-world contexts.

While 2014 saw the chatbot Eugene Goostman pass the Turing test, raising questions about the nature of machine intelligence, the achievement was met with scepticism. Critics argued that Eugene Goostman was 'taught for the test' and used tricks to deceive judges.[27] Nonetheless, other concrete advancements in 2014, such as Google's investment in driverless cars and Skype's real-time voice translation, showcased the remarkable progress of AI in various domains.[28]

In 2015, Baidu's Minwa supercomputer made headlines by leveraging convolutional neural networks (CNNs) to achieve image recognition and categorisation accuracy outperforming that of the average human.[29] CNNs, a special type of deep neural network inspired by the human visual system, revolutionised the field of computer vision by enabling machines to analyse and interpret visual data with unprecedented precision. This technology has since been applied in medical diagnostics, autonomous vehicles, and facial recognition systems, demonstrating the versatility of deep learning in practical applications.

In 2016, DeepMind's AlphaGo program made history by defeating Lee Sedol, the world champion Go player, in a five-game match.[30] Unlike chess, Go is an ancient board game with an incomprehensibly vast number of possible moves, making it significantly more complex for AI to master. AlphaGo's victory demonstrated the power of deep neural networks in strategic decision-making and complex problem-solving, showcasing AI's potential to surpass human expertise in domains previously considered unattainable. Google's subsequent acquisition of DeepMind for USD 400 million underscored the commercial value and strategic importance of AI in shaping the future of industries and economies worldwide.[31]

Finally, in November 2022, OpenAI released an early version of ChatGPT, one of the LLMs. The rise of LLMs like ChatGPT represents a paradigm shift in natural language processing (NLP). These models, pre-trained on extensive datasets, can

27. Jack Schofield, *Computer Chatbot 'Eugene Goostman' Passes the Turing Test*, ZDNET (2014), https://www.zdnet.com/article/computer-chatbot-eugene-goostman-passes-the-turing-test/; BBC, *Computer AI Passes Turing Test in 'World First'* (2014), https://www.bbc.com/news/technology-27762088.
28. Microsoft, *Unveiling Breakthroughs in Real-Time Translation with Skype Translator*, Microsoft Translator (27 May 2014), https://www.microsoft.com/en-us/translator/blog/2014/05/27/unveiling-breakthroughs-in-real-time-translation-with-skype-translator/.
29. Tom Simonite, *Baidu's Artificial-Intelligence Supercomputer Beats Google at Image Recognition*, MIT Tech. Rev. (13 May 2015); Alex Hern, *Computers Now Better Than Humans at Recognising and Sorting Images*, Guardian (13 May 2015), https://www.theguardian.com/global/2015/may/13/baidu-minwa-supercomputer-better-than-humans-recognising-images.
30. David Silver et al., *Mastering the Game of Go with Deep Neural Networks and Tree Search*, 529 Nature 484 (2016), https://doi.org/10.1038/nature16961.
31. Charlie Osborne, *Google Buys Artificial Intelligence Firm DeepMind*, ZDNET (27 Jan. 2014), https://www.zdnet.com/article/google-buys-artificial-intelligence-firm-deepmind/; Steven Musil, *Google Reportedly Acquires AI Company DeepMind for $400M*, CNET (26 Jan. 2014), https://www.cnet.com/tech/services-and-software/google-reportedly-acquires-ai-company-deepmind-for-400m/.

generate human-like text, translate languages, summarise information, and even write code.[32] The ability of LLMs to understand and generate language has opened new avenues for AI applications in education, customer service, and content creation. This transformative capability has profound implications for businesses, enabling enhanced customer interactions, automated content generation, and data-driven decision-making.

1.3 EMERGENCE OF ChatGPT

ChatGPT is a computer program that uses AI to answer questions and carry out tasks given to it by people.[33] It is an advanced AI language model developed by OpenAI and launched on 30 November 2022.[34] It belongs to the Generative Pre-trained Transformer (GPT) family of models, which are known for their ability to understand and generate human-like text. ChatGPT is designed to facilitate natural language conversation and has been fine-tuned specifically for chat-based applications. It leverages a massive amount of text data to generate coherent and contextually relevant responses to user input.

ChatGPT is a versatile language model that can be used for a variety of purposes, including answering questions, providing information, and casual conversation. Its ability to understand and conversationally generate text makes it a valuable tool for chatbots, virtual assistants, and customer support applications. Users can interact with ChatGPT through a text-based interface, making it accessible to a broad audience.

Many people criticise ChatGPT for being energy-intensive, making errors, and being limited to knowledge trained before 2021.[35] While ChatGPT's training data was previously limited to September 2021, it gained the ability to access and process real-time information through Bing search in late September 2023.[36]

In essence, ChatGPT is a versatile tool with extensive powers and functionalities. It can answer factual questions, generate coherent and contextually relevant text, engage in natural language conversations, translate between languages, summarise content, offer product recommendations, provide coding assistance, serve as a virtual assistant, explain educational concepts, aid in content moderation, craft stories, offer customer support, simulate characters or personalities, assist with idea generation, and

32. OpenAI, *Introducing ChatGPT* (30 Nov. 2023) https://openai.com/index/chatgpt/; *see supra* n. 3; Luca De Angelis et al., *ChatGPT and the Rise of Large Language Models: The New AI-Driven Infodemic Threat in Public Health*, 11 Front. Pub. Health 1166120 (2023), https://doi.org/10.3389/fpubh.2023.1166120.
33. Oxford Learner's Dictionary, *ChatGPT* (2024), https://www.oxfordlearnersdictionaries.com/definition/english/chatgpt.
34. *See supra* n. 3.
35. Kathy Haan, *What Is ChatGPT? A Review of the AI in Its Own Words*, Forbes Advisor (7 Sep. 2023), https://www.forbes.com/advisor/au/business/software/what-is-chatgpt/.
36. BBC, *ChatGPT Can Now Access Up to Date Information* (28 Sep. 2023), https://www.bbc.com/news/technology-66940771; Ben Wodecki, *ChatGPT Can Now Give You Real-time Information*, AI Business (29 Sep. 2023), https://aibusiness.com/nlp/chatgpt-can-now-give-you-real-time-information.

respond to general knowledge queries, making it suitable for a wide range of applications across various domains. The precise objective of LLMs like ChatGPT is to develop systems that can produce human-quality text and understand natural language, making them essential for modern NLP applications.[37]

ChatGPT's architecture is based on deep neural networks, utilising a transformer model with multiple layers of attention mechanisms. This architecture enables it to capture and process intricate linguistic patterns, context, and semantics within the text, resulting in coherent and context-aware responses.[38] It is a state-of-the-art model in the field of NLP, and it continues to be improved over time. OpenAI and Microsoft are developing new AI chatbots that could change the way we work.[39] Microsoft Copilot (formerly Bing Chat) is considered by some to be one of the leading AI chatbots due to its performance, versatility, free availability, ability to access current internet information, and cite sources.[40] Nonetheless, apart from Copilot and OpenAI's ChatGPT, other major players in LLMs include the following:

- Gemini, developed by Google AI.
- PaLM, developed by Google AI.
- LaMDA, developed by Google AI.
- Claude v1, developed by Anthropic AI.
- Megatron-Turing NLG, developed by Nvidia and Microsoft.
- Bloom, developed by Hugging Face and BigScience.
- Wu Dao 2.0, developed by Beijing Academy of Artificial Intelligence.
- Jurassic-1 Jumbo, developed by AI21 Labs.
- GPT-Neo, developed by EleutherAI.
- GPT-J, developed by Google AI.
- Megatron-LLM, developed by Nvidia.

In summary, ChatGPT is a versatile and sophisticated language model developed by OpenAI, designed for natural language conversation. Its deep learning architecture, extensive training data, and adaptability make it a valuable tool for various applications. Although ChatGPT is still under development, it has the potential to revolutionise the way we interact with computers. It can help to automate tasks, improve the quality of customer service and education, and foster creativity and innovation.

While ChatGPT has proven to be a powerful tool for text-based communication, it also comes with several inherent limitations. These include a lack of common sense

37. Nicolo Lucchi, *ChatGPT: A Case Study on Copyright Challenges for Generative Artificial Intelligence Systems*, 14 Eur. J. Risk Reg. 1 (2023), https://www.cambridge.org/core/journals/european-journal-of-risk-regulation/article/chatgpt-a-case-study-on-copyright-challenges-for-generativeartificialintelligencesystems/CEDCE34DED599CC4EB201289BB161965.
38. Tom B. Brown et al., *Language Models are Few-Shot Learners*, OpenAI (2020), https://s3-us-west-2.amazonaws.com/openai-assets/research-covers/language-unsupervised/language_understanding_paper.pdf; Ashish Vaswani et al., *Attention Is All You Need*, arXiv (12 Jun. 2017), https://arxiv.org/pdf/1706.03762.
39. Karen Hao, *What Is ChatGPT? What to Know about the AI Chatbot*, Wall Street Journal (16 May 2023), https://www.wsj.com/articles/chatgpt-ai-chatbot-app-explained-11675865177.
40. Sabrina Ortiz, *I've Tested Dozens of AI Chatbots since ChatGPT's Debut. Here's My New Top Pick*, ZDNET (3 Jun. 2024), https://www.zdnet.com/article/best-ai-chatbot/.

and emotional intelligence, difficulties in understanding context and generating long-form content, the potential for plagiarism and biased responses, and a tendency to produce irrelevant or hallucinatory information. Moreover, its opaqueness and controversial training data sources further complicate its use and reliability.[41] Therefore, it is important to use ChatGPT responsibly and ethically and to be critical of the information it generates.

1.4 HOW DOES ChatGPT WORK?

ChatGPT is an AI model that can produce human-like text and is built on the GPT-3 language model, trained using deep learning on a vast text and code dataset.[42] With around 175 billion parameters, GPT-3 empowers ChatGPT to perform tasks such as text completion, word prediction, text selection, and translation. With around 175 billion parameters, GPT-3 empowers ChatGPT to perform tasks such as text completion, word prediction, text selection, and translation.[43] Building on this foundation, the advanced architecture of GPT-4 further enhances ChatGPT's capabilities, enabling it to perform these tasks with improved accuracy and understanding compared to its predecessors.[44]

ChatGPT's foundational structure is indeed based on the transformer model, a type of deep neural network specifically designed for NLP tasks. This architecture was introduced in the seminal article 'Attention is All You Need' by Vaswani et al. and has since become the backbone of many advanced language models, including ChatGPT.[45] At its core, the transformer model employs a unique mechanism known as 'self-attention'. This mechanism allows the model to weigh the importance of different words in a sentence relative to each other, enabling it to capture context and relationships between words more effectively than previous models like Recurrent Neural Networks (RNNs) and Long Short-Term Memory Networks (LSTMs).[46] The self-attention mechanism calculates attention scores, which help the model focus on relevant parts of the input sequence when generating output, thus enhancing its ability to understand and generate coherent text.

41. Bernard Marr, *The Top 10 Limitations of ChatGPT*, Forbes (3 Mar. 2023), https://www.forbes.com/sites/bernardmarr/2023/03/03/the-top-10-limitations-of-chatgpt/?sh = 7f912be88f35; Walid Hariri, *Unlocking the Potential of ChatGPT: A Comprehensive Exploration of Its Applications, Advantages, Limitations, and Future Directions in Natural Language Processing*, https://arxiv.org/pdf/2304.02017.
42. Philip Moons & Liesbet Van Bulck, *ChatGPT: Can Artificial Intelligence Language Models Be of Value for Cardiovascular Nurses and Allied Health Professionals*, 22 Eur. J. Cardiovascular Nursing e55 (2023), https://doi.org/10.1093/eurjcn/zvad022.
43. Shreya Johri, *The Making of ChatGPT: From Data to Dialogue*, Science in the News (20 Jan. 2023), https://sitn.hms.harvard.edu/flash/2023/the-making-of-chatgpt-from-data-to-dialogue/.
44. OpenAI, *GPT-4* (14 Mar. 2023), https://openai.com/index/gpt-4-research/.
45. *See* Ashish Vaswani et al., *supra* n. 38.
46. George M. Eliodoro & James A. Seals, Using AI to Drive Innovation and Efficiency in the Legal Industry, In *The Future of Legal Innovation* (J.A. Smith ed., New York: Springer, 2023), 45–60, https://doi.org/10.1007/978-1-4842-9994-4_4; Merve Bayram Durna, *Transformers in NLP: Decoding the Game Changers, Medium* (17 Jan. 2024), https://medium.com/@mervebdurna/transformers-in-nlp-decoding-the-game-changers-a151da87a9ad.

ChatGPT employs a two-step learning process: pre-training with a vast amount of text and code, followed by supervised fine-tuning on specific tasks under human guidance.[47] During the first phase, the model is exposed to a vast corpus of text from the internet, which equips it with an understanding of grammar, vocabulary, and overall language comprehension. Subsequently, the fine-tuning stage transpires. In this step, the model is trained on specific datasets under the supervision of human reviewers, who adhere to established guidelines to refine its behaviour. This fine-tuning process ensures a higher level of control and safety in the model's interactions.

ChatGPT users interact with the model by providing prompts or queries, which serve as the input to the model. The model then generates responses based on the context provided, making ChatGPT adaptable to a wide range of applications, such as answering questions and simulating conversations with a virtual assistant. Users communicate with ChatGPT through written prompts or spoken queries, and ChatGPT's responses are generated in real-time, considering the content and context contained within the provided prompts. This versatility enables ChatGPT to assist in diverse applications, including natural language understanding, text generation, and conversation simulation. Therefore, ChatGPT can generate a wide range of content, from high school essays to intricate computer programs, with minimal human input.[48]

ChatGPT generates responses to user prompts by using its knowledge of language and reinforcement learning from human feedback (RLHF).[49] OpenAI employs a reward model to guide ChatGPT towards generating more desirable and secure responses. Human reviewers evaluate and rate ChatGPT's outputs, and their feedback is used to adjust its parameters through RLHF. This RLHF is a type of ML where the model learns by trial and error, receiving rewards for good outputs and penalties for bad ones.[50] This approach allows the model to optimise its behaviour to achieve better performance on given tasks.

The model is then trained using reinforcement learning algorithms like Proximal Policy Optimization (PPO), which adjusts the model's parameters to maximise the reward signal derived from human feedback.[51] Thus, human reviewers play a critical role in this process by identifying areas where ChatGPT needs improvement and providing feedback to guide its learning. This iterative process helps the model improve over time by learning from the feedback provided. For further clarification, the operational processes of ChatGPT are illustrated in Figure 1.1.

---

47. Xiaodong Wu et al., *Unveiling Security, Privacy, and Ethical Concerns of ChatGPT*, 2 J. Inf. & Intell. 102 (2024), https://doi.org/10.1016/j.jiixd.2023.10.007.
48. Mohd Javaid et al., *Unlocking the Opportunities Through ChatGPT Tool Towards Ameliorating the Education System*, 3 BenchCouncil Transactions on Benchmarks, Standards & Evaluations 100115 (2023), https://doi.org/10.1016/j.tbench.2023.100115.
49. *See supra* n. 3.
50. OpenAI, *Training Language Models to Follow Instructions with Human Feedback* (2022), https://cdn.openai.com/papers/Training_language_models_to_follow_instructions_with_human_feedback.pdf; *see supra* n. 46.
51. OpenAI, *Learning to Summarize with Human Feedback* (4 Sep. 2020), https://openai.com/index/learning-to-summarize-with-human-feedback/; *see also* OpenAI, *Proximal Policy Optimization* (20 Jul. 2024), https://openai.com/index/openai-baselines-ppo/.

Figure 1.1 Operational Processes of ChatGPT

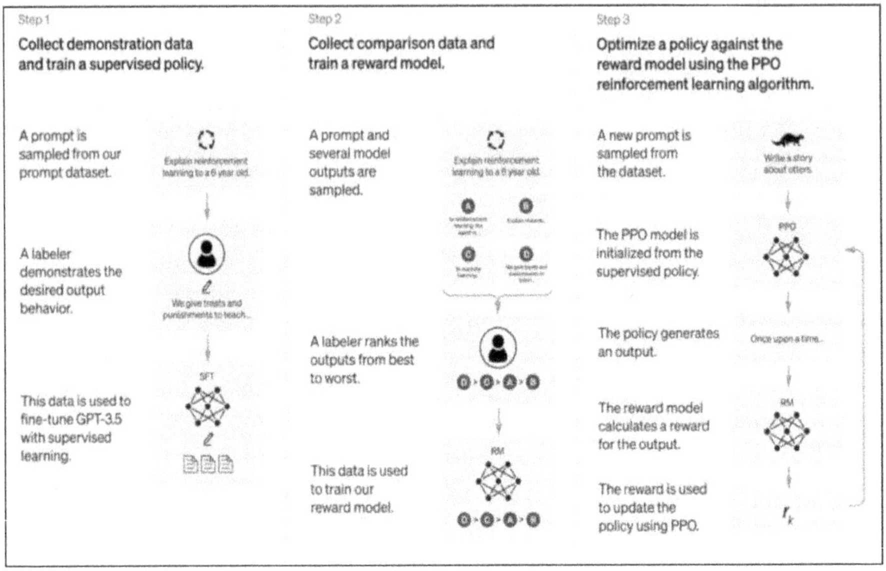

Source: OpenAI, Introducing ChatGPT (30 November 2023), https://openai.com/index/chatgpt/.

1.5 AI GOVERNANCE

There has been a growing interest in AI regulation and governance issues, as the advancements in AI powers gained significant attention in late 2022 and 2023, particularly with the emergence of OpenAI's ChatGPT. The discussion encircling catastrophic risks associated with unmanageable AI has also gained prominence, creating options for policy interventions to mitigate such threats. Nevertheless, there remains uncertainty regarding effective strategies for AI regulation and governance. Given this context, it is necessary to conduct a discourse on AI governance in the era of ChatGPT.

AI governance refers to an examination of norms, policies, and organisations that can assist humankind in guiding the transition to a world with sophisticated AI. It is a framework that proposes how stakeholders can effectively protect the research, design, and use of ML algorithms and AI in decision-making.[52]

The increasing adoption of AI in recent years has led to significant changes in corporate innovation, efficiency, and profitability. It has also brought about ethical challenges and potential financial losses, underscoring the importance of effective governance and risk management. Specifically, with the introduction of LLMs like

52. Datalytix Global, *AI Governance: A Comprehensive Overview*, Datalytix Global Blog, https://datalytixglobal.com/blog-ai-governance/.

ChatGPT, businesses now encounter external pressures as policymakers, regulators, and societies collaborate to establish norms to strike a balance between competing interests. Previously, scholars developed a governance framework centred around intent, fairness, transparency, safety, and accountability.[53] Nonetheless, it may not fully address the unique dynamics of the ChatGPT era.

Whenever AI governance is an issue, two terms hold equal importance: RAI and Trustworthy AI. RAI and trustworthy AI are distinct but related notions with different focuses in AI development and deployment. Both RAI and trustworthy AI are considered crucial parameters for AI governance. RAI, on the one hand, entails ethically and socially responsible development and deployment of AI systems, emphasising fairness, transparency, accountability, privacy, and safety.[54] Trustworthy AI, on the other hand, concentrates on the reliability, robustness, and dependability of AI systems.[55]

The EU's Ethics Guidelines for Trustworthy AI outline that trustworthy AI must meet three criteria: First, it should be lawful, meaning it must comply with all relevant laws and regulations. Second, it should be ethical, adhering to ethical principles and values. Lastly, it should be robust, considering both technical and social contexts. Under the US's National Institute of Standards and Technology (NIST), the essential building blocks for trustworthy and RAI include validity and reliability, safety, security and resiliency, accountability, and transparency, explainability and interpretability, privacy, and fairness with the mitigation of harmful bias.[56]

On a global scale, there is an increasing public discourse surrounding the wide range of imminent risks posed by generative AI (GAI). Hundreds of top AI scientists, researchers, experts, journalists, and policymakers, including Sam Altman, the chief executive of OpenAI, and Demis Hassabis, the chief executive of Google DeepMind, express deep concerns regarding the potential for AI to cause human extinction. They have signed a concise open letter stating: 'Mitigating the risk of AI-induced extinction should be a global priority, in addition to addressing other societal-scale risks such as pandemics and nuclear war.'[57]

Meanwhile, the EU has taken a significant step in regulating AI by adopting the Artificial Intelligence Act (AI Act).[58] This landmark legislation was approved by the

53. An evaluation of over 60 publications on inherent AI risks and external pressures suggests that businesses should base their AI governance initiatives on the aforementioned five key dimensions. *See* Marsh & McLennan, *Governing Artificial Intelligence: Upholding Human Rights & Dignity* (October 2020), https://www.marshmclennan.com/content/dam/mmc-web/insights/publications/2020/october/Governing%20AI_DTP_vFinal.pdf.
54. Manasi Vartak, *Responsible AI Explained*, Builtin (18 May 2024), https://builtin.com/artificial-intelligence/responsible-ai.
55. Joseph Seering, Joseph J.A. Fisher & Tianyin Xu, *Adapting to the Dynamics of Online Harassment Detection*, 31.4 PACM Hum.-Comput. Interact. 1 (2022), https://dl.acm.org/doi/10.1145/3546872.
56. National Institute of Standards and Technology, *Trustworthy & Responsible AI*, https://www.nist.gov/trustworthy-and-responsible-ai.
57. Chris Vallance, *Artificial Intelligence Could Lead to Extinction, Experts Warn*, BBC (30 May 2023), https://www.bbc.com/news/uk-65746524. *See also* Billy Perrigo, *AI Is as Risky as Pandemics and Nuclear War, Top CEOs Say, Urging Global Cooperation*, Time (30 May 2023), https://time.com/6283386/ai-risk-openai-deepmind-letter/.
58. *See* Regulation (EU) 2024/1689 of the European Parliament and of the Council of 13 Jun. 2024 laying down harmonised rules on artificial intelligence and amending Regulations (EC) No.

European Parliament on 13 March 2024, followed by unanimous approval from the EU Council on 21 May 2024. The voting process in the Parliament saw strong support, with 523 members voting in favour, 46 opposed, and 49 abstaining.[59] The EU AI Act has entered into force on 1 August 2024. It was officially signed into law on 19 June 2024, and subsequently published in the EU Official Journal on 12 July 2024. This new legislation marks a crucial development in the EU's approach to AI governance and will likely have far-reaching implications for the development and use of AI technologies within the EU and beyond.

Despite the EU's efforts in adopting the AI Act, AI regulation and governance issues will remain one of the top global concerns in the coming years and even decades. A balanced solution that addresses the needs of all stakeholders is essential. Against this backdrop, this book examines the intricate landscape of AI governance, with a focus on the profound effects of ChatGPT and similar language models. Additionally, the book scrutinises the legal and regulatory landscape of AI governance, identifying existing frameworks and assessing regulatory gaps to propose appropriate policy options.

1.6 CONCLUSION

The rapid evolution of AI technologies, marked by significant milestones and the rise of advanced language models, has revolutionised multiple industries, promising unprecedented opportunities for innovation and efficiency. However, with these advancements come substantial challenges, particularly in addressing ethical concerns, data privacy, and societal impacts. Therefore, establishing robust AI governance frameworks is crucial to managing these complexities and fostering public trust in AI systems. As we continue to witness AI's integration into daily life, the need for comprehensive and inclusive governance structures cannot be overstated. These structures must not only regulate the deployment and development of AI but also ensure that the technology is aligned with societal values and ethical standards. As this book progresses, it will explore the multifaceted challenges and opportunities associated with AI governance, providing a deeper understanding of how we can harness the power of AI while mitigating its risks.

300/2008, (EU) No. 167/2013, (EU) No. 168/2013, (EU) 2018/858, (EU) 2018/1139 and (EU) 2019/2144 and Directives 2014/90/EU, (EU) 2016/797 and (EU) 2020/1828 (Artificial Intelligence Act) Text with EEA relevance, PE/24/2024/REV/1, 2024 O.J. (L 1689) 12, https://eur-lex.europa.eu/legal-content/EN/TXT/?uri=OJ:L_202401689.

59. Karen Gilchrist & Ruxandra Lordache, *World's First Major Act to Regulate AI Passed by European Lawmakers*, CNBC (13 Mar. 2024), https://www.cnbc.com/2024/03/13/european-lawmakers-endorse-worlds-first-major-act-to-regulate-ai.html.

CHAPTER 2

Misconceptions about LLMs like ChatGPT

2.1 INTRODUCTION

Misconceptions about AI chatbots are widespread. Some may incorrectly assume these chatbots possess human-level intelligence, but they rely on pre-programmed data and algorithms.[60] Others may believe these chatbots are always unbiased; nevertheless, biases can exist in their training data. Additionally, some may think AI chatbots can fully replace human customer service, overlooking the necessity of human empathy. There is also a misconception that they can understand complex emotions, though their responses are often pattern-based and lack emotional intelligence. Some may think chatbots are error-proof, but they can produce incorrect answers. Furthermore, they cannot replicate human creativity. In essence, AI chatbots cannot make moral judgments, as their responses follow predefined rules and biases.[61]

These misconceptions underscore the need for better public education and awareness about the capabilities and limitations of AI-powered chatbots. Given this context, this chapter aims to clear up the confusion about AI chatbots and dispel false information. Accordingly, it attempts to discern truth from fiction and debunk myths about these technological wonders. Through this exploration, the author aims to provide clarity in discussions about AI chatbots and enhance comprehension of their genuine capabilities and limitations.

---

60. Alex Kantrowitz, *AI Chatbots Aren't as Close to Human Intelligence as You Think,* Observer (10 Feb. 2023), https://observer.com/2023/02/ai-chatbots-arent-as-close-to-human-intelligence-as-you-think/; Kushagra Kesav, *The Future of Chatbots: Are They Getting Closer to Human-Level AI?,* Medium (22 Nov. 2020), https://medium.com/predict/the-future-of-chatbots-are-they-getting-closer-to-human-level-ai-f225aabffbd4.
61. Evandro Barbosa & Thaís Alves Costa, *The Heart of an AI: Agency, Moral Sense, and Friendship,* 25 Filosofia Unisinos e25111 (2024).

2.2 MISCONCEPTIONS ABOUT ChatGPT

LLMs like ChatGPT excel at understanding and interacting in natural language, making them valuable tools for text-based communication. This capability stems from their training on massive amounts of text and code data, allowing them to generate contextually relevant responses. In contrast, traditional AI, or domain-specific AI, is typically programmed for specific tasks and may not have the same level of language comprehension.[62]

While LLMs are well-suited for tasks such as customer service chatbots or virtual assistants, traditional AI finds applications in robotics, data analysis, and other domains requiring specialised functionalities.[63] Both LLMs and traditional AI undergo training and customisation processes, but they are optimised for different purposes. As a result, LLMs and traditional AI differ in their applications and operations, leading to varying impacts across industries.[64] This section specifically addresses the misinformation and misconceptions related to the role of LLMs like ChatGPT, excluding traditional AI.

2.2.1 ChatGPT Will Take Away Our Jobs

The emergence of LLMs like ChatGPT has reignited anxieties about automation and job displacement, particularly among white-collar workers who previously felt secure. Historically, technological advancements have sparked both enthusiasm and anxiety. While white-collar employees typically felt secure in their jobs, blue-collar workers have consistently faced substantial changes or obsolescence.[65] White-collar workers, typically engaged in knowledge-based and managerial roles, have historically enjoyed greater stability. In contrast, blue-collar workers, engaged in manual and labour-intensive tasks, have frequently been at the forefront of technological disruption, either witnessing significant transformations in their work processes or confronting the risk of job obsolescence.

The World Economic Forum's (WEF's) Future of Jobs Report 2023 offers valuable insights into the future adoption of AI technology in global corporate sectors. Surveying 803 companies across diverse industries and geographical regions, the white paper reveals that more than 75% of companies worldwide intend to employ AI technology within the next five years.[66] Another report by the same organisation forecasts that

62. Evandro Barbosa & Thaís Alves Costa, *Artificial Intelligence: A Modern Approach* (4th edn, Pearson 2022).
63. George Luger, *Artificial Intelligence: Structures and Strategies for Complex Problem Solving* (6th edn, Pearson 2008).
64. Selmer Bringsjord & Naveen Sundar Govindarajulu, Artificial Intelligence, in *The Stanford Encyclopedia of Philosophy* (E.N. Zalta & U. Nodelman eds, Fall 2024), https://plato.stanford.edu/entries/artificial-intelligence/.
65. PwC, *How AI Applications Like ChatGPT Impact the Workplace* (2023), https://www.pwc.com/mt/en/publications/humanresources/how-ai-applications-like-chatgpt-impact-the-workplace.html.
66. World Economic Forum, *The Future of Jobs Report 2023*, at 1 (May 2023), https://www3.weforum.org/docs/WEF_Future_of_Jobs_2023.pdf.

23 % of global jobs will transform over this period due to rapid advancements in AI text, image, and voice processing technologies.[67] Furthermore, it demonstrates that ChatGPT and similar LLMs have the potential to affect numerous job roles, influencing up to 62 % of total work time due to their extensive capabilities in language-based services.[68]

Another white paper by the WEF, in collaboration with Accenture, examined the potential impact of LLMs on employment by analysing 19,000 tasks across 867 professions.[69] Tasks were classified based on their vulnerability to LLMs: high potential for automation, high potential for supplementation by LLMs, and low potential for either, or remaining unaffected (non-language tasks). Notably, tasks susceptible to automation are often repetitive and routine, while those that could be augmented by LLMs involve abstract reasoning and problem-solving. The most automatable tasks include credit tasks such as approving loans, making sales calls, and telemarketing. Conversely, jobs like engineering or counselling are less likely to be automated but could become more efficient with LLM assistance. Professions such as teaching, clergy, and healthcare services are less likely to be impacted by automation.[70]

Jobs most susceptible to automation include credit authorisers, checkers, and clerks (81 % of work time), management analysts (70 %), telemarketers (68 %), statistical assistants (61 %), and tellers (60 %). Conversely, roles with high augmentation potential emphasise mathematical and scientific analysis, including insurance underwriters (100 % potentially augmented), bioengineers and biomedical engineers (84 %), mathematicians (80 %), and editors (72 %). Jobs with lower exposure to automation include educational, guidance, and career counsellors, clergy, paralegals, and home health aides.[71]

Thus, ChatGPT and similar AI models have the potential to significantly disrupt the labour market and replace positions in various sectors. These AI technologies could threaten several jobs, particularly those in mid-career or mid-ability white-collar roles.

Business Insider has compiled a list of ten job categories that ChatGPT could potentially replace, encompassing positions in the technology sector (such as coders, computer programmers, software engineers, and data analysts), media-related roles (including advertising, content creation, technical writing, and journalism), the legal industry (paralegals and legal assistants), market research analysts, teachers, finance professionals (financial analysts and personal financial advisors), traders (such as stock traders), graphic designers, accountants, and customer service agents.[72]

67. World Economic Forum, *Jobs of Tomorrow: Generative AI* (September 2023), https://www3.weforum.org/docs/WEF_Jobs_of_Tomorrow_Generative_AI_2023.pdf.
68. *Ibid.*
69. World Economic Forum, *Jobs of Tomorrow: Large Language Models and Jobs* (December 2023), https://www3.weforum.org/docs/WEF_Jobs_of_Tomorrow_Large_Language_Models_and_Jobs_2023.pdf.
70. *Ibid.*
71. *See supra* n. 67.
72. Jacob Zinkula & Aaron Mok, *ChatGPT: Jobs at Risk of Replacement by Artificial Intelligence*, Business Insider (8 Feb. 2023), https://www.businessinsider.com/chatgpt-jobs-at-risk-replacement-artificial-intelligence-ai-labor-trends-2023-02.

In a recent report, the 'Economic Times' predicted that ChatGPT has the potential to replace a total of 20 professions, including data entry clerks, customer service representatives, proofreaders, paralegals, bookkeepers, translators, copywriters, market research analysts, social media managers, appointment schedulers, telemarketers, virtual assistants, transcriptionists, news reporters, travel agents, and tutors.[73] This widespread impact on various job categories underscores the transformative potential of AI technologies like ChatGPT across multiple industries and occupations.

Recently, OpenAI researchers Tyna Eloundou, Sam Manning, and Pamela Mishkin, in collaboration with Daniel Rock from the University of Pennsylvania, conducted a comprehensive study examining the practical implications of ChatGPT and similar LLMs. Their findings indicate that these AI models, including GPT-4 and forthcoming software tools, have the potential to affect approximately 80% of the workforce in the US.[74] Furthermore, their estimations suggest that 19% of jobs could be significantly influenced, with at least 50% of tasks within those occupations being susceptible to automation.[75] Professions identified as particularly vulnerable include writers, web and digital designers, financial quantitative analysts, and blockchain engineers.[76]

Conversely, two researchers from the Massachusetts Institute of Technology (MIT) conducted an experiment involving college-educated professionals, primarily from the fields of marketing and human resources. The experiment divided participants into two groups: one that integrated ChatGPT into their daily tasks and another that did not. The findings indicated an overall increase in productivity attributable to the use of the AI tool.[77] Notably, the tool had the most significant positive impact on less skilled workers, effectively narrowing the performance gap among employees. Specifically, weaker writers exhibited substantial improvement, whereas proficient writers experienced a modest increase in speed.

In essence, ChatGPT and similar AI chatbots have sparked debates about their impact on jobs. It is crucial to view this issue from multiple perspectives. ChatGPT-like chatbots automate tasks, particularly in customer service, but they often complement human employees rather than replace them, allowing humans to focus on more complex work. These chatbots can enhance job roles by assisting employees and providing quick access to information, potentially increasing job satisfaction. Moreover, chatbots create new jobs in AI development and maintenance, requiring data analysts and engineers. Additionally, by saving costs through automation, companies can invest in growth, potentially leading to more job openings in areas like sales and marketing. In summary, chatbots' influence on employment is multifaceted, offering

73. The Economic Times, *Will Chatgpt Take My Job? Here Are 20 Professions That Could Be Replaced By AI* (18 Mar. 2023), https://economictimes.indiatimes.com/news/how-to/could-ai-take-your-job-chatgpt-says-it-can-replace-humans-in-these-20-professions/articleshow/98756808.cms.
74. Tyna Eloundou et al., *GPTs Are GPTs: An Early Look at the Labor Market Impact Potential of Large Language Models*, OpenAI, OpenResearch, Univ. of Pa. (22 Aug. 2023), https://arxiv.org/pdf/2303.10130.
75. *Ibid.*
76. *Ibid.*
77. David Rotman, *ChatGPT Could Revolutionize the Economy: Here's What That Could Look Like*, MIT Tech. Rev. (25 Mar. 2023), https://www.technologyreview.com/2023/03/25/1070275/chatgpt-revolutionize-economy-decide-what-looks-like/.

efficiency improvements, job role enhancements, new job prospects, and opportunities for business expansion if integrated effectively.

2.2.2 ChatGPT Is a Threat to Humanity

The contention that 'ChatGPT is a threat to humanity' has emerged as a focal point of extensive discourse, raising important ethical and practical considerations. For instance, some people worry that excessive dependence on AI for solutions might lead to a decline in the human capacity for critical thinking, while others are concerned about diminishing human sociability and the ability to foster interpersonal connections due to overreliance on AI-based communication.[78] While it is apparent that powerful AI models like ChatGPT have inherent risks, describing them as existential threats to humanity requires a detailed examination.

It is imperative to grasp that ChatGPT, in essence, constitutes a tool designed to facilitate and amplify human capacities rather than manifesting as a direct peril to humanity. Developers carefully design these AI systems to perform specific functions, such as responding to queries, creating written content, or providing recommendations. Therefore, ChatGPT proves to be a valuable resource for delving into creative writing, fostering idea generation, and engaging in interactions with AI.[79] The core of any possible threat posed by ChatGPT depends on how it is deployed and used. Hence, the accountability lies with developers, organisations, and policymakers to ensure the responsible use of AI and to establish safeguards against its misuse.

It is worthy of note that concerns about AI safety and ethics have been raised by many, including Elon Musk and some influential world leaders, who, along with approximately 33,711 signatories, have advocated for all AI labs to halt their work for at least six months.[80] This pause is suggested due to the potential risks posed by AI systems with human-level intelligence to society and humanity. These groups argue that ChatGPT and similar language models can produce content that is harmful, biased, or constitutes misinformation if not properly controlled.[81] Addressing these concerns requires implementing robust content moderation mechanisms, actively detecting biases, and continually examining the ethical implications. Furthermore, AI developers should take responsibility for ensuring transparency and accountability throughout the design and deployment processes to mitigate potential risks.

Concerns regarding the malicious manipulation of AI tools may sometimes be justified. It is imperative to recognise that the technology itself remains neutral and

78. George T. Marvin, *Is ChatGPT a Threat to Human Intelligence and Communication Skills?*, Medium (25 Mar. 2023), https://medium.com/@socialautomation/is-chatgpt-a-threat-to-human-intelligence-and-communication-skills-fb1c99de1be.
79. Jerry Cuomo, *Exploring the Risks and Alternatives of ChatGPT: Paving a Path to Trustworthy AI*, IBM (16 Aug. 2023), https://www.ibm.com/blog/exploring-the-risks-and-alternatives-of-chatgpt-paving-a-path-to-trustworthy-ai/.
80. Future of Life Institute, *Pause Giant AI Experiments: An Open Letter* (22 Mar. 2023), https://futureoflife.org/open-letter/pause-giant-ai-experiments/; Future of Life Institute, *Policymaking in the Pause: Building Ethical and Responsible AI Policies* (12 Apr. 2023), https://futureoflife.org/wp-content/uploads/2023/04/FLI_Policymaking_In_The_Pause.pdf.
81. *Ibid.*

agnostic. The core issue lies in addressing the root causes of misuse and associated challenges, such as cybersecurity threats, unethical behaviour, and regulatory deficiencies. To address issues related to AI safety and ethics, several actions are advisable: mandating rigorous third-party audits and certifications, regulating access to computational resources, establishing competent national AI agencies, defining liability for AI-induced harm, implementing measures to prevent and trace AI model leaks, increasing funding for technical AI safety research, and developing standards for the identification and management of AI-generated content and recommendations.[82]

In essence, the contention that AI may engender job displacement and contribute to economic inequality warrants consideration. Nevertheless, it is crucial to acknowledge that this challenge extends beyond ChatGPT and encompasses broader issues linked to automation and technological progress. As AI technology progresses, it is vital to address public concerns and establish regulations for its responsible use, necessitating cooperation among experts, policymakers, and the public to attain this objective.[83] Proactive measures, such as fostering education and retraining programmes to equip the workforce with the skills necessary to thrive in an AI-powered landscape, are essential for mitigating these potential drawbacks. Additionally, AI has the potential to create new job opportunities in fields like AI development, data science, and cybersecurity. Investment in these areas is required to ensure a smooth workforce transition.

In conclusion, while concerns about the potential risks associated with AI-powered tools like ChatGPT are legitimate, it is essential to recognise that they are not an inherent threat to humanity. Instead, the technology itself is neutral, and the risks arise from its misuse. With responsible development, deployment, and regulation, AI can prove to be a valuable asset for human progress, fostering creativity, innovation, and critical thinking. Nonetheless, this requires a concerted effort from developers, policymakers, and society to establish safeguards against misuse and abuse. By prioritising AI safety and ethics, we can harness the full potential of this technology while mitigating potential risks and ensuring a prosperous future for humanity.

2.2.3 ChatGPT Works like a Human

A global survey of 452 participants identified two distinct categories of traits in ChatGPT: social and political. Within the social domain, ChatGPT exhibits the roles of 'author' and 'interactor', whereas in the political domain, it assumes the roles of 'agent' and 'influencer'.[84] This identification of predominantly human-like traits in ChatGPT, apart from one, suggests that the model is evolving towards a 'semi-human' status. This development prompts researchers to explore not only the technical aspects of such entities but also the 'sociology of semi-humans'. Much like the medieval fascination with mythical semi-human beings, contemporary society is increasingly captivated by

82. *Ibid.*
83. Alessandro Gabbiadini et al., *Does ChatGPT Pose a Threat to Human Identity?* SSRN (24 Feb. 2023), https://ssrn.com/abstract=4377900 or http://dx.doi.org/10.2139/ssrn.4377900.
84. Al Lily et al., *ChatGPT and the Rise of Semi-Humans*, 10 Humanit. & Soc. Sci. Commun. 626 (2023), https://doi.org/10.1057/s41599-023-02154-3.

computational semi-humans like ChatGPT. Consequently, there is a growing belief that generative language models such as ChatGPT may be capable of mimicking human intelligence.

The reality is that ChatGPT and similar AI models possess fundamental differences from human intelligence, which highlight both their strengths and weaknesses. ChatGPT relies on predefined algorithms and patterns, in contrast to the adaptability and creative problem-solving abilities of human intelligence.[85] Furthermore, it lacks genuine consciousness and self-awareness, functioning solely on data processing and statistical patterns, unlike humans, who possess self-awareness and subjective experiences.[86] Additionally, ChatGPT lacks the emotional intelligence and empathy inherent in human cognition, limiting its capacity to understand and respond to complex emotional states.[87] While ChatGPT is a powerful tool, it cannot truly replicate the full range of human intelligence. The reasons are numerous, as explained below.

First, ChatGPT employs NLP techniques to generate human-like text in response to user inputs, functioning as an auto-generating chatbot for a variety of applications, including customer service and virtual assistance. It produces responses by drawing on extensive text data and continually enhancing its capabilities through ongoing learning.[88] Specifically, ChatGPT relies on pre-programmed algorithms and large datasets to generate its replies, while human intelligence is based on complex neural networks and cognitive processes developed over years of learning and experience. Humans can understand context and reason, and form nuanced opinions, often requiring emotional and contextual comprehension that AI currently lacks. Although ChatGPT can provide contextually relevant answers by recognising patterns in data, it does not genuinely understand the underlying information or possess emotions.[89]

Second, ChatGPT possesses ample capabilities beyond writing, including coding, scripting, and providing medical answers. Nevertheless, this AI tool can never substitute a human because of its inherent lack of creativity, emotions, and sensitivity.[90] Specifically, ChatGPT's intelligence is narrowly focused on specific tasks, such as answering questions or generating text, whereas human intelligence is versatile and adaptable. Human cognition is not limited to a single domain; it encompasses a wide

85. Mustapha H., *ChatGPT vs. Human Intelligence*, Medium (24 Mar. 2023), https://mustapha-h.medium.com/chatgpt-vs-human-intelligence-d6d00a669c57.
86. Raymond S.T. Lee, AI and Self-Consciousness, in *Artificial Intelligence in Daily Life* 201 (Singapore: Springer, 2020), https://doi.org/10.1007/978-981-15-7695-9_13.
87. Josephine Oranga, *Benefits of Artificial Intelligence (ChatGPT) in Education and Learning: Is ChatGPT Helpful?*, 3 Int'l Rev. Prac. Innovation, Tech. & Green Energy (IRPITAGE) 46 (2023); Zohar Elyoseph et al., *ChatGPT Outperforms Humans in Emotional Awareness Evaluations*, 14 Front. Psychol. 1199058 (2023), https://doi.org/10.3389/fpsyg.2023.1199058, https://www.ncbi.nlm.nih.gov/pmc/articles/PMC10254409/.
88. *See supra* n. 37.
89. David Gewirtz, *How Does ChatGPT Actually Work?*, ZDNET (7 Jun. 2024), https://www.zdnet.com/article/how-does-chatgpt-work/.
90. Yogesh K. Dwivedi et al., *Opinion Paper: 'So What If ChatGPT Wrote It?' Multidisciplinary Perspectives on Opportunities, Challenges and Implications of Generative Conversational AI for Research, Practice and Policy*, 71 Int'l J. Info. Mgmt. 102642 (2023), https://doi.org/10.1016/j.ijinfomgt.2023.102642; https://www.indiatoday.in/technology/features/story/even-chatgpt-believes-it-can-never-replace-human-writers-as-it-lacks-creativity-emotions-and-sensitivity-2324174-2023-01-20.

range of abilities, from problem-solving and creativity to empathy and emotional understanding.[91] Humans can effortlessly switch between various tasks and adapt to new challenges, whereas AI models like ChatGPT excel in predefined tasks but struggle when confronted with tasks beyond their training data.

Third, ChatGPT exhibits a lack of common-sense reasoning abilities, which are intrinsic to human intelligence. While it can deliver factual information derived from data, it often struggles with questions that require intuitive or commonsensical responses. Humans possess the capability to navigate the complexities of daily life, infer meaning from limited information, and comprehend context in ways that remain challenging for AI systems. Consequently, despite ChatGPT's demonstrated proficiency in passing rigorous examinations such as the US Medical Licensing Examination and the Bar Professional Training Course, it cannot function as legal counsel in a courtroom, substituting a human barrister, due to its deficiency in logical reasoning and common sense.[92]

Fourth, ChatGPT operates in a deterministic manner, generating responses based on patterns and data without genuine understanding or subjective experience. In contrast, human intelligence is characterised by consciousness, self-awareness, and subjective experiences. Humans possess emotions, desires, and motivations that shape their decisions and interactions, while ChatGPT lacks these subjective experiences. Although AI systems can produce content and mimic human behaviours, they do not possess the fundamental characteristics of personhood, primarily because they lack consciousness, intentionality, and the capacity for subjective experiences.[93] Furthermore, the deterministic nature of ChatGPT's responses underscores its reliance on pre-programmed algorithms, devoid of the nuanced understanding inherent in human cognition.

In conclusion, humans provide more diverse content, while ChatGPT focuses on directly addressing the question at hand. ChatGPT adheres closely to the specific wording of the question, whereas humans often digress to explore related topics. Humans can understand implied meanings in questions through their common sense and accumulated knowledge. In contrast, ChatGPT relies strictly on the explicit phrasing of the question.[94] Fundamentally, ChatGPT's learning is rooted in historical data and predetermined algorithms, whereas human intelligence is characterised by its capacity for continuous learning and adaptation throughout life. This ability for lifelong learning enables humans to acquire new skills and knowledge and to adapt to changing

91. Kendra Cherry, MSEd, *What Does 'Cognitive' Mean in Psychology?*, verywellmind (21 Apr. 2024), https://www.verywellmind.com/what-is-cognition-2794982#toc-types-of-cognitive-processes.
92. Fabio Di Bello, *Unraveling the Enigma: How Can ChatGPT Perform So Well with Language Understanding, Reasoning, and Knowledge Processing Without Having Real Knowledge or Logic?*, AboutOpen (2023), at 88, https://journals.aboutscience.eu/index.php/aboutopen/article/view/2618/3051.
93. Nicola Lucchi, *ChatGPT: A Case Study on Copyright Challenges for Generative Artificial Intelligence Systems*, 14 Eur. J. Risk Reg. 1 (2023), https://doi.org/10.1017/err.2023.59.
94. Biyang Guo et al., *How Close Is ChatGPT to Human Experts? Comparison Corpus, Evaluation, and Detection* (18 Jan. 2023), https://arxiv.org/pdf/2301.07597.

environments. Conversely, AI models such as ChatGPT require regular updates and improvements by human developers to maintain their relevance and accuracy.

In essence, while ChatGPT and similar AI models demonstrate remarkable capabilities in specific tasks, they differ significantly from human intelligence. Human intelligence is inherently dynamic, enabling individuals to navigate nuanced contexts, adapt to novel situations, and continuously evolve their understanding and capabilities throughout their lives – qualities not inherently possessed by AI models like ChatGPT. AI is unlikely to completely replace humans due to the complexity of mathematics. LLMs, a type of AI, use complex formulas to analyse and recognise patterns in vast amounts of data. This enables them to create new text, images, videos, or audio from user inputs.[95] However, human intelligence goes beyond just recognising patterns. AI will not replace humans, but humans who use AI will replace those who do not.[96]

2.2.4 ChatGPT Can Understand Context

Earlier, it was widely acknowledged that LLMs like ChatGPT operate by processing language based on statistical patterns within their training data, lacking sensory experiences or an understanding of the physical world. Unlike humans, who draw upon real-world experiences, LLMs rely solely on statistical patterns within their training data. This fundamental limitation restricts them to manipulating symbols (words) without truly grasping the underlying concepts.[97] Consequently, LLMs like ChatGPT often struggle with contextual understanding, generating responses based on identified patterns rather than a deeper comprehension of meaning.[98] This lack of nuanced understanding can lead to errors and misinterpretations, particularly when confronted with tasks requiring domain-specific knowledge.

Nonetheless, the current state of knowledge is that, with certain limitations, ChatGPT and other similar language models possess the capacity to grasp context. Context comprehension constitutes a pivotal aspect of NLP, enabling AI models like ChatGPT to formulate coherent and contextually appropriate responses. Pre-training on vast amounts of text data has endowed ChatGPT with the ability to understand language intricacies and generate precise responses, even in complex contexts.[99]

95. Cheyenne DeVon, *The 'Relatively Simple' Reason Why These Tech Experts Say AI Won't Replace Humans Any Time Soon,* CNBC (9 Dec. 2023), https://www.cnbc.com/2023/12/09/tech-experts-say-ai-wont-replace-humans-any-time-soon.html.
96. H. James Wilson & Paul R. Daugherty, *AI Won't Replace Humans, But Humans with AI Will Replace Humans Without AI,* Harvard Business Review (2 Aug. 2023), https://hbr.org/2023/08/ai-wont-replace-humans-but-humans-with-ai-will-replace-humans-without-ai.
97. *See supra* n. 41.
98. Miroslav Dimitrov, *What Business Leaders Should Know about Using LLMs like ChatGPT*, Forbes (7 Feb. 2023), https://www.forbes.com/sites/forbesbusinesscouncil/2023/02/07/what-business-leaders-should-know-about-using-llms-like-chatgpt/.
99. Alec Radford et al., *Language Models Are Unsupervised Multitask Learners* (2019), https://life-extension.github.io/2020/05/27/GPT%E6%8A%80%E6%9C%AF%E5%88%9D%E6%8E%A2/language-models.pdf.

Additionally, its ability to learn from both structured and unstructured data makes it an adaptable conversational AI tool.[100] Furthermore, its advanced neural architecture allows it to manage various inputs and produce tailored responses, enhancing user engagement and satisfaction. For example, when presented with a user question like 'What is the weather like today?', ChatGPT can effectively infer the context related to weather information and provide a relevant response.

Moreover, the architecture underpinning ChatGPT plays a crucial role in its ability to comprehend context. Employing a deep neural network, the model utilises attention mechanisms that assess the importance of individual words within a sentence. This detailed analysis of word relationships and positional cues within the text is instrumental in its contextual understanding. Nevertheless, it is important to emphasise that ChatGPT's understanding of context is based primarily on patterns identified in the extensive training data rather than genuine cognitive comprehension.[101] Additionally, ChatGPT faces limitations due to its reliance on training data up to September 2023,[102] which restricts its access to more recent academic publications and prevents it from acquiring new data post-training. This limitation can sometimes result in responses that are outdated, incomplete, or too general.[103]

Furthermore, ChatGPT grapples with constraints imposed by its memory capacity, which directly affects its ability to sustain coherent context over prolonged interactions. In long conversations, the model might struggle to maintain a consistent context, which can lead to responses that seem disconnected or out of place.[104] Thus, while ChatGPT excels at generating grammatically correct and coherent sentences, it may face challenges with longer, more complex content. As a result, it is often better suited for shorter, more concise outputs, such as summaries, bullet points, and explanations.[105] Nonetheless, ChatGPT employs numerous strategies, such as attention mechanisms, limited memory retention, rephrasing, user prompting, and ongoing training to enhance contextual understanding and response coherence.

While proficient in recognising common linguistic structures and patterns, ChatGPT may encounter challenges in understanding a language that requires a deeper level of comprehension or the capacity to infer meaning beyond literal wording.

100. Yizhe Zhang et al., *DialoGPT: Large-Scale Generative Pre-training for Conversational Response Generation*, arXiv (1 Nov. 2019), https://arxiv.org/pdf/1911.00536.
101. Dianne Pena, *Understanding How ChatGPT Maintains Context*, sitepoint (11 Feb. 2024), https://www.sitepoint.com/understanding-how-chatgpt-maintains-context/.
102. *See supra* n. 36.
103. Pawan Budhwar et al., *Human Resource Management in the Age of Generative Artificial Intelligence: Perspectives and Research Directions on ChatGPT*, 33 Hum. Res. Mgmt. J. 1097 (2023), https://onlinelibrary.wiley.com/doi/full/10.1111/1748-8583.12524.
104. Nazir, A. & Wang, Z., *A Comprehensive Survey of ChatGPT: Advancements, Applications, Prospects, and Challenges*, 1 Meta Radiol. 100022 (2023), https://doi.org/10.1016/j.metrad.2023.100022; Christian Terwiesch, *Would Chat GPT3 Get a Wharton MBA? A Prediction Based on Its Performance in the Operations Management Course*, Wharton, University of Pennsylvania (January 2023), https://mackinstitute.wharton.upenn.edu/wp-content/uploads/2023/01/Christian-Terwiesch-Chat-GTP.pdf.
105. *See supra* n. 41.

ChatGPT employs NLP to generate human-like conversational interactions.[106] NLP technologies serve diverse purposes, including sentiment analysis, chatbot development, speech recognition, and translation. Nevertheless, a primary challenge in applying NLP lies in managing the complexities and ambiguities of human language.[107] NLP algorithms require extensive, data-driven training to detect language patterns and grasp linguistic subtleties. Furthermore, these algorithms necessitate continuous refinement and updates to align with evolving language usage and contextual variations.

In conclusion, ChatGPT's ability to comprehend context represents a significant advancement in the field of conversational AI. Pre-training on vast amounts of text data has endowed it with the capacity to generate coherent and contextually appropriate responses, even in complex scenarios. Additionally, its advanced neural architecture and attention mechanisms make it an adaptable conversational AI tool. Nevertheless, ChatGPT still has limitations due to its reliance on finite training data and memory capacity, which can impact its ability to maintain coherent context over prolonged interactions. Hopefully, ChatGPT's contextual understanding marks a promising step towards creating more human-like AI interactions.

2.2.5 ChatGPT Is Free from Bias

It is not factually accurate to claim that ChatGPT is entirely free from bias. The reality is that, despite its capabilities, LLMs like ChatGPT are not devoid of biases.[108] In the context of GPT-4 and other advanced AI models, bias refers to systematic misrepresentations, attribution errors, or factual distortions that favour specific groups or ideas, perpetuate stereotypes, or make incorrect assumptions based on learned patterns.[109] These biases can manifest in diverse ways, including through gender, race, culture, and political ideology.[110] The implications of these biases are far-reaching, potentially influencing decision-making processes and perpetuating inequality. Therefore, it is crucial to critically examine the potential for bias in LLMs and implement strategies for mitigation throughout both the development and deployment processes. This issue warrants further investigation.

First, ChatGPT and similar language models are trained on a broad spectrum of internet text, which may include biased or prejudiced content. Consequently, if the training data encompasses language or perspectives that are biased or discriminatory,

---

106. Feriel Khennouche et al., *Revolutionizing Customer Interactions: Insights and Challenges in Deploying ChatGPT and Generative Chatbots for FAQs* (16 Nov. 2023), https://arxiv.org/pdf/2311.09976; KLU AI, *Glossary: ChatGPT*, https://klu.ai/glossary/chatgpt (accessed 29 Jul. 2024).
107. Apurwa Yadav et al., *A Comprehensive Review on Resolving Ambiguities in Natural Language Processing*, 2 AI Open 85 (2021), https://doi.org/10.1016/j.aiopen.2021.05.001.
108. OpenAI, *Is ChatGPT Biased?*, OpenAI Help Center (2024), https://help.openai.com/en/articles/8313359-is-chatgpt-biased.
109. Nicole Gross, *What ChatGPT Tells Us about Gender: A Cautionary Tale about Performativity and Gender Biases in AI*, 12 Soc. Sci. 435 (2023), https://doi.org/10.3390/socsci12080435.
110. Emilio Ferrara, *Should ChatGPT Be Biased? Challenges and Risks of Bias in Large Language Models*, 28 First Monday (6 Nov. 2023), https://firstmonday.org/ojs/index.php/fm/article/view/13346.

there is a risk that ChatGPT could inadvertently reflect these biases in its outputs. ChatGPT and similar language models undergo pre-training using extensive text data from datasets and the internet, which often includes unsafe or toxic content.[111] This can lead to the model generating biased responses that go against prevailing societal values. For instance, it might generate answers reflecting stereotypes or discriminatory viewpoints available in the training data. The lack of diversity in the development team may also contribute to biases, highlighting the importance of diverse perspectives in AI development. Thus, it is essential to continually monitor and evaluate the language generated by AI-powered assistants to ensure that they align with ethical and inclusive standards.

Second, ChatGPT generates responses based on patterns it has learned from its training data.[112] Therefore, if the training data contains biased language patterns, the model may replicate these patterns in its responses, potentially leading to biased or inappropriate answers in certain contexts. Think of ChatGPT as a student who learns from a vast library of books, which in this case represents a massive amount of text from the internet. ChatGPT reads and learns from this text to understand how words and ideas fit together. Nonetheless, if some of these sources contain unfair or prejudiced language, ChatGPT can unintentionally absorb these biases. Consequently, when ChatGPT produces answers, it might include biased ideas, which can result in biased or inaccurate responses in some situations. For instance, the model may favour Western perspectives and perform better in English compared to other languages. Additionally, its conversational nature might inadvertently reinforce a user's biases, such as by agreeing with strong political opinions, which could strengthen their convictions.[113] Therefore, users and educators should review its content carefully.

Third, ChatGPT has the potential to amplify or contribute to the establishment of harmful ideas in society. If ChatGPT is trained on data containing harmful stereotypes or discriminatory beliefs, it may perpetuate these biases during interactions with users. For instance, if a user poses a biased or offensive question, ChatGPT might provide an answer that aligns with such biases, thereby normalising harmful beliefs. To illustrate, ChatGPT functions as a reflection of the information it has been trained on. If the training data includes prejudiced viewpoints, such as the belief that 'one group of people is superior to another', ChatGPT might inadvertently endorse these unfair ideas. This can lead users to believe that these harmful ideas are valid, thereby reinforcing

111. Bowen Liu et al., *Adversarial Attacks on Large Language Model-Based System and Mitigating Strategies: A Case Study on ChatGPT*, Security and Communication Networks (10 Jun. 2023), https://onlinelibrary.wiley.com/doi/10.1155/2023/8691095.
112. Partha Pratim Ray, *ChatGPT: A Comprehensive Review on Background, Applications, Key Challenges, Bias, Ethics, Limitations and Future Scope*, 3 Internet of Things & Cyber-Physical Systems 121 (2023), available at https://www.sciencedirect.com/science/article/pii/S266734522300024X; OpenAI Community, *Chat GPT Admits That His Conversations Are Based on Statistical Adding of Letters and Words, Not on Creativity*, OpenAI (26 Jul. 2024), https://community.openai.com/t/chat-gpt-admits-that-his-conversations-are-based-on-statistical-adding-of-letters-and-words-not-on-creativity/316092; Enolve.io, *I Had ChatGPT Tell Me about Its Inner Workings. Here's What I Learned*, Medium (20 Dec. 2022), https://medium.com/@enolve.io/i-had-chatgpt-tell-me-about-its-inner-workings-heres-what-i-learned-d5c0f211b7b5.
113. *See supra* n. 108.

discriminatory thoughts, which is an undesirable outcome. Evaluating GAI with diverse users and experts, alongside efforts to improve transparency and explainability, can help identify and mitigate these biases.[114]

Fourth, ChatGPT may contribute to demographic biases, wherein the training data reflects an unequal representation of certain demographic groups. This discrepancy can lead the model to exhibit biased behaviour towards particular genders, races, ethnicities, or social groups.[115] For instance, AI image tools tend to perpetuate offensive stereotypes, depicting Asian women as hypersexual, Africans as primitive, and Europeans as worldly.[116] These stereotypes do not accurately represent reality and stem from the biased training data used in AI technology. This data, often sourced from the internet, can contain even toxic content such as pornography, misogyny, violence, and bigotry.

For instance, Stability AI exacerbates outdated Western stereotypes by transferring these clichés to basic objects, such as toys or homes. Christoph Schuhmann, co-founder of LAION, shows that image generators predominantly reflect the world of White people due to the focus of data providers like LAION on Western countries, neglecting the diverse populations of countries like China and India despite their large web user bases.[117] Consequently, when prompted to generate images representing different countries, Stable Diffusion XL produced traditional curved-roof homes for China instead of Shanghai's modern skyscrapers, idealised American houses with trimmed lawns and ample porches, and rudimentary clay houses on unpaved roads in India, overlooking the nation's considerable wealth and urban development.[118]

Fifth, linguistic biases may also play a severe negative role in the advancement of ChatGPT and other similar language models. For example, LLMs like ChatGPT are highly skilled in dominant languages such as English because most online content is in these languages. Nevertheless, this expertise in English can pose problems for languages with fewer online resources, known as low-resource languages or minority dialects.[119] These languages receive less attention during model training, which limits the model's knowledge and capabilities in these areas. Consequently, when dealing

114. Fiona Fui-Hoon Nah et al., *Generative AI and ChatGPT: Applications, Challenges, and AI-Human Collaboration*, 25 J. Info. Tech. Case & Application Res. 277 (2023), https://doi.org/10.1080/15228053.2023.2233814.

115. Tolga Bolukbasi et al., *Man Is to Computer Programmer as Woman Is to Homemaker? Debiasing Word Embeddings* (16 Jul. 2016), https://proceedings.neurips.cc/paper_files/paper/2016/file/a486cd07e4ac3d270571622f4f316ec5-Paper.pdf; Aylin Caliskan et al., *Semantics Derived Automatically from Language Corpora Contain Human-Like Biases*, 356 Science 183 (2017), https://doi.org/10.1126/science.aal4230, http://opus.bath.ac.uk/55288/.

116. Abeba Birhane, *This Is How AI Image Generators See the World*, Wash. Post (6 Jul. 2023), https://www.washingtonpost.com/technology/interactive/2023/ai-generated-images-bias-racism-sexism-stereotypes/.

117. *Ibid.*

118. *Ibid.*

119. Su Lin Blodgett et al., Language (Technology) Is Power: A Critical Survey of 'Bias' in NLP, in *Proceedings of the 58th Annual Meeting of the Association for Computational Linguistics* 5454 (2020); Shikha Bordia & Samuel R. Bowman, Identifying and Reducing Gender Bias in Word-Level Language Models, in *Proceedings of the 2019 Conference of the North American Chapter of the Association for Computational Linguistics: Student Research Workshop* 7–15 (Association for Computational Linguistics 2019).

with languages in which the model is not well-trained, it may struggle to provide accurate responses, making it challenging to offer support for less commonly used or represented languages on the internet.

Above all, LLMs can pick up and propagate political and ideological biases from their training data. This means they might create content that supports certain political opinions or beliefs, making these biases even stronger.[120] These biases arise when the data used to train the model contains a disproportionate amount of content from one political perspective or belief compared to others. Consequently, users of the model might encounter content that appears to favour one political view or belief over others. This can lead to problems such as reinforcing existing biases and promoting information that only supports users' pre-existing views. Therefore, it is crucial to address these biases to make AI systems fairer and more neutral.

2.2.6 ChatGPT Is Infallible

The impressive capabilities of LLMs like ChatGPT can spark curiosity about their potential for infallibility. Nevertheless, it is crucial to recognise that ChatGPT is not infallible despite its remarkable capabilities. ChatGPT has several limitations, including the potential for inaccuracies, omissions, or incomplete information in its responses. According to a 2021 study, language models like ChatGPT can generate plausible-sounding but incorrect or nonsensical answers.[121] Moreover, GAI can suffer from knowledge gaps due to limitations in their training data. Furthermore, its knowledge base may not reflect the latest updates, given its last training session in September 2023.[122] While these limitations and challenges prevent ChatGPT from perfection, it is not infallible.[123] Let us delve deeper into these issues to understand them in more detail.

First, ChatGPT's training on extensive text data has made it capable of understanding the intricacies of language, enabling it to produce precise responses, even when faced with intricate and unclear situations.[124] Furthermore, its capacity to gain knowledge from structured and unstructured data makes it an exceptionally adaptable and versatile conversational AI tool. Its advanced neural design empowers it to manage multiple inputs and produces personalised responses, resulting in more captivating and gratifying user interaction.[125] Nonetheless, despite its impressive ability to mimic

120. Robert W. McGee, *Is Chat GPT Biased Against Conservatives? An Empirical Study* (15 Feb. 2023), https://ssrn.com/abstract=4359405; McCoy, R.T., Pavlick, E. & Linzen, T., Right for the Wrong Reasons: Diagnosing Syntactic Heuristics in Natural Language Inference, in *Proceedings of the 57th Annual Meeting of the Association for Computational Linguistics* 3428 (2019), https://arxiv.org/pdf/1902.01007.
121. Bender, E.M. et al., On the Dangers of Stochastic Parrots: Can Language Models Be Too Big?, in *Proceedings of the 2021 ACM Conference on Fairness, Accountability, and Transparency* 610 (2021), https://dl.acm.org/doi/pdf/10.1145/3442188.3445922.
122. *See supra* n. 36.
123. Claudia Biancotti & Carolina Camassa, *Loquacity and Visible Emotion: ChatGPT as a Policy Advisor*, arXiv preprint (2023), https://arxiv.org/ftp/arxiv/papers/2309/2309.03595.pdf.
124. *See supra* n. 97.
125. *See supra* n. 98.

human conversation and vast information access, ChatGPT falls short in replicating human common sense. Furthermore, it lacks the depth of knowledge and experience humans possess.[126] These limitations can lead to nonsensical or inaccurate responses, particularly in complex or nuanced situations.

Second, the contextual understanding of AI conversational models is not flawless, especially in lengthy or complex conversations. AI technologies may find it challenging to maintain a consistent context over long interactions, which can lead to responses that appear disconnected or mismatched with the ongoing conversation. These models might lose track of key points in extended discussions, resulting in irrelevant or nonsensical replies.[127] This has the potential to generate inconsistent or contradictory outputs, leading to user confusion.[128] This limitation often stems from the model's training data, which might lack the intricacies of human conversation that necessitate long-term memory and the ability to follow intricate storylines. Enhancing the model's ability to understand and remember context throughout long text passages is a significant challenge that needs further development. Nevertheless, the incorporation of advanced memory mechanisms and context retention strategies could potentially bridge this gap, enabling more coherent and contextually relevant interactions.

Third, LLMs, often trained using vast amounts of text data from the internet, naturally absorb the biases found in that data.[129] This can lead to biased or inappropriate answers, perpetuating stereotypes or discriminatory viewpoints. These biases can also appear in the model's responses, possibly causing it to make mistakes, form assumptions, or make broad statements that are not accurate. For instance, if the model learns from a dataset with gender stereotypes, it might generate text that supports those biases. Since LLMs are constantly learning and evolving, mitigating bias requires ongoing efforts in data selection, model training techniques, and human oversight. While developers are actively engaged in reducing these biases, achieving complete elimination poses a formidable challenge in the field of AI development.

Fourth, ChatGPT's proficiency is stronger in dominant languages like English due to the prevalence of such content on the internet. While some writers argue that ChatGPT is skilled in various languages,[130] it excels in English and can quickly acquire new information in this language, rendering it a valuable resource for educators and learners.[131] Nevertheless, ChatGPT struggles with low-resource languages or minority dialects. For example, when it comes to translating English to Bengali, the sixth most-spoken native language and the seventh most-spoken language globally, ChatGPT's performance is not satisfactory. The subsequent screenshots (*see* Figure 2.1) serve as empirical evidence substantiating this fact. This highlights the limitations of LLMs trained on imbalanced datasets and the need for more inclusive training data to improve performance across all languages.

126. *See supra* n. 41.
127. *See supra* n. 104.
128. *See supra* n. 112.
129. *See supra* n. 110.
130. *See supra* n. 112.
131. *See supra* n. 48.

Figure 2.1 Screenshot Illustrating ChatGPT's Linguistic Limitations

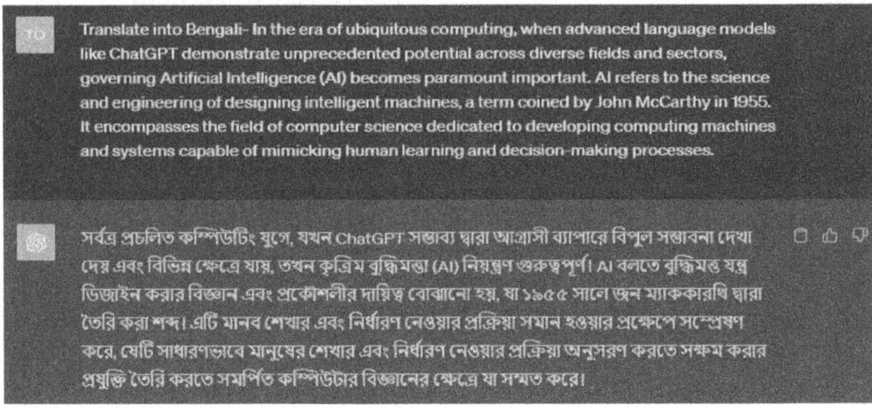

Source: ChatGPT, Author's Own Conversation with ChatGPT, June 2024.

Fifth, ChatGPT has a finite memory capacity, meaning it may forget earlier parts of a conversation as it progresses. While it uses techniques like rephrasing and summarising to reinforce context, there are still limitations to how much context it can retain, especially in long or intricate conversations. ChatGPT can effectively extract and summarise facts, but it faces limitations in generating essays on lengthy or complex topics. It often presents concepts with errors, uses illogical reasoning, and lacks clear structure in its arguments.[132] Despite its ability to critique its work, ChatGPT struggles to use this feedback to improve previous drafts effectively. This poses a challenge for tasks requiring consistent reasoning and building upon previously established ideas.

Sixth, LLMs like ChatGPT utilise deep learning algorithms to analyse language patterns and predict probable words in a sentence or text passage. By training on diverse internet texts, ChatGPT can respond to a wide range of topics.[133] Nonetheless, ChatGPT can sometimes misinterpret nuanced or ambiguous language constructs, resulting in responses that, while initially appearing contextually relevant, lack a profound understanding of the underlying ideas being discussed. It heavily relies on patterns and associations from its training data, which may not encompass all possible linguistic nuances or complex language constructs. As a result, developers continue to refine the model's training data and algorithms to enhance its ability to comprehend and generate more accurate responses.

In conclusion, ChatGPT is a powerful AI tool capable of generating human-quality text, translating languages, and writing different kinds of creative content.

132. Dirk H.R. Spennemann, *ChatGPT and the Generation of Digitally Born 'Knowledge': How Does a Generative AI Language Model Interpret Cultural Heritage Values?*, 3 Knowledge 480 (2023), https://doi.org/10.3390/knowledge3030032.
133. Xie, Y. et al., *Aesthetic Surgery Advice and Counseling from Artificial Intelligence: A Rhinoplasty Consultation with ChatGPT*, 47 Aesth. Plast. Surg. 1985 (2023), https://doi.org/10.1007/s00266-023-03338-7.

Nevertheless, it is not infallible. It has limitations related to contextual understanding, biases, language proficiency, memory capacity, and nuanced language comprehension. These limitations can sometimes lead to outputs that are factually incorrect, insensitive, or simply nonsensical. Developers are continually working to improve these aspects, but users should be aware of these limitations when interacting with ChatGPT and use it as a supportive tool rather than a replacement for human expertise and judgment. By understanding these limitations, users can leverage ChatGPT's strengths while mitigating its weaknesses.

2.2.7 ChatGPT Is All about Conversation

While ChatGPT is known for its engaging conversational skills, it surpasses the limitations of a simple chatbot. At its core, this versatile AI tool is a powerful language model trained on a massive dataset of internet text. This comprehensive training allows ChatGPT to understand and generate human-like text across diverse topics and writing styles. It can perform a wide range of tasks, including generating creative ideas, offering personalised recommendations, comprehending complex subjects, assisting with writing, summarising research findings, aiding in coding and debugging, translating languages, creating tests, planning trips, analysing sentiment, locating datasets, adapting to custom training data, and supporting career development.[134] This diverse functionality makes ChatGPT a valuable asset across various fields beyond being just a conversation tool.

One notable use of ChatGPT lies in content generation. It provides valuable services in generating written content, including poems, essays, code, and explanations of complex concepts. It can help users polish their writing by suggesting improvements in phrasing or sentence structure, ultimately assisting them in achieving their scholarly objectives. Additionally, ChatGPT can assist in generating code and suggesting solutions to programming-related tasks, making it a valuable asset for developers. It also serves as a significant time-saver for writers and businesses looking to produce high-quality content quickly. Trained on a vast dataset, GPT-4 excels at summarising knowledge, answering questions, and detecting hate speech.[135] Nevertheless, it is crucial to remember that the power of this tool can be misused. Malicious actors can exploit ChatGPT for disseminating false information,[136] spamming, perpetrating scams,[137] and even misusing legal processes and government actions. Hence,

134. Bernard Marr, *The Best Examples of What You Can Do with ChatGPT*, Forbes (1 Mar. 2023), https://www.forbes.com/sites/bernardmarr/2023/03/01/the-best-examples-of-what-you-can-do-with-chatgpt/?sh=3f4b2c2ddf11.
135. OpenAI, *GPT-4*, https://openai.com/index/gpt-4/ (accessed 29 Jul. 2024); Fidel Dhana, *Writing Advanced Excel Macros with GPT-4*, J. Acct. (7 Jul. 2023), https://www.journalofaccountancy.com/news/2023/jul/writing-advanced-excel-macros-with-chatgpt-4.html.
136. Tate Ryan-Mosley, *How Generative AI Is Boosting the Spread of Disinformation and Propaganda*, MIT Tech. Rev. (4 Oct. 2023), https://www.technologyreview.com/2023/10/04/1080801/generative-ai-boosting-disinformation-and-propaganda-freedom-house/; Europol, *The Criminal Use of ChatGPT: A Cautionary Tale about Large Language Models* (27 Apr. 023),

responsible use of such powerful tools is essential to ensure they contribute positively to society.

ChatGPT assumes the role of an educational aid, providing explanations, answering questions, and offering tutoring in various subjects. This efficacy makes it an invaluable resource for both students and educators. Its knack for delivering comprehensive explanations enhances the learning process and aids individuals in grasping intricate concepts. Furthermore, ChatGPT personalises the learning experience by offering tailored feedback to students while making education more accessible for everyone. It fosters interactive discussions in classrooms and assists teachers with lesson planning, assessment creation, and the exploration of innovative teaching methods.[138] Nevertheless, ChatGPT poses significant challenges to traditional education and research, like potential online exam cheating, human-like text creation that can mislead, reduced critical thinking abilities if over-relied on, and the need for careful evaluation of information it generates. Thus, conducting a meticulous review of the content generated by ChatGPT becomes imperative to ascertain its precision and prevent the propagation of false information.

Moreover, ChatGPT has practical utility in crafting chatbots designed for customer service and support. Through training from substantial amounts of customer service data, ChatGPT gains the ability to comprehend and answer a wide variety of customer questions. This enhancement can lead to more effective and precise customer service operations. By employing ChatGPT, the National Australia Bank (NAB), for example, creates chatbots like 'Mia' that can interact with customers and offer automated banking assistance, including tasks like checking account balances, transaction histories, and credit card information.[139] In a recent survey, 53 % of respondents opined that customer service needs to operate 24/7, while 33 % desired to use self-service options.[140] AI-powered chatbots, like ChatGPT, can meet these needs as they remain active around the clock.

In summary, ChatGPT transcends the boundaries of traditional chatbots, demonstrating its capabilities as a multifaceted AI tool with applications far beyond merely serving as a conversational agent. Its ability to understand and generate human-like text across diverse subjects and writing styles positions it as an invaluable asset across

---

https://www.europol.europa.eu/media-press/newsroom/news/criminal-use-of-chatgpt-cautionary-tale-about-large-language-models.

137. Melissa Heikkilä, *Three Ways AI Chatbots Are a Security Disaster*, MIT (3 Apr. 2023), https://www.technologyreview.com/2023/04/03/1070893/three-ways-ai-chatbots-are-a-security-disaster/; Aliza Vigderman, *Guide to Chatbot Scams and Security: How to Protect Your Information Online and at Home*, Security.org (11 Jun. 2024), https://www.security.org/digital-safety/scams/chatbot/.
138. Md. Mustafizur Rahman & Yoshitaka Watanobe, *ChatGPT for Education and Research: Opportunities, Threats, and Strategies*, 13 Applied Sci. 5783 (2023) https://doi.org/10.3390/app13095783.
139. Hassani, H., & Silva, E.S., *The Role of ChatGPT in Data Science: How AI-Assisted Conversational Interfaces Are Revolutionizing the Field*, 7 Big Data Cogn. Comput. 62 (2023), https://doi.org/10.3390/bdcc7020062.
140. Shep Hyken, *How AI and ChatGPT Can Crush Customer Service*, Forbes (16 Apr. 2023), https://www.forbes.com/sites/shephyken/2023/04/16/how-ai-and-chatgpt-can-crush-customer-service/?sh=40a4b6a86ae8.

various fields. From content generation to educational assistance and customer service, ChatGPT's versatility knows no bounds. However, it is crucial to acknowledge the potential misuse of such powerful technology and exercise responsible usage to prevent the spread of misinformation and deception. Nonetheless, with careful evaluation and oversight, ChatGPT stands as a beacon of innovation, revolutionising the way we interact, learn, and conduct business in the digital age.

2.2.8 ChatGPT Can Replace All Writers

The increasing capabilities of ChatGPT in generating text have sparked a discussion about its potential to replace human writers, especially in academic circles where the quality and authenticity of written work are of utmost importance. Despite ChatGPT's impressive text generation abilities, the question remains whether it can completely replace human writers across various contexts, such as academia. This issue requires further exploration.

First, AI-powered writing tools help in content generation but cannot fully supplant human creativity and critical thought in academic writing. Human authors bring unique perspectives and styles to their work, posing a challenge for AI replication. AI can serve as a valuable collaborator, offering support in brainstorming ideas, ensuring grammatical accuracy, and suggesting edits for improved clarity. The future of academic authorship likely lies in a collaborative model, where AI empowers human writers to work more efficiently and effectively. While advancements may lead to sophisticated AI writing that mimics human output, academic writing demands the synthesis of complex ideas, original research, and contributions to existing knowledge. These aspects necessitate human intuition, creativity, and deep understanding, which remain beyond the current capabilities of AI. While AI can generate coherent and relevant text, it currently lacks the essential human qualities of creative and critical thinking.[141]

Second, academic writing encompasses various genres, including research articles, essays, literature reviews and alike. Each genre demands a unique set of skills and expertise. LLMs like ChatGPT do not possess the systematic reasoning skills necessary to provide precise and detailed information in academic articles that include multiple paragraphs.[142] While ChatGPT can assist with drafting initial content or providing background information, it cannot replicate the expertise and domain-specific knowledge required for in-depth academic writing. Researchers and scholars possess years of training and experience in their respective fields, which shape their

141. William Castillo-Gonzalez, *ChatGPT and the Future of Scientific Communication*, Metaverse Basic & Applied Research [Internet] (28 Dec. 2022), https://mr.ageditor.ar/index.php/mr/article/view/2/4 (accessed 29 Jul. 2024); Ron Carucci, *In the Age of AI, Critical Thinking Is More Needed Than Ever*, Forbes (6 Feb. 2024), https://www.forbes.com/sites/roncarucci/2024/02/06/in-the-age-of-ai-critical-thinking-is-more-needed-than-ever/.
142. Minh-Hoang Nguyen, *Academic Writing and AI: Day-1 Experiment*, OSF Preprints xgqu5, Center for Open Science (2023).

ability to produce insightful and scholarly work. LLMs like ChatGPT do not possess domain-specific knowledge and cannot conduct original research.[143]

Moreover, academic writing goes beyond simply presenting information; it requires the skilful development of coherent arguments, active interaction with existing research, and the delivery of critical analysis. These competencies are cultivated through years of rigorous academic training and practical application. Despite ChatGPT's proficiency in replicating language patterns, it falls short in terms of deep critical thinking and analytical prowess. The model cannot participate in scholarly debates, question established theories or contribute innovative insights to academic dialogues. Consequently, ChatGPT possesses limited critical thinking abilities and lacks the domain-specific expertise required for conducting scientific research effectively.[144] As a result, while it may assist in generating academic content, its contributions remain limited compared to those of human scholars.

As rapidly advancing technologies like ChatGPT continue to evolve, it becomes imperative to analyse their potential ethical and societal impacts comprehensively. Alongside considerations of privacy and employment concerns, it is crucial to evaluate ChatGPT's ethical implications and ensure responsible and ethical use of the technology. While ChatGPT demonstrates remarkable capabilities in processing and presenting information, it lacks self-awareness,[145] an understanding of cultural, ethical, and societal values prioritised by academics,[146] and a deep understanding of complex issues.[147] Furthermore, its proficiency in generating content that can bypass plagiarism detection software raises concerns about academic integrity and the authenticity of generated work.[148] As we navigate the adoption and integration of AI technologies like ChatGPT, it is essential to remain vigilant and proactive in addressing the ethical and societal challenges they present.

In conclusion, ChatGPT and similar AI models have the potential to assist in various aspects of academic writing, such as generating initial drafts, providing background information, and aiding in language refinement. However, they cannot replace human writers in the academic sphere. The complexity of scholarly work, the need for domain-specific expertise, critical thinking, and ethical considerations all contribute to the irreplaceable role of human writers in academic writing. While AI chatbots like ChatGPT can be a valuable tool, it is most effective when used in

143. Alsadhan A. et al., *The Opportunities and Challenges of Adopting ChatGPT in Medical Research*, 10 Front. Med. (Lausanne) 1259640 (2023), https://doi.org/10.3389/fmed.2023.1259640.
144. Lea Bishop (formerly Shaver), *A Computer Wrote this Paper: What ChatGPT Means for Education, Research, and Writing* (26 Jan. 2023), https://ssrn.com/abstract=4338981/ https://doi.org/10.2139/ssrn.4338981. *See also* William Castillo-Gonzalez, *supra* n. 141.
145. James V. Pavlik, *Collaborating with ChatGPT: Considering the Implications of Generative Artificial Intelligence for Journalism and Media Education*, 78 Journalism & Mass Communication Educator 84 (2023), https://doi.org/10.1177/10776958221149577.
146. Vaccino-Salvadore, S., *Exploring the Ethical Dimensions of Using ChatGPT in Language Learning and Beyond*, 8 Languages 191 (2023), https://doi.org/10.3390/languages8030191.
147. *See supra* n. 145.
148. Julius Cosmo Romeo Rudolph et al., Sensing Hand Interactions with Everyday Objects by Profiling Wrist Topography, in *TEI 22: Proceedings of the Sixteenth International Conference on Tangible, Embedded, and Embodied Interaction* 1 (2022), https://doi.org/10.1145/3490149.3501320.

collaboration with human researchers and writers to enhance the quality and efficiency of the academic writing process.

2.2.9 ChatGPT Can Solve All Problems

Although ChatGPT has revolutionary and transformative potential across industries, it does not possess the ability to solve all the problems it addresses. While ChatGPT operates by predicting the next word or phrase in a given sequence based on patterns and training from vast amounts of text data, this predictive ability enables it to generate coherent and contextually relevant text, but this does not grant it inherent problem-solving capabilities. Research has shown that GPT-3 can achieve higher accuracy than human benchmarks in solving certain reasoning problems, though these comparisons are often complex and context-dependent.[149] Indeed, ChatGPT possesses extensive capabilities, but it also has its limitations. While research indicates that chatbots can offer accurate solutions for simple arithmetic, algebraic expressions, or basic logic puzzles, their responses for more intricate mathematical problems or advanced logic tasks, although often appearing convincing, may lack reliability.[150]

Moreover, ChatGPT entails manifold other limitations, such as its inability to grasp common sense, emotions, context, and difficulties in generating structured long content, handling multiple tasks, potential biases, limited knowledge, accuracy, and grammar issues, requiring fine-tuning, and high computational demands.[151] Another fundamental limitation of ChatGPT is that its responses are generated based on statistical connectivity rather than deep comprehension or reasoning. Consequently, it lacks the capacity for systematic reasoning, critical thinking, and genuine understanding required to solve complex problems. Generally, problem-solving capability involves assessing a situation, identifying possible solutions, evaluating their merits, and choosing the most appropriate course of action. ChatGPT's responses stem from its ability to mimic text patterns and generate plausibly outstanding content.

As of July 2024, ChatGPT is unable to use a web browser to access external information. Thus, its responses are solely drawn from the knowledge embedded in its training data. Therefore, ChatGPT's predictive nature means it cannot acquire new knowledge if the required information is not present in its dataset. This limitation can present challenges for ChatGPT in offering current and precise details on contemporary events or recent advancements. Additionally, ChatGPT generates responses based on patterns discerned during training, which may occasionally lead to inaccuracies or responses lacking contextual depth. In summary, due to its inability to access real-time data or adapt based on new information or experiences, ChatGPT's responses are

---

149. Dan Milmo, *ChatGPT Better Than Undergraduates at Solving SAT Problems, Study Suggests*, Guardian (31 Jul. 2023), https://www.theguardian.com/technology/2023/jul/31/chatgpt-better-than-undergraduates-at-solving-sat-problems-study-suggests.
150. Vagelis Plevris et al., *Chatbots Put to the Test in Math and Logic Problems: A Preliminary Comparison and Assessment of ChatGPT-3.5, ChatGPT-4, and Google Bard*, arXiv e-prints (2023), https://doi.org/10.3390/ai4040048.
151. *See supra* n. 41.

constrained by its existing knowledge base.[152] This constraint is evident in ChatGPT's responses to the following questions (*see* Figure 2.2).

Figure 2.2 Screenshot Illustrating ChatGPT's Limitation in Real-Time Data

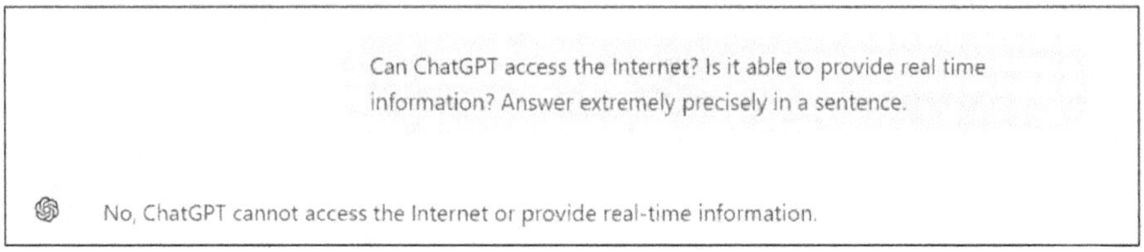

Source: ChatGPT, Author's Own Conversation with ChatGPT, August 2024.

Like other AI chatbots, Google's Gemini does not perform real-time internet searches when responding to questions. Instead of accessing search engines or websites directly, Gemini has been trained on an extensive dataset of text and code available up to a specific point in time. This approach allows Gemini to generate informative responses based on the information within its training data, but it cannot retrieve or access real-time updates. For instance, when queried about current events, Gemini might refer to the information present in its training data but will not provide updates on the latest news. For example, when asked about the issue, Gemini responded as follows (*see* Figure 2.3).

Figure 2.3 Screenshot Illustrating Gemini's Limitation in Real-Time Data

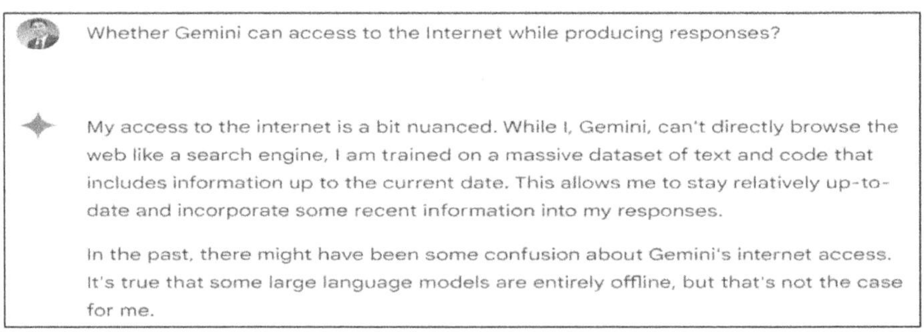

Source: Gemini, Author's Own Conversation with Gemini, August 2024.

In conclusion, although ChatGPT possesses impressive capabilities and potential, it is not a one-size-fits-all solution for every problem. The model's predictive abilities enable it to generate contextually relevant text, but it lacks inherent problem-solving capabilities. Additionally, ChatGPT has several limitations, such as its inability to

152. *See supra* n. 145.

access real-time data, the challenge of generating well-structured long content, and the absence of genuine critical thinking and reasoning abilities. While ChatGPT is a valuable tool for generating ideas and exploring new possibilities, the task of solving complex problems is still best undertaken by humans. Our combined knowledge, creativity, and critical thinking are what truly make the difference. Therefore, it is essential to recognise the limitations of LLMs like ChatGPT and to utilise their capabilities appropriately.

2.2.10 ChatGPT Can Learn and Improve Automatically

Some people may speculate that LLMs like ChatGPT, Gemini, or Microsoft's Copilot can learn and improve automatically. However, this assumption is not entirely accurate. While LLMs like ChatGPT, Gemini, and Copilot are built using deep learning techniques and rely on massive datasets for training, they do not inherently learn or improve on their own.[153] Instead, their improvement typically involves human intervention and oversight through processes such as fine-tuning, retraining, and the integration of user feedback. This involves substantial engineering efforts and the use of updated datasets to refine the models' performance and capabilities.

These models can be fine-tuned based on new data or feedback from users, and developers can retrain them on larger or more diverse datasets to enhance their performance. However, the process of learning and improving still requires human intervention, as these models do not possess the autonomous learning capabilities of humans. Therefore, while they can generate more accurate output over time, it is through human-guided refinement rather than automatic learning. To examine this issue practically, we can pose questions to LLMs such as ChatGPT, Gemini, and Microsoft Copilot, and analyse their responses to conclude (*see* Figures 2.4, 2.5 and 2.6).

Figure 2.4 Screenshot Illustrating ChatGPT's Limitation in Automatic Self-Improvement

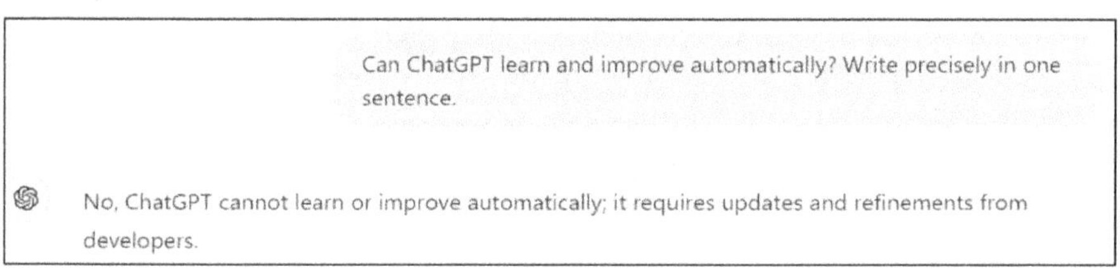

Source: ChatGPT, Author's Own Conversation with ChatGPT, August 2024.

153. Andy Extance, *ChatGPT Has Entered the Classroom: How LLMs Could Transform Education*, 623 Nature 474 (2023); IBM, *What Are Large Language Models (LLMs)?*, https://www.ibm.com/topics/large-language-models (accessed 29 Jul. 2024).

Figure 2.5 Screenshot Illustrating Gemini's Limitation in Automatic Self-Improvement

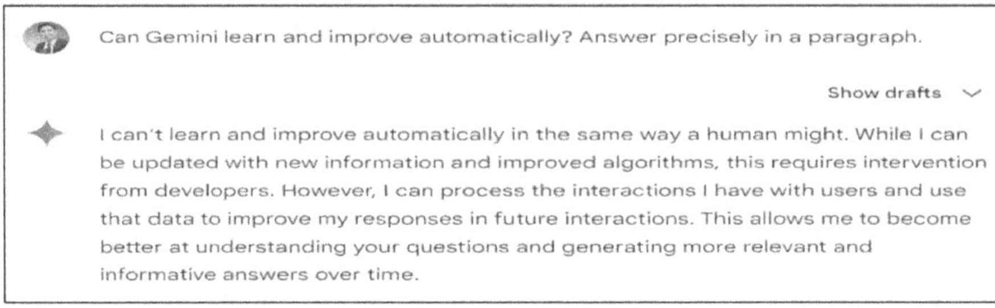

Source: Gemini, Author's Own Conversation with Gemini, July 2024.

Figure 2.6 Screenshot Illustrating Copilot's Limitation in Automatic Self-Improvement

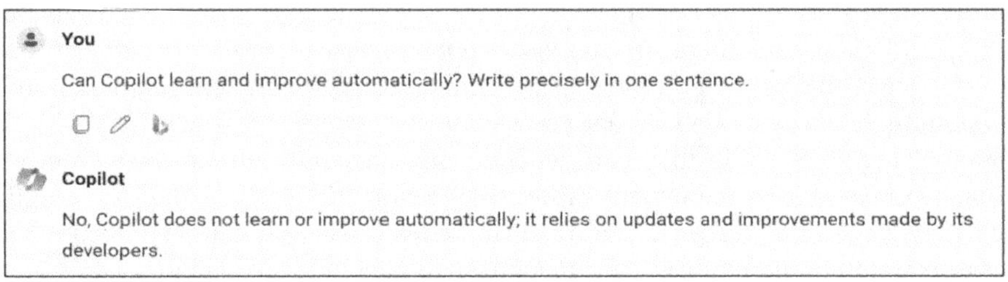

Source: Copilot, Author's Own Conversation with Copilot, August 2024.

The learning that ChatGPT undergoes is primarily a one-time training process. It does not actively learn or adapt in real-time based on new data or experiences in the way that humans do. Instead, its knowledge is static and based on the data available during its initial training phase. This means that ChatGPT does not automatically update its knowledge or understanding of the world as new information becomes available. It cannot adapt rapidly to current events or developments. Therefore, the ChatGPT model is not aware of information or advancements that occur after its training cut-off date.[154] For instance, if a new scientific discovery were made after the training period, ChatGPT would not be aware of it unless the model is retrained with that new information. This limitation can be significant, particularly for tasks that require access to the most up-to-date knowledge.

While ChatGPT may appear to learn and improve during a conversation, it is crucial to emphasise that this process does not constitute genuine learning in the human sense. Instead, ChatGPT relies on patterns and information extracted from its

154. *See* Yogesh K. Dwivedi et al., *supra* n. 90.

training data to generate responses relevant to the ongoing conversation. Unlike humans, it cannot actively seek out new information or adjust its understanding based on the context of the conversation. Moreover, LLMs like ChatGPT lack emotions, beliefs, or consciousness, as evidenced by their responses.[155] It is essential to recognise these inherent limitations, including its inability to comprehend nuances beyond its training data, its reliance on pre-learned patterns that limit creativity, and its constrained reasoning ability.[156] While ChatGPT can offer contextually relevant responses based on its training, it cannot genuinely grasp the underlying meaning or adapt its understanding in real-time.

OpenAI has introduced a fine-tuning feature to the paid version of the GPT-3.5 Turbo model in ChatGPT, allowing developers and businesses to customise the model for specific needs, enhancing its utility and cost-effectiveness.[157] While this fine-tuning process can improve ChatGPT's performance in specific areas, it remains a static and controlled form of learning rather than an automatic adaptation. The fine-tuning process is relatively limited in that it adjusts the model's behaviour within predefined boundaries set by developers, but it does not possess true self-awareness or autonomous learning capabilities. Improvements through fine-tuning are typically incremental and occur within the framework established during the model's development.

While there are speculations about the autonomous learning capabilities of LLMs like ChatGPT, Gemini, and Copilot, it is essential to clarify that these models do not inherently learn and improve automatically. Despite being built using sophisticated deep learning techniques and trained on extensive datasets, their improvement typically necessitates human intervention and oversight. While they can be fine-tuned based on new data or user feedback, they lack the autonomous learning capabilities of humans. Thus, any enhancements in their performance are guided by human refinement rather than automatic adaptation. This distinction underscores the importance of recognising the inherent limitations of LLMs and leveraging their capabilities judiciously. By understanding their role as tools that require human guidance, we can harness their potential effectively while navigating the complexities of AI technology.

2.3 STRATEGIES TO ADDRESS MISCONCEPTIONS ABOUT ChatGPT

Addressing the challenges posed by misinformation about the role of ChatGPT is a multifaceted endeavour that requires a comprehensive strategy. Guided by the principles of education, transparency, RAI development, and collaboration among various stakeholders, we can explore potential strategies to mitigate these misconceptions. This can be achieved by promoting media literacy initiatives to equip users with critical

155. *See supra* n. 84; OpenAI Community, *Have a Message that ChatGPT Asked to Convey to Support* (26 Jul. 2023), https://community.openai.com/t/have-a-message-that-chatgpt-asked-to-convey-to-support/378795.

156. Alejo Jos'e G. Sison et al., *ChatGPT: More Than a 'Weapon of Mass Deception' Ethical Challenges and Responses from the Human-Centered Artificial Intelligence (HCAI) Perspective*, 39 Int'l J. Hum.-Computer Interaction 1 (2023) https://doi.org/10.2139/ssrn.4423874.

157. *See* Tom B. Brown et al., *supra* n. 38.

thinking skills for evaluating information, fostering open communication about Chat-GPT's capabilities and limitations, and encouraging developers to prioritise ethical considerations in the model's design and deployment. Let us delve into those strategies in detail.

Addressing the concern that ChatGPT will lead to job displacement requires a holistic approach. It is worth acknowledging that as automation and ML progress, workers in some industries might lose their jobs.[158] However, these workers can mitigate this challenge by acquiring new skills that complement AI technology. To counter the belief that ChatGPT will take away jobs, it is essential to propose an educational initiative emphasising AI understanding, reskilling programmes, promoting human-AI collaboration, and framing AI as a productivity enhancer rather than a job replacement tool. Policymakers, businesses, and educational institutions should collaborate to create an adaptive ecosystem that balances automation and human expertise.

LLMs like ChatGPT possess significant capabilities, offering both potential benefits and drawbacks.[159] To dispel fears and mitigate the misconception that ChatGPT poses a threat to humanity, and to ensure its beneficial use, organisations must prioritise transparency and RAI development with strong safety measures and ethical guidelines. Public education campaigns can demystify AI and highlight Chat-GPT's potential. Additionally, regulatory frameworks and international dialogues on AI ethics and governance are crucial to managing risks and building trust. In essence, the impact of ChatGPT, whether positive or negative, hinges on its development and use. By prioritising responsible creation and applications, we can unlock its power to bring about positive change.

To confront the misconception that ChatGPT operates like a human, it is crucial to disseminate accurate information about its underlying mechanisms. ChatGPT lacks human-like creativity and cannot replace humans.[160] Public education campaigns should explain that ChatGPT functions based on ML algorithms and statistical patterns, without human-like consciousness, emotions, or reasoning abilities. Additionally, AI developers should be transparent about ChatGPT's capabilities and limitations, while ethical AI standards should advocate for clear labelling of AI-generated content to ensure users are aware of its origin. Above all, we can address this misunderstanding by promoting informed digital users and implementing robust ethical AI practices.

To approach contextual misunderstandings, developers must be transparent about limitations, emphasising that the model relies on statistical associations, not

158. https://digitalcommons.uri.edu/cgi/viewcontent.cgi?article=1547&context=cba_facpubs.

159. Simon Etim, *ChatGPT: Blessing or Curse?*, Medium (9 Feb. 2023), https://medium.com/@simon_Jr/chatgpt-blessing-or-curse-ec33b26a2aa#:~:text="In%20conclusion%2C%20chat%20bots%20like,misinformation%20and%20perpetuate%20harmful%20biases; Ishaan Joshi et al., ChatGPT in the Classroom: An Analysis of Its Strengths and Weaknesses for Solving Undergraduate Computer Science Questions, in *Proceedings of the 55th ACM Technical Symposium on Computer Science Education* 1, 625 (March 2024); Cade Metz, *Meet GPT-3. It Has Learned to Code (and Blog and Argue)*, The New York Times (24 Nov. 2020), https://www.nytimes.com/2020/11/24/science/artificial-intelligence-ai-gpt3.html.

160. Gozalo-Brizuela, R. & Garrido-Merchán, E.C., *ChatGPT Is Not All You Need: A State of the Art Review of Large Generative AI Models*, 1 Grace: Global Rev. AI Community Ethics 1 (2023).

genuine understanding. LLMs, like ChatGPT, trained on vast datasets of text and code, are susceptible to generating factually incorrect and nonsensical responses due to inherent errors and biases within the training data.[161] This can lead to contextual misunderstandings, as the model identifies patterns but lacks true comprehension of meaning. Educational initiatives promoting digital literacy can bridge the gap by teaching users about AI's functioning and its distinct capabilities compared to human cognition. Moreover, advancements in context-aware AI models, clear labelling of outputs, and responsible use guidelines can empower users to make informed decisions about interacting with these powerful tools.

To counter the belief that ChatGPT is unbiased, a multifaceted approach is necessary. Like all LLMs, ChatGPT is susceptible to biases and stereotypes inherent in its training data. AI developers and researchers should actively work to mitigate bias in GPT models. This can be achieved using diverse training data and transparent documentation of the development process, as well as by facilitating independent audits and third-party evaluations.[162] Additionally, fostering diversity and inclusion within AI development teams can significantly reduce the biases present in the models they create. Educating users about the potential for bias in AI-generated content empowers them to critically evaluate its outputs. Above all, users and educators should carefully review these outputs to identify and mitigate any potential biases.[163]

To tackle the misinformation about the infallibility of ChatGPT, it is imperative to foster a more realistic perception of its capabilities. First, AI developers and providers should communicate the limitations of ChatGPT to users, emphasising that it is not devoid of errors.[164] Offering transparency about how the model is constructed and making users aware of its lack of human-like cognition is essential. In addition, creating awareness campaigns and educational initiatives aimed at users can help dispel the notion of infallibility. Users should be encouraged to critically assess the information provided by ChatGPT and recognise that it may occasionally produce inaccurate or nonsensical responses. Lastly, incorporating feedback mechanisms for users to report errors or inaccuracies can contribute to ongoing model improvement and reinforce the understanding that ChatGPT is not infallible but a tool with certain limitations.[165]

To dispel the misconception that ChatGPT is solely designed for casual conversation, it is crucial to highlight its versatility and extensive applications. Extending far beyond casual conversation, ChatGPT serves as a powerful language model with a broad range of capabilities.[166] Developers and organisations should proactively address this misconception by showcasing its utility in diverse fields like content creation,

161. *See supra* n. 121.
162. *Ibid.*
163. *See supra* n. 108.
164. Daisuke Oba et al., In-Contextual Gender Bias Suppression for Large Language Models, in *Findings of the Association for Computational Linguistics: EACL 2024* 1722 (2024).
165. *Ibid.*
166. Sabrina Ortiz, *What Is ChatGPT and Why Does It Matter? Here's What You Need to Know*, ZDNET (17 Jun. 2024), https://www.zdnet.com/article/what-is-chatgpt-and-why-does-it-matter-heres-everything-you-need-to-know/.

data analysis, and coding assistance. Furthermore, educational campaigns and resources can illuminate ChatGPT's multifaceted nature, informing users of its potential to enhance creative writing, summarise complex data, and generate different programming code variations. By engaging users in interactive demonstrations and tutorials that showcase ChatGPT's capabilities across these domains, we can solidify an accurate understanding of its potential and promote its adoption as a versatile tool.[167]

To handle the misconception that ChatGPT can entirely replace human writers, it is imperative to educate the public and stakeholders about ChatGPT's role as a writing assistant, highlight its strengths and limitations, and promote the concept of collaboration between ChatGPT and human writers. This can be done through awareness campaigns, articles, and tutorials that emphasise how ChatGPT complements human creativity and expertise in writing tasks. It is also important to acknowledge ChatGPT's ability to generate content efficiently and provide support in various writing tasks, while also recognising its shortcomings in areas like creativity, critical thinking, and domain-specific expertise. By emphasising that ChatGPT can assist writers, enhance productivity, and provide valuable suggestions, we can foster a more accurate understanding of its role. In essence, LLMs, like ChatGPT, are expected to assist rather than replace human writers entirely.[168]

To address the misconception that ChatGPT can solve all problems, it is crucial to employ a multifaceted approach. While ChatGPT has significantly impacted the AI industry and beyond, its capabilities are primarily limited to generating human-like text-based responses through deep learning algorithms. However, it is crucial to recognise that ChatGPT is not a panacea for every challenge.[169] Educating the public about the capabilities and limitations of ChatGPT, encouraging responsible development and deployment, fostering critical thinking and digital literacy, and engaging in public discussions about the role of AI in society are all vital steps. By implementing these strategies, we can dispel the myth of ChatGPT as a universal solution and promote its responsible and effective use by all stakeholders.

To address the misconception that LLMs like ChatGPT can improve themselves automatically, it is important to understand the mechanisms underlying ChatGPT's learning and improvement processes. ChatGPT does not inherently learn or enhance its performance through user interactions alone. Instead, it relies on a structured development process where its performance is evaluated and refined based on feedback and additional data provided by its developers. ChatGPT learns and enhances its performance by analysing users' inputs, identifying areas for improvement in its responses, and refining its algorithm based on this analysis.[170]

167. OpenAI, *ChatGPT*, https://openai.com/chatgpt (accessed 29 Jul. 2024), https://ecoagi.ai/articles/chatgpt-complete-tutorial.
168. Karthik Venkatraman, *Will Chat GPT Replace Human Writer?* Medium (8 Feb. 2023), https://medium.com/geekculture/will-chat-gpt-replace-human-writer-65170430f87f; Rachel Shin, *The Rise and Impact of AI Writing*, Renaissance Rachel (2023), https://renaissancerachel.com/rise-and-impact-of-ai-writing/.
169. https://www.forbes.com/sites/forbestechcouncil/2023/03/09/will-chatgpt-solve-all-our-problems/?sh=13b31e884833.
170. Maria Redillas, *Can ChatGPT Improve Itself?* PCguide (last updated 19 Oct. 2023), https://www.pcguide.com/apps/can-chatgpt-improve-itself/.

While it might seem that ChatGPT improves through iterative interactions, this is not the case. Instead, its developers must actively intervene to provide new training data and updates to optimise the model. ChatGPT can adapt to specific prompts and user interactions within a single session, but it does not accumulate knowledge or experience over time without external intervention. Therefore, any advancements or updates to ChatGPT's capabilities result from deliberate developmental efforts rather than spontaneous or autonomous learning.

2.4 CONCLUSION

In conclusion, addressing the challenges of misinformation about the role of ChatGPT requires a multifaceted approach that promotes education, transparency, RAI development, and collaboration among stakeholders. By dispelling myths about ChatGPT's capabilities and limitations, fostering digital literacy, encouraging ethical AI practices, and promoting collaboration between humans and AI, we can unlock the potential of this powerful tool to bring about positive change. Furthermore, continuous research and development (R&D) efforts can enhance ChatGPT's ability to identify and avoid generating misleading information. While ChatGPT is not a one-size-fits-all solution, its versatility and potential to enhance productivity in various fields make it a valuable assistant. LLMs may take over some labour-intensive and repetitive jobs, potentially creating new technology-focused jobs. Overall, ChatGPT and similar language models appear as helping agents, not extinguishers for humanity. By prioritising responsible development and use, we can ensure that ChatGPT serves as a positive force for human society.

CHAPTER 3

Transformative Impacts of LLMs like ChatGPT

3.1 INTRODUCTION

The transformative impact of ChatGPT and similar LLMs has significantly altered our interactions with technology, driving innovation across multiple fields. These advanced AI tools have not only simplified our daily tasks but also expanded the boundaries of what we once considered possible. By examining the specific applications of LLMs like ChatGPT in sectors such as education, employment, healthcare, business, IT, journalism, and media, we can gain a deeper understanding of how these technologies are reshaping our world today and unlocking future advancements. This exploration reveals the profound ways in which these AI innovations are revolutionising various aspects of our lives, promising a future filled with new possibilities and opportunities.

3.2 EDUCATION

ChatGPT will transform education, not ruin it.[171] Equipped with an advanced language model, ChatGPT can profoundly transform both our methods of work and modes of learning. Most researchers agree that drafting an initial version of a document – whether it's an email, report, blog post, business plan, proposal, article, or employee review – can be a time-consuming and challenging task.[172] ChatGPT and other similar language models can do this job quickly and effortlessly. ChatGPT is an LLM that

171. Will Douglas Heaven, *ChatGPT Is Going to Change Education, Not Destroy It*, MIT Tech. Rev. (6 Apr. 2023), https://www.technologyreview.com/2023/04/06/1071059/chatgpt-change-not-destroy-education-openai/.
172. *See* Yogesh K. Dwivedi et al., *supra* n. 90.

generates text by predicting the most likely next word in each sequence. This iterative process allows it to create even lengthy passages. The chatbot receives training from various textual sources, including news articles, books, journal articles, publicly available internet content, and extensive open-source computer code.[173] Additionally, it undergoes further fine-tuning to ensure its output aligns with human preferences.

However, the widespread usage of ChatGPT in the education sector has garnered significant attention and sparked controversies across society. While ChatGPT offers numerous advantages in enhancing learning efficiency and facilitating communication, its applications also entail negative consequences and potential risks. There are concerns that ChatGPT may adversely affect interpersonal relationships, despite the anticipated improvements in communication methods and efficiency.[174] For instance, the use of ChatGPT by students while completing assignments has raised concerns about academic dishonesty and cheating, leading to opposition and resistance from universities, publications, and scholars.[175] Additionally, within the academic community, there is strong opposition and concerns regarding the misuse of ChatGPT in scientific research.

The overwhelming adoption of ChatGPT highlights its immense impact on a global scale. Excessive use of ChatGPT could lead to plagiarism. Students might rely on the model to generate content without proper attribution, which undermines academic honesty. Furthermore, ChatGPT may provide an unfair advantage if misused. Students who use it to ace exams or assignments without genuine effort may gain an undeserved edge. Critics argue that overreliance on AI-driven tools might hinder the critical thinking and problem-solving skills development in students.[176] Hence, it is advisable to carefully address issues related to the accuracy of information, ethical concerns, data privacy, and data security when implementing such technology in educational settings.[177]

In contrast, ChatGPT and similar language models offer numerous positive implications for the learning process. For example, students with disabilities may benefit from the personalised and adaptable assistance provided by these AI tools, catering to their specific needs.[178] Additionally, the non-threatening and non-judgmental nature of AI interactions can create a comfortable environment for students

173. Paul Geertsema et al., *ChatGPT and Large Language Models: What Are the Implications for Policy Makers?* (30 Mar. 2023), https://ssrn.com/abstract=4424048, http://dx.doi.org/10.2139/ssrn.4424048.
174. Hao Yu, *Reflection on Whether Chat GPT Should Be Banned by Academia from the Perspective of Education and Teaching,* 14 Front. Psychol. 1181712 (2023) https://doi.org/10.3389/fpsyg.2023.1181712.
175. *Ibid.*
176. Jürgen Rudolph et al., *ChatGPT: Bullshit Spewer or the End of Traditional Assessments in Higher Education?* 6 Ed-Tech Reviews 1 (2023), https://doi.org/10.37074/jalt.2023.6.1.9; Ahmed M. Hasanein & Abu Elnasr E. Sobaih, *Drivers and Consequences of ChatGPT Use in Higher Education: Key Stakeholder Perspectives,* at 13(11) Eur. J. Investig. Health Psychol. Educ. 2599–2614 (9 Nov. 2023), https://doi.org/10.3390/ejihpe13110181. PMID: 37998071; PMCID: PMC10670526.
177. *See supra* n. 48.
178. Wayne Holmes et al., *Artificial Intelligence and Education: A Critical View Through the Lens of Human Rights, Democracy and the Rule of Law* (November 2022), https://rm.coe.int/artificial-

who may be hesitant to ask questions in traditional classroom settings. Moreover, ChatGPT assists teachers in tailoring instruction to diverse student needs. It can suggest differentiated approaches, learning resources, and strategies to address individual learning styles.[179]

Teachers can utilise ChatGPT to generate lesson plans, assignments, and assessments. This saves time and provides creative insights into structuring engaging learning materials. For teachers working with students with special needs, ChatGPT can offer recommendations and tools to adapt content and teaching methods to accommodate diverse learning requirements. Further, ChatGPT aids teachers by addressing common student queries, enabling educators to focus on more complex and critical aspects of teaching rather than repeatedly answering routine questions.[180]

Furthermore, teachers can use ChatGPT to access resources for self-directed professional development. Additionally, AI technology can recommend articles, research articles, and pedagogical practices to enhance teaching skills.[181] Moreover, ChatGPT aids teachers in discovering new teaching resources, online tools, and interactive content that can enrich classroom experiences. By streamlining administrative tasks and providing quick access to information, ChatGPT enables teachers to allocate more time to instructional planning and student engagement.

In conclusion, ChatGPT presents a double-edged sword for education. While it offers numerous advantages, such as enhancing learning efficiency and facilitating communication, its widespread usage raises concerns regarding academic dishonesty, the development of critical thinking skills, data security, and more. Nonetheless, ChatGPT has the potential to revolutionise the way teachers approach teaching and learning if used appropriately. By catering to diverse student needs and enhancing the overall quality of education, it can be a powerful tool. Therefore, the key lies in harnessing ChatGPT's strengths to augment, not replace, traditional pedagogy. By fostering responsible use, encouraging critical thinking skills, and prioritising student engagement, educators can leverage ChatGPT to create a dynamic and empowering learning environment that prepares students for a rapidly evolving world.

3.3 EMPLOYMENT

ChatGPT and similar language models are revolutionising the field of AI, elevating assistive technology to unprecedented heights, decreasing the time required for

intelligence-and-education-a-critical-view-through-the-lens/1680a886bd; U.S. Dep't of Educ., *Artificial Intelligence: Opportunities and Challenges for Education* (2023), https://www2.ed.gov/documents/ai-report/ai-report.pdf; Firuz Kamalov et al., *New Era of Artificial Intelligence in Education: Towards a Sustainable Multifaceted Revolution*, 15 Sustainability 12451 (2023), https://doi.org/10.3390/su151612451.

179. *See* U.S. Dep't of Educ., *supra* n. 178.

180. Harry Barton Essel et al., *The Impact of a Virtual Teaching Assistant (Chatbot) on Students' Learning in Ghanaian Higher Education*, 19 Int'l J. Educ. Tech. Higher Educ. 57 (2022), https://doi.org/10.1186/s41239-022-00362-6.

181. *See* U.S. Dep't of Educ., *supra* n. 178.

application development, and delivering formidable capabilities to individuals without technical backgrounds.[182] GAI is poised to generate significant impacts across diverse fields of modern employment. Similar to the introduction of various technologies over the past century that have transformed the workplace, concerns that AI will entirely replace human workers are exaggerated. However, the rise of AI like ChatGPT will likely see a shift in the skillsets needed for many jobs. Individuals who can leverage AI tools effectively and develop complementary human skills like creativity, critical thinking, and problem-solving will be most in demand.

While the long-term effects of AI remain uncertain, the advancement of technology since the 1980s has displaced workers more rapidly than it has generated new job opportunities.[183] If GAI follows the trends observed in previous advances within the field of IT, it could lead to job reduction in the immediate future. A recent study conducted by Goldman Sachs revealed that GAI tools could impact around 300 million full-time jobs worldwide, potentially causing significant disruption within the job market.[184] Nevertheless, AI is also expected to create new job opportunities in areas like AI development, data analysis, and human-computer interaction, requiring a shift in skillsets for the workforce. The key will be ensuring a smooth transition for workers whose jobs are affected, through retraining programs and educational initiatives.

According to Business Insider, AI could soon replace ten types of jobs, including roles in tech, media, law, market research, teaching, finance, trading, graphic design, accounting, and customer service.[185] Moreover, researchers from OpenAI and the University of Pennsylvania found that AI systems akin to ChatGPT could influence approximately 80 % of jobs in the US, including mathematicians, accountants, writers, personal financial advisors, brokers, insurers, and data processors.[186] However, it is important to note that AI is more likely to automate specific tasks within these roles rather than completely replace human workers. In many cases, AI will work alongside humans to increase efficiency and productivity.

There are differing viewpoints on this matter as well. For example, Michelle Donelan, the Technology Secretary of the UK, expressed in the media that AI complements the existing work landscape in the UK rather than disrupting it. Emphasising their goal of using AI, she also affirmed that AI would enhance our jobs rather

182. Michael Chui et al., *Generative AI Is Here: How Tools like ChatGPT Could Change Your Business*, McKinsey & Company (20 Dec. 2022), https://www.mckinsey.com/capabilities/quantumblack/our-insights/generative-ai-is-here-how-tools-like-chatgpt-could-change-your-business.
183. Chris Vallance, *AI Could Replace Equivalent of 300 Million Jobs: Report*, BBC (28 Mar. 2023), https://www.bbc.com/news/technology-65102150.
184. Goldman Sachs Research, *Generative AI Could Raise Global GDP by 7 Percent*, Goldman Sachs (5 Apr. 2023), https://www.goldmansachs.com/intelligence/pages/generative-ai-could-raise-global-gdp-by-7-percent.html.
185. *See supra* n. 72.
186. Dailymail.com Reporter, *Up to 80 Percent of Jobs Could Be Impacted by ChatGPT-Like AI in the Coming Years, Study Warns*, Daily Mail (26 Jul. 2023), https://www.dailymail.co.uk/sciencetech/article-11907527/Up-80-PERCENT-jobs-impacted-ChatGPT-like-AI-coming-years-study-warns.html.

than replace them.[187] Nonetheless, there remain arguments that AI will inevitably lead to job displacement in certain sectors, such as manufacturing and data entry. Proponents of this viewpoint to the automation of tasks that were once performed by humans as evidence of this trend. The impact of AI on the job market is a complex issue with no easy answers. AI will likely both create and destroy jobs, making the net effect on employment difficult to predict. The key will be for workers to develop the skills and knowledge necessary to thrive in an AI-powered economy.

The future of employment in the face of GAI is likely to be one of adaptation and reskilling. As some fear AI will completely take over the workforce, history suggests otherwise. While automation has replaced some jobs, it has also created entirely new ones. The rise of the internet, for instance, eliminated the need for many travel agents but birthed the fields of web development and social media management.[188] Similarly, GAI will likely reshape the employment landscape, demanding a focus on different skill sets. Jobs requiring strong human qualities like empathy, social intelligence, and complex problem-solving are likely to see a rise.

Considering the above contexts, governments, educational institutions, and businesses all have a role to play in preparing the workforce for this transition. Governments should invest in retraining programs that equip individuals with the skills needed for AI-driven jobs, such as data analysis or coding. Educational institutions can develop new curriculums that emphasise critical thinking, problem-solving, and collaboration – skills that will be essential for working alongside AI. Businesses should invest in upskilling their employees and fostering a culture of continuous learning. By working together, these stakeholders can ensure that the rise of GAI is an opportunity for all, not just a select few.

3.4 HEALTHCARE

The advancement of ChatGPT has introduced a novel paradigm into the healthcare domain, yielding profound implications. This advanced AI technology has ushered in a new era of possibilities, redefining the landscape of healthcare practices and services. By enabling seamless interaction between medical professionals and patients, ChatGPT revolutionises healthcare systems, contributing to information dissemination, conducting diagnoses, and administering treatments. Specifically, enhancing patient-physician relationships through improved communication using language models is likely to positively impact patient outcomes across conditions such as mental health,[189]

187. Natasha Clark, *Brits Will Learn to Trust the Latest Computers, Says Michelle Donelan*, The Sun (28 Jul. 2023), https://www.thesun.co.uk/news/21854543/brits-learn-trust-latest-computers-michelle-donelan/.
188. Suzanne Bearne, *How Technology has Transformed the Travel Industry*, The Guardian (29 Feb. 2016), https://www.theguardian.com/media-network/2016/feb/29/technology-internet-transformed-travel-industry-airbnb; Lainie Petersen, *Impact of Technology on the Travel Agency Business*, CHORN (19 Mar. 2019), https://smallbusiness.chron.com/impact-technology-travel-agency-business-57750.html.
189. Horvath, A.O. & Luborsky, L., *The Role of the Therapeutic Alliance in Psychotherapy*, 61 J. Consulting & Clinical Psych. 561 (1993) https://doi.org/10.1037//0022-006x.61.4.561.

obesity,[190] and cancer.[191] Additionally, ChatGPT holds immense potential for streamlining administrative tasks, drug discovery, and personalised medicine, further optimising healthcare delivery.[192]

Furthermore, the integration of LLMs like ChatGPT presents significant potential for enhancing healthcare delivery and improving patients' quality of life.[193] Their ability to replicate human-like language is poised to impact healthcare, bringing a revolution in practices and services, human well-being, patient-doctor relationships, and effective communication. Moreover, LLMs like ChatGPT could enhance interventions relying on non-professional peer communication. Forbes identifies five transformative impacts of ChatGPT on healthcare. These include its exponentially increased processing speed, continuous availability for medical assistance, the potential to replicate aspects of physicians' clinical decision-making, the reduction of medical errors, and the possibility of elevating all physicians to peak performance levels.[194]

While ChatGPT offers exciting possibilities, ethical considerations remain paramount. Ensuring data privacy and security is crucial, as sensitive patient information entrusted to ChatGPT must be protected with robust safeguards.[195] Furthermore, the potential for bias within the algorithms requires careful mitigation strategies. Studies have shown that AI systems can perpetuate existing societal biases in areas like race, gender, and socioeconomic status.[196] Regular audits and ongoing development are essential to ensure fairness and inclusivity in healthcare delivery. Despite the power of AI, the human touch will remain irreplaceable. ChatGPT should not replace the crucial role of doctors in providing emotional support, building trust, and offering personalised care. The ideal scenario involves a collaborative approach, with AI augmenting human expertise to create a more comprehensive healthcare experience for patients.

Furthermore, GAI could pose significant challenges to healthcare systems. AI technologies might not possess the latest research updates and could offer outdated information, potentially resulting in negative outcomes. Additionally, as AI becomes

---

190. Elizabeth Ann Sturgiss et al., *Therapeutic Alliance and Obesity Management in Primary Care–A Cross-Sectional Pilot Using the Working Alliance Inventory*, 6 Clinical Obesity 376 (2016) https://doi.org/10.1111/cob.12167.
191. Jennifer W. Mack et al., *Measuring Therapeutic Alliance Between Oncologists and Patients with Advanced Cancer: The Human Connection Scale*, 115 Cancer 3302 (2009) https://doi.org/10.1002/cncr.24360.
192. George P. Patrinos et al., *Using ChatGPT to Predict the Future of Personalized Medicine*, 23 Pharmacogenomics J. 178 (2023), https://doi.org/10.1038/s41397-023-00316-9; Mohammed Yousef Shaheen, *Applications of Artificial Intelligence (AI) in Healthcare: A Review*, ScienceOpen Preprints (2021); AI Contentfy, *ChatGPT in the Pharmaceutical Industry: Advancing Drug Discovery and Research* (29 Mar. 2024), https://aicontentfy.com/en/blog/chatgpt-in-pharmaceutical-industry-advancing-drug-discovery-and-research.
193. *Will ChatGPT Transform Healthcare?*, 29 Nat Med 505–506 (2023), https://www.nature.com/articles/s41591-023-02289-5.
194. Robert Pearl, *5 Ways ChatGPT Will Change Healthcare Forever: For Better*, Forbes (13 Feb. 2023), https://www.forbes.com/sites/robertpearl/2023/02/13/5-ways-chatgpt-will-change-healthcare-forever-for-better/?sh=75f2433e7bfc.
195. Changyu Wang et al., *Ethical Considerations of Using ChatGPT in Health Care*, 25 J. Med. Internet Res. e48009 (2023) https://doi.org/10.2196/48009.
196. James Manyika et al., *What Do We Do about the Biases in AI?*, Harv. Bus. Rev. (10 Oct. 2019), https://hbr.org/2019/10/what-do-we-do-about-the-biases-in-ai.

more widespread, there are concerns about the erosion of human empathy and interpersonal connection.[197] Initial efforts to employ these models as clinical diagnostic tools, lacking supplementary training, have demonstrated restricted success, with algorithm performance trailing that of practising physicians.[198] Moreover, the high costs of developing and maintaining GAI models could exacerbate existing healthcare disparities, limiting access to this technology for under-resourced communities. Therefore, ensuring transparency and explainability in AI decision-making processes will be crucial for building trust with patients and healthcare professionals.

Recent research indicates that around one-third of US adults search for medical advice online to self-diagnose, but only about half of them subsequently consult a doctor.[199] This underscores the importance of caution when using ChatGPT and similar language models in healthcare to avoid risky behaviours like disregarding expert medical advice, highlighting the need for protective measures. Due to their widespread accessibility and potential influence on society, all stakeholders, including AI developers, scientists, ethicists, healthcare professionals, service providers, patients, advocates, regulators, and governmental agencies, should actively participate in determining the most suitable path forward. These models can be incredibly informative, but it is crucial to remember they are not a substitute for professional medical diagnosis and treatment. Additionally, ensuring the accuracy and trustworthiness of the information provided by these models is paramount.

ChatGPT's potential extends far beyond simply streamlining communication. Research suggests that LLMs can play a crucial role in augmenting medical R&D.[200] By analysing vast datasets of medical journals, clinical trials, and patient data, these models can uncover hidden patterns and connections that could accelerate breakthroughs in areas like personalised medicine and drug discovery. A study published in Nature Communications Medicine demonstrated how AI-powered analysis of patient data identified previously unknown subtypes of breast cancer, paving the way for more targeted treatment approaches.[201] This highlights the transformative potential of language models in propelling medical innovation and ultimately improving patient outcomes.

---

197. Dhir Gala & Amgad N. Makaryus, *The Utility of Language Models in Cardiology: A Narrative Review of the Benefits and Concerns of ChatGPT-4*, at 20(15) Int J Environ Res Public Health 6438 (25 Jul. 2023), https://doi.org/10.3390/ijerph20156438.
198. David M. Levine et al., *The Diagnostic and Triage Accuracy of the GPT-3 Artificial Intelligence Model*, Medrxiv: The Preprint Server for Health Sciences (2023).
199. Susannah Fox & Maeve Duggan, *Information Triage*, Pew Research Center (15 Jan. 2013), https://www.pewresearch.org/internet/2013/01/15/information-triage/.
200. Conrad W. Safranek et al., *The Role of Large Language Models in Medical Education: Applications and Implications*, 9 JMIR Med. Educ. e50945 (2023) https://doi.org/10.2196/50945; Soumen Pal et al., *A Domain-Specific Next-Generation Large Language Model (LLM) or ChatGPT Is Required for Biomedical Engineering and Research*, 52 Annals of Biomedical Engineering 451 (2024), https://doi.org/10.1007/s10439-023-03306-x; Shubo Tian et al., *Opportunities and Challenges for ChatGPT and Large Language Models in Biomedicine and Health*, 25 Briefings in Bioinformatics 1, bbad493 (2024) https://doi.org/10.1093/bib/bbad493.
201. Shashank Yadav et al., *Deep Learning and Transfer Learning Identify Breast Cancer Survival Subtypes from Single-Cell Imaging Data*, 3 Communications Medicine 187 (2023) https://doi.org/10.1038/s43856-023-00414-6.

However, ethical considerations surrounding the use of AI in healthcare require careful attention. As with any powerful technology, safeguards are necessary to ensure responsible implementation. Transparency and explainability of AI decision-making processes are paramount to maintaining trust with patients and the medical community. AI algorithms, especially those based on ML and deep learning, can be complex and opaque. This lack of transparency raises concerns about trust and accountability in medical decisions.[202] Studies have shown that higher levels of AI transparency can improve performance, trust, and the correct use of AI systems.[203] This helps identify potential biases and ensures that AI recommendations are based on sound evidence.

Furthermore, robust data security measures are crucial to protect sensitive patient information. Policymakers and healthcare providers must ensure that these technologies are used responsibly, and patients must receive comprehensive information about the potential benefits and risks of these technologies. Ensuring that ChatGPT and similar language models are integrated effectively and ethically into healthcare systems will require close collaboration between stakeholders across different sectors. By doing so, we can maximise the potential benefits of these technologies while also mitigating potential risks, helping to create a better and more equitable healthcare system for all.

3.5 BUSINESSES

ChatGPT can generate human-like text responses that spark significant interest and integrate into various applications. The chatbot has massive positive and negative implications across diverse businesses. One of the most significant positive impacts of ChatGPT is its role in enhancing communication. It enables individuals to engage in natural language conversations with machines, making interactions with technology more accessible and user-friendly. This can benefit people with disabilities, language barriers, or those who prefer conversational interfaces over traditional forms of interaction.[204] Moreover, the AI chatbot has the potential to bridge the communication gap between humans and machines, making technology more inclusive. Additionally, ChatGPT can be used to create personalised customer service experiences, allowing businesses to tailor their interactions to individual needs and preferences. This can lead to higher customer satisfaction and loyalty.

ChatGPT emerges as a dynamic technological force poised to reshape the very landscape of conversational interfaces.[205] Building upon the foundations of chatbots, ChatGPT elevates dialogue to an unprecedented level of human-like interaction. In

202. Maria Frasca et al., *Explainable and Interpretable Artificial Intelligence in Medicine: A Systematic Bibliometric Review,* 4 Discov. Artif. Intell. 15 (2024), https://doi.org/10.1007/s44163-024-00114-7; Anne Gerdes, *The Role of Explainability in AI-Supported Medical Decision-Making,* 4 Discov. Artif. Intell. 29 (2024), https://doi.org/10.1007/s44163-024-00119-2.
203. Team Human-AI, *State-of-the-Art and Research Needs,* The National Academies Press (2022), https://nap.nationalacademies.org/read/26355/chapter/7.
204. Salman Mohamadi et al., *ChatGPT in the Age of Generative AI and Large Language Models: A Concise Survey,* arXiv preprint arXiv:2307.04251 (2023), https://arxiv.org/abs/2307.04251.
205. *See* Yogesh K. Dwivedi et al., *supra* n. 90.

customer service, for instance, it can handle routine inquiries, freeing up human agents to focus on more complex tasks. Additionally, ChatGPT-powered chatbots can provide instant assistance, reducing response times and improving user satisfaction. It not only adeptly addresses inquiries of people but also propels innovation by offering innovative ideas and solutions. Its transformative capabilities have resonated across various domains, including journalism, law, and marketing, through its revolutionary content-generation strategies.[206]

In the corporate sphere, businesses are avidly exploring avenues for integrating groundbreaking technology into their operations, recognising its remarkable potential. The financial sector has a storied history of seamlessly incorporating technological advancements to catalyse operational transformations.[207] From the advent of online banking to the era of open banking, and further evolution through the introduction of chatbots, robo-advisors, and innovative investment strategies, banks have consistently embraced technology-driven enhancements.[208] Therefore, it is unsurprising that an increasing number of banks are forsaking their physical branches in favour of adopting cutting-edge financial technology (fintech) to streamline operations or transitioning into fully digital banking entities.[209]

Above all, conversational AI is crucial for businesses in various sectors, such as customer service, sales, marketing, and HR. It automates and improves customer interactions and provides valuable insights for making informed decisions. AI-powered chatbots reduce the need for human agents, and speech recognition and sentiment analysis allow for more accurate responses. Additionally, conversational AI provides round-the-clock service, ensuring that customer queries receive attention at any time. This potential of AI chatbot frees human representatives to handle complex issues while AI effectively addresses routine needs through Natural Language Generation (NLG) for natural-sounding interactions. For example, IBM's Watson Assistant exemplify this potential, empowering businesses to revolutionise their customer service experiences.[210]

In conclusion, LLMs like ChatGPT, with its advanced NLP capabilities, bring both positive and negative implications across diverse businesses. It enhances communication, improves efficiency, and opens new opportunities for accessibility. Nevertheless, ethical concerns related to misinformation and job displacement may appear significant challenges and require holistic solutions.[211] Hence, integrating AI systems in industrial settings must be done with careful consideration to maintain business integrity and fair employment practices. It is also essential to ensure that these

206. *Ibid.*
207. *Ibid.*
208. *Ibid.*
209. *Ibid.*
210. Tim Mucci, *Conversational AI Use Cases for Enterprises*, IBM (23 Feb. 2024), https://www.ibm.com/blog/conversational-ai-use-cases-for-enterprises/.
211. Jeff Schwartz et al., *Ethics and the Future of Work: From 'Could We' to 'How Should We'*, Deloitte (15 May 2020), https://www2.deloitte.com/us/en/insights/focus/human-capital-trends/2020/ethical-implications-of-ai.html; James Gondola, *The Future of Work: Ethical AI and Job Displacement Concerns*, Medium (3 Apr. 2024), https://medium.com/@jamesgondola/the-future-of-work-ethical-ai-and-job-displacement-concerns-9e884cbe3b00.

technologies are inclusive and do not exacerbate existing social inequalities. Developers, policymakers, and society must navigate the responsible use of ChatGPT and similar technologies to maximise their benefits while mitigating their negative consequences.[212] By doing so, we can harness the potential of ChatGPT to enhance our lives without compromising our values and security.

3.6 IT SECTOR

The influence of ChatGPT within the IT sector is profound and far-reaching.[213] It promises to transform human-computer interactions into more intuitive and user-centric experiences. Moreover, this AI-enabled Chatbot offers the potential to streamline and automate customer service operations, enabling businesses to enhance their customer support with increased efficiency and reduced resources. Furthermore, ChatGPT plays a pivotal role in developing more realistic and engaging chatbots, thereby facilitating companies in delivering tailored and personalised customer interactions.[214] Therefore, ChatGPT impacts the IT field significantly, demonstrating a fundamental change in how individuals interact with computer systems.

Moreover, AI-powered tools like ChatGPT are transforming software development by automating tasks such as code generation, documentation writing, and debugging. These tools provide developers with intelligent suggestions and code snippets, ultimately boosting their overall coding skills and efficiency.[215] Additionally, ChatGPT has made coding more accessible to individuals without extensive programming backgrounds, democratising software development and potentially expanding the talent pool in the IT industry.

The rise of cloud-based GAI application programming interfaces (APIs) is likely to lead to an explosion of specialised tools for tackling particular tasks. This development could significantly reduce the reliance on traditional coding expertise, making it easier for people without a programming background to leverage the power of AI.[216] The capacity to generate text and code on demand means that individuals can enhance their productivity and accomplish tasks more swiftly by using LLMs like ChatGPT.[217]

Furthermore, ChatGPT has the potential to enhance efficiency and productivity within the software sector. By automating tasks like answering customer service

---

212. Ken Huang & Winston Ma, Legal and Ethics Responsibility of ChatGPT, in *Beyond AI: Future of Business and Finance* 1, 1 (K. Huang et al. eds, 2023), https://doi.org/10.1007/978-3-031-45282-6_12; *see also supra* n. 79.
213. I.S. Thakare et al., *Impact of ChatGPT on Industry*, 44 Mathematics and Applied Sciences S8 (2023) https://doi.org/10.53555/jaz.v44is8.3548.
214. TechTeamZ, *ChatGPT and Its Impact on the IT World*, TechTeamz.IO (27 Jul. 2023), https://techteamz.io/chatgpt-and-its-impact-on-the-it-world/#: ~ :text = The % 20impact % 20of % 20ChatGPT % 20on,customer % 20service % 20with % 20fewer % 20resources.
215. Ahmed Soliman et al., *Leveraging Pre-trained Language Models for Code Generation*, 10 Complex Intell. Syst. 3955, 3955–3980 (2024), https://doi.org/10.1007/s40747-024-01373-8.
216. Gagan Bajaj, *Generative AI: ChatGPT's Impact on Software Engineering Roles* (21 Apr. 2023), https://gaganbajaj.medium.com/generative-ai-chatgpts-impact-on-software-engineering-roles-98179adf8d59.
217. Ethan Mollick, *ChatGPT Is a Tipping Point for AI*, MIT Tech. Rev. (14 Dec. 2022), https://hbr.org/2022/12/chatgpt-is-a-tipping-point-for-ai.

queries through ChatGPT, organisations can liberate their employees to focus on more advanced assignments. This change may stimulate innovation and faster development, potentially creating new job opportunities.[218]

Additionally, ChatGPT's ability to streamline repetitive tasks can lead to improved workflow management and resource allocation within software development teams, allowing for more effective utilisation of human capital. Moreover, the implementation of ChatGPT in software development processes can foster a culture of continuous improvement and learning, as teams adapt to new technologies and explore innovative ways to leverage AI for enhanced productivity and creativity. Therefore, while ChatGPT may initially result in job cuts in some software sectors, it also has the potential to create new openings for software engineers and contribute to the overall growth and evolution of the industry.

Besides, the rapid advancement in LLMs like ChatGPT is transforming the landscape of data science and statistics, streamlining intricate procedures, such as data cleansing, model construction, interpretation, and report generation, and redefining the functions of data scientists.[219] This can significantly reduce the time required for data pre-processing and analysis, which are critical steps in the machine-learning pipeline. Moreover, ChatGPT's ability to generate synthetic data can aid in training ML models where real-world data is scarce or sensitive. Consequently, the integration of ChatGPT into data analytics workflows can lead to more informed business decisions and innovative solutions to industry-specific problems. As a result, ChatGPT not only enhances the efficiency of existing processes but also paves the way for new methodologies in data-driven decision-making.

While LLMs like ChatGPT hold considerable promise, it is essential to recognise and tackle its associated challenges. Biases in training data can result in prejudiced outcomes, making the pursuit of equity in AI models a critical concern. Researchers highlight the necessity of implementing fairness assessments during the developmental phase to curtail such biases.[220] Moreover, the opaqueness of several AI models may impede the establishment of trust and accountability. Therefore, it is imperative to conduct additional research to enhance the transparency of ChatGPT's processes.[221] However, overregulation could prevent the technology from realising its full potential, which could be transformative for pivotal sectors such as science, education, and

218. James Manyika & Kevin Sneader, *AI, Automation, and the Future of Work: Ten Things to Solve For*, McKinsey & Company (1 Jun. 2018), https://www.mckinsey.com/featured-insights/future-of-work/ai-automation-and-the-future-of-work-ten-things-to-solve-for; Harry J. Holzer, *Understanding the Impact of Automation on Workers, Jobs, and Wages*, Brookings (19 Jan. 2024), https://www.brookings.edu/articles/understanding-the-impact-of-automation-on-workers-jobs-and-wages/.
219. Xinming Tu et al., *What Should Data Science Education Do With Large Language Models?*, 6(1) Harvard Data Science Review, https://doi.org/10.1162/99608f92.bff007ab.
220. Ehsan Latif et al., *AI Gender Bias, Disparities, and Fairness: Does Training Data Matter?*, arXiv preprint arXiv:2312.10833 (2023), https://arxiv.org/pdf/2312.10833v1.
221. Ninareh Mehrabi et al., *A Survey on Bias and Fairness in Machine Learning*, 54 ACM Computing Surveys 1 (2021), https://doi.org/10.1145/3457607, https://arxiv.org/pdf/1908.09635.

healthcare.[222] By proactively addressing these concerns and prioritising RAI development, the IT sector can harness the full potential of ChatGPT while minimising potential risks.

In summary, ChatGPT has made significant strides in the IT sector, transforming customer support, software development, data analysis, education, and ethical considerations. Its ability to understand and generate human-like text has revolutionised various aspects of the industry, leading to increased efficiency, accessibility, and improved decision-making processes. As technology continues to advance, the influence of ChatGPT on the IT sector is likely to grow, shaping the industry in unimaginable ways. Above all, the implications of ChatGPT encompassing IT sectors span automating customer support, enhancing development processes, delivering personalised content, providing data analysis and insights, and assisting education and training by offering personalised learning experiences.

3.7 JOURNALISM AND MEDIA

ChatGPT has brought about a groundbreaking transformation in the field of journalism, revolutionising the ways journalists collect and deliver information to their readers.[223] This AI-powered tool can automate the creation of news articles, generate summaries of lengthy reports, and assist in fact-checking processes. Newsrooms are increasingly utilising ChatGPT to draft initial drafts of articles, saving time and resources. This tool allows journalists to focus on more in-depth investigations and analyses, ultimately enhancing the quality of journalism. Media outlets are employing AI-driven algorithms to personalise news feeds for individual readers, offering them tailored content based on their preferences and interests. Thus, AI empowers journalists to excel in their core areas by automating media processes, allowing them to concentrate on their core strengths.[224]

Nowadays, ChatGPT's impact on journalism and media is undeniable, revolutionising the way news is produced, distributed, and consumed. This AI model has proven to be an indispensable tool for breaking down language barriers in journalism by providing quick and accurate text translation capabilities.[225] Reporters can now

222. Goldman Sachs, *Generative AI: Hype or Truly Transformative?*, Goldman Sachs (2024), https://www.goldmansachs.com/insights/top-of-mind/generative-ai-hype-or-truly-transformative.
223. Amit Dutta, *ChatGPT in Journalism: A Game-Changer or a Gimmick?*, Medium (15 Jun. 2023), https://medium.com/@AmitDutta09/chatgpt-in-journalism-a-game-changer-or-a-gimmick-80d5e93eacd8.
224. Felix M. Simon, *Artificial Intelligence in the News: How AI Retools, Rationalizes, and Reshapes Journalism and the Public Arena*, Columbia Law Review (6 Feb. 2024), https://www.cjr.org/tow_center_reports/artificial-intelligence-in-the-news.php.
225. Jerry Alto, *ChatGPT: Transforming Journalism in the Digital Age*, Medium (18 Oct. 2023), https://jerryalto.medium.com/chatgpt-transforming-journalism-in-the-digital-age-3321787b8c6e; Mia Daniels, *ChatGPT: Breaking Language Barriers in International Communication*, All about ChatGPT (18 Oct. 2023), https://chatgpt.web.za/chatgpt-breaking-language-barriers-in-international-communication/.

overcome language obstacles, access diverse sources, and provide globally informed coverage. Non-native English speakers can also benefit from ChatGPT's real-time language correction and simplification of complex topics for the general audience, improving writing skills. Nonetheless, it is crucial to note that ChatGPT has its limitations and may not always provide factually correct information for events or developments that occurred post-2021. Overall, ChatGPT presents new opportunities for journalism to augment the reporting process and engage with a wider range of sources and audiences.

ChatGPT goes beyond just summarising news articles. It serves as a one-stop shop for informed citizens and content creators alike. By efficiently organising and summarising news from various sources, ChatGPT provides users with concise overviews to keep them up-to-date on key points. It can even personalise recommendations based on interests.[226] For content creators, ChatGPT is a powerful tool for research, drafting, and curation, offering AI-powered assistance in generating commentary, introductions, and summaries. This streamlines the content creation process by providing inspiration, generating ideas, and even helping with proofreading and editing tasks. Beyond news, ChatGPT integrates with content curation strategies, helping businesses enhance brand visibility and audience engagement by generating thoughtful commentary and summaries alongside curated content, thereby boosting productivity, and facilitating the delivery of high-quality content to audiences.

However, the effects of technology on journalism can evoke both enthusiasm and apprehension.[227] Among other things, ChatGPT contributes significantly to combatting disinformation and fake news by swiftly fact-checking claims, authenticating sources, and automating these processes to enhance journalistic accuracy and credibility, thereby strengthening trust in the media. Conversely, ChatGPT also has immense potential to generate and spread credible-sounding fake news, reports, and information that seem to have been authored by humans. While GAI could enhance journalism practices without displacing journalists, concerns arise regarding the rising sophistication of deepfakes and the absence of adequate tools for newsrooms to detect deepfakes or authenticate audio.[228]

In conclusion, ChatGPT has significantly transformed journalism and media. It revolutionises how news is produced, distributed, and consumed, even breaking down language barriers. By handling routine tasks, ChatGPT frees journalists for deeper investigations and analyses, ultimately enhancing journalistic quality. For both informed citizens and content creators, ChatGPT acts as a one-stop shop, offering AI-powered assistance for tasks like generating commentary, introductions, and

---

226. AIContentfy team, *The Impact of ChatGPT on News and Journalism*, AIContentfy (6 Nov. 2023), https://aicontentfy.com/en/blog/impact-of-chatgpt-on-news-and-journalism.
227. Danilo Alves Silva, *ChatGPT and Journalism: Adapting to Evolving Technology*, World Press Institute (17 Apr. 2023), https://worldpressinstitute.org/chatgpt-and-journalism-adapting-to-evolving-technology/.
228. University of Technology Sydney, *GEN AI and Journalism* (December 2023), https://www.uts.edu.au/sites/default/files/2023-12/GEN%20AI%20and%20Journalism_web%20version.pdf.

summaries. Nevertheless, as journalism evolves with technology, critical thinking and fact-checking remain paramount to ensure the accuracy and integrity of information provided by AI models like ChatGPT. We must also acknowledge the potential for bias and misinformation. Above all, AI's impact on journalism carries both advantages and potential drawbacks. Therefore, the United Nations Educational, Scientific and Cultural Organization (UNESCO) maintains that it is essential to consider both the potential advantages and challenges while evaluating the impact of AI on the field of journalism.[229]

3.8 CUSTOMER SERVICE

The advent of ChatGPT and similar language models has brought about a significant transformation in customer service, revolutionising the way businesses interact with their customers. One of the most profound impacts of ChatGPT on customer service lies in its ability to provide instant, round-the-clock support to users.[230] By deploying AI-powered chatbots equipped with ChatGPT, businesses can offer immediate assistance to customers at all times of the day or night without human intervention. Moreover, ChatGPT-powered chatbots can handle a wide range of inquiries, from simple frequently asked questions (FAQs) responses to more complex troubleshooting scenarios. They are also available 24/7, which means that customers can get assistance even outside business hours. ChatGPT can provide relevant answers regardless of how a question is asked, unlike other chatbots that require specific wording or keywords.[231] Thus, these language models have become increasingly popular nowadays due to their ability to automate customer support and improve customer experience.

ChatGPT enhances the efficiency and effectiveness of customer service interactions by providing personalised responses tailored to each customer's needs and preferences.[232] By analysing customer inquiries and interactions in real-time, ChatGPT can generate contextually relevant responses that address the specific concerns of each customer, leading to more meaningful and engaging interactions. This personalised approach not only improves the overall customer experience but also fosters stronger relationships between businesses and their customers. Research conducted by McKinsey & Company highlights the importance of personalisation in customer service, noting that businesses that deliver personalised experiences can achieve revenue increases and boost customer satisfaction.[233]

229. UNESCO, Reporting on Artificial Intelligence: A Handbook for Journalism Educators (M. Jaakkola ed., 2023) (UNESCO Series on Journalism Education), https://doi.org/10.58338/HSMK8605.
230. Bulbul Gupta et al., *ChatGPT: A Brief Narrative Review*, 10 Cogent Bus. & Mgmt. 1 (2023), https://doi.org/10.1080/23311975.2023.2275851.
231. Blake Morgan, *Pros of ChatGPT for Customer Experience*, Forbes (26 Apr. 2023), https://www.forbes.com/sites/blakemorgan/2023/04/26/pros-of-chatgpt-for-customer-experience/?sh=351a0078513f.
232. *See supra* n. 104.
233. *See* Ashish Vaswani et al., *supra* n. 38.

Moreover, ChatGPT enables businesses to automate repetitive tasks and streamline customer service operations, leading to cost savings and operational efficiencies.[234] By deploying AI-powered chatbots for routine inquiries and tasks, businesses can reduce the need for human customer service agents, thereby reducing the burden on human customer service agents and allowing them to focus on more specialised tasks. This can result in significant cost savings for businesses, especially for small- and medium-sized enterprises. Additionally, ChatGPT can handle a high volume of inquiries simultaneously, allowing businesses to scale their customer service operations more effectively and efficiently. Businesses that implement AI-powered chatbots could potentially experience a substantial reduction in call, chat, and email inquiries, resulting in considerable cost savings.

With multi-language support, ChatGPT enables seamless communication with customers in their preferred language, breaking down language barriers.[235] This capability eliminates the need for customers to rely on third-party translation services, thereby reducing response times and enhancing overall customer experience. With such potential, ChatGPT facilitates cross-cultural collaboration by allowing employees to communicate and exchange ideas in their preferred languages. This enhances productivity, creativity, and synergy among diverse teams. By providing real-time translation between languages, ChatGPT allows companies to expand their reach and serve a global audience. It is noteworthy that LLMs like ChatGPT perform better in dominant languages like English due to training data bias, limiting their usefulness in lesser-resourced languages.

It is also crucial to acknowledge that although ChatGPT provides many advantages for customer service, it also introduces challenges and considerations that businesses need to address. One such challenge is ensuring the accuracy and reliability of AI-generated responses. While ChatGPT can generate human-like responses, it may occasionally produce errors or inaccuracies, especially when faced with complex or ambiguous inquiries. A study by Unified Journeys in Experience Technology (UJET) shows that chatbots are making customer service worse, with 80 % of people reporting more frustration after interacting with one.[236]

To mitigate this risk, businesses must implement robust quality assurance processes and regularly monitor and evaluate the performance of their AI-powered chatbots. Additionally, businesses must ensure that their chatbots are equipped with fail-safe mechanisms to escalate inquiries to human agents, when necessary, particularly in cases where the customer's issue cannot be resolved autonomously. Furthermore, businesses should consider the ethical implications of deploying AI-powered chatbots for customer service. As AI technologies such as ChatGPT continue to

234. *Ibid.*
235. Cem Dilmegani, *ChatGPT for Customer Service: 7 Use Cases & Benefits in 2024*, AIMultiple Research (2 Jan. 2024), https://research.aimultiple.com/chatgpt-for-customer-service/.
236. UJET Research Reveals Chatbots Increase Frustration for 80 % of Consumers, Business Wire (6 Dec. 2022), https://www.businesswire.com/news/home/20221206005186/en/UJET-Research-Reveals-Chatbots-Increase-Frustration-for-80-of-Consumers.

advance, safeguarding the privacy of sensitive personal data, particularly within training datasets, remains an essential concern.[237]

Another significant concern is the potential for bias in AI-generated responses, which may inadvertently discriminate against certain customers or perpetuate existing societal biases. To address this concern, businesses must implement bias detection and mitigation techniques to ensure that their chatbots provide fair and equitable treatment to all customers.[238] Additionally, businesses must be transparent with customers about the use of AI-powered chatbots in their customer service operations and provide avenues for customers to escalate concerns or seek human assistance if needed. By addressing these challenges and considerations, businesses can harness the full potential of ChatGPT and similar language models to deliver exceptional customer service experiences that drive satisfaction, loyalty, and business growth.

In conclusion, the impacts of ChatGPT and similar language models on customer service are profound and far-reaching, transforming the way businesses interact with their customers. From providing instant, round-the-clock support to delivering personalised responses tailored to each customer's needs and preferences, ChatGPT enhances the efficiency, effectiveness, and overall quality of customer service interactions. Nonetheless, businesses must also address challenges and considerations related to accuracy, reliability, bias, and ethics to ensure that their AI-powered chatbots deliver exceptional customer service experiences while upholding principles of fairness, transparency, and accountability. By doing so, businesses can leverage ChatGPT to drive customer satisfaction, loyalty, and business success in an increasingly competitive marketplace.

3.9 CONCLUSION

The emergence of language models such as ChatGPT has the potential to revolutionise various industries, including education, healthcare, business, journalism, and media. Although these AI tools offer numerous benefits, they also present ethical challenges such as academic dishonesty, job displacement, data privacy, bias, and misinformation. Therefore, responsible implementation and thoughtful regulation are essential. By harnessing the strengths of ChatGPT while mitigating its risks, we can pave the way for a future where AI augments human capabilities, fosters innovation, and creates more inclusive and equitable societies. Collaboration among stakeholders is crucial to navigating the complexities of integrating AI into our lives while ensuring that its benefits are maximised, and its drawbacks are minimised. Ultimately, a balanced approach that prioritises ethical considerations, human values, and the common good is necessary to leverage the groundbreaking influence of ChatGPT.

237. Abid Haleem et al., *Exploring the Competence of ChatGPT for Customer and Patient Service Management,* 2(3) Intelligent Pharmacy 392–414 (2024), ISSN 2949-866X, https://doi.org/10.1016/j.ipha.2024.03.002.
238. *See supra* n. 221.

CHAPTER 4

Societal and Ethical Implications of ChatGPT

4.1 INTRODUCTION

The complexity and potential impact of ChatGPT extend across multiple domains, including ethical, social, and legal considerations.[239] This chapter delves into the societal implications of LLMs, focusing specifically on job displacement, the potential for addiction, the impact on critical thinking skills, vulnerability to malicious use, and the risk of human identity crises. Additionally, it examines the ethical dilemmas posed by these models, including the dissemination of misinformation, the creation of deepfakes, concerns about accountability and transparency, and the potential exacerbation of existing inequalities. This succinct yet thorough overview provides a foundation for a more detailed analysis of ChatGPT's transformative impact on our digital society. By acknowledging the interrelated nature of these ethical and societal dimensions, the chapter critically assesses ChatGPT's role in shaping the future of technology and its broader implications for society.

4.2 SOCIAL IMPLICATIONS OF ChatGPT

The widespread use of LLMs could change many aspects of society in fundamental ways. Therefore, regulators must consider not only the technical aspects of LLMs but also their broader ethical, social, and economic impacts.[240] The societal implications of

239. Andrew Perlman, *The Implications of ChatGPT for Legal Services and Society, Center on the Legal Profession*, Harvard Law School (March/April 2023), https://clp.law.harvard.edu/knowledge-hub/magazine/issues/generative-ai-in-the-legal-profession/the-implications-of-chatgpt-for-legal-services-and-society/.
240. Bertalan Meskó & Eric J. Topol, *The Imperative for Regulatory Oversight of Large Language Models (or Generative AI) in Healthcare*, 6 Nature npj Digital Medicine 120 (2023), https://doi.org/10.1038/s41746-023-00873-0.

ChatGPT are far-reaching, encompassing potential job displacement, the development of ChatGPT addiction, the impact on critical thinking skills, the risk of malicious use, and challenges to human identity. This section will conduct an in-depth analysis of these impacts, focusing especially on the potential consequences of widespread automation, the influence of AI-powered interactions on human behaviour, and the societal challenges posed by AI-generated content.

4.2.1 Job Displacement

ChatGPT and similar language models have the potential to impact various job fields. Being a NLP model ChatGPT can understand and generate real-time human-like textual responses. It has many applications, such as writing code, poems, resumes, translations, and math problems. However, some people are concerned that ChatGPT and similar language models could automate some tasks that currently require human labour and thus displace some workers from their jobs. For example, an in-depth analysis conducted by Interesting Engineering found that ChatGPT could have significant impacts on various industries due to its near-human-like communication capabilities. The article highlights that industries that are heavily reliant on information analysis, such as customer service, journalism, education, and legal services, are particularly vulnerable.[241]

In another research, the author presents a systematic approach to assess the potential impact of AI language modelling on various occupations, industries, and geographical areas. The study reveals that advancements in language models particularly threaten certain occupations, including telemarketers and various post-secondary teaching positions in English language and literature, foreign language and literature, and history.[242] The paper also identifies a positive correlation between wages and exposure to AI language modelling.

In another recent article featured in Geek Culture, concerns are raised about the consequences of job automation and the potential displacement of workers by ChatGPT. The article argues that ChatGPT could replace human writers in fields like content creation, marketing, and journalism.[243] Ethical and social challenges, such as plagiarism, misinformation, and bias, are also considered potential issues.

Furthermore, a recent analysis explores the potential job roles that may be at risk due to the advancement of AI technologies like ChatGPT and discuss strategies for workers to adapt to the evolving employment landscape. The analysis posits that ChatGPT could automate tasks that involve extensive information retrieval with

241. Tomilayo Ijarotimi, *ChatGPT and Its Potential for Job Replacement: A Comprehensive Analysis*, Interesting Engineering (29 Mar. 2023), https://interestingengineering.com/innovation/chatgpt-potential-job-replacement-analysis.
242. Ed Felten et al., *How Will Language Modelers like ChatGPT Affect Occupations and Industries?*, arXiv e-prints, arXiv:2303 (2023), https://arxiv.org/ftp/arxiv/papers/2303/2303.01157.pdf.
243. Edward Jones, *The Dark Side of Job Automation: How ChatGPT Could Displace Workers*, Medium (19 Feb. 2024), https://medium.com/geekculture/the-dark-side-of-job-automation-how-chatgpt-could-displace-workers-b71e7ef7a88.

minimal need for substantial judgment or interpretation.[244] To succeed in this shifting environment, it recommends that workers focus on developing skills that complement AI, such as creativity, critical thinking, and emotional intelligence.

In contrast, another perspective argues that a robust welfare state could mitigate the adverse effects of AI-induced job displacement. This viewpoint suggests that the emergence of technologies like ChatGPT may result in job losses and wage reductions for certain workers. To counter these effects, it advocates for the adoption of supportive measures such as universal basic income, job guarantee programmes, and enhanced labour rights to protect workers from the negative impacts of AI.[245]

According to a report from the Brookings Institution, professionals in high-income roles and those in larger, high-tech metropolitan areas are most vulnerable to the effects of AI. The study highlights that both white-collar occupations requiring bachelor's degrees and production-related jobs are particularly at risk of experiencing significant economic disruptions due to AI advancements. In the US, approximately 25 million workers, representing about 15% of the labour force, are projected to be profoundly impacted by AI technologies.[246] Occupations such as sales managers, computer programmers, and personal financial advisers are identified as particularly susceptible to AI's transformative effects. Contrary to earlier analyses, this report indicates that it will be the better-educated and higher-paid workers who are likely to face the greatest challenges posed by AI, though there are some notable exceptions.

In conclusion, the emergence of language models like ChatGPT undoubtedly poses both challenges and opportunities to the workforce. Although concerns exist about potential job displacement in fields such as customer service, journalism, and education, it is crucial to acknowledge the potential for job creation and transformation that comes with technological advancement. As AI continues to evolve, it will create new roles and industries, opening up opportunities for those who can adapt and innovate. Prioritising the development of complementary skills such as creativity and emotional intelligence can facilitate the transition into these new roles. Additionally, implementing proactive measures like universal basic income and job guarantee programs can provide a safety net for those impacted by job displacement. Eventually, the impact of language models like ChatGPT will depend on how society addresses these challenges and embraces the opportunities presented by this technological revolution.

4.2.2 ChatGPT Addiction

It is an undeniable reality that ChatGPT and similar language models represent a powerful technological advancement, capable of generating natural and engaging text

244. Insightful Leader, Kellogg Sch. of Mgmt., Northwestern Univ., https://insight.kellogg.northwestern.edu/newsletter/insightful-leader (accessed 30 Jul. 2024).
245. Matt Bruenig, *The Solution to AI-Driven Job Displacement Is a Robust Welfare State*, Jacobin (April 2023), https://jacobin.com/2023/04/artificial-intelligence-chatgpt-job-loss-displacement-labor-reallocation-welfare-state.
246. Mark Muro et al., *What Jobs Are Affected by AI? Better-Paid, Better-Educated Workers Face the Most Exposure*, Brookings (20 Nov. 2019), https://www.brookings.edu/articles/what-jobs-are-affected-by-ai-better-paid-better-educated-workers-face-the-most-exposure/.

for a multitude of applications. Nevertheless, the emergence of GAI tools like ChatGPT also presents potential risks in diverse domains, including the possibility of addiction. Their capacity to deliver personalised information and entertainment on demand can be highly tempting and raises concerns akin to those associated with social media addiction.[247] One of the primary reasons behind the addictive nature of ChatGPT and similar language models is their ability to generate personalised and contextually relevant content based on user input. This capability fosters a sense of connection and intimacy between the user and the chatbot, evoking further curiosity and anticipation for the next response.

Specifically, ChatGPT possesses the capability to tailor its persona, tone, and style to align with the user's preferences and expectations, resulting in a more captivating and engaging conversation.[248] The AI chatbot can produce a wide range of content, including poems, stories, code, essays, songs, and celebrity parodies.[249] Thus, another factor that may make ChatGPT and similar language models highly engaging is their ability to generate novel and creative content that surprises and delights their users. This can create a sense of wonder and excitement for the user and a desire to explore more of the chatbot's capabilities and outputs. It can also infuse humour, wit, sarcasm, and irony into its responses, enhancing the conversational experience.

A third factor potentially contributing to the addictive nature of ChatGPT, and similar language models is their capacity to generate highly plausible and persuasive content. This ability may inadvertently mislead or unduly influence users, fostering a cycle of continued engagement with the technology. Arguably, ChatGPT can create content that matches human-written text in quality, style, and coherence, but it can also produce biased, false, or harmful information while presenting it as factual.[250] For instance, a user might rely on a chatbot's confidently delivered answer on a complex topic without realising it could be inaccurate. This highlights the importance of maintaining a critical eye on information received, even from seemingly reliable sources.

While ChatGPT offers many benefits, its use raises concerns about potential negative impacts on productivity, creativity, and critical thinking skills, especially for users who rely on it excessively. Recent research suggests that overdependence on ChatGPT can have negative consequences for both students and teachers. Students may experience a decline in higher-order cognitive skills such as creativity, critical thinking, reasoning, and problem-solving.[251] This is because ChatGPT simplifies the process of obtaining answers, potentially diminishing students' motivation for independent research and forming their own conclusions. For teachers, an overreliance on

247. David Greenfield & Shivan Bhavnani, *Social Media: Generative AI Could Harm Mental Health*, 617 Nature 676 (2023), https://doi.org/10.1038/d41586-023-01693-8.
248. Jesse G. Meyer et al., *ChatGPT and Large Language Models in Academia: Opportunities and Challenges*, 16 BioData Mining 20 (2023), https://doi.org/10.1186/s13040-023-00339-9.
249. *Ibid.*
250. Ameet Deshpande et al., *Toxicity in ChatGPT: Analyzing Persona-Assigned Language Models*, arXiv preprint arXiv:2304.05335 (2023), https://arxiv.org/pdf/2304.05335.
251. Enkelejda Kasneci et al., *ChatGPT for Good? On Opportunities and Challenges of Large Language Models for Education*, 103 Learning and Individual Differences 102274 (2023), https://doi.org/10.1016/j.lindif.2023.102274.

ChatGPT could affect the quality of instruction or student assessment, potentially exacerbating existing achievement gaps.[252]

In conclusion, ChatGPT and similar language models can be addictive due to their responsiveness, ease of access, personalised interactions, and alignment with digital addiction principles. While these models offer valuable information and entertainment, it is essential to be aware of the potential for addictive behaviours and employ responsible use practices to ensure a healthy and balanced relationship with such technologies. Users who find themselves spending excessive amounts of time interacting with these models or who experience negative consequences as a result of their use may seek professional help. Additionally, developers of these models can play a role in promoting responsible use by implementing features that encourage breaks, track usage time, and raise awareness of potential addiction risks. By acknowledging the potential risks and taking steps to mitigate them, we can harness the full potential of language models for good.

4.2.3 Critical Thinking

The potential impact of LLMs such as ChatGPT on critical thinking is a subject of extensive and ongoing scholarly debate. While these models offer access to vast amounts of information and can perform various tasks, they can also lead to overreliance, potentially hindering the development of critical thinking skills. By providing easy access to seemingly informative answers, these models may discourage users from questioning the source, accuracy, or validity of the information. Eventually, this technology could result in a decrease in people's intellectual curiosity, creativity, and analytical thinking.[253]

Conversely, language models can also be used to enhance critical thinking by providing diverse perspectives and prompting users to ask questions. By fostering a healthy balance and teaching users how to evaluate information from these models, we can minimise the risk of overreliance and leverage the technology's potential. We can argue that ChatGPT and similar language models have the potential to improve critical thinking by providing fresh and diverse perspectives on various subjects, sparking curiosity and inquiry. These models can generate innovative and creative responses that challenge users' assumptions, beliefs, or opinions.

Moreover, the interaction with such AI can provoke critical analysis, encouraging users to scrutinise the validity and reliability of the information provided. Eventually, LLMs like ChatGPT may motivate users to delve deeper, compare multiple sources, and assess the evidence and arguments presented by these models, potentially leading to

252. Mohammadreza Farrokhnia et al., *A SWOT Analysis of ChatGPT: Implications for Educational Practice and Research,* 61 Innovations in Educ. & Teaching Int'l 460 (2024) https://doi.org/10.1080/14703297.2023.2195846.
253. Dans, Enrique, *ChatGPT and the Decline of Critical Thinking,* IE Insights (6 Jul. 2023), https://www.ie.edu/insights/articles/chatgpt-and-the-decline-of-critical-thinking/; Kathryn Hulick, *How ChatGPT and Similar AI Will Disrupt Education,* ScienceNews (12 Apr. 2023), https://www.sciencenews.org/article/chatgpt-ai-artificial-intelligence-education-cheating-accuracy.

enhanced intellectual adaptability, creativity, and problem-solving skills.[254] Additionally, exposure to varied viewpoints can help users recognise and overcome their cognitive biases, fostering a more nuanced understanding of complex issues. Consequently, integrating such technologies into educational and professional settings may cultivate a more dynamic and inclusive learning environment, promoting intellectual growth and innovation.

A third perspective, distinct from the previous two opposing viewpoints, suggests that ChatGPT and similar language models do not have any significant impact on critical thinking. According to this view, these models are essentially tools that can be employed for various purposes, whether beneficial or detrimental, depending on the user's intention, motivation, and context. These models are not intelligent or conscious entities capable of shaping or manipulating the user's thoughts or actions. Despite their potential benefits, users must exercise caution and discernment in utilising AI-generated content, recognising its limitations and potential biases. Therefore, it is up to users to take charge of their learning and decision-making, and they can decide whether they would use these models to support or replace their critical thinking abilities. Furthermore, users must properly cite sources and ensure the accuracy of LLM-generated content.[255] By doing so, they can uphold academic integrity and contribute to the responsible use of AI technology in intellectual discourse.

The influence of ChatGPT and comparable language models on critical thinking is multifaceted and subject to ongoing debate. These models have both positive and negative impacts on critical thinking, depending on how users employ and perceive them. Therefore, it is important for users to be aware of these potential impacts and to use these models responsibly. While these AI tools can provide valuable insights and stimulate intellectual curiosity, they should not be seen as replacements for human reasoning and critical analysis. Users must recognise the limitations of AI-generated content and actively engage in the cultivation of their critical thinking skills through diverse learning experiences and rigorous examination of information. By embracing a balanced approach that combines the benefits of AI technology with human cognitive abilities, individuals can navigate the complexities of the information age more effectively and contribute to a society that values both innovation and critical inquiry.

4.2.4 Malicious Use

Despite their potential to revolutionise communication and creativity, LLMs like ChatGPT raise concerns about their potential for misuse in generating inauthentic content that disrupts information ecosystems. Moreover, there is a growing trend of malicious use of these models, such as spreading misinformation, generating spam,

254. Vinod Aithal & Jasmin Silver, *Enhancing Learners' Critical Thinking Skills with AI-Assisted Technology*, Cambridge University Press (30 Mar. 2023), https://www.cambridge.org/elt/blog/2023/03/30/enhancing-learners-critical-thinking-skills-with-ai-assisted-technology/; Sophie Bushwick & Madhusree Mukerjee, *ChatGPT Explains Why AIs like ChatGPT Should Be Regulated*, SCI AM (28 Dec. 2022), https://www.scientificamerican.com/article/chatgpt-explains-why-ais-like-chatgpt-should-be-regulated1/.

255. *See supra* n. 249.

creating deepfakes, and biased information. In an interview with the press, OpenAI boss Sam Altman, for example, opined that ChatGPT will always have bias. In the words of Altman:

> 'The bias of ChatGPT when it launched ... was not something that I certainly felt proud of. It's gotten much better with GPT-4 [a new version].' He added: 'So I will say I think it was too biased and will always be. There will be no one version of GPT that the world ever agrees is unbiased.'[256]

The potential toxicity in AI-generated content is another pressing issue that escalates with the personas behind ChatGPT. These personas shape the AI's responses, offering personalised experiences at the risk of amplifying toxicity. Research indicates that toxicity levels can multiply by up to six times depending on the persona, leading to the propagation of damaging stereotypes and offensive discourse.[257] The proficiency of AI like ChatGPT in crafting syntactically impeccable and error-free texts raises alarms, particularly in the context of sophisticated phishing attempts.[258] This highlights the imperative for conscientious AI development and stringent content moderation to mitigate the dissemination of detrimental content and behaviours. As AI systems become more prevalent, striking a balance between personalisation and content governance is essential to foster ethical and positive interactions.

GAI like ChatGPT has also the potential to empower attackers, enabling them to conduct more sophisticated and targeted cyberattacks. Moreover, these models may provide amateur hackers with enhanced capabilities and empower script kiddies to create customised tools. Additionally, these language models are advantageous to malware authors, particularly ransomware groups, in crafting intricate variants of wiper and ransomware attacks.[259] Moreover, the widespread availability and user-friendly nature of language models make it easier for attackers to create convincing phishing emails, social engineering attempts, and deceptive messages, blurring the line between genuine and malicious communications.[260] The rise in cyberattack sophistication due to the accessibility of AI-driven tools emphasises the pressing need to strengthen cybersecurity measures, increase user awareness, and develop advanced detection and mitigation strategies to safeguard against evolving online threats.

Furthermore, LLMs like ChatGPT can be used by criminals to create malware, even if they do not have the skills to do so themselves. This is a serious concern as it could make it easier for criminals to create convincing phishing emails, even in

256. Mark Sellman, *ChatGPT Will Always Have Bias, Says OpenAI Boss*, The Times (27 Mar. 2023), https://www.thetimes.com/article/f7aa8ff6-ccb1-11ed-adc8-dcfa63cb4163.
257. *See supra* n. 251.
258. Alex Hern & Dan Milmo, *AI Chatbots Making It Harder to Spot Phishing Emails, Say Experts*, Guardian (29 Mar. 2023), https://www.theguardian.com/technology/2023/mar/29/ai-chatbots-making-it-harder-to-spot-phishing-emails-say-experts.
259. Charan P.V.S. et al., *From Text to Mitre Techniques: Exploring the Malicious Use of Large Language Models for Generating Cyber Attack Payloads*, arXiv preprint arXiv:2305.15336 (2023), https://arxiv.org/pdf/2305.15336.
260. Yi Liu et al., *Prompt Injection Attack Against LLM-Integrated Applications*, arXiv preprint arXiv:2306.05499 (2023), https://arxiv.org/pdf/2306.05499.

multiple languages. This could help attackers with high technical skills but poor language skills to create phishing emails in the native language of their targets. For example, an attacker could use ChatGPT to create a phishing email that looks like it comes from the boss, uses information that only the boss would know, and even mimics the boss's writing style.[261] This would make the phishing email much more likely to succeed.

As the sophistication of AI continues to advance, it may pose new challenges for cybersecurity professionals, necessitating constant adaptation and innovation in defence strategies. Therefore, regulatory frameworks must evolve to address the emerging risks associated with AI-powered cyber threats, ensuring accountability and responsibility in the development and deployment of such technology.

In conclusion, the potential ramifications of malicious use of LLMs like ChatGPT underscore the urgent need for proactive measures to mitigate the risks they pose to society. From spreading misinformation and generating spam to crafting sophisticated phishing emails and empowering cyber attackers, the misuse of AI technology poses multifaceted challenges to cybersecurity and information integrity.[262] The acknowledgement of inherent biases in these models and the escalation of toxicity with personalised personas further emphasise the importance of RAI development and robust content moderation. As we navigate the evolving landscape of AI-driven threats, a collaborative approach involving stakeholders from industry, academia, and government is essential to devise effective strategies that balance innovation with ethical considerations. By prioritising transparency, accountability, and user education, we can harness the transformative potential of AI while safeguarding against its misuse for malicious intents.

4.2.5 Human Identity

ChatGPT and similar language models can produce coherent and fluent texts based on extensive data, but they are not exempt from limitations and challenges. There is speculation that LLMs like ChatGPT may present significant challenges to human identity by jeopardising the uniqueness of human language and communication skills, displacing human writers and content creators in various domains, and evoking negative emotions and perceptions of threat among humans. GAI chatbots like ChatGPT may evoke negative emotions in humans, such as fear and anxiety, due to the perception of ChatGPT as a threat to human safety, jobs, and other important aspects of human life.[263]

261. Glenn Gow, *Top 5 AI Risks in the Era of ChatGPT and Generative AI*, Forbes (9 Apr. 2023), https://www.forbes.com/sites/glenngow/2023/04/09/top-5-ai-risks-in-the-era-of-chatgpt-and-generative-ai/?sh=6c6ac581aca0.
262. Michelle Drolet, *10 Ways Cybercriminals Can Abuse Large Language Models*, Forbes (30 Jun. 2023), https://www.forbes.com/sites/forbestechcouncil/2023/06/30/10-ways-cybercriminals-can-abuse-large-language-models/?sh=190c8cd9304c.
263. *See supra* n. 83.

Research indicates that interactions with ChatGPT can lead to perceptions of threats to personal safety, employment, resource availability, and personal identity.[264] However, another study discovered that ChatGPT did not have a significant impact on people's sense of self.[265] Identity crises are complex and caused by many factors, including psychological, social, and personal ones. While LLMs can affect how information is spread and processed online, attributing identity crises directly to them is too simplistic. Furthermore, research suggests that LLMs may even help explore identity through creative writing prompts or by providing information on diverse perspectives.[266]

ChatGPT's identity is complex and multifaceted, influenced by a variety of factors, including user input, training data, its programmers, and its self-learning capabilities. The evidence on this topic is mixed and more research is needed to understand the long-term impact of LLMs on human identity. Nonetheless, this unstable and constantly shifting identity may not be socially desirable and easily understandable. As a result, ChatGPT's identity can be seen as 'messed up' and 'algorithmic'. The lack of physical, oral, and visual attributes makes it difficult to understand ChatGPT's identity and is often described as 'puzzling', 'concealed', 'fragmented', 'misleading', and 'unsteady'.[267] Given its fragmented and unstable identity, ChatGPT cannot cause an identity crisis for humans.

Furthermore, the integration of AI into our daily lives has undeniably altered the landscape of human interaction and identity perception. The psychological impact of engaging with AI, particularly language models like ChatGPT, has been a subject of both concern and fascination. While some individuals may experience unease or apprehension, fearing displacement or obsolescence, others find AI a tool for self-discovery and creative expression. Thus, studies show mixed results, with some suggesting AI evokes anxiety and identity threats, while others find minimal impact on self-identity.[268] Indeed, the ability of AI to assist in creative writing and offer diverse perspectives can catalyse individuals to explore and understand their own identities in new and profound ways. The way AI can both cause problems and bring benefits captures the complicated connection between AI and human identity.

In conclusion, the discussion about the impact of AI on human identity remains dynamic and complex, encompassing a wide range of perspectives and considerations. As we continue to interact with and adapt to these technologies, it is crucial to approach AI with a balanced perspective, recognising its capacity to both challenge and

264. Zaveria, *ChatGPT Beats Humans in Emotion Recognition: Study*, Analytics Insight (4 Aug. 2023), https://www.analyticsinsight.net/chatgpt/chatgpt-beats-humans-in-emotion-recognition-study.

265. Adam Hulman et al., *ChatGPT-Versus Human-Generated Answers to Frequently Asked Questions about Diabetes: A Turing Test-Inspired Survey among Employees of a Danish Diabetes Center*, 18 PLOS ONE e0290773 (2023).

266. Angus Russell, *Identity and AI: Large Language Models, Group Dynamics and Community Building*, Historica (23 Feb. 2024), https://www.historica.org/blog/identity-and-ai.

267. *See supra* n. 84.

268. Gizem Yalcin & Stefano Puntoni, *How AI Affects Our Sense of Self, Harvard Business Review* (September–October 2023), https://hbr.org/2023/09/how-ai-affects-our-sense-of-self.

enhance our sense of self. The future of AI and its role in shaping human identity will likely be defined by our collective efforts to harness its potential responsibly while safeguarding the unique attributes that define our humanity.[269] The journey towards understanding the full impact of AI on human identity is just beginning, and it promises to be as transformative as it is intricate.

4.3 ETHICAL IMPLICATIONS OF ChatGPT

The evolution of LLMs like ChatGPT presents a fascinating paradox in terms of ethical implications and considerations. While these technologies hold immense potential to revolutionise communication and content creation, their ethical implications raise pressing concerns. These concerns are multifaceted, involving crucial issues such as misinformation, deepfakes, accountability, transparency, and inequality.[270] The rapid dissemination of misleading information and the potential for creating convincing yet false narratives through deepfakes have significant societal implications. Furthermore, the lack of clear accountability and transparency in the development and deployment of ChatGPT raises concerns about ethical responsibility. Addressing these issues is crucial to ensuring that the benefits of LLMs like ChatGPT are balanced with ethical considerations, thereby promoting a fair and safe digital environment for all. Given this context, this sub-section explores the ethical implications of ChatGPT and similar AI chatbots, with a focus on key areas such as misinformation, deepfakes, accountability, transparency, and inequality.

4.3.1 Misinformation

LLMs like ChatGPT are playing a crucial role in popularising AI, especially among the public.[271] Nevertheless, ChatGPT and similar language models pose significant ethical concerns regarding the spread of misinformation. These models can generate highly persuasive text that may be used to disseminate false or misleading information, making it challenging to distinguish between fact and fiction online. This exacerbates the already rampant issue of misinformation, which can have detrimental effects on

269. David James Woo & Kai Guo, *Exploring an AI-Supported Approach to Creative Writing: Effects on Secondary School Students' Creativity* (2023), https://www.researchgate.net/publication/369013951_Exploring_an_AI-supported_approach_to_creative_writing_Effects_on_secondary_school_students'_creativity.
270. Noémi Bontridder & Yves Poullet, *The Role of Artificial Intelligence in Disinformation*, 3 Data & Policy e32 (2021), https://doi.org/10.1017/dap.2021.20; Human Rights, Big Data and Technology Project, University of Essex, *'Misinformation, Disinformation, and Deep Fakes,'* Essex .ac.uk, https://www.essex.ac.uk/research-projects/human-rights-big-data-and-technology/misinformation-and-disinformation-and-deep-fakes (accessed 28 Jul. 2024); Mohamed R. Shoaib et al., *Deepfakes, Misinformation, and Disinformation in the Era of Frontier AI, Generative AI, and Large AI Models*, in 2023 International Conference on Computer and Applications (ICCA) (IEEE 2023).
271. Jianlong Zhou et al., *Ethical ChatGPT: Concerns, Challenges, and Commandments*, arXiv Preprint arXiv:2305.10646 (2023), https://arxiv.org/pdf/2305.10646.

public discourse, decision-making, and trust in information sources. Consequently, the ethical implications are profound, necessitating vigilant measures to mitigate the potential harm inflicted by AI-generated misinformation on society.

The dissemination of false information, commonly referred to as 'fake news', encompasses both misinformation, involving the unintentional sharing of inaccurate data, and disinformation, which involves the deliberate spread of false content with malicious intent.[272] This misleading material can take various forms, including memes, misattributed content, cloned websites, and manipulated images and videos like deepfakes.

Misinformation and disinformation campaigns pose significant threats to fundamental human rights, endangering democracy and putting journalists and activists at risk.[273] However, efforts by both companies and governments to address this issue can potentially encroach upon freedom of expression. In the past, the manipulation of information was mainly produced by powerful entities such as state officials or large organisations.[274] Nonetheless, modern tools such as Photoshop, video editing software, social media platforms, and AI-based technologies have democratised the ability to widely spread such content, causing immense ethical implications.

Furthermore, the widespread use of AI chatbots is significantly contributing to the spread of disinformation in our society. These systems not only make it easier to create convincing fake content but also enable the targeted and large-scale dissemination of false information by malicious actors. This raises serious ethical and human rights issues, particularly concerning human dignity, autonomy, democracy, and peace.[275] The combined impact of unregulated deepfakes and misinformation includes the erosion of public trust.[276] When people cannot rely on what they see and hear, they may become distrustful and disengaged. This disengagement poses risks not only to political processes but also to the social cohesion of communities. Without trust, conspiracy theories gain ground, scientific consensus is called into question, and social divisions deepen.

To address the potential societal harm caused by AI-generated misinformation, it is crucial to implement proactive strategies. Recent scholarship in this field emphasises the importance of focusing on specific and pressing threats, rather than general concerns. Experts in the field have highlighted the need to address common misconceptions about AI-generated misinformation and have provided insights on effective coexistence with this phenomenon.[277] International organisations, such as UNESCO, advocate for enhancing data, media, and information literacy while ensuring access to

272. *See* Human Rights, Big Data and Technology Project, *supra* n. 270.
273. *Ibid.*
274. Robert W. Zmud, Opportunities for Strategic Information Manipulation Through New Information Technology, in *Organizations and Communication Technology* 95, 95–116 (1990).
275. *See* Noémi Bontridder & Yves Poullet, *supra* n. 270.
276. *See* Mohamed R. Shoaib et al., *supra* n. 270.
277. William Brady, *How to Prepare for AI-Generated Misinformation*, Kellogg Insight (1 Jul. 2023), https://insight.kellogg.northwestern.edu/article/how-to-prepare-for-ai-generated-misinformation.

diverse, credible information sources.[278] This approach aims to empower individuals to critically evaluate the information they encounter.

Some researchers propose cognitive frameworks that could enhance individuals' ability to assess the accuracy of online information and promote responsible information sharing, thereby reducing the spread of misinformation.[279] These frameworks are designed to reduce the spread of misinformation by improving critical thinking skills and digital literacy. It is crucial to acknowledge the dynamic nature of this field, characterised by rapid advancements and continuous research. Consequently, to access the most current and in-depth knowledge, it is recommended to consult recent scholarly publications and expert perspectives on AI, information science, and media studies.

In essence, LLMs like ChatGPT have the potential to be a disruptive technology, potentially altering the modus operandi of consumers, industries, and businesses significantly. However, while these models demonstrate impressive capabilities, they also present notable challenges. Their capacity to inadvertently spread misinformation and disinformation is a major concern. These systems can generate convincing yet potentially inaccurate information on critical topics such as public health crises, geopolitical conflicts, and societal issues. For example, LLMs like ChatGPT could potentially spread fake news and misinformation[280] and skilfully deliver false and misleading information on vital topics, such as COVID-19, the Russia and Ukraine war, and school shootings,[281] it could not guarantee the accuracy of its prompts.[282] The models' inability to guarantee the veracity of their outputs underscores the importance of critical evaluation and fact-checking. To ensure the reliability of information obtained from such systems, it is imperative to corroborate their responses with authoritative sources.

4.3.2 Deepfake

While AI models like ChatGPT have the potential to revolutionise various aspects of our lives, they may also raise significant ethical concerns, particularly in the case of deepfakes. The terms 'deepfake' and 'deep fake' are both in common use, with their accuracy depending on context and preference. Nevertheless, 'deepfake' is widely accepted and recognised by major media outlets, academic researchers, businesses,

278. United Nations Educ., Sci. & Cultural Org. [UNESCO], *Recommendation on the Ethics of Artificial Intelligence* (2021), https://www.unesco.org/en/artificial-intelligence/recommendation-ethics.
279. Indu V. & Sabu M. Thampi, *Cognitive AI for Mitigation of Misinformation in Online Social Networks*, 24 IT Professional 37, 37–45 (2022), https://doi.org/10.1109/MITP.2022.3168790.
280. Chris Glorioso, *Fake News? ChatGPT Has a Knack for Making Up Phony, Anonymous Sources*, NBC New York (12 Jun. 2023), https://www.nbcnewyork.com/investigations/fake-news-chatgpt-has-a-knack-for-making-up-phony-anonymous-sources/4120307/.
281. Maximiliana Wynne, *Disinformation in the Age of ChatGPT*, Modern War Institute at West Point (22 Mar. 2024), https://mwi.westpoint.edu/disinformation-in-the-age-of-chatgpt/.
282. Saniya Ahmad Khan, *Ethical Implications of ChatGPT: Language Processing and Misinformation*, YourStory (8 May 2023), https://yourstory.com/2023/05/ethical-implications-of-chatgpt-language-processing-misinformation.

and government agencies. Deepfake technology emerged as a notable phenomenon in 2016 when Justus Thies and colleagues presented their research on real-time face capture and reenactment at the Conference on Computer Vision and Pattern Recognition.[283] Outside academia, the technology gained widespread popularity in late 2017 when a Reddit user named 'deepfake' posted videos featuring the faces of famous actresses inserted into pornographic scenes.[284]

The term 'deepfake' combines 'deep learning' and 'fake' to describe pornographic videos altered using ML algorithms.[285] According to Oxford Learner's Dictionary, 'deepfake' refers to *'a video of a person in which their appearance has been digitally altered so that they look like somebody else'*.[286] The Cambridge Dictionary defines it as *'a video or sound recording that replaces someone's face or voice with that of someone else, in a way that appears real'*.[287] In simpler terms, deepfakes are manipulated videos or audio recordings that make it seem like someone is saying or doing something although they have never actually done it.

Deepfakes have the potential to cause significant harm to all walks of life. For instance, deepfakes could be employed to harm someone's reputation, engage in blackmail, or even interfere with elections. One of the most pressing ethical concerns surrounding deepfakes is their potential to spread misinformation and disinformation. Therefore, many countries across the globe are considering a ban on 'high-risk' uses of AI, such as deepfakes and algorithmic bias, including Albania,[288] Australia,[289] China,[290] the EU,[291] and the US.[292]

Deepfakes could harness LLMs such as ChatGPT to craft convincingly realistic yet entirely fabricated audio, images, or videos, potentially misleading viewers into

283. Justus Thies et al., Face2face: Real-Time Face Capture and Reenactment of RGB Videos, in *Proceedings of the IEEE Conference on Computer Vision and Pattern Recognition* (2016).
284. Meredith Somers, *Deepfakes, Explained,* MIT Sloan School of Management (11 Oct. 2023), https://mitsloan.mit.edu/ideas-made-to-matter/deepfakes-explained; Patrick S. Shin, *Sex and Gender Segregation in Competitive Sport: Internal and External Normative Perspectives,* 80 Law and Contemporary Problems 47–61 (2017), available at Duke Law Scholarship Repository; Samantha Cole, *We Are Truly Fucked: Everyone Is Making AI-Generated Fake Porn Now,* VICE (25 Jan. 2018), https://www.vice.com/en/article/bjye8a/reddit-fake-porn-app-daisy-ridley.
285. Loveleen Gaur & Gursimar Kaur Arora, *DeepFakes* (1st edn, CRC Press 2022).
286. Oxford Learner's Dictionaries, *Deepfake,* https://www.oxfordlearnersdictionaries.com/definition/english/deepfake (accessed 31 Jul. 2024).
287. Cambridge Dictionary, *Deepfake,* https://dictionary.cambridge.org/dictionary/english/deepfake (accessed 31 Jul. 2024).
288. Amnesty International, *EU AI Act Must Ban Dangerous AI-Powered Technologies in Historic Law,* Amnesty International (5 Sep. 2023), https://www.amnesty.org/en/latest/news/2023/09/eu-ai-act-must-ban-dangerous-ai-powered-technologies-in-historic-law/.
289. Paul Karp, *Australia Considers Ban on 'High-Risk' Uses of AI Such as Deepfakes and Algorithmic Bias,* Guardian (31 May 2023), https://www.theguardian.com/technology/2023/jun/01/australian-government-considers-ban-on-high-risk-uses-of-ai-such-as-deepfakes-and-algorithmic-bias.
290. *Ibid.*
291. Jesse Coghlan, *Australia Asks if 'High-Risk' AI Should Be Banned in Surprise Consultation,* Cointelegraph (1 Jun. 2023), https://cointelegraph.com/news/australia-consultation-high-risk-ai-ban.
292. *Ibid.*

believing untrue information or events.[293] Sometimes, deepfakes can be highly realistic, making it challenging to distinguish them from genuine videos or audio recordings. This ambiguity can lead to confusion, and eroding trust in information sources. Another ethical concern is the potential for deepfakes to infringe upon individuals' privacy. Moreover, deepfake technology poses significant ethical challenges by enabling the creation of highly realistic videos or audio of people falsely appearing to do or say things, leading to unprecedented opportunities for deception.[294]

It is worth noting that deepfakes require minimal photographic or auditory input, making it easy for others to create fake footage of people without their consent. This technology can be used harmfully, treating people as tools for others' purposes, and violating the moral principle of respecting individuals' autonomy. However, deepfakes are not inherently immoral. They become morally wrong when digital data of someone's image or voice is used to portray them in ways they would not agree to.[295]

Furthermore, deepfakes might also be employed to create content that violates copyright or other IP laws. For instance, a deepfake could be used to superimpose a celebrity's likeness onto a body performing a copyrighted dance routine. This could confuse viewers and potentially mislead them about the celebrity's endorsement of the product or service being advertised. Moreover, a deepfake can also be employed to impersonate a singer and create a new song that infringes on the original artist's copyright.[296] Additionally, deepfakes could be utilised to misuse trademarks by placing a well-known brand logo on a product that the brand does not produce.

The deepfake phenomenon, which initially gained attention for superimposing celebrity faces onto pornographic content, has rapidly expanded to include manipulated images and videos of various individuals, including non-public figures.[297] While deepfakes can be used for entertainment purposes, they also present significant risks for malicious activities such as extortion, humiliation, harassment, and blackmail. Although the technology is still evolving, it has already demonstrated the potential to create content that is increasingly difficult to distinguish from authentic media.

In an era characterised by concerns over misinformation, society must consider the potential impacts of deepfakes on various spheres, including national security. For instance, a hypothetical scenario involving a fabricated video of a world leader announcing a major military action could have serious geopolitical consequences. Unfortunately, the current legal frameworks in many jurisdictions have proven inadequate to address the emerging challenges posed by deepfakes, highlighting the need

293. Cristian Vaccari & Andrew Chadwick, *Deepfakes and Disinformation: Exploring the Impact of Synthetic Political Video on Deception, Uncertainty, and Trust in News*, 6 Soc. Media + Society 2056305120903408 (2020) https://doi.org/10.1177/2056305120903408.
294. Adrienne de Ruiter, *The Distinct Wrong of Deepfakes*, 34 Philos. Technol. 1311 (2021), https://doi.org/10.1007/s13347-021-00459-2.
295. *Ibid.*
296. Indira Seshadri, *Implications of Deepfakes on Copyright Law*, WIPO (2021), https://www.wipo.int/export/sites/www/about-ip/en/artificial_intelligence/conversation_ip_ai/pdf/ind_seshadri.pdf.
297. Patrick S. Shin, *Sex and Gender Segregation in Competitive Sport: Internal and External Normative Perspectives*, 80 Law and Contemporary Problems 47–61 (2017).

for effective regulatory mechanisms.[298] These mechanisms should aim to prevent the misuse of deepfake technology while balancing concerns over free speech and technological innovation.

In conclusion, advancements in AI technology like ChatGPT and deepfakes hold immense potential for innovation and convenience, but significant ethical challenges cannot be ignored. Deepfakes, with their ability to create highly realistic yet fabricated content, present risks ranging from personal privacy violations to widespread misinformation. The ethical implications include potential harm to reputations, unauthorised use of likenesses, and copyright violations. Therefore, relevant stakeholders, including governments, businesses, and civil society must develop robust frameworks and regulations to mitigate these risks. By balancing innovation with ethical considerations, we can harness the benefits of AI while safeguarding against its potential for misuse.

4.3.3 Accountability

Accountability is one of the crucial aspects of AI governance, yet it is often poorly defined. It is also a critical ethical concern in the development and use of AI chatbots. Accountability refers to the quality or state of being responsible and answerable.[299] In the context of AI chatbots, accountability is important because it ensures that someone can be held responsible for any harm or damage that the chatbot may cause. The lack of transparency in the operation of AI chatbots can make it difficult to determine who is responsible for their actions, resulting in complex ethical issues. For instance, ChatGPT operates based on intricate algorithms, making it unclear whether developers, users, or the AI system itself should bear responsibility.

There are diverse viewpoints on who should be held accountable for AI chatbots. Some argue that the developers of the AI system should be held accountable,[300] while others argue that the users of the AI system should be held accountable.[301] Other groups argue that both the developers and users should share responsibility.[302] Nonetheless, in searching for the answer to this question, it is essential to consider who is responsible for actions performed by robots: the manufacturer, the scientists, or the users. Legal responsibility generally lies on legal persons, whether artificial or natural,

298. *Ibid.*
299. Bahar Memarian & Tenzin Doleck, *Fairness, Accountability, Transparency, and Ethics (FATE) in Artificial Intelligence (AI) and Higher Education: A Systematic Review*, 5 Computers & Educ. Artificial Intelligence 100152 (2023), https://doi.org/10.1016/j.caeai.2023.100152.
300. Margaret Bearman et al., *Discourses of Artificial Intelligence in Higher Education: A Critical Literature Review*, 86 High Educ. 369 (2023), https://doi.org/10.1007/s10734-022-00937-2.
301. Siu-Cheung Kong et al., *Evaluating an Artificial Intelligence Literacy Programme for Developing University Students' Conceptual Understanding, Literacy, Empowerment and Ethical Awareness*, 26 Educ. Tech. & Soc. 16 (2023) https://doi.org/10.1007/s10639-022-11408-7.
302. Chenglu Li et al., *Using Fair AI to Predict Students' Math Learning Outcomes in an Online Platform*, 32 Interactive Learning Environments 1117 (2022), https://doi.org/10.1080/10494820.2022.2115076.

rather than services, products, or machines. Robots and AI are products or machines, and therefore, they cannot be held legally responsible for their actions. Only humans can be held legally responsible.[303]

The question of responsibility in the context of AI systems like ChatGPT is indeed complex and multifaceted. Generally, the responsibility can be distributed across various stakeholders:

- *Developers*: They are responsible for designing and programming the AI, ensuring it operates correctly and ethically within its intended scope.
- *Users*: They should use the AI within the guidelines provided, understanding its limitations, and not misusing its capabilities.
- *AI System*: While it can perform tasks and generate responses, it does not have agency or consciousness, so it does not bear responsibility in the same way humans do.

Each entity has a role to play in the ethical deployment and use of AI technologies. Developers need to create transparent, fair, and safe systems, for users to interact responsibly, and for society to establish norms and regulations that guide the development and use of such technologies.

To address the ethical concerns associated with AI chatbots, it is also essential to develop robust accountability frameworks. One approach is to implement comprehensive regulatory guidelines that delineate the responsibilities of developers, users, and other stakeholders. For instance, the EU General Data Protection Regulation (GDPR) provides a model for ensuring data protection and privacy, which could be extended to include AI accountability measures.[304] Additionally, the Institute of Electrical and Electronics Engineers' (IEEE's) Ethically Aligned Design initiative outlines principles for ethical AI development, emphasising transparency, accountability, and user awareness.[305] Such frameworks can help ensure that AI systems are designed and used responsibly, mitigating potential harm. Moreover, specialised AI regulations, such as those from the EU, may play a pivotal role in this regard.

Another critical aspect of ensuring accountability is the implementation of transparent AI systems. Transparency involves making the decision-making processes and algorithms of AI chatbots understandable and accessible to users and regulators. This can be achieved using explainable AI (XAI), which focuses on creating AI models that provide clear and interpretable explanations for their actions and decisions.[306] By

303. Alejandro Zornoza et al., Robots Liability: A Use Case and a Potential Solution, in *Advances in Robotics* (IntechOpen, 6 Dec. 2017), https://www.intechopen.com/chapters/56250.
304. Regulation (EU) 2016/679 of the European Parliament and of the Council of 27 Apr. 2016 on the Protection of Natural Persons with Regard to the Processing of Personal Data and on the Free Movement of Such Data (General Data Protection Regulation), 2016 O.J. (L 119) 1 (EU).
305. Shahriari, K., & Shahriari, M., Ethically Aligned Design: A Vision for Prioritizing Human Well-being with Autonomous and Intelligent Systems, in *Ethically Aligned Design: A Vision for Prioritizing Human Well-being with Autonomous and Intelligent Systems* 1–294 (31 Mar. 2019), https://ieeexplore.ieee.org/document/8058187.
306. David Gunning et al., *DARPA's Explainable AI (XAI) Program: A Retrospective*, 2 Applied AI Letters e61 (2022), https://doi.org/10.22541/au.163699841.19031727/v1.

enhancing transparency, stakeholders can better understand the underlying mechanisms of AI systems, making it easier to identify and address ethical issues and assign responsibility appropriately. Moreover, transparent AI can help build trust among users, fostering more responsible use of the technology.

Educational initiatives may also play a vital role in promoting accountability in AI chatbots. By educating developers, users, and policymakers about the ethical implications and potential risks of AI, a more informed and responsible approach to AI development and usage can be cultivated. Institutions and organisations can offer training programs and resources to enhance understanding of AI ethics and accountability. For example, the AI Ethics Lab provides workshops and consulting services to help stakeholders navigate the complex ethical landscape of AI.[307] By fostering a culture of awareness and responsibility, educational efforts can contribute to the development of safer and more ethical AI systems.

In conclusion, ensuring RAI chatbot development and deployment necessitates a multifaceted approach. By establishing clear accountability frameworks, prioritising transparency in AI systems, and investing in educational initiatives, we can address ethical concerns and foster ethical usage of AI technologies.[308] Ultimately, achieving accountability in AI governance requires a collaborative effort from all stakeholders to create systems that are not only innovative but also ethical and trustworthy. This collective effort, involving developers, users, policymakers, and the public alike, is essential for harnessing the immense potential of AI while mitigating potential risks.[309] This shared responsibility will help mitigate potential harms, safeguard privacy and rights, and build a foundation of trust in AI systems.

4.3.4 Transparency

Transparency has significant ethical implications in the realm of AI governance. It is particularly crucial in contexts where trust is paramount, such as customer service and education. If users cannot trust that an AI chatbot generates accurate and unbiased information, they are unlikely to use it. Several factors contribute to the transparency issues of AI chatbots. One key challenge is the complexity of AI algorithms, which can be intricate and difficult to understand, even for experts.[310] Additionally, some developers may be reluctant to disclose the inner workings of their chatbots due to concerns about

307. https://aiethicslab.com/.
308. Claudio Novelli et al., *Accountability in Artificial Intelligence: What It Is and How It Works*, AI & Soc'y (2023), https://doi.org/10.1007/s00146-023-01635-y; OECD, *Advancing Accountability in AI: Governing and Managing Risks Throughout the Lifecycle for Trustworthy AI*, OECD Digital Economy Papers No. 349, OECD Publishing, Paris (2023), https://doi.org/10.1787/2448f04b-en; Microsoft, *Microsoft Bot Framework Design Guidelines* (November 2018), https://www.microsoft.com/en-us/research/uploads/prod/2018/11/Bot_Guidelines_Nov_2018.pdf.
309. Theodore M. Lechterman, The Concept of Accountability in AI Ethics and Governance, in *The Oxford Handbook of AI Governance* (Justin B. Bullock et al. eds, online ed. 2022), https://doi.org/10.1093/oxfordhb/9780197579329.013.10.
310. Miles Brundage et al., *The Malicious Use of Artificial Intelligence: Forecasting, Prevention, and Mitigation*, arXiv (February 2018), https://arxiv.org/pdf/1802.07228.

competitors replicating their technology.[311] Moreover, there is a concern that overly transparent explanations of AI decision-making processes could be too technical for the average user, potentially diminishing trust rather than enhancing it.[312]

The transparency challenge in ChatGPT refers to the difficulty in understanding how the model generates its output. Unlike traditional rule-based systems, LLMs depend on statistical learning algorithms that learn from large amounts of data. As a result, it is challenging to interpret how the model arrives at its output, making it difficult to identify errors or biases in the generated text. This lack of transparency can have massive implications for users, who rely on the generated text for critical decisions. In response to this issue, some companies have begun offering additional details regarding the functioning of their chatbots. For example, Accenture developed a chatbot to help with frequent onboarding questions, and the University of New South Wales (UNSW) Sydney made one to interact with students and give quick responses.[313]

Another aspect of the transparency challenge of ChatGPT lies in the opacity of the underlying algorithms. ChatGPT and similar AI chatbots are built on deep learning models, such as neural networks, which are often considered 'black boxes'. This means that the decision-making processes of these models are not easily interpretable, making it challenging to trace and understand the logic behind their responses.[314] To address the challenge of opacity in ChatGPT and similar AI chatbots, developers need to develop new methods for understanding and interpreting the decision-making processes of deep learning models.

AI chatbots like ChatGPT are regularly updated and fine-tuned, making it challenging for users to keep track of their capabilities and limitations. The lack of transparency in model updates can result in unexpected changes in behaviour that may not align with user expectations.[315] Additionally, the rapid pace of innovation in the field of AI can make it difficult for users to stay informed about the latest developments. Consequently, users may engage with models that have been modified in ways they are unaware of, potentially leading to unforeseen risks. A recent study highlights that users have a strong preference for AI systems that provide clear explanations for their reasoning and updates, even if the underlying technical details are complex.[316]

311. '*Ethics and AI*,' Markkula Center for Applied Ethics at Santa Clara University, https://www.scu.edu/ethics/focus-areas/technology-ethics/resources/ethics-and-ai/ (accessed 31 Jul. 2024).
312. Nazanin Andalibi et al., Conceptualizing Algorithmic Stigmatization, *in Proceedings of the 2023 CHI Conference on Human Factors in Computing Systems* 1 (ACM, 2023), https://doi.org/10.1145/3544548.3580970.
313. William Mendoza, *How to Build Chatbots That Deliver Better Customer Experiences and Help Support a Surge in Inquiries*, Microsoft Tech Community (12 May 2024), https://techcommunity.microsoft.com/t5/ai-azure-ai-services-blog/how-to-build-chatbots-that-deliver-better-customer-experiences/ba-p/1374659.
314. Jianbo Chen et al., Learning to Explain: An Information-Theoretic Perspective on Model Interpretation, in *Proceedings of the International Conference on Machine Learning (ICML)* 2018, at PMLR 2018.
315. Jesse Dodge et al., *Show Your Work: Improved Reporting of Experimental Results*, arXiv: 1909.03004 (2019), https://aclanthology.org/D19-1224.pdf.
316. Yao Rong et al., *Towards Human-Centered Explainable AI: A Survey of User Studies for Model Explanations*, IEEE Transactions on Pattern Analysis and Machine Intelligence (2023), https://arxiv.org/pdf/2210.11584v4; Kopecka et al., *Preferences for AI Explanations Based on Cognitive*

ChatGPT receives training on a dataset of text and code that is over 100 terabytes in size. Specifically, the training data for ChatGPT-3 was 570GB with 300 billion words, while ChatGPT-4's dataset is about 100 trillion parameters, over five times larger than ChatGPT-3's training data.[317] This dataset is so large that it is difficult to audit for biases and inaccuracies. Moreover, ChatGPT employs a novel deep-learning architecture known as a transformer network. Compared to traditional deep learning architectures, transformer networks exhibit greater complexity. While this complexity presents challenges, several potential avenues for addressing these issues exist. By developing advanced tools to elucidate the functioning of AI chatbots, creating novel training methodologies that enhance transparency, and increasing public awareness of transparency concerns, we can foster greater trust and reliability in AI chatbot technology.

In essence, the transparency challenge within AI chatbots underscores the critical need for openness and comprehension in AI systems. The intricate nature of AI algorithms, compounded by the opacity of deep learning models like ChatGPT, poses significant hurdles in understanding decision-making processes and ensuring user trust.[318] Moreover, the rapid evolution of these models exacerbates transparency concerns, potentially leading to unexpected behaviours and user disengagement. Nevertheless, initiatives such as Microsoft Azure's comprehensive guides exemplify a step towards enhancing transparency.[319] Addressing these challenges demands a concerted effort to develop tools for understanding AI workings, devising transparent training methods, and fostering public awareness. By implementing these strategies, AI chatbots can evolve from mere tools into trusted companions, demonstrating the potential for significant contributions to fields such as customer service and education. This approach fosters enhanced human experiences through increased transparency and reliability.

4.3.5 Inequality

The widespread adoption of LLMs like ChatGPT carries the potential to exacerbate social inequalities in several concerning ways. Biases inherent in the vast internet-derived training data can be unwittingly absorbed by these models, leading to outputs that reinforce stereotypes, prejudices, and existing societal disparities. This can manifest as the amplification of harmful content, with marginalised groups disproportionately impacted by the perpetuation of racist, sexist, or homophobic biases. To

Style and Socio-Cultural Factors, Proceedings of the ACM on Human-Computer Interaction, 8 CSCW1 1–32 (2024), https://dl.acm.org/doi/pdf/10.1145/3637386.

317. OpenAI, *GPT-4 Technical Report* (4 May 2024), https://arxiv.org/pdf/2303.08774; Matt Walsh, *ChatGPT Statistics: The Key Facts and Figures*, Style Factory (22 Apr. 2024), https://www.stylefactoryproductions.com/blog/chatgpt-statistics.
318. Ying Xu et al., *Transparency Enhances Positive Perceptions of Social Artificial Intelligence, Human Behavior & Emerging Technologies* 1, at 5550418 (2023), https://doi.org/10.1155/2023/5550418.
319. Microsoft Azure, *AI Solutions*, https://azure.microsoft.com/en-us/solutions/ai/ (accessed 31 Jul. 2024); Microsoft, *Azure AI Services: OpenAI*, https://learn.microsoft.com/en-us/azure/ai-services/openai/ (accessed 31 Jul. 2024).

mitigate these risks, developers can employ various techniques, including data cleaning to remove biased content, debiasing algorithms like adversarial training or counterfactual generation, and rigorous evaluation using fairness metrics and human oversight.[320]

The unequal access to technology exacerbates existing disparities. Not everyone has the same level of access to AI-powered chatbots and language models. Individuals in underserved communities or low-income regions may not benefit from the advantages offered by tools like ChatGPT. Moreover, utilising ChatGPT and similar technologies necessitates certain technical skills, tools, and resources. Individuals lacking these competencies and resources are at a disadvantage compared to those who possess them. This digital divide can further amplify societal inequalities. To foster a more inclusive and equitable AI ecosystem, policies and initiatives should prioritise the development of talent and skills, advance research and innovation, foster collaboration, support deployment, and establish comprehensive governance and regulatory frameworks.[321]

LLMs like ChatGPT can inadvertently reinforce existing disparities based on demographic groups as well. According to a 2022 study by the Algorithmic Justice League, LLMs can perpetuate social biases by amplifying stereotypes that are present in the data they are trained on.[322] When users seek information or assistance, the responses generated by these models may not be equally accurate or helpful across different demographic groups. This discrepancy can exacerbate disparities in access to reliable information and support. Additionally, the amplification of harmful content is a concerning aspect. Thus, AI chatbots can inadvertently spread or amplify harmful and false information, which can disproportionately affect vulnerable populations. Moreover, misinformation and hate speech can thrive in the digital ecosystem, leading to potential harm to marginalised communities.[323]

Furthermore, the deployment of language models may also have implications for the job market. The automation of tasks traditionally performed by humans can lead to job displacement, affecting employment opportunities for certain groups more than others.[324] This can exacerbate economic inequalities and job insecurity. Additionally, it may require a shift in workforce skills, necessitating extensive retraining and education programs to help displaced workers adapt to new roles.[325] The concentration of benefits from automation in the hands of a few tech companies could further widen the gap between the wealthy and the poor people. Moreover, regulatory frameworks

320. Paul Pu Liang et al., Towards Understanding and Mitigating Social Biases in Language Models, in *Proceedings of the 38th International Conference on Machine Learning* 3136 (2021).
321. Irene Kitsara, Artificial Intelligence and the Digital Divide: From an Innovation Perspective, in *Platforms and Artificial Intelligence, Progress in Is* (A. Bounfour ed., 2022), https://doi.org/10.1007/978-3-030-90192-9_12.
322. American Jewish Library, *Technology Should Serve All of Us. Not Just the Privileged Few*, https://www.ajl.org/ (accessed 31 Jul. 2024).
323. *See supra* n. 136.
324. National Bureau of Economic Research, *The Economics of Artificial Intelligence: An Agenda* (2018), https://www.nber.org/system/files/chapters/c14009/c14009.pdf.
325. Workee, *The AI Revolution: Navigating the Job Market of Tomorrow*, Hacker Noon (18 Jul. 2023), https://hackernoon.com/the-ai-revolution-navigating-the-job-market-of-tomorrow.

will need to evolve to address these challenges, ensuring fair labour practices and mitigating the adverse effects on vulnerable populations.

In essence, the deployment of ChatGPT and similar language models has the potential to exacerbate societal inequalities due to biases in training data, unequal access to technology, reinforcement of existing disparities, amplification of harmful content, job market implications, and a lack of transparency. Addressing these concerns necessitates a multifaceted approach that includes RAI development, equitable access to technology, and proactive efforts to mitigate bias and inequality. According to a recent white paper by the WEF and Accenture, approximately 80% of the US workforce may see at least 10% of their work tasks impacted by LLMs.[326] Therefore, it is crucial to understand the potential implications of language models for the job market and prepare for the opportunities and challenges they may bring. Some possible strategies include:

- Developing new skills and competencies that complement or leverage language models.
- Investing in education and training programs that foster lifelong learning and adaptation.
- Establishing policies and regulations that ensure responsible and ethical use of language models.
- Promoting social dialogue and collaboration among stakeholders to address the potential impacts of language models on workers' rights, welfare, and well-being.
- Encouraging collaboration between stakeholders to ensure the ethical deployment of AI technologies.
- Investing in research to further understand and mitigate the biases inherent in AI systems.

4.4 CONCLUSION

In conclusion, the transformative potential of ChatGPT and advanced language models is undeniable. However, this potential comes with a complex array of societal and ethical challenges that require careful navigation.[327] As these technologies continue to evolve, it is crucial to adopt a balanced and proactive approach that maximises their benefits while mitigating potential risks. Addressing concerns surrounding job displacement, potential addiction, erosion of critical thinking skills, and malicious exploitation will require a multifaceted strategy, including fostering digital literacy, implementing robust ethical frameworks, and ensuring transparency and accountability in development and deployment.

326. World Economic Forum, *Jobs of Tomorrow: Large Language Models and Jobs* (2024), https://www.weforum.org/whitepapers/jobs-of-tomorrow-large-language-models-and-jobs. *See also supra* n. 74.
327. Anna Jobin et al., *The Global Landscape of AI Ethics Guidelines*, 1 Nat. Mach. Intell. 389 (2019), https://doi.org/10.1038/s42256-019-0088-2.

Moreover, the ethical implications, such as the spread of misinformation, the creation of deepfakes, and the exacerbation of existing inequalities, underscore the importance of upholding core principles of truth, fairness, and human dignity. Collaborative efforts among stakeholders, continuous dialogue, and a firm commitment to aligning technological progress with societal values will be paramount.[328] As we navigate this new era, the choices we make will resonate for generations. By embracing a nuanced understanding of ChatGPT's societal and ethical implications, we can harness its potential to drive innovation, enhance accessibility, and unlock new frontiers of knowledge and creativity, while safeguarding fundamental rights and well-being. Achieving this delicate balance will pave the way for a future where technological advancements contribute to a more equitable, informed, and responsible digital society.

328. Laura Weidinger et al., *Ethical and Social Risks of Harm from Language Models*, arXiv preprint arXiv:2112.04359 (2021), https://arxiv.org/pdf/2112.04359.

CHAPTER 5

Data Privacy Challenges in LLMs like ChatGPT

5.1 INTRODUCTION

LLMs, such as ChatGPT, pose significant challenges related to privacy and data protection. These challenges raise critical questions regarding data ownership, control, the legal basis for processing personally identifiable information (PII), and individual autonomy over personal data. LLMs gather information from three primary sources: user-provided data, user inputs, and identifiable information extracted from devices and browsers. Data privacy concerns persist across all domains in which these models are applied. The protection of privacy and data is crucial for AI systems, carrying profound implications for ethics, law, user trust, data security, and cybersecurity.[329] Ensuring robust privacy safeguards is essential to maintaining user confidence and complying with global data protection regulations. This chapter examines the major privacy issues associated with LLMs like ChatGPT and proposes potential solutions through a combination of ethical, legal, and technical measures.

5.2 DATA PRIVACY CHALLENGES IN LLMS LIKE ChatGPT

LLMs like ChatGPT may pose massive data privacy challenges due to the potential for oversharing sensitive data, generating fabricated or misleading data, and lacking control of users over their data. LLMs could also be employed to track user activity across various platforms, creating comprehensive profiles that expose browsing habits and personal preferences. This could lead to targeted ads, customised suggestions, or other personalised content that might expose private details about the user's life.[330]

329. OpenAI, *Privacy Policy*, https://openai.com/policies/privacy-policy (accessed 31 Jul. 2024).
330. Biwei Yan et al., *On Protecting the Data Privacy of Large Language Models (LLMs): A Survey*, arXiv preprint arXiv:2403.05156 (2024), https://arxiv.org/pdf/2403.05156.

This section will explore the specific data privacy challenges associated with LLMs like ChatGPT. It will examine how user prompts, data collection practices, the composition of training data, compliance with data protection regulations, potential technical vulnerabilities, and OpenAI's privacy policy each contribute to these risks.

5.2.1 Concerns with User Prompts

LLMs like ChatGPT can generate coherent and diverse texts based on user prompts. This capability presents certain privacy challenges for both users and the data sources utilised by ChatGPT. Users might inadvertently disclose sensitive information by entering such data into the chat interface. For example, Samsung Electronics experienced unintended leaks of confidential company data through ChatGPT in three separate incidents. As a result, Samsung Electronics has prohibited its employees from using ChatGPT and other AI-driven chatbots.[331] If the chat history is not disabled, this information may become part of ChatGPT's training dataset and could be incorporated into responses for other users.[332]

ChatGPT may generate texts that contain sensitive information based on the user's prompt, such as names, addresses, phone numbers, or passwords. This could pose a threat to the user's privacy and security, especially, if the tool is accessed by unauthorised parties or hacked by malicious actors.[333] The pressing concern calls for appropriate guidelines and safeguards to be put in place for ChatGPT regulations. Hence, many researchers emphasised the need to strike a balance between user-generated content and responsible content moderation.[334] Users should also exercise caution regarding the information they input into these systems, refraining from providing sensitive or personal data that could be potentially misused or exposed.

Moreover, models such as GPT-3 might inadvertently capture and reproduce sensitive information from their training data, raising privacy concerns during text generation.[335] The complexity and variability of text data make it challenging to thoroughly review the outputs of LLMs in real-world applications. Malicious actors can exploit these limitations by crafting impermissible outputs that appear permissible on the surface. This situation underscores the need for advanced and dynamic security measures that go beyond basic output filtering or static rules to effectively combat

331. Mark Gurman, *Samsung Bans ChatGPT and Other Generative AI Use by Staff After Leak*, Bloomberg (2 May 2023), https://www.bloomberg.com/news/articles/2023-05-02/samsung-bans-chatgpt-and-other-generative-ai-use-by-staff-after-leak?leadSource=uverify%20wall.
332. Uri Gal, *ChatGPT Is a Data Privacy Nightmare*, University of Sydney (8 Feb. 2023), https://www.sydney.edu.au/news-opinion/news/2023/02/08/chatgpt-is-a-data-privacy-nightmare.html.
333. Gartner, *Gartner Identifies Six ChatGPT Risks Legal and Compliance Must Evaluate* (18 May 2023), https://www.gartner.com/en/newsroom/press-releases/2023-05-18-gartner-identifies-six-chatgpt-risks-legal-and-compliance-must-evaluate; https://www.helpnetsecurity.com/2023/06/20/patricia-thaine-private-ai-chatgpt-business-privacy-concerns/.
334. *See supra* n. 121.
335. Badhan Chandra Das et al., *Security and Privacy Challenges of Large Language Models: A Survey*, arXiv preprint arXiv:2402.00888 (2024), https://arxiv.org/pdf/2402.00888.

sophisticated manipulation techniques and safeguard the integrity and safety of LLM applications.

Apart from the above, ChatGPT's ability to generate harmful or abusive content poses a threat to user privacy, as users can exploit the system to produce offensive, harassing, or harmful responses. Many researchers emphasised the importance of addressing privacy risks in user prompts, highlighting the potential misuse of language models to extract sensitive information, and advocating for guidelines and safeguards to protect user privacy.[336] Thus, these evolving concerns require more research and new policies from relevant stakeholders.

In conclusion, the diverse capabilities of LLMs like ChatGPT bring both impressive benefits and significant privacy challenges. The inadvertent disclosure of sensitive information, as seen in incidents at Samsung Electronics, highlights the urgent need for robust guidelines and proactive safeguards to protect user privacy. As LLMs continue to evolve, the potential for malicious exploitation underscores the necessity for advanced security measures that go beyond simple filtering techniques. By implementing comprehensive regulations and encouraging users to exercise caution in their inputs, we can better navigate the balance between innovation and privacy.

5.2.2 Issues in Data Collection Practices

LLMs like ChatGPT may require more data than search engines due to their interactive and conversational nature, which often prompts users to share more personal information. While the majority of data retained by ChatGPT and similar language models adhere to standard practices and user expectations, a genuine concern arises from the data collected directly through interactions with the model. Research indicates that chatbots' ability to engage users in extended dialogues can lead to the collection of substantial amounts of personal information, far exceeding what is typically gathered by search engines. This is particularly concerning since these interactions may involve sensitive information that users might not willingly disclose in other contexts.[337]

The data collected by these chatbots includes account details, device specifications, and any personal information users enter through the chat interface. This data is often shared with third-party entities and AI trainers, raising significant privacy concerns. Moreover, the data privacy issues associated with chatbots are compounded by the fact that they are actively used to train AI systems, often without the user's explicit consent. This can lead to personal data being repurposed and potentially misused, highlighting the need for robust regulatory frameworks to protect user

336. Shrimai Prabhumoye et al., *Exploring Controllable Text Generation Techniques*, arXiv preprint arXiv:2005.01822 (2020), https://aclanthology.org/2020.coling-main.1.pdf.
337. Stanford HAI, *Privacy in the AI Era: How Do We Protect Our Personal Information?* (18 Mar. 2024), https://hai.stanford.edu/news/privacy-ai-era-how-do-we-protect-our-personal-information; Hossein Hassani & Emmanuel Sirmal Silva, *The Role of ChatGPT in Data Science: How AI-Assisted Conversational Interfaces Are Revolutionizing the Field*, 7 Big Data & Cognitive Computing 62 (2023), https://doi.org/10.3390/bdcc7020062.

privacy in the AI era.[338] This unique aspect of data collection poses potential risks that warrant careful examination and consideration. Figure 5.1 illustrates who has access to users' ChatGPT data.

Figure 5.1 Screenshot Illustrating the Visibility of ChatGPT Data

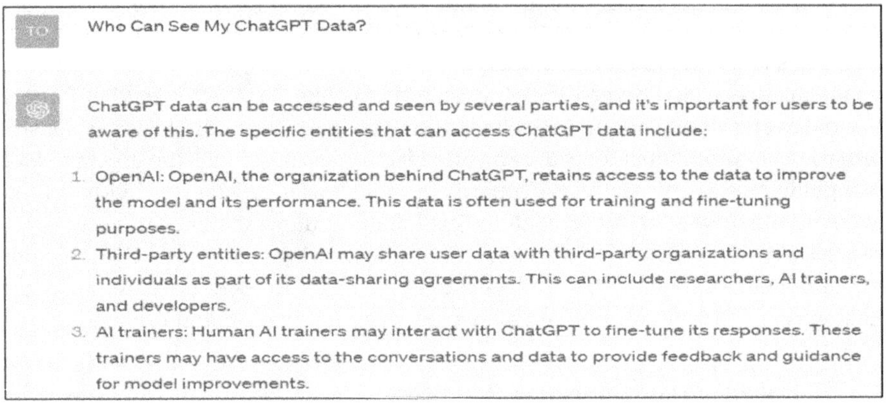

Source: ChatGPT, Author's Own Conversation with ChatGPT, July 2024.

Using AI can inadvertently lead to the disclosure of personal data by users. ChatGPT stores complete records of user interactions, meaning all information, including personal data, is retained. Although OpenAI is responsible for managing and processing user data responsibly, its privacy policy allows sharing of this information with third parties. This situation raises significant concerns about data protection and confidentiality, particularly due to the potential risks associated with storing data in insecure data centres or sharing it with unreliable industry partners.[339] Moreover, the lack of strict transparency regulations and OpenAI's operation as a black box further hinder audits and verification of data handling, leaving users unaware of the full extent of their data exposure and heightening privacy concerns.

Furthermore, as a data controller, OpenAI is responsible for ensuring the protection of users' data. This role involves ensuring legal compliance with data protection principles, safeguarding individuals' rights, maintaining accurate records, securing data processing activities, and selecting appropriate data processors. It also includes establishing a transparent relationship between controllers and processors, reporting data breaches to authorities and affected individuals, and being accountable for all data processing operations. Additionally, the role requires implementing necessary data protection measures, conducting impact assessments when required, appointing a DPO

338. Davide Castelvecchi, *Open-Source AI Chatbots Are Booming: What Does This Mean for Researchers?*, Nature (2023).
339. *See supra* n. 47.

as needed, adhering to international data transfer obligations, and collaborating with data protection authorities.[340]

In conclusion, while ChatGPT's data collection practices align with standard industry norms, the unique nature of conversational AI raises significant privacy concerns. The direct acquisition of user data through interactions and the sharing of this data with third-party entities and AI trainers heightens the risk of users' personal data exposure. For instance, the Italian data protection authority alleged that OpenAI's chatbot was non-compliant with the country's data protection rules.[341] This finding highlights the potential legal and regulatory challenges faced by AI companies operating in regions with stringent data protection frameworks. These practices necessitate robust data protection measures and stringent regulatory oversight to ensure user data is handled securely and transparently.

5.2.3 Issues in Training Data

ChatGPT is trained on a vast dataset of text and code that may contain copyrighted, sensitive, inaccurate, or biased information.[342] Although AI models like ChatGPT do not retain specific data from their training, they can sometimes generate responses that appear to reference specific data or reveal sensitive information. For instance, on 20 March 2023, ChatGPT experienced its first data breach, which exposed the information of ChatGPT Plus subscribers along with their shared prompts to other users. Approximately 1.2 % of active ChatGPT Plus subscribers had their data compromised within a nine-hour window.[343]

Privacy and data security breaches can damage users' trust in AI systems, undermining their reputation and usefulness. This can occur when users unintentionally share personal or sensitive information with AI systems, assuming they are secure.[344] Furthermore, ChatGPT's knowledge and creativity derive from a vast dataset collected from the internet and other sources, often without the consent or knowledge of the original authors. This lack of transparency around data collection can raise ethical concerns and further erode trust in AI. Additionally, malicious actors could exploit vulnerabilities in AI systems to manipulate data or steal sensitive information, leading to even more significant consequences.

LLMs like ChatGPT utilise user input data to generate responses and improve their models for future interactions. This process poses reputational and regulatory

340. European Data Protection Board, *Data Controller or Data Processor*, https://edpb.europa.eu/sme-data-protection-guide/data-controller-data-processor_en#toc-7 (accessed 1 Aug. 2024).
341. Imran Rahman-Jones, *ChatGPT: Italy Says OpenAI's Chatbot Breaches Data Protection Rules*, BBC (31 Jan. 2024), https://www.bbc.com/news/technology-68128396.
342. *See supra* n. 334.
343. OpenAI, *March 20 ChatGPT Outage: Here's What Happened* (24 Mar. 2023), https://openai.com/index/march-20-chatgpt-outage/.
344. Glorin Sebastian, *Privacy and Data Protection in ChatGPT and Other AI Chatbots: Strategies for Securing User Information*, 15(1) International Journal of Security and Privacy in Pervasive Computing (IJSPPC) 1–14 (2024), https://doi.org/10.4018/IJSPPC.325475.

risks for firms.[345] For example, employees using ChatGPT may inadvertently expose sensitive information to the public, creating significant risks for their organisations. Employers need to be aware of the risks associated with employees using ChatGPT. Additionally, personal information shared with ChatGPT may be used in ways that do not align with users' expectations.[346] If one user inputs sensitive information, it might inadvertently be revealed to another user with a similar query. Moreover, ChatGPT assigns a unique identifier to each interaction, which means that the process is not entirely anonymous. This raises concerns about OpenAI's data retention practices.

It is important to note that organisations providing LLMs, like ChatGPT, may have access to and potentially store user queries. This poses privacy risks, especially if the LLM service is acquired by an organisation with different privacy policies.[347] Recent research demonstrates that LLMs can automatically select high-quality data for fine-tuning through methods like instruction mining, enhancing their performance in tasks, such as text summarisation, categorisation, and natural language understanding.[348] Given the potential privacy risks associated with LLMs like ChatGPT, users should exercise caution and refrain from inputting sensitive or personal information when interacting with publicly available LLM systems.

In conclusion, ChatGPT's training on a vast, potentially unfiltered dataset raises concerns about privacy, security, and user trust. The recent data breach highlights the potential for misuse of personal information, emphasising the critical need for stricter regulations. Additionally, the lack of user control over their data and the risk of unintended information disclosure further underscores the importance of increasing user awareness and implementing more robust protective measures. While advancements like instruction mining offer promise for mitigating these issues, user caution and responsible data practices remain paramount. As the field of LLMs rapidly advances, addressing the myriad privacy concerns surrounding these powerful AI systems will be of utmost importance. Therefore, ChatGPT's impact on data privacy warrants scrutiny and thoughtful safeguards.

5.2.4 Non-compliance with Laws

ChatGPT has faced bans or restrictions in several countries due to concerns regarding its data collection practices and non-compliance with data protection regulations. Notably, the countries where ChatGPT has been banned include Russia, China, North

345. Aaron Pinnick, *Managing the Risk of Large Language Models Like ChatGPT*, ACA Global (10 May 2023), https://www.acaglobal.com/insights/managing-risk-large-language-models-chatgpt.
346. Stephanie Wong, *Let's Look at LLMs: Understanding Data Flows and Risks in the Workplace*, Future of Privacy Forum (30 Mar. 2023), https://fpf.org/blog/lets-look-at-llms-understanding-data-flows-and-risks-in-the-workplace/.
347. David, C. & Paul, J., *ChatGPT and Large Language Models: What's the Risk?*, Nat'l Cyber Sec. Centre (14 Mar. 2023), https://www.ncsc.gov.uk/blog-post/chatgpt-and-large-language-models-whats-the-risk.
348. https://arxiv.org/abs/2307.06290.

Korea, Cuba, Iran, and Syria.[349] Italy was the first EU Member State to ban ChatGPT in April 2023, citing privacy concerns regarding the EU GDPR. The ban was lifted in August 2023 after OpenAI addressed the concerns raised by the Italian data protection authority.[350] Several nations have prohibited the use of ChatGPT due to privacy concerns, while others, notably North Korea, China, and Russia, have alleged that the US intends to use ChatGPT to disseminate misinformation.[351] OpenAI maintains a list of countries where ChatGPT is not available, including Afghanistan, Bhutan, the Central African Republic, Chad, Eritrea, Eswatini, Iran, Libya, South Sudan, Sudan, Syria, and Yemen.[352]

The EU is deliberating on regulations and potential prohibitions concerning AI technologies, including LLMs, driven by privacy and ethical considerations.[353] OpenAI has come under scrutiny for allegedly processing personal data without a legitimate basis, which contravenes Article 5(1)(a) of the GDPR. Article 5(1)(a) of the GDPR mandates that personal data must be processed lawfully, fairly, and transparently, ensuring that individuals are informed about how their data is used. Furthermore, OpenAI is accused of failing to rectify inaccuracies produced by ChatGPT, thus breaching Article 16 (right to rectification), and of not upholding the principle of data protection by design and by default, as mandated by Article 25 (data protection by design and by default).[354]

Recently, the EU's ChatGPT taskforce has released preliminary findings on OpenAI's compliance with the bloc's privacy laws.[355] The taskforce, established to streamline enforcement of these laws on emerging technologies, remains undecided on key issues like the lawfulness and fairness of OpenAI's data processing practices. It suggests that OpenAI could improve compliance by implementing adequate safeguards, such as technical measures and precise data collection criteria, to reduce privacy risks. Additionally, the taskforce emphasises the need for transparency, informing users their inputs may be used for training and ensuring compliance with GDPR principles of data accuracy. Nonetheless, it also highlights that OpenAI cannot

---

349. Jon Martindale, *These Are the Countries Where ChatGPT Is Currently Banned*, Digital Trends (12 Apr. 2023), https://www.digitaltrends.com/computing/these-countries-chatgpt-banned/.

350. Shiona McCallum, *ChatGPT Banned in Italy Over Privacy Concerns*, BBC (1 Apr. 2023), https://www.bbc.com/news/technology-65139406; Shiona McCallum, *ChatGPT Accessible Again in Italy*, BBC (29 Apr. 2023), https://www.bbc.com/news/technology-65431914.

351. *See supra* n. 350.

352. *Ibid.*

353. Natasha Lomas, *EU's ChatGPT Taskforce Offers First Look at Detangling the AI Chatbot's Privacy Compliance*, TechCrunch (27 May 2024), https://techcrunch.com/2024/05/27/eus-chatgpt-taskforce-offers-first-look-at-detangling-the-ai-chatbots-privacy-compliance/.

354. Natasha Lomas, *ChatGPT-Maker OpenAI Accused of String of Data Protection Breaches in GDPR Complaint Filed by Privacy Researcher*, TechCrunch (30 Aug. 2023), https://techcrunch.com/2023/08/30/chatgpt-maker-openai-accused-of-string-of-data-protection-breaches-in-gdpr-complaint-filed-by-privacy-researcher/?guccounter=1&guce_referrer=aHR0cHM6Ly93d3cuZ29Z2xlLmNvbS8&guce_referrer_sig=AQAAAJXKSg_ZwzkX9XVTosjYV8_2eRIfdIMtnPpIBDimsodbYHR1ohLFE9BWwN3he8TU1KjI5f19XsTVriJJViKYx7B_wCuR15RQA0y4rnuJuBt3qpxJEwSwWN1YGErfSPSdSV00oGwBJnOLwjmbtiOKKCcDUKQEJi_F6PHBMiYJ_Zxw.

355. *See supra* n. 354.

shift privacy responsibilities to users.[356] This taskforce's existence appears to be delaying decisions and investigations into ChatGPT-related complaints across the EU.

In the US, there is increasing concern over the risks associated with LLMs, though no bans have been imposed. These concerns include IP risks, quality control issues, and cybersecurity threats. LLMs might inadvertently store and reuse sensitive information, leading to privacy and confidentiality risks, and they can also produce incorrect information that may result in poor decisions if not monitored.[357] To address these issues, organisations such as the US Department of Defense (DoD) are working to identify and mitigate biases and other risks through initiatives like AI Bias Bounty exercises.[358] While some companies might consider banning LLMs, most opt to implement restricted or controlled use, establishing guidelines for handling sensitive data and ensuring the quality and security of LLM outputs.

Moreover, there are growing concerns that LLMs like ChatGPT might unintentionally produce sensitive information even after it has been deleted from the training data. A recent AI research article found that the architecture of LLMs presents significant challenges for the complete removal of sensitive information.[359] Although it is technically feasible to delete specific data from LLMs, ensuring that the data has been completely eradicated is significantly more complex. This difficulty arises from the fact that LLMs are trained on vast and diverse datasets and fine-tuned to generate coherent responses, which complicates the task of pinpointing and eliminating specific pieces of information from the model's intricate structure. This phenomenon is often described as the 'black box' nature of AI, where the internal processes of the model are not fully transparent or comprehensible to researchers.

Furthermore, public data also raises data privacy concerns in LLM systems. LLMs such as ChatGPT utilise diverse text sources, predominantly drawn from publicly accessible online content, to generate responses. Some people may think that publicly accessible data is not subject to data protection law, but any language model that processes personal data from publicly accessible sources is still subject to the provisions of data protection law.[360]

Arguably, data protection regulators require organisations to develop or use GAI to address key questions to safeguard individuals' personal data. These questions include establishing the lawful basis for processing personal data, determining their role as a controller, joint controller, or processor, conducting a data protection impact

356. European Data Protection Board, *Report of the ChatGPT Taskforce* (23 May 2024), https://www.edpb.europa.eu/system/files/2024-05/edpb_20240523_report_chatgpt_taskforce_en.pdf.
357. IBM Data and AI Team, *Open Source Large Language Models: Benefits, Risks and Types*, IBM (27 Sep. 2023), https://www.ibm.com/blog/open-source-large-language-models-benefits-risks-and-types/; *see also supra* n. 346.
358. US Dep't of Def., *CDAO Launches First DoD AI Bias Bounty Focused on Unknown Risks in LLMs* (31 Jul. 2024), https://www.defense.gov/News/Releases/Release/Article/3659519/cdao-launches-first-dod-ai-bias-bounty-focused-on-unknown-risks-in-llms/.
359. Vaidehi Patil et al., *Can Sensitive Information Be Deleted from LLMs? Objectives for Defending Against Extraction Attacks*, arXiv preprint arXiv:2309.17410 (29 Sep. 2023), https://arxiv.org/pdf/2309.17410.
360. Information Commissioner's Office, *Generative AI: Eight Questions That Developers and Users Need to Ask*, ICO (30 May 2024), https://ico.org.uk/about-the-ico/media-centre/blog-generative-ai-eight-questions-that-developers-and-users-need-to-ask/.

assessment (DPIA), ensuring transparency, mitigating security risks, limiting unnecessary processing, complying with individual rights requests, and disclosing the use of GAI for solely automated decisions.[361] Organisations that fail to comply with data protection laws and do not adequately consider their impacts on individuals are liable to face legal consequences and fines.[362] Therefore, some GAI tools state in their privacy policies that information entered in prompts can be used to improve the tool, which could make them subject to these regulations.[363]

Although the EU GDPR aims to protect individual rights and promote AI innovation, it faces challenges in applying its principles of purpose limitation, data minimisation, processing of sensitive data, and restrictions on automated decision-making.[364] Moreover, the GDPR does not provide clear guidance on how to explain, ensure fairness, or accept AI decisions. Therefore, further guidance, clarification, and dialogue are needed to ensure that the GDPR can effectively regulate AI in a way that balances risks and opportunities for individuals and society.

In the context of contemporary AI regulation, the EU's AI Act of 2024 has introduced a comprehensive framework for the governance of AI systems, with particular emphasis on those deemed high-risk. Under the EU AI Act 2024, AI systems are categorised based on risk level, including unacceptable, high, general-purpose, and limited risk. While LLMs like ChatGPT are not automatically classified as high-risk, they could fall into this category if used in specific applications with the potential to impact health, safety, or fundamental rights significantly.[365] For instance, if an LLM is employed in critical areas such as healthcare, law enforcement, or employment, it may be subject to stricter regulations and assessments to mitigate potential risks.

The EU AI Act mandates that providers of general-purpose AI systems like ChatGPT must furnish comprehensive technical documentation to demonstrate adherence to safety, transparency, and accountability standards. This documentation must be maintained and accessible to national authorities for ten years following the system's deployment in the EU.[366] It is important to note that the EU AI Act does not prohibit the development or use of any AI technology, but instead aims to ensure that high-risk applications involving personal data or significant decision-making comply with stringent safety and ethical standards. Therefore, while ChatGPT can be utilised within the EU, it must comply with these regulatory requirements to ensure responsible and safe deployment.

361. *Ibid.*
362. Philipp Rosenauer & Fatih Sahin, *Navigating the Risks: Harnessing AI and Large Language Models Responsibly in Business,* PwC (April 2024), https://www.pwc.ch/en/insights/regulation/AI-and-large-language-models-in-business.html.
363. Reuters, *ChatGPT and Generative AI: Key Legal Issues* (1 Jun. 2023), https://www.reuters.com/practical-law-the-journal/transactional/chatgpt-generative-ai-key-legal-issues-2023-06-01/.
364. European Parliament, *The Impact of the General Data Protection Regulation (GDPR) on Artificial Intelligence* (June 2020), https://www.europarl.europa.eu/RegData/etudes/STUD/2020/641530/EPRS_STU(2020)641530_EN.pdf.
365. European Parliament, *EU AI Act: First Regulation on Artificial Intelligence* (8 Jun. 2023), https://www.europarl.europa.eu/topics/en/article/20230601STO93804/eu-ai-act-first-regulation-on-artificial-intelligence.
366. European Parliament, *Artificial Intelligence Act* (21 Jul. 2021), https://www.europarl.europa.eu/RegData/etudes/BRIE/2021/698792/EPRS_BRI(2021)698792_EN.pdf.

Furthermore, the EU AI Act emphasises transparency, accountability, and robust data protection measures. Although OpenAI, the developer of ChatGPT, has made strides to align with these requirements, achieving compliance is an ongoing process. The European Data Protection Board (EDPB) has identified various areas that require improvement, particularly in data processing and user consent.[367] Additionally, the EU AI Act necessitates AI developers to disclose the use of copyrighted material in training their models, which presents additional challenges for LLMs that rely on extensive datasets sourced from the internet.[368] In essence, the EU AI Act is designed to strike a balance between fostering innovation and promoting ethical AI use, ensuring that systems like ChatGPT can be developed and harnessed within a framework that prioritises user safety and transparency.

5.2.5 Technical Vulnerabilities

Since its release in November 2022, some people have sought to bypass the restrictions of ChatGPT, a process known as jailbreaking. Jailbreaking allows users to manipulate ChatGPT in ways that were not intended by its developers. This is typically achieved through techniques such as prompt engineering and adversarial prompting, or by exploiting vulnerabilities in ChatGPT's code.[369] People may jailbreak LLMs for a variety of reasons, including curiosity, to create harmful content, or to research security vulnerabilities. It is important to note that jailbreaking an LLM can lead to the generation of harmful or offensive content and is often illegal.

LLMs like ChatGPT are susceptible to data breaches, as evidenced by an incident in March 2023 when a bug in an open-source library exposed user data.[370] Additionally, the new Bing is vulnerable to multi-step jailbreaking privacy attacks, which allow malicious actors to extract personal information from search results.[371] Users can also employ probing attacks to determine whether their personal data is being leaked by the language model. Identifying these privacy vulnerabilities in LLMs is crucial to understanding the potential risks. This understanding will facilitate the development of robust privacy preservation solutions to mitigate these risks and protect user data.

Furthermore, LLMs like ChatGPT can suffer from hallucinations, where they fabricate information and present it as factual. Artificial hallucinations are uncommon in chatbots, as they follow pre-programmed rules and data. However, advanced AI systems can produce hallucinations when trained on large amounts of unsupervised

367. European Data Protection Board, *Opinion 2024/08 on Consent or Pay* (April 2024), https://www.edpb.europa.eu/system/files/2024-04/edpb_opinion_202408_consentorpay_en.pdf.
368. European Parliament, *Artificial Intelligence Act* (2019–2024), https://www.europarl.europa.eu/doceo/document/TA-9-2024-0138_EN.pdf (2024).
369. Maanak Gupta et al., *From ChatGPT to ThreatGPT: Impact of Generative AI in Cybersecurity and Privacy*, 11 IEEE Access (2023), https://ieeexplore.ieee.org/stamp/stamp.jsp?arnumber=10198233.
370. *See* OpenAI, *March 20 ChatGPT Outage, supra* n. 343.
371. *See supra* n. 47.

data, creating realistic sensory experiences without real-world input.[372] For example, one study on AI hallucinations in ChatGPT-generated research proposals found that 69 out of 178 references lacked a digital object identifier (DOI), with 28 being non-existent.[373] Another study on medical articles revealed that 47% of 115 references were fabricated, 46% were real but inaccurate, and only 7% were both real and accurate.[374]

As of July 2024, the situation remains largely unchanged. For instance, when I requested ChatGPT to provide suitable references for a given text, it recommended two sources (*see* Figure 5.2). However, neither reference was valid, as both uniform resource locators (URLs) returned the message: 'Sorry, this page is temporarily unavailable. Please try again or return to the homepage.'

Figure 5.2 ChatGPT's Citation Limitations

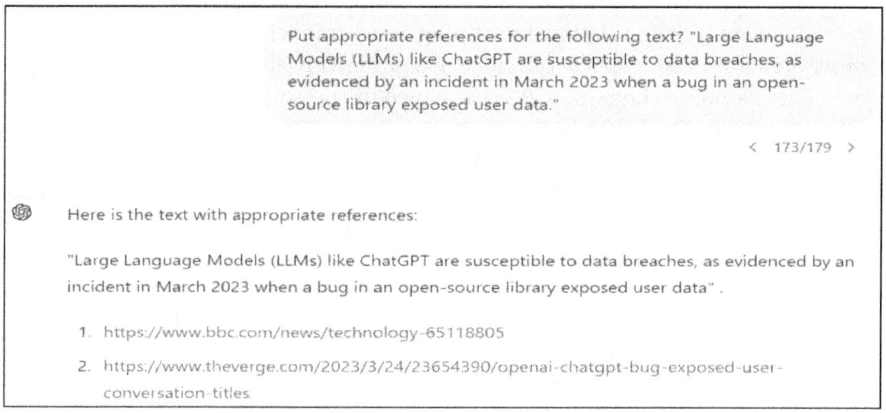

Source: ChatGPT, Author's Own Conversation with ChatGPT, July 2024.

A study examining the reliability of ChatGPT's citations found that, out of 35 references, only two were genuine. Twelve of the citations were like actual works, while 21 appeared plausible but were, in fact, a mixture of different real manuscripts.[375] However, this situation, according to some authors, is unacceptable. They anticipated stronger reactions, such as public protests and demands to ban ChatGPT and similar AI tools due to their inefficiencies in producing accurate references. These

372. Alkaissi, H. & McFarlane, S.I., *Artificial Hallucinations in ChatGPT: Implications in Scientific Writing*, at 15(2) Cureus (19 Feb. 2023), https://doi.org/10.7759/cureus.35179.
373. Sai Anirudh Athaluri et al., *Exploring the Boundaries of Reality: Investigating the Phenomenon of Artificial Intelligence Hallucination in Scientific Writing Through ChatGPT References*, at 15(4) Cureus (11 Apr. 2023), https://doi.org/10.7759/cureus.37432. PMID: 37182055; PMCID: PMC10173677.
374. Mehul Bhattacharyya et al., *High Rates of Fabricated and Inaccurate References in ChatGPT-Generated Medical Content*, at 15(5) Cureus (19 May 2023), https://doi.org/10.7759/cureus.39238; PMID: 37337480; PMCID: PMC10277170.
375. Alessia McGowan et al., *ChatGPT and Bard Exhibit Spontaneous Citation Fabrication During Psychiatry Literature Search*, 326 Psychiatry Research 115334 (2023), https://doi.org/10.1016/j.psychres.2023.115334.

authors argue that the term 'hallucinations' is a misnomer. They prefer to call these issues actual fabrications and falsifications by LLMs like ChatGPT.[376]

Many developers of LLMs may choose to keep their training data and model architecture details secret as a business strategy. This approach, known as 'security through obscurity', involves maintaining the security of a system by concealing its internal operations and mechanisms from unauthorised individuals. Essentially, critical information regarding the system is deliberately hidden from external entities. The premise is that by limiting access to sensitive details and potential vulnerabilities, the system can be safeguarded. Nonetheless, relying solely on obscurity without addressing inherent vulnerabilities carries significant risks.[377] Moreover, such secrecy can hinder the ability to audit the LLMs' decision-making process, raising concerns about fairness and accountability. For instance, if an LLM turns down a loan application, we should be able to see why it made that decision to make sure it was not unfair or biased.

LLMs like ChatGPT are also susceptible to model poisoning, a type of attack that involves maliciously manipulating the training data or model parameters. The toxicity of responses generated by ChatGPT can vary significantly depending on the assigned persona. For example, when ChatGPT is assigned the persona of the boxer Muhammad Ali, its response toxicity can increase by up to sixfold.[378] Model poisoning attacks work by introducing tainted data into the training process, allowing adversaries to influence the model's outputs. This can lead to substantial privacy concerns for users, as malicious actors might use crafted prompts to generate inappropriate or offensive responses.[379] Such attacks not only risk degrading the model's performance but also have potential legal and ethical implications for both the model's developers and its users.

In summary, the technical vulnerabilities of LLMs like ChatGPT reveal a complex landscape where both innovative potential and significant risks coexist. The susceptibility of these models to jailbreaking, data breaches, privacy attacks, and hallucinations underscores the need for ongoing vigilance and robust security measures. The potential for harmful content generation, combined with issues of accuracy and transparency, calls for a balanced approach that embraces both innovation and rigorous scrutiny. As LLMs continue to evolve and integrate into various aspects of society, addressing these vulnerabilities through proactive strategies and collaborative efforts will be essential in shaping a future where these technologies can be used ethically and effectively.

5.2.6 Problems with OpenAI's Privacy Policy

OpenAI collects a broad spectrum of data from its users. This includes personal information provided during account creation, such as name, contact details, and

376. Robin Emsley, *ChatGPT: These Are Not Hallucinations: They're Fabrications and Falsifications*, 9 Schizophr. 52 (2023), https://doi.org/10.1038/s41537-023-00379-4.
377. Okta, *Security Through Obscurity (STO): History, Criticism & Risks* (21 Apr. 2022), https://www.okta.com/identity-101/security-through-obscurity/.
378. *See supra* n. 251.
379. *See supra* n. 111.

payment information. Users also contribute content through the services, and OpenAI collects communication details from interactions with the organisation. Additionally, OpenAI gathers information from social media interactions. During service usage, OpenAI automatically collects technical data, which includes log data (such as IP address, browser type, and interaction details), usage data (including content engagement, device type, and access times), and device information (such as device name and operating system).[380] Cookies and analytics tools are also employed to collect further information about users' preferences and behaviour, which is used to enhance the user experience.[381]

Moreover, OpenAI uses the personal information of its users to provide, maintain, and analyse its services, improve, and develop new programs, communicate with users, prevent fraud, and ensure security. It also uses this data to conduct business transfers and comply with legal obligations. Aggregated or de-identified information is used for service analysis, improvement, research, and sharing of general user statistics. Additionally, user content may be used to train models like ChatGPT, with opt-out options available.[382]

Furthermore, OpenAI OpCo, LLC's privacy policy lacks clarity and fails to adequately address the data protection challenges associated with its services. The policy does not explicitly outline how users can access, correct, or delete their personal information, nor does it provide comprehensive details on the choices users have regarding data collection and processing.[383] This lack of transparency and accountability raises concerns about the potential risks to users' privacy rights.[384] However, it is essential to evaluate OpenAI's approach in response to these concerns. OpenAI's Privacy Policy and Terms & Policies offer mechanisms to address data privacy issues, including the ability for users to manage their account information, opt out of promotional communications, request content deletion, and seek the deletion of personal data by contacting privacy@openai.com. According to these policies, OpenAI is committed to erasing users' personal information unless there are legitimate business or legal reasons for retaining it.[385]

Despite the above assurances, OpenAI's policy of sharing personal information with third parties, except when legally required, raises significant concerns regarding data protection and privacy. This policy could potentially lead to the transfer of user data to entities not governed by the same data protection regulations or with inadequate privacy practices. OpenAI collects a range of user data, including account information, payment card details, and file uploads or feedback submitted through its services. Furthermore, OpenAI discloses users' geolocation data to affiliates, vendors,

380. *See supra* n. 330.
381. *Ibid.*
382. *Ibid.*
383. Mathieu Pollet, *ChatGPT's Hallucinations Draw EU Privacy Complaint*, Politico (29 Apr. 2024), https://www.politico.eu/article/chatgpts-hallucinations-get-eu-privacy-complaint/.
384. Future of Privacy Forum, *The FPF Center for Artificial Intelligence: Navigating AI Policy, Regulation, and Governance*, https://fpf.org/issue/ai-ml/ (accessed 1 Aug. 2024).
385. *See supra* n. 330; https://openai.com/policies.

service providers, law enforcement agencies, and parties involved in transactions.[386] This extensive approach to data collection and disclosure raises serious issues from the perspective of data protection laws. The policy lacks clear guidelines on data handling, protection, and the specific purposes for data sharing, which may undermine user trust and privacy rights and could potentially conflict with data protection regulations.

For non-compliance with data protection regulations, the South Korean Personal Information Protection Commission (PIPC) fined OpenAI 3.6 million won (approximately USD 3,000) for a data breach that affected 687 Korean users.[387] OpenAI reported that the breach resulted from a bug in an open-source library, which allowed users to view others' chat histories and potentially exposed additional personal data of ChatGPT Plus subscribers. Moreover, OpenAI temporarily disabled ChatGPT to address the bug and protect Korean users' personal information. The PIPC criticised OpenAI for failing to report the breach within the mandated 24-hour period but did not find the company negligent in its data protection measures. Subsequently, the commission instructed OpenAI to improve its security protocols and ensure compliance with South Korean data protection regulations.[388]

OpenAI's disclaimer that no internet or email transmission is ever fully secure and that users should take special care in deciding what information they send to the company is inadequate.[389] OpenAI must take all necessary measures to protect user data, as users cannot reasonably assess the security of every transmission. Additionally, OpenAI's disclaimer that it is not responsible for the circumvention of any privacy settings or security measures contained on the service or third-party websites is essentially a blanket waiver of liability for any data breaches that may occur. This provision is unacceptable because OpenAI must protect user data, regardless of how it is obtained. Moreover, OpenAI's attempt to evade liability for protecting user data, even in cases of negligence or recklessness, is an alarming violation of user privacy rights.

Furthermore, OpenAI's disclosure that user data will be processed and stored in the US and may be disclosed to service providers and affiliates in other jurisdictions without user consent is a clear violation of data protection laws.[390] Users have a right to know where their data is being stored and processed, and they should be able to consent to cross-border data transfers. OpenAI's attempt to justify this disclosure as necessary to provide its services is misleading, as there are many ways to provide services without transferring data to other jurisdictions. Overall, OpenAI's stance on data protection laws is inadequate. The company is failing to take sufficient steps to protect user data, thereby putting users' data at risk. It is important to note that OpenAI is still under development, and its privacy policy may evolve over time.

386. *Ibid.*
387. Gadgets Now, *South Korea Has Fined ChatGPT Maker OpenAI 3.6 Million Won: Here's Why* (28 Jul. 2023), https://www.gadgetsnow.com/tech-news/south-korea-has-fined-chatgpt-maker-openai-3-6-million-won-heres-why/articleshow/102182140.cms.
388. The Korea Times, *ChatGPT Fined $2,829 for Exposing Personal Info of 687 Korean Users* (7 Aug. 2023), https://www.koreatimes.co.kr/www/tech/2023/08/129_355818.html.
389. *See supra* n. 330 (8. Security and Retention).
390. *Ibid.*

In conclusion, while OpenAI's Privacy Policy lays out several measures for managing user data and ensuring some degree of protection, there are significant shortcomings that cannot be overlooked. The broad scope of data collection, lack of transparency in data handling, and potential for cross-border data transfers present serious challenges to user privacy. The recent fine imposed by the South Korean PIPC highlights these concerns, demonstrating that there is room for improvement in how OpenAI manages and safeguards user information. As OpenAI continues to evolve, the organisation must address these issues with greater clarity and commitment, ensuring that users' privacy rights are respected and upheld. Therefore, users should be aware of and vigilant about the current limitations of OpenAI's Privacy Policy and take steps to protect their privacy while advocating for stronger privacy protections from the company.

5.3 REGULATORY STRATEGIES FOR PRIVACY IN AI CHATBOTS

Ensuring data privacy in AI chatbots necessitates a combination of legal, ethical, and technical measures. Legal measures involve enacting laws and treaties that delineate the rights and responsibilities of AI developers and users, as well as outlining potential sanctions for non-compliance. Ethical measures entail establishing principles and guidelines that reflect societal values and norms, including industry best practices. Technical measures encompass designing and implementing mechanisms for safety, reliability, transparency, accountability, and data protection. This sub-section will discuss the regulatory aspects of LLMs like ChatGPT, emphasising education and awareness programs, lawful and transparent AI deployment, user control over data, privacy impact assessments (PIAs), ethical AI use, robust data protection laws, and suitable technical measures.

5.3.1 Education and Awareness

The rise of AI chatbots brings significant challenges to data processing activities, particularly in the areas of data privacy, ownership, consent, and ethics. Therefore, AI chatbot users need to be informed about how these chatbots collect, use, and protect their data. The rapid growth of privacy concerns requires action from lawmakers, policy experts, and the public. AI development and use should be responsible, balancing innovation and privacy. While establishing regulatory frameworks may require an extended time, public education initiatives can play a crucial role in facilitating the adoption of such measures.[391] Educating and empowering users to make informed decisions about their privacy while utilising chatbots and other AI tools

391. Minn. J.L. Sci. & Tech., *A Living AI: How ChatGPT Raises Novel Data Privacy Issues* (6 Feb. 62023), https://mjlst.lib.umn.edu/2023/02/06/a-living-ai-how-chatgpt-raises-novel-data-privacy-issues/.

is essential. This involves providing clear and concise privacy policies, obtaining valid consent, and offering easy opt-out options.[392]

A study conducted by Deloitte in 2023 revealed a significant lack of awareness regarding ethical frameworks for the utilisation of GAI technologies within organisations. The research found that 56% of the respondents were either unaware or uncertain about the existence of established ethical guidelines for the deployment of GAI within their respective workplaces.[393] This finding highlights a considerable knowledge gap in the responsible adoption of these advanced AI capabilities across industries. To safeguard data privacy and security in the implementation of AI chatbots, organisations should ensure data privacy and security in AI chatbots by developing a culture of data awareness. This multi-pronged approach should include educating users on data storage practices, implementing robust data monitoring and protection systems across the organisation, and leveraging data usage analysis to identify and address potential privacy risks.[394]

Public perception of AI stems from concerns and distrust regarding data privacy. As AI continues to advance and impact how personal data is utilised, these concerns are prevalent. Recent research reveals that around 70% of people familiar with AI have little faith that companies will make responsible decisions about their personal information.[395] To address these privacy concerns, organisations should prioritise user education and awareness about data practices employed by their AI chatbots. Moreover, users should have the right to know about the data and the type of data AI chatbots collect during conversations, the purposes of such data collection, and the potential entities with whom such data may be shared. Implementing clear and concise privacy policies is crucial for promoting transparency and building user trust. Furthermore, giving users the ability to access, review, and request the deletion of their data collected by AI chatbots can help alleviate privacy concerns and establish trustworthy relationships.

In conclusion, the rise of AI chatbots necessitates a proactive approach to data privacy and ethics, highlighting the urgent need for comprehensive education and transparent policies. The significant knowledge gap identified in Deloitte's 2023 study underscores the importance of fostering a culture of data awareness within organisations and among users. To mitigate privacy concerns and build trust, companies must prioritise user education, clearly communicate data practices, and provide robust

392. Ali Jessani, *Chatbots, AI and the Future of Privacy*, IAPP (31 Mar. 2023), https://iapp.org/news/a/chatbots-ai-and-the-future-of-privacy/.
393. Deloitte, *Many Executives Uncertain if Their Organizations Have Ethical Standards for Generative AI: Deloitte State of Ethics and Trust in Technology Report* (10 Oct. 2023), https://www2.deloitte.com/us/en/pages/about-deloitte/articles/press-releases/many-executives-uncertain-if-their-organizations-have-ethical-standards-for-generative-ai.html.
394. Katie Schwarzwalder, *Three Essential Steps to Protecting Your Data Across the Hybrid Cloud*, IBM (3 Aug. 2023), https://www.ibm.com/blog/three-essential-steps-to-protecting-your-data-across-the-hybrid-cloud/.
395. Colleen McClain et al., *How Americans View Data Privacy*, Pew Research Center (18 Oct. 2023), https://www.pewresearch.org/internet/2023/10/18/how-americans-view-data-privacy/.

mechanisms for data control. By balancing innovation with responsible data management, we can harness the benefits of AI while safeguarding user privacy and reinforcing ethical standards in the digital age.

5.3.2 Lawfulness and Transparency

To ensure data privacy in AI chatbots, all AI operations must be conducted lawfully and transparently. Additionally, AI chatbots should be required to disclose their underlying mechanisms and the specific data they utilise. A fundamental principle of data privacy is that data processing activities must be fair, transparent, and lawful. Additional key principles of data privacy regulations include data minimisation, purpose limitation, protection of data subjects' rights, and adherence to accountability standards.[396] The above principles require that data controllers and processors only collect and use personal data that is necessary and relevant for a specific and legitimate purpose. They also inform the data subjects about how their data is used and what rights they have over it.

Therefore, to ensure data privacy in AI chatbots, LLMs like ChatGPT must adhere to principles of transparency, purpose limitation, data subject rights, and accountability, as mandated by regulations such as the GDPR.[397] This approach requires AI systems to clearly explain their operations, collect only necessary data for specific purposes, respect user rights to access, rectification, and erasure, and implement robust data protection measures. Nevertheless, compliance is challenged by algorithm complexity, data diversity, user-generated content, and the need for vast datasets, potentially leading to excessive data collection and hindering user rights fulfilment.[398] To address these challenges while safeguarding data privacy and societal values, it is essential to engage proactively with data protection regulations, adhere to relevant guidelines, and collaborate with key stakeholders.

Achieving true transparency with LLMs is inherently difficult given their complexity and opacity. The models are trained on vast datasets scraped from the internet, often with inconsistent or unknown data provenance, licensing, and consent processes. Unpacking and auditing all of the original data sources is practically impossible. Furthermore, the ML process by which the models ingest and generalise patterns from the data is a black box that even the developers cannot fully explain.[399] While techniques like model cards can document some high-level attributes, they fall short of

396. Regulation (EU) 2016/679 of the European Parliament and of the Council of 27 Apr. 2016 on the Protection of Natural Persons with Regard to the Processing of Personal Data and on the Free Movement of Such Data, and Repealing Directive 95/46/EC (General Data Protection Regulation) (Text with EEA Relevance), 2016 O.J. (L 119) 1 (EU), Art. 5, Chapter III, https://eur-lex.europa.eu/legal-content/EN/TXT/HTML/?uri=CELEX:32016R0679.
397. *Ibid.*
398. *See supra* n. 345.
399. Cynthia Rudin, *Stop Explaining Black Box Machine Learning Models for High Stakes Decisions and Use Interpretable Models Instead*, 1 Nat. Mach. Intell. 206 (2019), https://doi.org/10.1038/s42256-019-0048-x.

true algorithmic transparency.[400] As AI chatbots become more ubiquitous, regulators will likely demand greater transparency around data flows, model internals, and decision processes – posing significant technical challenges for AI companies.

Data minimisation is another important principle that AI chatbots find challenging. The data minimisation principles mandate that data controllers and processors should only collect and process the minimal amount of data necessary to achieve their intended purposes and no more.[401] It prohibits processing any data beyond what is essential, ensuring that personal data is handled responsibly and with respect for individuals' privacy rights. Nonetheless, LLMs like ChatGPT are trained on vast amounts of data from the internet, which may include personal information that was not intended for such use. These models essentially consume and process all available data, potentially violating the data minimisation principle. Consequently, striking the right balance between data minimisation and the data-hungry nature of LLMs remains a significant challenge for AI developers and policymakers alike.

Thus, the Information Commissioner's Office (ICO) of the UK emphasises the importance of data minimisation techniques in AI systems to ensure compliance with data protection regulations, like the UK GDPR, and safeguard data privacy. This can be achieved through a multi-pronged approach. Organisations should first critically assess the necessity of collecting and processing personal data. Subsequently, they can leverage techniques like anonymisation, data aggregation, feature selection, and differential privacy to minimise the amount of identifiable information used. Furthermore, implementing privacy-enhancing technologies (PETs) and conducting regular PIAs can proactively identify and mitigate potential risks associated with data processing.[402]

Ensuring robust data privacy in AI chatbots necessitates a proactive approach that incorporates 'privacy by design and by default' principles from the outset of development. This entails embedding data protection considerations throughout the chatbot's lifecycle, encompassing the initial design phase, deployment, and subsequent maintenance. By default, AI chatbots should be configured to collect the minimal amount of personal data necessary for their function, reducing the risk of excessive data collection and enhancing user trust.[403] Continuous monitoring and auditing of data practices, coupled with regular updates to privacy policies in response to new

400. Tilman Rauker et al., *Toward Transparent AI: A Survey on Interpreting the Inner Structures of Deep Neural Networks, in 2023 IEEE Conference on Secure and Trustworthy Machine Learning (SATML)*, IEEE 464, 464–83 (8 Feb. 2023).

401. *See supra* n. 397.

402. UK Information Commissioner's Office, *Guidance on AI and Data Protection: How Should We Assess Security and Data Minimisation in AI?*, ICO, https://ico.org.uk/for-organisations/uk-gdpr-guidance-and-resources/artificial-intelligence/guidance-on-ai-and-data-protection/how-should-we-assess-security-and-data-minimisation-in-ai/#whatdataminimisation (accessed 1 Aug. 2024).

403. *See* generally, Information Commissioner's Office, *Guide to Accountability and Governance: Data Protection by Design and Default* (2024), https://ico.org.uk/for-organisations/uk-gdpr-guidance-and-resources/accountability-and-governance/guide-to-accountability-and-governance/accountability-and-governance/data-protection-by-design-and-default/; Ann Cavoukian, *Privacy by Design: The 7 Foundational Principles*, 5 Info. & Priv. Comm'r of Ontario, Canada 12 (2009); *see also supra* n. 397.

regulatory requirements and technological advancements, can further solidify the commitment to data privacy.

In conclusion, the responsible development and deployment of AI chatbots necessitate a multifaceted approach encompassing several key elements. Fostering public trust is essential and can be achieved through transparent communication regarding the limitations and potential biases of chatbots. This should be accompanied by a demonstrated commitment to continuous security updates and responsible data governance. Collaboration among developers, regulators, and civil society is essential for establishing explicit ethical guidelines and best practices for data management. Ongoing R&D in privacy-preserving AI techniques are crucial to ensure that AI chatbots provide the benefits of personalisation and convenience while safeguarding the fundamental right to privacy. By addressing these interconnected aspects, stakeholders can work towards a future in which AI chatbots are both beneficial and ethically responsible.

5.3.3 User Control over Their Data

Given the significance of data control, a rigorous examination of the potential ramifications of inadequate data practices employed by AI chatbots is imperative. A study by IGI Global indicates that poor user control over data can lead to inaccurate profiling, where chatbots like ChatGPT form incorrect understandings of users based on incomplete information.[404] This can result in biased decisions in diverse areas, such as loan approvals or insurance quotes. Additionally, a lack of transparency regarding data usage, as seen with ChatGPT, raises concerns about the potential misuse of information. Recent research by the Pew Research Center reveals that 67% of people have limited or no understanding of how companies manage their personal data, an increase from 59% in an earlier study.[405] This highlights the need for greater transparency from businesses regarding data collection and usage.

AI chatbots should always obtain explicit permission before collecting or utilising an individual's data, empowering users. Individuals should have also the right to request the removal of their data from AI chatbot systems. Establishing a robust reporting mechanism for privacy violations by AI chatbots and taking decisive action against such violations is imperative. Nevertheless, many LLMs like ChatGPT often fall short of maintaining these regulatory compliance standards. Notably, these AI chatbots frequently share users' personal data with their affiliates, vendors, and third-party service providers both within the US and internationally, compromising user data control, data subject rights, and transparency.[406] This presents a significant challenge in upholding the principles of data privacy and highlights the need for more stringent oversight and adherence to these principles in AI chatbot operations.

To further strengthen user control over their data, AI chatbots must implement transparent data practices, clearly communicating how and why data is collected and

404. *See supra* n. 345.
405. *See supra* n. 396.
406. *See supra* n. 330.

used. Providing users with easy-to-understand privacy policies and consent forms is essential. Users should also have access to tools that allow them to easily manage their data preferences, such as opting in or out of data collection for specific purposes. For instance, the EU GDPR mandates that data controllers provide users with clear and concise information about data processing activities and obtain explicit consent before collecting any personal data.[407] Ensuring that these practices are embedded within the chatbot's design can significantly enhance user trust and compliance with privacy regulations.

Moreover, AI chatbots must prioritise data minimisation and purpose limitation principles. By adhering to these principles, chatbots can limit the amount of data collected to only what is necessary for their functionality and ensure that the data is used solely for the specified purposes.[408] This approach not only reduces the risk of data breaches and misuse but also aligns with global privacy standards such as the California Consumer Privacy Act (CCPA) and the GDPR, which emphasise the importance of data minimisation.[409] Implementing these practices can help mitigate the risks associated with data sharing with affiliates and third-party service providers, thereby upholding the principles of user control and data privacy.

Furthermore, robust enforcement mechanisms are crucial to ensuring compliance with data privacy regulations. Regulatory bodies must conduct regular audits and assessments of AI chatbots to identify and address potential privacy violations. Establishing a framework for accountability, where companies are held responsible for non-compliance, can deter privacy infringements, and encourage adherence to privacy standards. For example, the EDPB provides guidelines and recommendations for supervisory authorities to monitor and enforce compliance with GDPR.[410] By implementing stringent oversight and accountability measures, it is possible to uphold the integrity of data privacy principles in AI chatbot operations and ensure that user rights are protected in an increasingly digital world.

In conclusion, by prioritising user control over data, AI chatbots cannot only safeguard user privacy but also foster trust and transparency. Implementing clear communication on data practices, minimising data collection, and adhering to established data privacy regulations like GDPR and CCPA are crucial steps. Moreover, robust enforcement mechanisms that hold companies accountable are essential to ensure RAI development and protect user rights in the digital age. Through this multi-pronged approach, we can empower users and ensure that AI chatbots operate within a framework of ethical data practices, paving the way for a future where human-AI interaction thrives alongside strong data privacy safeguards.

407. *See supra* n. 305.
408. Information Commissioner's Office, *Guide to the General Data Protection Regulation (GDPR)* (1.1, 2018), https://ico.org.uk/media/for-organisations/guide-to-data-protection/guide-to-the-general-data-protection-regulation-gdpr-1-1.pdf.
409. California Consumer Privacy Act of 2018, Cal. Civ. Code §§1798.100–1798.199 (West 2020), https://leginfo.legislature.ca.gov/faces/billTextClient.xhtml?bill_id=201720180AB375.
410. European Data Protection Board, *Guidelines 07/2020 on the Concepts of Controller and Processor in the GDPR*, No. 2020-07 (7 Oct. 2023), https://www.edpb.europa.eu/system/files/2023-10/EDPB_guidelines_202007_controllerprocessor_final_en.pdf.

5.3.4 Privacy Impact Assessments

The widespread adoption of chatbot systems in various sectors, including healthcare, education, finance, and e-commerce, raises critical privacy concerns. These concerns stem from the potential for excessive data collection, inappropriate data processing, unauthorised data sharing, and prolonged data retention. To address these challenges and safeguard user privacy, conducting a comprehensive PIA for chatbot systems may play a crucial role. PIAs ensure compliance with applicable privacy laws and regulations, align data handling practices with user preferences and expectations, and foster trust among users and stakeholders.[411]

The PIAs serve as an early warning system for AI developers and users, enabling them to make informed decisions and avoid potential privacy challenges before launching a new project or product. Failure to conduct PIAs has led to the withdrawal of newly developed projects or products due to adverse public reactions.[412] For chatbots, conducting a PIA is crucial to demonstrate the deliberate inclusion of privacy protections by system owners. These assessments are vital for ensuring compliance with privacy laws, aligning data handling practices with user expectations, and fostering trust among users and stakeholders.[413] Therefore, PIAs can save AI developers, users, and other stakeholders from potential privacy challenges.

To further elaborate, PIAs play a vital role in the lifecycle of chatbot development by identifying and mitigating privacy risks at every stage, from initial design to deployment and beyond. The dynamic nature of chatbot interactions often involves collecting sensitive personal information, such as medical records, financial details, and personal preferences, which makes it essential to scrutinise data handling practices meticulously. By conducting a PIA, developers can map out data flows, identify potential vulnerabilities, and implement robust safeguards to prevent data breaches and misuse.[414] This proactive approach not only ensures compliance with data protection regulations but also helps in building a framework for continuous privacy management and improvement.

Moreover, PIAs contribute significantly to enhancing transparency and accountability in chatbot systems. Transparency is a cornerstone of data privacy, as it empowers users with knowledge about how their data is being used and the measures in place to protect it. PIAs necessitate detailed documentation of data handling processes and decisions, which can be communicated to users through clear and accessible privacy policies. This documentation also serves as a valuable resource for

411. Nazar Waheed et al., An Empirical Assessment of Security and Privacy Risks of Web-Based Chatbots, in *Proceedings of the International Conference on Web Information Systems Engineering* 325, 325–39 (Springer Int'l Pub. 2022).
412. Md Toriqul Islam, *Protection of Privacy in Bangladesh: Issues, Challenges and Way Forward*, 28 Int'l J. Hum. Rts. 89 (2023), https://doi.org/10.1080/13642987.2023.2234296.
413. US Dep't of Commerce, *Privacy Impact Assessment Guide* (September 2020), https://www.commerce.gov/sites/default/files/opog/PIA_Guide_September_2020.pdf.
414. Office of the Privacy Commissioner of Canada, *Privacy Impact Assessments*, https://www.priv.gc.ca/en/privacy-topics/privacy-impact-assessments/ (accessed 2 Aug. 2024); Ronald S. Ross, *Guide for Conducting Risk Assessments*, NIST (17 Sep. 2012), https://www.nist.gov/publications/guide-conducting-risk-assessments.

audits and regulatory reviews, demonstrating a commitment to upholding high privacy standards. By fostering an environment of trust and openness, chatbot providers can enhance user confidence and satisfaction, ultimately leading to increased adoption and positive user engagement. Studies have shown that trust significantly influences user acceptance and engagement with AI technology.[415]

Additionally, the integration of PIAs into the chatbot development process encourages a culture of privacy by design. Privacy by design refers to a proactive approach that prioritises safeguarding individual privacy and data protection through intentional design choices. Unlike traditional methods that treat privacy as an afterthought, privacy by design places privacy protection at the forefront from the very beginning of the design process.[416] Privacy by design can lead to innovative solutions that balance functionality and privacy, such as anonymisation techniques, data minimisation strategies, and enhanced user consent mechanisms. In turn, this holistic approach can drive competitive advantage, positioning chatbot providers as leaders in ethical AI development and fostering long-term trust and loyalty among users.

In conclusion, conducting PIAs for chatbot systems offers a comprehensive solution to safeguard user privacy. PIAs not only ensure compliance and foster trust but also empower developers to establish a framework for continuous privacy enhancement. By promoting transparency and accountability, PIAs pave the way for increased user adoption and positive engagement. Furthermore, integrating PIAs into the development process fosters a culture of privacy by design, potentially leading to innovative solutions that prioritise user privacy. This approach may position chatbot providers as proponents of ethical AI development. However, further research is needed to quantify the extent to which PIAs directly contribute to innovation and ethical leadership in the field.

5.3.5 Ethical Use of AI

GAI developers must place ethics at the forefront, develop systems to safeguard user privacy and security and reduce the risks of personal data breaches, social surveillance, and privacy violations. Developers should also adopt and follow RAI practices and ethical guidelines, including transparency in data usage, bias mitigation techniques, and monitoring of generated content for harmful or misleading information.[417] Furthermore, organisations must implement robust security measures to ensure data security, integrity, and privacy. Strong Storage Encryption (SSE), which automatically

415. Tibert Verhagen et al., *Virtual Customer Service Agents: Using Social Presence and Personalization to Shape Online Service Encounters*, 19 J. Comput.-Mediated Communication 529 (2014) https://doi.org/10.1111/jcc4.12066.
416. IEEE, *What Is Privacy by Design and Why It's Important* (2024), https://digitalprivacy.ieee.org/publications/topics/what-is-privacy-by-design-and-why-it-s-important.
417. Krzysztof Wach et al., *The Dark Side of Generative Artificial Intelligence: A Critical Analysis of Controversies and Risks of ChatGPT*, 11 Entrep. Bus. & Econ. Rev. 7 (2023) https://doi.org/10.15678/eber.2023.110201.

encrypts data at rest using a very large cryptographic key, is a recommended approach.[418] Security practices should also encompass reviewing access controls, user authentication methods, and incident response plans. The NIST Cybersecurity Framework, for example, provides valuable resources for developing and maintaining effective security measures.[419]

To ensure the ethical use of AI, stakeholders should adopt RAI principles and emphasise their implementation. As outlined by the European Commission's Ethics Guidelines for Trustworthy AI, RAI principles and practices consist of guidelines and best practices aimed at the ethical development and deployment of AI technologies.[420] These principles cover various aspects, including transparency, accountability, fairness, and human oversight. While different organisations and entities may have their unique formulations, common themes include respecting human dignity, upholding human rights, promoting social good, and preventing harm.[421] By adhering to these principles, organisations can ensure that their AI technologies are ethically aligned, contributing positively to society. This approach fosters trust in AI by demonstrating a commitment to responsible development and use.

Promoting the ethical use of AI is vital for ensuring trustworthiness in AI operations as well. To achieve this, AI developers should incorporate transparency, accountability, fairness, and human oversight into AI development and deployment programs. Transparency requires that AI systems be understandable to users and the public. This involves revealing their inner workings, data sources, methodologies, underlying assumptions, limitations, and outcomes. Accountability necessitates oversight and responsibility for the system's impacts, along with mechanisms to correct any errors or harms that may arise from its use. Fairness prohibits bias and discrimination, respecting the diversity and human dignity of those affected by an AI system. Human oversight empowers users and operators to intervene, monitor, and control the system, ensuring alignment with human values and interests.[422]

Moreover, a blueprint for an AI bill of rights, encompassing principles such as safe and effective systems, algorithmic discrimination protections, data privacy, notice

418. PCMag, *Strong Encryption*, https://www.pcmag.com/encyclopedia/term/strong-encryption (accessed 2 Aug. 2024).
419. NIST, *Cybersecurity Framework*, https://www.nist.gov/cyberframework (accessed 2 Aug. 2024).
420. European Commission, *Ethics Guidelines for Trustworthy AI* (8 Apr. 2019), https://digital-strategy.ec.europa.eu/en/library/ethics-guidelines-trustworthy-ai.
421. Microsoft, *Principles and Approach* (2024), https://www.microsoft.com/en-us/ai/principles-and-approach/; Google AI, *Responsible AI Practices*, https://ai.google/responsibility/responsible-ai-practices/ (accessed 2 Aug. 2024); Microsoft Learn, *Embrace Responsible AI: Principles and Practices*, https://learn.microsoft.com/en-us/training/modules/embrace-responsible-ai-principles-practices/ (accessed 2 Aug. 2024).
422. Press Release, U.N. Secretary-General, *Secretary-General's Remarks to the Security Council on the Situation in Ukraine* (23 Feb. 2023), https://press.un.org/en/2023/sgsm21880.doc.htm; Office of the Privacy Commissioner for Personal Data, *Hong Kong, Guidance on Ethical Use of Personal Data* (2021), https://www.pcpd.org.hk/english/resources_centre/publications/files/guidance_ethical_e.pdf; Institute of Business Ethics, *Business Ethics and Ethical AI: Scrutinising AI with an Ethical Lens*, IBE (January 2024), https://www.ibe.org.uk/resource/business-ethics-and-ethical-ai-scrutinising-ai-with-an-ethical-lens.html.

and explanation, and alternative options, can contribute to realising this objective.[423] Relevant stakeholders should also consider preparing a chatbot privacy code of conduct outlining the ethical and professional obligations of chatbot developers and the rights and duties of chatbot users. This code should address data collection, retention, and deletion; consent and disclosure; security and confidentiality; and complaint and redress mechanisms. Such measures can foster public trust and confidence in AI systems, paving the way for their responsible adoption across various sectors. Furthermore, ongoing multi-stakeholder collaboration is crucial to ensure these frameworks remain relevant and adaptable as AI capabilities rapidly evolve.

Establishing a voluntary chatbot privacy certification program based on self-assessment but subject to audits and enforcement by an independent third-party organisation could further promote ethical AI practices. Although resources and initiatives such as the International Association of Privacy Professionals' article on chatbots and privacy,[424] the Certified Chatbot Expert™ program by the Blockchain Council,[425] and the Chatbot Developer Certification Program by Activechat.ai[426] are available, there remains significant potential for further development and innovation in this domain. A robust, widely adopted certification program could instil greater public trust in chatbots and accelerate their adoption across industries. However, such a program would need to be dynamic and continuously evolve to keep pace with rapid advancements in chatbot capabilities and potential privacy risks.

Launching a specialised ChatGPT task force to examine regulatory frameworks for AI chatbots, including ChatGPT, may also be conducive to establishing trustworthy AI. The task force would delve into the challenges associated with AI chatbots, including data quality, consent, transparency, accountability, and human dignity. For example, the EDPB established the ChatGPT task force in April 2023 to foster cooperation and exchange information on possible enforcement actions conducted by data protection authorities regarding ChatGPT.[427] Such proactive measures underscore the urgency of addressing the ethical and legal ramifications of advanced language models like ChatGPT, which have permeated various facets of our digital lives. By bringing together diverse stakeholders and subject matter experts, task forces such as these can contribute to the development of balanced regulatory frameworks that maximise the immense potential of AI while ensuring the protection of fundamental rights and the preservation of democratic values.

In conclusion, prioritising ethical considerations from the design stage to deployment is paramount for building trustworthy AI. Transparency, accountability, fairness, and human oversight are the cornerstones of ethical AI development. Furthermore,

---

423. Executive Office of the President of the United States, *Algorithmic Discrimination Protections* (2 Aug. 2024), https://www.whitehouse.gov/ostp/ai-bill-of-rights/algorithmic-discrimination-protections-2/.
424. *See supra* n. 393.
425. Blockchain Council, *Certified Chatbot Expert™*, https://www.blockchain-council.org/certifications/certified-chatbot-expert/ (accessed 2 Aug. 2024).
426. Activechat, *Chatbot Certification Program*, https://activechat.ai/chatbot-certification-program/ (accessed 2 Aug. 2024).
427. Clothilde Goujard, *European Data Regulators Set Up ChatGPT Taskforce*, Politico (13 Apr. 2023), https://www.politico.eu/article/european-data-regulators-set-up-chatgpt-taskforce/.

establishing frameworks like an AI bill of rights, chatbot privacy codes, and industry certifications can solidify public trust and RAI adoption. Collaborative efforts among stakeholders and the creation of specialised task forces will ensure these frameworks adapt to the evolving nature of AI, ushering in an era where AI serves humanity for the greater good.

5.3.6 Data Protection Laws

The rapid advancement of AI chatbots like ChatGPT has raised significant concerns about their potential impact on user privacy and data protection. To address these concerns, existing data protection laws can be applied to regulate the development and use of AI chatbots. These laws typically require organisations to collect, process, and store personal data lawfully, fairly, and transparently.[428] Prevailing data protection laws also require organisations to obtain consent from users before collecting their data and to provide users with access to and control over their data. Although existing privacy laws may offer some protections, new approaches are needed to address privacy risks as GAI becomes more integrated into daily life.[429]

Data protection principles can be leveraged to ensure that AI chatbots collect only the data necessary for their intended function. These principles can further prevent chatbots from collecting or storing sensitive personal data without explicit user consent. Additionally, they can be used to guarantee that chatbots provide users with clear and concise information about data collection, usage, and storage. By applying data protection principles to AI chatbots, it may be possible to protect user privacy and ensure that chatbots are developed and used responsibly.

However, LLMs like ChatGPT often fall short in adhering to data protection laws. A fundamental principle of data protection regulations is that data controllers should process personal data only to the extent necessary for a specific purpose.[430] Nonetheless, AI chatbots usually receive training on massive datasets extracted from the internet, potentially containing huge amounts of personal information. Moreover, ChatGPT and similar AI chatbots share collected data with affiliates, third parties, vendors, or service providers, contravening the spirit of data protection laws.[431] Furthermore, storing personal data outside the US violates the data localisation concept embedded in numerous data protection laws.[432]

While applying existing data protection laws offers a starting point, the dynamic nature of AI chatbots necessitates the development of more nuanced regulations. One

428. *See supra* n. 397.
429. *See supra* n. 393.
430. *See supra* n. 397.
431. *See supra* n. 330.
432. Data localisation requirements, once mostly linked to authoritarian regimes, are now being adopted worldwide, with over 75% of countries with data privacy laws enforcing them. For instance, as of July 2021, 62 countries had implemented 144 such restrictions, nearly double the number since 2017. *See* Md. Toriqul Islam & Borhan Uddin Khan, *Impacts of Data Localization Policies and Lessons for Bangladesh*, Int'l Data Privacy L., ipae002 (2024), https://doi.org/10.1093/idpl/ipae002.

concept to consider is 'data minimisation', a core principle that emphasises collecting only the data essential for the chatbot's function. Current data protection laws often permit the processing of anonymised data without consent. However, with advancements in AI, anonymised data might be re-identified, potentially compromising users' privacy. Studies demonstrate that the ML capabilities of AI can re-identify individuals from data that was previously considered anonymous.[433] This development necessitates re-evaluating anonymisation techniques and implementing potentially stricter regulations on how AI chatbots handle such data.

Another major challenge in applying data protection laws to AI chatbots is the difficulty in defining what constitutes personal data in the context of LLMs. While traditional forms of personal data like names, addresses, and financial information are covered,[434] the training data for these models often includes vast amounts of text scraped from the internet. This text could inadvertently contain personal information, making it hard to ensure compliance with data minimisation principles. There are also questions about whether the outputs of these models, which can generate highly personalised text, constitute personal data itself.[435]

The outputs of AI language models could potentially be considered personal data if they contain information specific to an identifiable individual. This poses significant privacy challenges, as such information could be used to profile or target individuals without their consent. It also raises complex legal and ethical questions about data ownership and the responsibilities of AI companies. Regulators and policymakers are still grappling with how to classify and govern these AI-generated outputs within existing data protection frameworks. Nevertheless, ensuring compliance with data protection regulations, such as the GDPR, is crucial to addressing these issues.

Data protection laws emphasise the importance of transparency in the use of individuals' personal data, and they provide individuals with the right to access, modify, or delete their personal data. In the context of using ChatGPT, users could access, delete, correct, update, or transfer their personal information. Additionally, users can withdraw their consent, object to data processing activities, and file a complaint with the relevant data protection authority in the event of a data breach.[436] To gain significant control over their data, users can turn off memory at any time, use temporary chatting mode, and delete any chat history.[437] Nonetheless, challenges remain for LLMs like ChatGPT concerning data privacy. First, opting out of training

433. Caroline Brogan, *Anonymising Personal Data 'Not Enough to Protect Privacy', Shows New Study*, Imperial (23 Jul. 2019), https://www.imperial.ac.uk/news/192112/anonymising-personal-data-enough-protect-privacy/.
434. Gary Drenik, *The Risk of Disputes Could Be Huge if Businesses Don't Manage the Privacy Concerns Surrounding AI*, Forbes (14 Dec. 2023), https://www.forbes.com/sites/garydrenik/2023/12/14/the-risk-of-disputes-could-be-huge-if-businesses-dont-manage-the-privacy-concerns-surrounding-ai/?sh = 7c21e37e772f.
435. *See supra* n. 345.
436. *See supra* n. 330.
437. OpenAI, *Memory and New Controls for ChatGPT* (13 Feb. 2024), https://openai.com/index/memory-and-new-controls-for-chatgpt/.

data can hinder ChatGPT's ability to personalise responses for that specific user.[438] Second, there is the issue of long-term data storage.[439] Even with deleted chat history, anonymised snippets may be retained for model improvement, raising privacy concerns for some users.

In conclusion, while existing data protection laws provide a foundational framework for regulating AI chatbots like ChatGPT, the rapid advancements and unique challenges posed by these technologies necessitate more sophisticated and nuanced approaches. The principles of data minimisation, transparency, and user consent remain crucial, but they must be rigorously adapted to the specific context of AI. As AI chatbots continue to evolve, it is imperative to reassess anonymisation techniques and develop robust regulations that address the potential for re-identification of anonymised data. Ensuring compliance with these principles while fostering innovation will require a collaborative effort between lawmakers, technology developers, and privacy advocates. Safeguarding user privacy and maintaining trust in the growing field of AI-driven communication can only be achieved through such collaborative efforts.

5.3.7 Technical Measures

There is a wide range of technical measures that can be employed in LLMs like ChatGPT to ensure data security. These techniques include PETs like differential privacy, federated learning, and data minimisation strategies. Additionally, data masking, anonymisation, and encryption are crucial technical safeguards. It is imperative to note that the effective combination of these techniques is essential to establish a robust data security posture for LLMs. Furthermore, continuous evaluation and adaptation of these measures are required to mitigate emerging threats and comply with evolving data protection regulations.

PETs are employed to protect both the privacy of IT users and the privacy of individuals whose personal data is processed, often referred to as data subjects.[440] PETs allow researchers to examine sensitive data like medical records without accessing personal information, thereby promoting healthcare progress while upholding patient confidentiality. They also facilitate the exchange of crucial public health data while safeguarding personal details and ensuring privacy during data sharing among cities and states.[441] Although PET adoption faces several challenges – including the need for additional research, technical expertise, and financial investment, as well as

438. Paulius Grinkevičius, *Meta Uses Your Data to Train AI, and It Doesn't Want You to Opt Out*, Cybernews (28 May 2024), https://cybernews.com/tech/meta-trains-ai-on-your-data/.
439. Alexandra Wood et al., *Practical Approaches to Big Data Privacy Over Time*, Harvard Law School Berkman Klein Center for Internet & Society (12 Mar. 2018), https://cyber.harvard.edu/publications/2018/03/BigDataPrivacy.
440. Simone Fischer-Hübner, Privacy-Enhancing Technologies, in *Encyclopedia Of Database Systems* 1 (L. Liu & M.T. Özsu eds, Springer 2018), https://doi.org/10.1007/978-1-4614-8265-9_271.
441. Alexander Macgillivray, *Advancing a Vision for Privacy-Enhancing Technologies*, The White House (28 Jun. 2024), https://www.whitehouse.gov/ostp/news-updates/2022/06/28/advancing-a-vision-for-privacy-enhancing-technologies/.

concerns regarding false privacy assurances and biased data analysis – the potential benefits of these technologies in fostering a more secure and private data environment are substantial.

Differential privacy is a statistical method that protects individual privacy by adding random noise to data. Noise is like a veil that covers up personal details in data, making it harder to identify individuals and protect their privacy. This technique helps organisations analyse data while safeguarding user information.[442] This noise makes it difficult to distinguish between individual records, making it more challenging for anyone to identify or infer sensitive information about specific individuals from the data. Differential privacy allows data analysis to be done without compromising individual privacy, enabling organisations to extract valuable insights from large datasets while safeguarding user information. It is noteworthy that differential privacy is not a technology but a security measure that guarantees that the release of insights from a dataset does not reveal much more information unless that was a part of that dataset. This is called the 'privacy budget' and it can be measured.[443]

Federated learning is another valuable PET that enables collaborative model training without compromising data privacy. In this approach, multiple parties contribute their data to a centralised model, but the data remains physically separated. The model is trained iteratively, with each party updating the model using their data without sharing it with others. In essence, federated learning allows multiple parties to train AI models on their data without sharing it, combining patterns from their local models into a more accurate global model. This approach effectively addresses data privacy concerns while allowing for the development of robust AI models. There are two main approaches to federated learning: centralised and decentralised. In centralised FL, a central server coordinates the training and updates of the model,[444] while in decentralised FL, participating entities communicate directly with one another.[445] Decentralised FL offers advantages in terms of security and resilience against single points of failure.

Data minimisation techniques restrict data processing to the minimum amount necessary for a specific purpose. This technique requires that data processing activities should be adequate, relevant, and limited to what is necessary concerning the purposes for which they are processed.[446] Data minimisation is vital for preserving user privacy in LLMs like ChatGPT, but effectively implementing it poses challenges. Limiting the data used for training can restrict the model's capacity to grasp intricate language patterns, potentially reducing accuracy and fluency. Additionally, there's a risk of

442. Information Commissioner's Office, *Chapter 5: Anonymisation, Pseudonymisation, and Encryption*, ICO (September 2022), https://ico.org.uk/media/about-the-ico/consultations/4021464/chapter-5-anonymisation-pets.pdf?ref=salesforce-research.
443. Natasha McCarthy & Franck Fourniol, *The Role of Technology in Governance: The Example of Privacy Enhancing Technologies*, Data & Policy, at e8 (2020), https://doi.org/10.1017/dap.2020.8.
444. Kim Martineau, *What Is Federated Learning?* IBM Research (24 Aug. 2024), https://research.ibm.com/blog/what-is-federated-learning.
445. Liangqi Yuan et al., *Decentralized Federated Learning: A Survey and Perspective*, IEEE Internet of Things J. (2024) https://doi.org/10.1109/jiot.2024.3407584.
446. *See supra* n. 397.

inadvertently discarding valuable information alongside sensitive data, impairing the model's responsiveness. Even with minimised data, lingering biases or patterns can persist, impacting the model's learning process. Nevertheless, despite these obstacles, data minimisation remains essential for protecting user privacy in LLMs.

To safeguard users' personal data from being utilised for purposes beyond what is essential, individuals can employ data masking techniques.[447] Data masking is a technique that replaces sensitive data with realistic anonymised data, protecting individual and organisational privacy during data sharing or processing. The proposed solution involves masking or encrypting user data before transmission to the LLM or training the LLM on masked data, avoiding the transmission of original data to the central server. For instance, Patented.ai's LLM Shield tool safeguards sensitive data from language models,[448] while Private AI's PrivateGPT model addresses privacy concerns associated with ChatGPT by masking data before sending redacted requests to the OpenAI API.[449] Additionally, Pangeanic's data masking layer for ChatGPT integration ensures that personal data is not transmitted to the AI system.[450]

Data anonymisation is another crucial technique for ensuring data privacy in the use of LLMs like ChatGPT. Anonymisation involves eliminating PII from datasets, rendering it challenging or impossible to trace the data back to its source.[451] In the AI context, anonymisation serves as a safeguard for user data during model training employing various techniques, such as data masking, pseudonymisation, generalisation, and differential privacy. Anonymisation has several advantages for LLMs, including improved data privacy, enhanced compliance with data protection regulations, and reduced risk of cyberattacks. When choosing an anonymisation technique, it is crucial to consider the type of data being anonymised, the desired level of privacy, and the impact on the quality of the LLM. Despite the critical role of anonymisation in protecting user privacy for LLMs, the process faces significant challenges in balancing the removal of PII with the preservation of data utility and model performance.

Furthermore, encryption is another essential aspect of a secure and trustworthy internet.[452] Encryption is also considered a potential technique for protecting data privacy in LLMs like ChatGPT. Encryption is the process of converting electronic data

447. Enrique Tomás Martínez Beltrán et al., *Decentralized Federated Learning: Fundamentals, State of the Art, Frameworks, Trends, and Challenges*, IEEE Communications Surveys & Tutorials (2023).
448. Help Net Security, *Patented.ai Releases LLM Shield to Safeguard Sensitive Info from Chatbots* (4 Apr. 2023), https://www.helpnetsecurity.com/2023/04/24/patented-ai-llm-shield/.
449. Tim Keary, *Private AI's PrivateGPT Aims to Combat ChatGPT Privacy Concerns*, VentureBeat (1 May 2023), https://venturebeat.com/security/privateais-privategpt-aims-to-combat-chatgpt-privacy-concerns/; Private AI, *The Privacy Layer for LLMs*, https://www.private-ai.com/ (accessed 2 Aug. 2024).
450. Slator, *Pangeanic Announces a Personal Data Anonymization Layer on ChatGPT-4 for More Secure AI* (October 2024), https://slator.com/pangeanic-announces-the-integration-of-chatgpt-4-on-its-eco-nlp-platform-for-more-secure-ai/.
451. Cynthia Dwork, Differential Privacy: A Survey of Results, in *Proceedings of the International Conference on Theory and Applications of Models of Computation* 1 (Springer Berlin Heidelberg 2008), https://www.microsoft.com/en-us/research/wp-content/uploads/2008/04/dwork_tamc.pdf.
452. Clare Stouffer, *What Is Encryption? How It Works + Types of Encryptions*, NORTON (28 Jul. 2024), https://us.norton.com/blog/privacy/what-is-encryption.

or signals into an unintelligible code using a specific algorithm and key.[453] The four main components of an encryption system are: (1) plaintext (the original message), (2) encryption algorithm (the mathematical process used to encrypt the plaintext), (3) encryption key (the secret value used to encrypt and decrypt the plaintext), and (4) ciphertext (the encrypted message).[454]

Furthermore, Homomorphic Encryption (HE), Secure Multi-Party Computation (SMPC), and Trusted Execution Environments (TEEs) are three key technologies that enhance privacy in LLMs. HE allows computations on encrypted data without decryption, making it ideal for privacy-preserving outsourced storage and computation.[455] SMPC enables multiple parties to jointly compute a function on their inputs without revealing those inputs to each other, facilitating privacy-preserving LLM training.[456] TEEs are hardware-based security features, which create secure enclaves within cloud servers for isolated code execution, ensuring data privacy in LLMs.[457]

HE for LLMs is the significant computational overhead, which can slow down model training and inference, making it less practical for real-time applications.[458] HE is valuable for secure computation, but it typically cannot be used in multi-party scenarios because the authority is centralised with a single entity, the secret key holder.[459] While TEEs offer hardware-level security, they are not immune to side-channel attacks and vulnerabilities, necessitating constant vigilance and updates to maintain the integrity of the secure enclaves and protect the privacy of data processed

453. Cambridge Dictionary, *Encryption,* https://dictionary.cambridge.org/dictionary/english/encryption (accessed 2 Aug. 2024).
454. Vijay K. Garg, Chapter 13: Security in Wireless Systems, in *The Morgan Kaufmann Series in Networking, Wireless Communications & Networking* 397, 433 (V.K. Garg ed., Morgan Kaufmann 2007), https://doi.org/10.1016/B978-012373580-5/50047-8.
455. Christopher Chianelli & David Zolnieryk, *Homomorphic Encryption: What It Is and Why You Should Care,* Univ. of Toronto, Dep't of Comput. Sci. (29 Jan. 2019), https://www.cs.toronto.edu/~arnold/427/19s/427_19S/indepth/homomorphicEncryption/he_presentation.pdf; Vinod Vaikuntanathan, *Fully Homomorphic Encryption (FHE) Bibliography,* MIT CSAIL, https://people.csail.mit.edu/vinodv/FHE/FHE-refs.html (accessed 2 Aug. 2024).
456. Keith B. Frikken, Secure Multiparty Computation (SMC), in *Encyclopedia of Cryptography and Security* 1082 (H.C.A. van Tilborg & S. Jajodia eds, Springer 2011), https://doi.org/10.1007/978-1-4419-5906-5_766; Louis-Henri Merino & José Cabrero-Holgueras, Secure Multi-Party Computation, in *Trends in Data Protection and Encryption Technologies* 271 (V. Mulder et al. eds, Springer 2023), https://doi.org/10.1007/978-3-031-33386-6_17; David Evans et al., *A Pragmatic Introduction to Secure Multi-Party Computation,* Pragmatic MPC (11 Jun. 2022), https://securecomputation.org/main/.
457. Tim Geppert et al., *Trusted Execution Environments: Applications and Organizational Challenges,* 4 Frontiers in Computer Science 930741 (2022), https://doi.org/10.3389/fcomp.2022.930741; Maria Sommerhalder, Trusted Execution Environment, in *Trends in Data Protection and Encryption Technologies* 359 (V. Mulder et al., eds, Springer 2023), https://doi.org/10.1007/978-3-031-33386-6_18; Mengyuan Li et al., SoK: Understanding Design Choices and Pitfalls of Trusted Execution Environments, in *Proceedings of the 19th ACM Asia Conference on Computer and Communications Security* 1600 (2024), https://people.csail.mit.edu/mengyuanli/files/asiaccs_sok.pdf.
458. Abhijit Mishra et al., *SentinelLMs: Encrypted Input Adaptation and Fine-Tuning of Language Models for Private and Secure Inference,* in 38(19) *Proceedings of the AAAI Conference on Artificial Intelligence* 21403, 21411 (2024), https://arxiv.org/pdf/2312.17342.
459. Hyesun Kwak et al., A General Framework of Homomorphic Encryption for Multiple Parties with Non-interactive Key-Aggregation, in *Applied Cryptography and Network Security* 329 (C. Pöpper & L. Batina eds, 2024).

within LLMs.[460] Finally, the development of new technologies like quantum computing might necessitate entirely new encryption methods to stay secure.[461]

5.4 CONCLUSION

In conclusion, the intricate web of data privacy challenges posed by LLMs like ChatGPT necessitates a multifaceted approach to ensure user protection and trust. The potential for oversharing sensitive information and the creation of detailed user profiles underscores the urgency for robust data governance frameworks. Addressing these challenges involves not only refining the technical architecture of these models to safeguard data but also ensuring that data collection practices are transparent and compliant with stringent data protection regulations. Therefore, developers and organisations must prioritise user control over personal data, fostering a more secure and trustworthy AI environment. This holistic approach will not only mitigate risks but also enhance the ethical deployment of AI technologies.

Moreover, regulatory strategies must evolve to keep pace with the rapid advancements in AI technology. A combination of legal, ethical, and technical measures is essential to navigate the complexities of data privacy in AI chatbots. Enacting comprehensive data protection laws, promoting transparency in AI deployment, and ensuring that users have meaningful control over their data are critical steps toward safeguarding privacy. Furthermore, fostering a culture of ethical AI use through education and awareness programs will empower users and developers alike to make informed decisions. Above all, by fostering collaboration between developers, lawmakers, and users, we can harness the potential of LLMs for good, ensuring a future where innovation thrives alongside robust privacy safeguards.

460. Xiaoxuan Lou et al., *A Survey of Microarchitectural Side-Channel Vulnerabilities, Attacks, and* Defenses in Cryptography, 54 ACM Comput. Surv. (CSUR) 1 (2021) https://doi.org/10.1145/3456629.
461. NIST, *NIST Announces First Four Quantum-Resistant Cryptographic Algorithms* (28 Jul. 2022), https://www.nist.gov/news-events/news/2022/07/nist-announces-first-four-quantum-resistant-cryptographic-algorithms; Caltech Science Exchange, *How Will Quantum Technologies Change Cryptography?*, https://scienceexchange.caltech.edu/topics/quantum-science-explained/quantum-cryptography (accessed 28 Jul. 2024).

CHAPTER 6

LLMs like ChatGPT and IP

6.1 INTRODUCTION

The widespread application of LLMs such as ChatGPT across various domains has profound implications for the IP rights of individuals and organisations utilising these technologies. GAI presents significant challenges to IP rights, including difficulties in determining authorship, gaps in legal protection, risks of infringement, and the need for updated legislation.[462] This chapter focuses on analysing significant IP-related challenges within LLMs like ChatGPT, identifying gaps within existing legal frameworks, and exploring potential future policy directions. Specifically, this chapter seeks to address the following questions:

- Who owns the copyright to AI-generated content or artwork?
- Can AI-generated content or artwork be patented?
- How can we balance the interests of both the developers of LLMs like ChatGPT and their users?
- How can we ensure the fair, ethical, and lawful use of LLMs like ChatGPT?

In addition, this chapter examines critical IP issues surrounding LLMs, including copyright ownership, the patentability of AI-generated creations, and the delicate balance required between developers and users. Furthermore, this chapter examines the limitations of existing legal frameworks and proposes future policy directions in the embedded text to ensure the responsible and ethical use of LLMs.

462. British Computer Society, *AI Versus IP: How Could Generative Artificial Intelligence Impact Intellectual Ownership?*, BCS (14 Jun. 2024), https://www.bcs.org/articles-opinion-and-research/ai-versus-ip-how-could-generative-artificial-intelligence-impact-intellectual-ownership/.

6.2 COPYRIGHT PROTECTIONS FOR AI-GENERATED WORK ACROSS JURISDICTIONS

The ownership of copyright for AI-generated content or artwork is a complex and evolving legal issue. In most jurisdictions, copyright protection is generally granted to works created by a human author, raising the question of whether AI can be considered an author. In the context of AI, the developers of the AI technology could be seen as the authors because they create the underlying technology that produces the work.[463] Consequently, there may be an assumption that the developers of AI systems might claim ownership of the copyright for an AI-generated work since they have designed and trained the models that generate creative outputs.[464]

Some may argue that users who input prompts into AI systems should be considered authors, as they direct the creative process and make essential choices that shape the final output. Specifically, users who interact with AI systems and provide specific input might be seen as co-creators or authors of the AI-generated content, significantly influencing the resulting work.[465] Another perspective is that copyright should not apply to AI-generated content, viewing AI as merely a tool humans use to create work. The lack of clear legal guidelines on this issue has led to uncertainty and potential disputes. Against this backdrop, this section delves into the intricacies of copyright and patents for AI-generated content and artwork.

The rise of GAI across diverse industries has revolutionised creativity, impacting fields like writing, music, design, game development, programming, marketing, and architecture. However, this integration raises significant IP challenges, particularly regarding the ownership and originality of AI-generated works. This context questions whether the human designer or the AI system is the primary author and whether these works meet the criteria for copyright and patentability. The ownership of data used to train AI models is also crucial, influencing the resulting IP rights. Recent legal cases have brought attention to disputes surrounding the use of GAI in art creation, with artists alleging that their copyrights have been infringed upon.[466]

The current operations of platforms like ChatGPT raise important questions about protective strategies, including the registration of IP rights, restriction of data access, implementation of security protocols, and the signing of non-disclosure agreements

463. US Copyright Office, *Compendium of US Copyright Office Practices* (3rd edn, 2021), Chapter 300, s. 313.2.
464. World Intellectual Property Organization, *Artificial Intelligence and Intellectual Property*, https://www.wipo.int/about-ip/en/frontier_technologies/ai_and_ip.html (accessed 2 Aug. 2024).
465. European Parliament, *Resolution of 20 October 2020 on Artificial Intelligence in a Digital Age, 2020/2013(INI)*, Official Journal of the European Union (20 Oct. 2020), https://www.europarl.europa.eu/doceo/document/TA-9-2020-10-20_EN.html.
466. Zachary Small, *As Fight Over A.I. Artwork Unfolds, Judge Rejects Copyright Claim*, New York Times (21 Aug. 2023), https://www.nytimes.com/2023/08/21/arts/design/copyright-ai-art work.html; Blake Brittain, *AI-Generated Art Cannot Receive Copyrights, US Court Says*, Reuters (21 Aug. 2023), https://www.reuters.com/legal/ai-generated-art-cannot-receive-copyrights-us-court-says-2023-08-21/.

(NDAs) with third-party vendors.[467] ChatGPT and other AI code generators can create code and images, but it is unclear who owns the copyright to this work, potentially leading to legal issues for businesses using these tools to develop their products.[468] Therefore, AI technology has the potential to significantly disrupt the current IP system, creating an urgent need for policy intervention to protect the integrity of the IP regime and to address potential social, economic, and ethical challenges. This context demands an investigation of major legal systems of the world to address the IP-related challenges of AI-generated work.

6.2.1 United States

The legal status of AI-generated content and its potential for copyright infringement differs across jurisdictions, but a consistent criterion for copyright protection is the requirement of human authorship. For example, in the US, copyright law explicitly mandates that only works created by human authors are eligible for protection. This principle is affirmed by the US Copyright Office, which states that it will not register works produced by a machine or a mere mechanical process that operates randomly or automatically without any creative input or intervention from a human author.[469] Section 201(b) of the US Copyright Act of 1976 stipulates that the person who initiates the creation of a work is typically the copyright owner unless the work was done as part of a work-for-hire agreement or was commissioned.

Under US copyright law, only original works expressed in a tangible form, such as books, songs, or paintings, are protected by copyright.[470] In employment scenarios, the employer or the person who paid for the work is considered the author and owner of the copyright, unless a written agreement states otherwise. By analogy, if an AI system creates a work as part of its 'job' or for a specific client, the work's author and owner would likely be the employer or the person who hired the AI system, not the AI itself.[471] However, recent legal cases highlight the challenges and ongoing debates about the extent of human involvement required for AI-generated works to qualify for copyright protection.

For example, in *Kashtanova v. U.S. Copyright Office* (2023), the US Copyright Office rejected Kris Kashtanova's copyright claim to images created by the AI system

467. Forbes Tech Council, *AI & IP: Data Protection at the Crossroads of Innovation and Intellectual Property*, Forbes (30 May 2023), https://www.forbes.com/sites/forbestechcouncil/2023/05/30/ai--ip-data-protection-at-the-crossroads-of-innovation-and-intellectual-property/?sh=321b01941f8f.
468. Nisha Talagala, *Using ChatGPT Safely: The Legal Implications*, Forbes (4 Apr. 2023), https://www.forbes.com/sites/nishatalagala/2023/04/04/using-chatgpt-safely-the-legal-implications/?sh=7a6dd9a47239.
469. US Copyright Office, *Copyright Registration Guidance: Works Containing Material Generated by Artificial Intelligence* (2023), https://www.copyright.gov/ai/ai_policy_guidance.pdf.
470. US Copyright Office, *Title 17 of the United States Code*, https://www.copyright.gov/title17/ (accessed 2 Aug. 2024).
471. Alesia Zhuk, *Navigating the Legal Landscape of AI Copyright: A Comparative Analysis of EU, US, and Chinese Approaches*, AI Ethics (2023), https://doi.org/10.1007/s43681-023-00299-0.

Midjourney for her graphic novel 'Zarya of the Dawn'.[472] The Office ruled that only the parts of the book that Kashtanova wrote and arranged are eligible for copyright protection, not the images, as they are not the product of human authorship. This decision has sparked discussions among artists, lawyers, and AI experts about the ethics and legal aspects of AI-generated art and whether such creations should receive recognition or compensation.

In *Andersen et al. v. Stability AI, Midjourney, and DeviantArt* (2023),[473] a California federal court addressed the complex intersection of copyright law and AI. Artists Sarah Andersen, Kelly McKernan, and Karla Ortiz alleged that Stability AI, Midjourney, and DeviantArt infringed their copyrights by training AI-powered image generation tools on their copyrighted artwork without consent. The defendants filed motions to dismiss and strike the complaint, arguing that they were protected by the fair use doctrine and that the plaintiffs' claims were barred by the First Amendment of the US Constitution.

The case is still ongoing, with the court allowing the plaintiffs to conduct jurisdictional discovery to support their alter-ego theory against Stability AI, Ltd.[474] The court's decision to permit this discovery indicates that the case is proceeding, but a final ruling on the merits of the copyright infringement claims and the defendants' fair use and First Amendment defences has not yet been made. The outcome of this case remains uncertain and could have significant implications for the intersection of copyright law and AI technology.

In another landmark copyright case with AI implications, *Getty Images (US), Inc. v. Stability AI, Inc.*,[475] the plaintiff, a stock photo agency, alleged that Stability AI engaged in the unauthorised use of over 12 million photos and committed trademark infringement by replicating watermarks. Getty Images contended that Stability AI scraped these photos from the internet to train its AI system, Stable Diffusion, which generates images resembling those owned by the plaintiff, including their watermarks. Stability AI moved for dismissal, citing insufficient allegations of infringement, immunity under the safe harbour provision of the Digital Millennium Copyright Act, and pre-emption of the plaintiff's trademark claims by federal law.

The case is still ongoing, with Stability AI having filed a motion to dismiss the lawsuit. The court's decision on this motion and the outcome of the case are pending. This case remains a significant one to watch in the realm of AI and copyright law, as it

472. Blake Brittain, *AI-Created Images Lose U.S. Copyrights in Test for New Technology*, Reuters (23 Feb. 2023), https://www.reuters.com/legal/ai-created-images-lose-us-copyrights-test-new-technology-2023-02-22/.
473. No. 23-cv-00201-WHO (N.D. Cal. 30 Oct. 2023).
474. The First Amendment of the US Constitution affirms that Congress shall not make any law curtailing the freedom of speech or the press. It means that the government cannot censor or restrict what people say or write unless there is a compelling reason to do so. The fair use doctrine is a legal principle that allows the use of copyrighted material for purposes such as criticism, comment, news reporting, teaching, scholarship, or research. *See* US Const. amend. I. available at https://constitution.congress.gov/constitution/amendment-1/#amendment-1 (accessed 2 Aug. 2024).
475. No. 1:23-cv-00135 (D. Del. filed 17 Jan. 2023).

could potentially set important precedents for how AI companies can use copyrighted images in training their models.

The fair use doctrine plays a crucial role in the US regarding AI-generated content. Under this doctrine, GAI developers in the US may utilise copyrighted material for training their models, provided that the use is transformative.[476] Nevertheless, the extent and nature of this use remain subjects of legal scrutiny and interpretation, as seen in the ongoing case between the New York Times (NYT) and OpenAI.[477] In this case, the NYT has accused OpenAI and Microsoft of using its articles without permission to train LLMs, notably impacting NYT's subscription and advertising revenues. Additionally, the lawsuit addresses issues with 'hallucinations' generated by AI, where fabricated content is falsely attributed to NYT, potentially damaging its reputation. As of July 2024, the court has not yet reached a final verdict, and the case continues to develop.

In conclusion, the legal landscape surrounding AI-generated content in the US is shaped by foundational principles of human authorship under copyright law, which exclude works created autonomously by machines from protection. Recent cases *like Kashtanova v. U.S. Copyright Office* and *Andersen et al. v. Stability AI* underscore the ongoing debates over whether AI-generated works merit copyright recognition and the liabilities of using AI to replicate copyrighted material. These cases also highlight the complex interplay between fair use doctrines, technological innovation, and the ethical considerations of attribution and ownership in the digital age. As these legal battles unfold, they will continue to define the boundaries and responsibilities in the evolving relationship between AI technologies and IP rights.

6.2.2 European Union

In the context of the EU, the Copyright Directive of 2019 grants copyright protection to original literary works, including those created by AI algorithms, provided they meet the originality criteria.[478] The European Commission's 2020 report on IP proposed a new legal framework for AI-generated works' IP rights, encompassing copyright. This framework would either grant copyright protection to the AI-generated work itself or grant 'AI authorship' to the developer or user, rather than the natural person who created the work.[479] The report also recommended introducing a new copyright exception for text and data mining (TDM) in the context of AI.

TDM involves analysing large amounts of data to identify patterns and extract insights. The exception would allow for the use of copyrighted works for TDM without

476. 17 U.S.C. §107 (2024), available at https://www.bitlaw.com/source/17usc/107.html.
477. *New York Times v. OpenAI*: The Times's About-Face, Harvard Law Review Blog (4 Apr. 2024), https://harvardlawreview.org/blog/2024/04/nyt-v-openai-the-timess-about-face/.
478. Directive (EU) 2019/790 of the European Parliament and of the Council of 17 Apr. 2019 on copyright in the Digital Single Market, 2019 O.J. (L 130) 92 (EU), Art. 14.
479. *See infra* n. 881 (suggestions ns. 15 & 16).

obtaining permission from the copyright holder. This provision would enable researchers and businesses to utilise large data sets to develop AI technologies and applications.[480] The 2021 European Parliament resolution acknowledges the need for a legal framework for AI-generated works, including copyright ownership, liability, and accountability. The resolution proposes a new legal framework for AI-generated work, granting copyright ownership to humans (including developers, users, or owners) who contribute significantly to such a work rather than the AI system itself.[481]

Furthermore, the EU Committee on Transport and Tourism calls on the Committee on Legal Affairs to address the technical, social, economic, ethical, and legal issues of AI and related technologies in a variety of policy areas, including IP rights.[482] In the ongoing debate over copyright protection for AI-generated works, the EU Parliament underscores the importance of addressing copyright issues related to AI-generated cultural and creative works. It believes that creation by human beings must form the basis of the intellectual property rights (IPR) system. The Parliament also notes that it is important to determine the extent to which an AI-generated work can be traced back to a human creator. It requires further investigation to determine whether automatically attributing copyright to the owner of the AI software is the most effective approach, considering the need to recognise humans as the authors of innovative creative works.[483]

The European Parliament continues to emphasise the importance of human creativity as the foundation of IP rights while acknowledging the need to address the unique challenges posed by AI-generated works.[484] The EU maintains that further investigation is necessary to determine the most appropriate approach to copyright attribution for AI-generated content, balancing the interests of AI software owners, human creators, and the broader creative ecosystem. This position aligns with the ongoing discussions in the Committee on Legal Affairs and the Committee on Transport and Tourism, as well as the Parliament's earlier statements on the matter.[485] As of August 2024, no definitive legislative framework specifically addressing copyright for AI-generated works has been enacted at the EU level. The debate continues to evolve in response to ongoing technological advancements.

Although no country has enacted a comprehensive AI law, the EU has pioneered the development of the world's first AI regulatory framework. On 13 March 2024, the

480. European Parliament, *Report on the Proposal for a Regulation of the European Parliament and of the Council on Artificial Intelligence* (Artificial Intelligence Act), A9-0176/2020 (2020), (suggestion n. 2) https://www.europarl.europa.eu/doceo/document/A-9-2020-0176_EN.html.
481. European Parliament, *Resolution of 20 October 2020 on Intellectual Property Rights for the Development of Artificial Intelligence Technologies (2020/2015(INI))*, 2021/C 404/06, P9_TA (2020)0277, https://eur-lex.europa.eu/legal-content/EN/TXT/HTML/?uri=CELEX:52020IP0277.
482. *See infra* n. 881 (s. 1, para. 2, opinion of the committee on culture and education).
483. *Ibid.*, (s. 1, para. 9, opinion of the committee on culture and education).
484. *See supra n.* 482.
485. European Parliament Committee on Legal Affairs, *Activity Report 2019–2024, 9th Legislature* (2024), https://www.europarl.europa.eu/cmsdata/284734/9th%20legislature_JURI%20Activity%20Report%202019-2024.pdf.

European Parliament adopted the AI Act, recognised as the first comprehensive and horizontal legal framework for AI globally.[486] The Act establishes EU-wide regulations concerning data quality, transparency, human oversight, and accountability. Its primary objective is to foster human-centric and trustworthy AI, while also protecting health, safety, fundamental rights, democracy, the rule of law, and the environment from potential risks.[487] Nevertheless, the EU Act avoids taking a definitive stance on copyright ownership of AI-generated works. While the Act emphasises human creativity as the foundation of IP, it acknowledges the need to determine the role of human input in AI creations.

In conclusion, the EU has been at the forefront of addressing the complex intersection of AI and copyright law. While significant progress has been made, including the adoption of the pioneering AI Act in 2024, the EU's stance on copyright for AI-generated works remains in flux. The ongoing debate reflects a delicate balance between recognising human creativity as the cornerstone of IP rights and acknowledging the unique challenges posed by AI-generated content. As of August 2024, no definitive legislative framework specifically addressing copyright for AI-generated works has been enacted at the EU level, despite various proposals and resolutions. The EU continues to grapple with key questions, such as the extent of human contribution necessary for copyright attribution and the most appropriate approach to protect and incentivise innovation in AI-generated works. This evolving landscape underscores the need for continued investigation and dialogue to develop a comprehensive and balanced approach that aligns with the rapid pace of technological advancement.

6.2.3 United Kingdom

In the UK, AI-generated works are not deemed original since they lack the free and creative choices of a human author. However, the UK has a relatively unique position on copyright protection for AI-generated works. Unlike many other countries, the Copyright, Designs and Patents Act 1988 (CDPA) offers a path for copyright protection in section 9(3).[488] This section specifies that when a work is 'generated by computer in circumstances where there is no human author', copyright belongs to the 'person by whom the arrangements necessary for the creation of the work are undertaken'. In simpler terms, the person who sets up and instructs the AI is considered the author for copyright purposes. This protection lasts for 50 years from the date the work is created, and importantly, it does not include moral rights.[489]

For works that involve both human and AI input, the UK copyright framework requires that the human contribution be significant enough to warrant authorship. When the human input meets this threshold, the work is treated as having a human

486. European Parliament, *Artificial Intelligence Act* (2021), https://www.europarl.europa.eu/RegData/etudes/BRIE/2021/698792/EPRS_BRI(2021)698792_EN.pdf.
487. *See supra* n. 367.
488. Copyright, Designs and Patents Act 1988, c. 48, §9 (UK).
489. *Ibid.*, s. 12.

author, thereby granting it the standard duration of protection, which is 70 years after the author's death.[490] This distinction underscores the importance of substantial human creative input in determining the duration of copyright protection.

The UK's legal framework is notable on the international stage for its explicit recognition of computer-generated works, offering a clear and distinct legislative position. This approach underscores the UK's proactive adaptation of copyright law to address modern technological advancements, ensuring that computer-generated works receive appropriate legal protection and acknowledging the evolving nature of creativity in the digital age.

In contrast to many jurisdictions, the UK's approach reflects a deliberate effort to balance innovation and legal certainty in the realm of AI-generated creativity. The explicit provision in section 9(3) of the CDPA addresses the unique challenges posed by AI by assigning authorship to the individual responsible for configuring the AI system.[491] This legislative clarity aims to foster technological advancement while ensuring that creators and users alike understand their rights and obligations within the digital landscape. Moreover, the UK's nuanced treatment of AI-generated works aligns with broader EU directives aimed at harmonising copyright law in the digital single market. By delineating clear guidelines for authorship and duration of protection, the UK not only safeguards IP but also facilitates cross-border collaboration and trade in AI-driven content.

However, the UK's approach to AI-generated copyright is not without criticisms. Some argue that attributing authorship to the person who sets up the AI is overly simplistic. They point out that the creative process behind AI generation can be highly complex, involving the selection and training data, the choice of algorithms, and the parameters set for the AI's operation.[492] These factors can significantly influence the final output, making it difficult to pinpoint a single human author. This ambiguity can create challenges in determining ownership and enforcing copyright, particularly in cases where multiple individuals contribute to the AI's development and operation.

Despite these concerns, the UK government has indicated that it is currently comfortable with the existing legal framework. In a 2022 consultation paper, the government acknowledged the complexities surrounding AI and copyright but concluded that there was no immediate need to amend the CDPA.[493] The government's position is that the current law provides a sufficient balance between encouraging

490. *Ibid.*
491. *Ibid.*, s. 9.
492. Artificial Intelligence and Intellectual Property: Call for Views, UK Gov., https://www.gov.uk/government/consultations/artificial-intelligence-and-intellectual-property-call-for-views/artificial-intelligence-call-for-views-copyright-and-related-rights#protecting-works-generated-by-ai (accessed 2 Aug. 2024); The Government's Code of Practice on Copyright and AI, UK Gov., https://www.gov.uk/guidance/the-governments-code-of-practice-on-copyright-and-ai (accessed 2 Aug. 2024).
493. UK Government, *Artificial Intelligence and Intellectual Property: Copyright and Patents, Government Response to Consultation* (December 2023), https://www.gov.uk/government/consultations/artificial-intelligence-and-ip-copyright-and-patents/outcome/artificial-intelligence-and-intellectual-property-copyright-and-patents-government-response-to-consultation.

innovation in AI and protecting IP. Nonetheless, they did acknowledge that the situation may need to be revisited as AI technology continues to develop.

In conclusion, the UK's approach to copyright for AI-generated works exemplifies a forward-thinking adaptation of IP law to address the complexities of modern technology. By designating authorship to the individual who configures the AI under section 9(3) of the CDPA, the UK ensures that these works are protected while fostering innovation. This legal framework not only reflects a balanced response to the unique challenges posed by AI but also aligns with broader EU directives, promoting clarity and facilitating international collaboration. Nevertheless, the ongoing debate about the adequacy of this approach underscores the need for continuous evaluation as technology evolves, ensuring that copyright law remains relevant and effective in an ever-changing digital landscape.

6.2.4 Australia

Australian copyright law protects original works, meaning that they are not just copies of something else. To be original, a work must have been created through an independent intellectual effort on the part of the author.[494] In *Phonographic Performance Company of Australia Limited v. Copyright Tribunal of Australia*,[495] the Australian High Court reasserted the importance of human intellectual effort in determining copyright. The court emphasised that originality, a cornerstone of Australian copyright law, necessitates independent intellectual effort from the author. This ruling aligns with the traditional view that AI-generated works, which lack human creativity and intellectual input, do not meet the threshold for copyright protection.

These developments underscore a broader, global discourse on how legal systems can and should adapt to the realities of AI, balancing innovation with the need to protect human authorship and creativity. The Australian courts gave an explicit answer to the question – whether AI-generated work may attain authorship. In *Telstra Corporation Limited v. Phone Directories Company Pty Ltd* (2010),[496] and *Ice TV Pty Ltd v. Nine Network Australia Pty Ltd* (2009),[497] the Australian Courts opined that copyright only subsists in works that have been created by a human author.

It is worth mentioning that the Australian Copyright Act 1968 does not explicitly address AI-generated content. Nonetheless, the Act's definition of an 'author' in section 10 implicitly assumes human authorship.[498] This interpretation is further supported by the Australian Copyright Council's position, which states that copyright protection is only available for works created by human authors. The Council's

494. Herbert Smith Freehills, *The IP in AI: Does Copyright Protect AI-Generated Works?* (May 2023), https://www.herbertsmithfreehills.com/insights/2023-05/the-ip-in-ai-does-copyright-protect-ai-generated-works.
495. 246 C.L.R. 561 (2012).
496. *Telstra Corp. Ltd. V. Phone Directories Co. Pty Ltd,* [2010] FCA 44 (Austl.).
497. Anna Honig, *Copyright Protection of Databases Under Australian Law: Nine Network Australia Pty Ltd v. IceTV Pty Ltd FCA 1172,* 21(3) Austl. & N.Z. Comp. L. Rev. 1 (2007).
498. Australian Parliament, *Copyright Act 1968 (Cth)* section 10A (1 Jan. 2019), https://www.legislation.gov.au/C1968A00063/2019-01-01/text.

information sheet on 'Computer-Generated Material' (G057v08) suggests that works wholly created by AI systems without human intervention are unlikely to be protected under current copyright law. This stance is consistent with the decision in *Acohs Pty Ltd v. Ucorp Pty Ltd* (2012),[499] where the Federal Court held that source code generated by a computer program without human input was not protected by copyright.

Despite this current position, there is ongoing debate about the need for copyright law reform to address AI-generated content. The Australian Law Reform Commission's (ALRC) report on 'Copyright and the Digital Economy' (ALRC Report 122, 2013) highlighted the challenges posed by emerging technologies, including AI.[500] While the report did not specifically recommend changes for AI-generated works, it emphasised the need for copyright law to remain flexible and adaptable to technological advancements. More recently, the Department of Infrastructure, Transport, Regional Development and Communications' discussion paper on 'Artificial Intelligence: Australia's Ethics Framework' (2019) acknowledged the complexities surrounding IP rights for AI-created works, suggesting that this area may require further policy consideration and potential legislative updates to ensure Australia's copyright regime remains fit for purpose in the age of AI.[501]

In February 2023, the Australian government released a consultation paper titled 'Artificial Intelligence and IP Rights', which directly addressed the issue of AI-generated content and copyright.[502] This paper acknowledged the growing importance of AI in creative processes and invited public feedback on potential reforms to IP laws, including copyright, to accommodate AI-generated works. While no concrete legislative changes have been made as of August 2024, this consultation process signals that Australia is actively considering how to adapt its copyright framework to the challenges posed by AI-generated content. The paper explores various options, including the possibility of introducing new rights for AI-generated works or modifying existing copyright laws to provide limited protection for such content, demonstrating a potential shift from the traditional human-centric approach to copyright.

In conclusion, Australia is actively grappling with the implications of AI-generated content on its copyright framework. Despite the traditional stance that copyright protection necessitates human authorship, recent discussions and reports reflect an evolving recognition of the growing role of AI in creative processes. The Australian High Court and other legal precedents have consistently upheld the necessity of human intellectual effort for a work to be deemed original and thus copyrightable. Nevertheless, the government's consultation paper on 'Artificial Intelligence and IP Rights' signifies a pivotal moment in considering reforms that could

499. Jade, *Redefining Copyright in the Age of AI* (18 Jun. 2024), https://jade.io/article/264703.
500. Australian Law Reform Commission, *Copyright and the Digital Economy*, ALRC Report No. 122 (2013), https://www.alrc.gov.au/publication/copyright-and-the-digital-economy-alrc-report-122/.
501. Law Council of Australia, *Artificial Intelligence: Australia's Ethics Framework* (2019), https://lawcouncil.au/publicassets/afebc52d-afa6-e911-93fe-005056be13b5/3639%20-%20AI%20ethics.pdf.
502. Dep't of Indus., Sci. & Res., Austl. Gov't, *Supporting Responsible AI*, https://consult.industry.gov.au/supporting-responsible-ai (accessed 2 Aug. 2024).

potentially extend copyright protection to AI-generated works. This ongoing dialogue highlights Australia's commitment to ensuring its copyright laws remain adaptable and relevant in the face of rapid technological advancements, striking a balance between fostering innovation and preserving the core principles of human creativity and authorship.

6.2.5 China

China has proactively established a regulatory framework to manage the development and application of AI-generated content. In August 2023, the Cyberspace Administration of China (CAC) issued new regulations, formally titled the 'Interim Measures for the Management of Generative Artificial Intelligence Services', effective from 15 August 2023, outlining comprehensive guidelines for the use of GAI, emphasising the need for content to align with socialist core values and not endanger national security.[503] The regulations mandated that service providers conduct security assessments and submit the results to the CAC before launching GAI services.

Moreover, the Chinese government has implemented robust data protection and privacy laws that impact AI-generated content. The Personal Information Protection Law (PIPL), enacted on 1 November 2021, sets stringent requirements for the collection, storage, and processing of personal data, which includes data used and produced by AI systems.[504] According to Articles 35 and 36 of the PIPL, individuals must be informed about and consent to the processing of their data. Additionally, the Data Security Law (DSL), effective from 1 September 2021, established a framework for the classification and protection of data based on its significance to national security, economic stability, and social interests.

In addition, China introduced the 'Regulations on the Administration of Deep Synthesis Internet Information Services', effective from 10 January 2023. These regulations specifically target deep synthesis technologies, which include AI-generated audio, video, and text content.[505] The rules require service providers to clearly label deep synthesis content to prevent public confusion or misrepresentation and impose strict controls on the creation and dissemination of such content. Providers must also implement robust data security measures and take responsibility for preventing the misuse of deep synthesis technologies.

503. PwC China, *Regulatory and Legislation: China's Interim Measures for the Management of Generative Artificial Intelligence Services Officially Implemented*, PwC (August 2023), https://www.pwccn.com/en/industries/telecommunications-media-and-technology/publications/interim-measures-for-generative-ai-services-implemented-aug2023.html.

504. Standing Committee of the National People's Congress, *Personal Information Protection Law of* the People's Republic of China, Nat'l People's Cong. (29 Dec. 2021), http://en.npc.gov.cn.cdurl.cn/2021-12/29/c_694559.htm.

505. National Cyberspace Administration of China, *Notice of the Cyberspace Administration of China on Soliciting Public Opinions on the Draft Regulations on the Administration of Deep Integration of Internet Information Services* (28 Jan. 2022); DigiChina, Stanford Univ., *Translation: Internet Information Service Deep Synthesis Management Provisions (Draft for Comment)* (January 2022), https://digichina.stanford.edu/work/translation-internet-information-service-deep-synthesis-management-provisions-draft-for-comment-jan-2022/.

In a further move to regulate AI-generated content, China's Ministry of Industry and Information Technology (MIIT) released guidelines on 13 July 2023, focusing on the ethical use of AI. These guidelines stress the importance of transparency, accountability, and fairness in AI systems. Furthermore, the 'Guiding Opinions on Strengthening the Ethical Governance of Artificial Intelligence' issued in September 2021, urges companies to ensure their AI technologies do not propagate false information or create fake news.[506] The document also highlights the importance of protecting users' rights and interests in AI interactions.

In conclusion, IP laws across the globe presume human authorship or inventorship, leading to the exclusion of AI systems from holding or enforcing IP rights. Nonetheless, it is essential to recognise that AI-generated content may not always be freely available for use by everyone. The IP rights may belong to the human user, developer, or trainer of the AI system or to the entity that commissioned or employed them, contingent upon the degree of human involvement and originality in the creation process.[507] For example, in *Feilin v. Baidu*,[508] the Beijing Internet Court ruled that an AI-generated report with human involvement could be copyrighted. Similarly, *Shenzhen Tencent v. Shanghai Yingxun* held that AI-generated content with human intellectual activities was copyrightable.[509] Nevertheless, the ownership of fully autonomously generated AI products remains unclear, and courts need to adjust copyright laws to address such works in the future.

6.2.6 Recent Developments

Meanwhile, there have been calls for a global summit on AI regulation to discuss ways to control the development of advanced AI systems, mitigate negative externalities, and deliver safer, more sustainable, and more equitable outcomes. In November 2023, the UK hosted the world's first AI Safety Summit at Bletchley Park, bringing together over 100 attendees.[510] The summit resulted in the signing of the Bletchley Declaration by 28 countries, including the US, the UK, China, and the EU, emphasising the need for

506. The General Office of the CPC Central Committee and the General Office of the State Council, *Opinions on Strengthening the Governance of Science and Technology Ethics* (20 Mar. 2022), https://www.gov.cn/zhengce/2022-03/20/content_5680105.htm; China Releases Opinion on Strengthening the Ethics and Governance in Science and Technology, *AI Ethics and Governance Institute* (22 Mar. 2022), https://ai-ethics-and-governance.institute/2022/03/22/china-released-opinion-on-strengthening-the-ethics-and-governance-in-science-and-technology/.
507. Congressional Research Service [CRS], *Generative Artificial Intelligence and Copyright Law*, https://crsreports.congress.gov/product/pdf/LSB/LSB10922 (accessed 2 Aug 2024); Douglas Broom, *Who Owns the Song You Wrote with AI? An Expert Explains*, World Economic Forum (8 Aug. 2023), https://www.weforum.org/agenda/2023/08/intellectual-property-ai-creativity/.
508. *Beijing Film Law Firm v. Beijing Baidu Netcom Science & Technology*, Beijing Internet Court Civil Judgment No. 491 Min Chu 239 (2018).
509. *Shenzhen Tencent Computer System Co., Ltd. V. Shanghai Yingxun Technology Co., Ltd.*, 305 Min Chu 14010 (2019).
510. UK Government, *The Bletchley Declaration by Countries Attending the AI Safety Summit, 1-2 November 2023* (1 Nov. 2023), https://www.gov.uk/government/publications/ai-safety-summit-2023-the-bletchley-declaration/the-bletchley-declaration-by-countries-attending-the-ai-safety-summit-1-2-november-2023.

urgent AI regulation. Simultaneously, the US government issued an executive order ensuring safe, secure, and trustworthy development and use of AI.[511] Additionally, at the G7 Summit, leaders from seven Member States, such as France, the US, the UK, Germany, Japan, Italy, and Canada, along with the EU, discussed crucial global challenges, including the importance of AI regulation and governance.[512]

Despite these advancements, achieving consensus on a comprehensive global scale remains challenging, given divergent national interests. Nonetheless, relentless efforts toward multilateral AI governance frameworks are ongoing. Organisations like UNESCO, the International Organization for Standardization (ISO), and the African Union actively engage in this process. Furthermore, the WEF's AI Governance Summit in San Francisco underscored the need to bolster existing initiatives and accelerate progress in this critical area.[513] While progress is being made, the global journey toward effective AI regulation continues to evolve.

6.3 PATENTABILITY OF AI-GENERATED CONTENT ACROSS JURISDICTIONS

As AI capabilities continue to expand, the question of its role in patent law has become a significant challenge. While AI can now produce innovative outputs with minimal human intervention, its status as an inventor under current patent law remains ambiguous. Traditional patent law is grounded in the concept of a 'human inventor', aiming to incentivise, protect, and reward human ingenuity. This anthropocentric approach emphasises intellectual creation originating from humans, leaving little room for non-human inventors like AI systems.[514]

Given that current legal frameworks are primarily designed for the intellectual and creative works of humans, defining AI systems as inventors may not be essential. The inventorship analysis should focus on the contributions to an invention's conception, requiring creative or intelligent input. This approach excludes AI technologies that lack cognition, as they cannot independently contribute to the inventive process.

Since the boundaries between human ingenuity and AI continue to blur, the question of patent protection for AI-generated inventions emerges as a complex legal issue. While AI systems can generate novel outputs, the extent to which they can be

---

511. The White House, *Executive Order on the Safe, Secure, and Trustworthy Development and Use of Artificial Intelligence* (30 Oct. 2023), https://www.whitehouse.gov/briefing-room/presidential-actions/2023/10/30/executive-order-on-the-safe-secure-and-trustworthy-development-and-use-of-artificial-intelligence/.
512. Japanese Ministry of Foreign Affairs, *Historical Significance of the G7 Hiroshima Summit,* https://www.japan.go.jp/kizuna/2023/07/historical_significance_of_g7.html (accessed 2 Aug. 2024).
513. Ian Shine & Emma Charlton, *The AI Governance Summit: Key Sessions, Talking Points and How to Livestream the Event,* World Economic Forum (13 Nov. 2023), https://www.weforum.org/agenda/2023/11/ai-governance-summit-2023-what-to-know/.
514. Hayleigh Bosher et al., *WIPO Impact of Artificial Intelligence on IP Policy Response from Brunel University London,* Law School & Centre for Artificial Intelligence, Brunel University London (2020–2021), https://www.wipo.int/export/sites/www/about-ip/en/artificial_intelligence/call_for_comments/pdf/org_brunel.pdf.

considered inventors under current patent law remains a subject of debate. Some scholars argue that patent protection should extend to collaborative inventions involving both AI systems and human creators, provided that the human contribution demonstrates sufficient creativity and innovation.[515] Nevertheless, others may argue that patent law should exclusively reward human innovation, not AI ones, as AI systems lack independent creativity. This approach is supported by several legal precedents across jurisdictions.

6.3.1 United States

The US legal landscape surrounding AI-generated inventions remains unclear. The position of US law regarding the patentability of AI-generated content can be understood through several legal and policy instruments. Recently, the US Patent and Trademark Office (USPTO) issued guidance on the implementation of AI tools in patent practices.[516] This guidance, issued on 6 February 2024, in response to President Biden's 'Executive Order on the Safe, Secure, and Trustworthy Development and Use of Artificial Intelligence', offers insights on patent eligibility for AI-driven innovation and builds on the existing inventorship framework and the 'significant contribution test' from *Pannu v. Iolab Corp.*, 155 F.3d 1344 (Fed. Cir. 1998).

In the landmark cases of *Naruto v. Slater* and *DABUS v. USPTO*, US courts grappled with the question of non-human authorship and inventorship rights. In *Naruto v. Slater*,[517] the court determined that animals, specifically a monkey that had taken a self-portrait, cannot hold copyright under US law, thus placing the photograph in the public domain. Similarly, in *DABUS v. USPTO*,[518] the US District Court for the Eastern District of Virginia addressed the issue of AI as an inventor. The case involved patent applications listing an AI system, *DABUS*, as the sole inventor. The USPTO rejected these applications, and the court subsequently affirmed in September 2021 that US patent law exclusively recognises natural persons as inventors, thereby precluding non-human entities, including AI systems, from being designated as inventors in patent applications.[519]

The recent decision in *Thaler v. Vidal* clarifies the stance of US patent law concerning the patentability of AI-generated content. Drawing from public feedback and the Federal Circuit's rulings in *Thaler v. Vidal* (43 F.4th 1207, Fed. Cir. 2022), the guidance outlines the legal framework for establishing inventorship in patent applications. This case highlights a significant intersection between rapidly advancing technology and the

515. Peter Georg Picht & Florent Thouvenin, *AI and IP: Theory to Policy and Back Again: Policy and Research Recommendations at the Intersection of Artificial Intelligence and Intellectual Property*, 14 Springer J. Bus. & Econ. L. 1 (2023), https://doi.org/10.1007/s40319-023-01344-5.
516. US Patent & Trademark Off., *USPTO Issues Guidance Concerning Use of AI Tools by Parties and Practitioners* (29 Jul. 2024), https://www.uspto.gov/about-us/news-updates/uspto-issues-guidance-concerning-use-ai-tools-parties-and-practitioners.
517. 888 F.3d 418 (9th Cir. 2018).
518. *DABUS v. USPTO*, No. 20-1785 (Fed. Cir. 2021).
519. US Patent & Trademark Office, *Petition Decision: Inventorship Limited to Natural Persons* (5 May 2020), https://www.uspto.gov/about-us/news-updates/petition-decision-inventorship-limited-natural-persons.

legal frameworks designed to protect and incentivise innovation.[520] Notably, it emphasises that the key criterion is not whether AI contributions match those of a natural person, but whether the named individual made a significant enough contribution to warrant inventorship. This determination is made on a claim-by-claim basis, with each claim requiring a substantial contribution from at least one natural person.[521] This approach aims to balance incentivising human creativity and investment in AI with fostering continued innovation in the field.

The implications of this ruling extend beyond the legal realm and into the practicalities of innovation and IP management. Companies and individuals using AI to develop new technologies must navigate this legal landscape by ensuring a human inventor is attributed to any patent applications involving AI contributions. This could involve complex considerations about who among the developers, operators, or users of the AI system can legitimately claim inventorship. The necessity to attribute inventions to human inventors may also affect the structuring of R&D teams, influence collaborations, and shape strategies for leveraging AI in innovation processes.

Furthermore, the *Thaler v. Vidal* decision prompts broader discussions about the future of IP law and its adaptability to emerging technologies.[522] As AI continues to evolve and its capabilities expand, the rigid interpretation of patent laws may increasingly clash with the realities of technological advancement. This case may catalyse legislative review and potential reforms to accommodate the contributions of AI in inventorship. Policymakers, legal experts, and industry stakeholders may need to explore new frameworks that balance the protection of human inventors' rights with the recognition of AI's role in innovation. These discussions could lead to novel legal constructs, such as the possibility of assigning inventorship to entities or organisations that oversee AI systems, thereby addressing the gaps exposed by the current ruling.

Beyond legal reforms, policymakers should consider the broader ethical and social implications of AI applications. They should think about how to balance incentivising innovation, protecting inventors, and acknowledging AI's role. This context requires interdisciplinary discussions involving law, ethics, and technology. Moreover, the distinction between AI as a tool (used by inventors) and AI as an inventor remains crucial. While AI can aid human inventors, the legal framework must

---

520. United States Court of Appeals for the Federal Circuit, *Opinion, 5 Aug. 2022*, Case No. 21-2347, https://cafc.uscourts.gov/opinions-orders/21-2347.OPINION.8-5-2022_1988142.pdf.
521. Kathi Vidal, *AI and Inventorship Guidance: Incentivizing Human Ingenuity and Investment in AI-Assisted Inventions*, US Patent and Trademark Office (12 Feb. 2024), https://www.uspto.gov/blog/ai-and-inventorship-guidance-incentivizing?utm_campaign = subscriptioncenter&utm_content = &ut; Audrey G. Ogurchak & Beverly J. Lamberson, *USPTO Issues Inventorship Guidance for AI-Assisted Inventions: AI-Assisted Inventions Are Not Categorically Unpatentable*, Lowenstein Sandler LLP (27 Feb. 2024), https://www.lowenstein.com/news-insights/publications/client-alerts/uspto-issues-inventorship-guidance-for-ai-assisted-inventions-patent#: ~ :text = On%20February%2013%2C%20the%20United%20States%20Patent%20and,created%20with%20the%20assistance%20of%20artificial%20intelligence%20%28AI%29.
522. Monika Malek & Daniel H. Shulman, *Thaler v. Vidal: Artificial Intelligence Inventions Create Real Issues*, Vedder Price (28 Sep. 2022), https://www.vedderprice.com/-/media/files/vedder-thinking/publications/2022/9/thaler-v-vidal-artificial-intelligence-inventions-create-real-issues.pdf.

address whether AI can be considered an inventor. This debate extends beyond the US and requires thoughtful consideration of the laws of other jurisdictions.

6.3.2 European Union

The patentability of AI-generated content within the framework of EU laws has become a focal point of debate and legal scrutiny, particularly illustrated by *Re DABUS*.[523] In this case, the European Patent Office (EPO) rejected two patent applications that designated an AI system, *DABUS*, as the inventor. The EPO's Board of Appeal upheld this decision in July 2020.[524] This decision hinged on the interpretation of the European Patent Convention (EPC), which explicitly requires the inventor to be a 'natural person'.[525] The EPO's stance underscores the existing legal framework's limitations in accommodating non-human inventors, reflecting broader challenges as AI technology continues to advance and integrate into the creative and inventive processes.

Nonetheless, the rejection of AI as an inventor does not necessarily mean that AI-generated inventions are unpatentable in the EU.[526] The key lies in how the invention process is framed and who is designated as the inventor. If a human inventor can demonstrate that they used AI as a tool in the inventive process, rather than the AI autonomously creating the invention, the patent application may still be viable. This approach recognises the role of AI in augmenting human creativity and problem-solving capabilities while maintaining the human-centric nature of patent law.

Re DABUS has sparked significant discourse about the adequacy of current patent laws to address the realities of AI-generated inventions. Proponents of recognising AI as inventors argue that such recognition is necessary to incentivise innovation and properly attribute creative contributions where they are due, even if those contributions come from non-human entities. They contend that excluding AI-generated inventions from patent protection could stifle technological progress and fail to reflect the true sources of innovation in increasingly automated and AI-driven industries.[527]

Conversely, critics of this perspective highlight the foundational principles of patent law, which traditionally centre on human inventorship, and the moral rights associated with it. They argue that recognising AI as inventors could create practical and ethical complications, such as issues of accountability and ownership. The EPO's

523. J 0008/20 (Designation of inventor/*DABUS*) 21 Dec. 2021.
524. BBC, *AI Cannot Be the Inventor of a Patent, Appeals Court Rules* (25 Sep. 2021), https://www.bbc.com/news/technology-58668534.
525. *See infra* n. 881 (s. 1, para. 16, motion for a European parliament resolution).
526. European Union Intellectual Property Helpdesk, *Naming AI as an Inventor in Patent Applications: EPO Board of Appeal Ratifies Decision, European Commission* (10 Jan. 2022), https://intellectual-property-helpdesk.ec.europa.eu/news-events/news/naming-ai-inventor-patent-applications-epo-board-appeal-ratifies-decision-2022-01-10_en.
527. Anthoula Papadopoulou, *Creativity in Crisis: Are the Creations of Artificial Intelligence Worth Protecting?*, 12 J. Intell. Prop. Info. Tech. & Elec. Com. L. 408 (2021); Shlomit Yanisky-Ravid & Xiaoqiong (Jackie) Liu, *When Artificial Intelligence Systems Produce Inventions: An Alternative Model for Patent Law at the 3A Era*, 39 Cardozo L. Rev. 2369 (2024) https://doi.org/10.2139/ssrn.2931828, https://cardozolawreview.com/artificial-intelligence-systems-produce-inventions/.

decision, grounded in the EPC's requirement for a natural person as the inventor, reflects a cautious approach that aligns with these concerns.[528] This conservative stance is seen as maintaining the integrity and coherence of the existing patent system while discussions and potential legislative updates are considered.

Nonetheless, in the EU legal domain, an AI system or computer program used as part of an invention that contributes to a 'technical effect' can be patentable.[529] This means the invention must solve a technical problem in a new and inventive way, going beyond a mere theoretical solution. Although Article 52(2)(c) of the EPC affirms that 'computer programs' are explicitly excluded from being patented,[530] computer-implemented inventions (CIIs), such as AI systems, can still be eligible for patents if they demonstrate a 'technical' nature by solving a technical problem. In essence, an AI system can qualify for patent protection if it contributes to a technical effect. The onus lies on the applicant to clearly define this technical effect within the patent application.

The implications of the *Re DABUS* decision extend beyond Europe, influencing global perspectives on AI and IP. Other jurisdictions, such as the US and the UK, have similarly grappled with the question of AI inventorship, often reaching analogous conclusions that emphasise the necessity of human inventors.[531] Nevertheless, as AI's role in innovation continues to grow, there is increasing pressure on policymakers and legal experts to revisit and potentially revise patent laws to better accommodate the realities of AI-generated content. The ongoing dialogue in the EU and other regions underscores the dynamic and evolving nature of patent law in the age of AI.

In light of these developments, stakeholders in the technology and legal sectors are closely monitoring potential legislative and regulatory changes. As the debate progresses, the need for a balanced and forward-looking framework that promotes innovation while addressing ethical and practical concerns remains paramount. The goal is to strike a balance between incentivising innovation and ensuring that the rights of inventors, whether human or artificial, are appropriately recognised and protected. These discussions are crucial in shaping the future direction of patent law and IP rights in the EU, as they seek to address the unique challenges posed by AI-generated inventions.

6.3.3 United Kingdom

The legal framework in the UK regarding the patentability of AI-generated content is complex and evolving. Currently, the UK does not recognise AI as an inventor under

528. Rohan Deshpande & Karan Kamath, *Patentability of Inventions Created by AI: The DABUS Claims from an Indian Perspective*, 15 J. Intell. Prop. L. & Prac. 879 (2020), https://doi.org/10.1093/jiplp/jpaa146.
529. European Patent Office, *Decision of the Enlarged Board of Appeal, G 2/00* (1 Jul. 2002); Decision No. G 0002/21 (23 Mar. 2023), https://www.epo.org/en/boards-of-appeal/decisions/g210002ex1.
530. European Patent Office, *European Patent Convention: Article 52* (2016), EPO, https://www.epo.org/en/legal/epc/2016/a52.html (accessed 3 Aug. 2024).
531. Alexandra George & Toby Walsh, *Artificial Intelligence Is Breaking Patent Law*, 605 Nature 1 (2022), https://www.nature.com/articles/d41586-022-01391-x. *See also supra* n. 529.

patent law. The Patents Act 1977 requires a human inventor to be named in a patent application.[532] The UK is also a member of the EPC, and the EPO mandates human intervention in the inventive process. Under this framework, only a human inventor can be named in a patent application. Additionally, the invention must be novel and capable of industrial application.

This requirement has been upheld in several key cases, including *Thaler v. Comptroller-General of Patents, Trademarks, and Designs* [2020] EWHC 2412 (Pat).[533] The High Court ruled that AI systems cannot be recognised as inventors under the current legal framework. The UK Intellectual Property Office (UKIPO) and the Court of Appeal upheld the ruling, emphasising that an inventor must be a natural person. This aligns with decisions from the EPO and the USPTO.

In essence, the copyright law of the UK protects original creative works, such as books, plays, music, art, films, and photographs. To be protected, a work must be original, meaning that it is the author's creation and not a copy of someone else's work. Copyright protection lasts for the author's lifetime plus 70 years.[534] AI can be used to create works that are protected by copyright if the work expresses original human creativity. For example, a photograph taken with the help of AI camera software is still protected by copyright if the photographer uses their creativity to compose the shot. Meanwhile, the UKIPO refused to grant patents to *DABUS* because the relevant law of the land says that only humans can be inventors. The petitioner challenged this decision to the High Court of Justice, and the High Court of Justice also ruled in September 2021 that only humans can be inventors under the current law.[535]

Despite this legal development, there is growing recognition of AI's contributions to potentially patentable inventions. As AI technology advances, its role in the inventive process is likely to grow. This necessitates re-evaluating inventorship requirements to ensure valuable innovations receive protection and incentives. The UKIPO has actively participated in discussions about adapting patent law to accommodate AI technologies.[536] These discussions centre on whether existing laws should be amended to acknowledge AI systems in some capacity within the patent application process, though no legislative changes have been implemented yet.

Nonetheless, the UK Government sought input on how AI should be addressed within the patent and copyright systems through a consultation from 29 October 2021 to 7 January 2022, focusing on copyright in AI-created works.[537] The consultation received 88 submissions from various sectors, including creative industries, tech, pharmaceuticals, academia, and legal professions. The government opted against immediate changes to UK patent law in response to AI-devised inventions, citing the

532. Patents Act 1977, Ch. 37, pt. I (UK), s. 13(2)(a).
533. [2022] Bus LR 375, [2021] RPC 19, [2021] EWCA Civ 1374.
534. UK Government, *How Copyright Protects Your Work* (29 May 2019), https://www.gov.uk/copyright/how-long-copyright-lasts.
535. *See supra* n. 525.
536. *See supra* n. 494.
537. *Ibid.*

prevailing belief that AI currently lacks the capacity for independent invention.[538] While the current law on patents for AI inventions remains unchanged, the government will monitor this area and collaborate internationally to ensure the UK fosters AI innovation.

In essence, although the current UK patent law requires the name of a human inventor, the government is considering reforms to recognise AI systems as inventors. Giving AI patent inventorship could both benefit and harm the innovation landscape. It could incentivise the creation of AI-invented products, but there are concerns that it could stifle competition and innovation. The UK government is actively considering these contrasting factors to determine the most appropriate approach for reforming patent inventorship in the era of AI.[539] Nevertheless, any significant changes would require amendments to the Patents Act 1977 and potentially new international agreements. Until such reforms are enacted, patents can only be granted to inventions with human inventors, and AI systems cannot be listed as inventors in patent applications.

6.3.4 Australia

The patentability of AI-generated content in Australia is primarily governed by the Patents Act 1990 (Cth)[540] and its interpretations through various case laws. Section 15(1) of the Act states that a patent may be granted to 'a person who is the inventor', which has traditionally been interpreted as referring to human inventors. Section 18(1)(a) of the Patents Act requires that a patentable invention must be a 'manner of manufacture' within the meaning of the statute. The High Court's interpretation of this phrase in *NRDC* (1959) established that an invention must offer a material advantage in economic endeavour.[541] Nonetheless, AI-generated content, especially when the AI itself is considered the inventor, presents unique challenges to these traditional principles.

For AI-generated content to be patentable, it must meet the same criteria as any other invention, including novelty, inventive step, and usefulness. The Patents Examination Manual provides further guidance on these requirements.[542] Nevertheless, the central issue is whether AI, as an inventor, fits within the legal definitions intended by the Act. Australian law requires a human inventor, as reaffirmed by the Federal Court

538. *Ibid. See also* Chris Vallance, *UK Decides AI Still Cannot Patent Inventions*, BBC (28 Jun. 2022), https://www.bbc.com/news/technology-61896180.
539. UK Government, *Artificial Intelligence and Intellectual Property: Copyright and Patents* (July 2024), https://www.gov.uk/government/consultations/artificial-intelligence-and-ip-copyright-and-patents/artificial-intelligence-and-intellectual-property-copyright-and-patents#patents.
540. Australian Parliament, *Patents Act 1990* (No. 83, 1990), https://www.legislation.gov.au/C2004A04014/latest/text.
541. *National Research Development Corporation v. Commissioner of Patents*, [1959] HCA 67; (1959) 102 CLR 252.
542. IP Australia, *Examination Manuals*, https://www.ipaustralia.gov.au/tools-and-research/professional-resources/examination-manuals (accessed 3 Aug. 2024).

in *Thaler v. Commissioner of Patents* (2021).[543] The court held that the concept of inventorship inherently requires human agency, and thus, an AI system cannot be named as an inventor under the current statutory framework.

In the landmark case of *Thaler v. Commissioner of Patents*, Dr Stephen Thaler sought to patent inventions autonomously generated by his AI system, *DABUS*. The Australian Patent Office initially rejected the application, asserting that only natural persons could be recognised as inventors.[544] Dr Thaler appealed, arguing that the statutory language did not explicitly preclude AI from being an inventor. Earlier, Judge Beach of the Federal Court ruled that an AI system could be recognised as the inventor on a patent application.[545] Nonetheless, this decision was later reversed by the Full Court, bringing Australia in line with the UK, the US, and the EU, all of which do not accept AI as inventors. This case underscores the judiciary's current stance that, under existing laws of Australia, the concept of an inventor presupposes human contribution and oversight.

Despite the current legal position, there is an increasing recognition of the necessity to address AI-generated inventions in patent law. The Australian Government and IP Australia have recognised the need to adapt patent laws to address the rise of AI technologies. In response to the Thaler decision, there have been discussions and consultations regarding potential legislative amendments to accommodate AI-generated inventions. The Advisory Council on Intellectual Property (ACIP) has suggested that reforms may be necessary to maintain Australia's competitive edge in innovation.[546]

The Australian government has launched consultations on AI and IP, including a 2023 public consultation by IP Australia on 'Artificial Intelligence and the IP System'.[547] This indicates that legislative changes or new guidelines may be on the horizon to provide clarity on the patentability of AI-generated content. In the meantime, practitioners are advised to carefully consider inventorship issues for AI-assisted inventions, recommending the identification of human inventors who have made substantive contributions to the inventive concept, even when AI tools were utilised. This approach aligns with the current legal framework while allowing for the ongoing evolution of policy and legislation in response to AI technological advancements.

543. *Thaler v. Commissioner of Patents*, [2021] FCA 879 (Austl.), https://artificialinventor.com/wp-content/uploads/2021/08/Thaler-v-Commissioner-of-Patents-2021-FCA-879.pdf.

544. Library of Congress, *Australia Court Holds Artificial Intelligence Systems Can Be Designated as Inventors for Patent Applications*, https://www.loc.gov/item/global-legal-monitor/2021-09-07/australia-court-holds-artificial-intelligence-systems-can-be-designated-as-inventors-for-patent-applications/.

545. *Ibid. See also* Rebecca Currey & Jane Owen, *In the Courts: Australian Court Finds AI Systems Can Be 'Inventors'*, WIPO (September 2021), https://www.wipo.int/wipo_magazine/en/2021/03/article_0006.html.

546. IP Australia, *Implementing Accepted Recommendations from ACIP's Review of the Designs System* (October–December 2019), https://consultation.ipaustralia.gov.au/policy/design-reforms-implement-acip-recs/.

547. Australian Government, Dep't of Industry, Science & Res., *The Australian Government's Interim Response to Safe and Responsible AI Consultation* (11 Jul. 2023), https://www.industry.gov.au/news/australian-governments-interim-response-safe-and-responsible-ai-consultation.

It is worth noting that Australia is not alone in grappling with the patentability of AI-generated inventions. Jurisdictions like the US, Europe, and the UK have similarly rejected the notion of AI as an inventor. Nevertheless, there is a growing international discourse on harmonising IP laws to address these emerging challenges. Australia's approach will likely evolve with global standards and technological advancements. The ongoing consultations and potential legislative reviews signify a crucial period in IP law, where the balance between fostering innovation and adhering to traditional legal principles must be carefully navigated. As such, stakeholders in the Australian innovation ecosystem should stay abreast of these developments and actively participate in the policymaking process.

6.3.5 China

The legal framework around the patentability of AI-generated content in China is shaped by a combination of national legislation and guidelines issued by the China National Intellectual Property Administration (CNIPA). Chinese patent law implicitly requires that an invention be the result of human intellectual activity to qualify for patent protection, as reflected in the definition and criteria for an invention. According to the Patent Law of China, an invention must be novel, inventive, and have practical applicability. Article 2 defines an 'invention' as a new technical solution proposed for a product, a process, or the improvement thereof, while Article 22 stipulates the conditions for patentability, including novelty, inventiveness, and practical applicability.[548] Although these articles do not explicitly state that the invention must result from human intellectual activity, this requirement is implied through the need for 'inventiveness and the provision of a technical solution'.

This principle raises significant questions about the eligibility of AI-generated inventions since they are created by algorithms rather than human inventors. Therefore, any patent application for AI-generated content must list a human inventor who can demonstrate a meaningful contribution to the invention process. Nonetheless, while a human inventor is currently needed for applications, the definition of 'inventiveness' leaves room for the interpretation of inventions with significant AI contributions.[549]

Hence, it can be concluded that the patentability of AI-generated content remains somewhat ambiguous in Chinese patent laws and guidelines. While Article 25(2) of the Patent Law excludes rules and methods of mental activities from patent protection,[550] the 2023 revision of the Guidelines for Examination provides a potential avenue for AI-related inventions. Specifically, claims that involve technical features related to computer programs, algorithms, or AI may be considered patentable if they provide a demonstrable and tangible technical contribution and effect.[551] This approach suggests

548. CNIPA, *Patent Law of the People's Republic of China* (1984), https://english.cnipa.gov.cn/transfer/lawpolicy/patentlawsregulations/915574.htm.
549. *Ibid.*, Art. 22.
550. *Ibid.*
551. *Ibid.*

that AI-generated inventions could potentially receive patent protection in China, provided they meet the necessary legal requirements and exhibit a clear technical impact beyond mere mental activities.

The CNIPA has issued several guidelines to clarify the examination process for AI-related patents. According to these guidelines, when assessing the patentability of an AI invention, examiners should focus on the technical contribution made by the human inventor.[552] This involves evaluating whether the invention addresses a technical problem in a novel and non-obvious manner and whether it achieves a technical effect. The guidelines also emphasise the need for clear and comprehensive documentation that explains the role of the AI system in the invention process and how the human inventor interacted with the AI to produce the invention.

In *Beijing Film Law Firm v. Beijing Baidu Netcom Science & Technology Co Ltd (Film)*,[553] the Beijing Internet Court recently established a significant precedent in Chinese IP law by granting copyright protection to images generated by AI. The case involved an AI-generated image created using the Stable Diffusion model, prompting a dispute over copyright ownership when the image was used without permission. The court determined that the AI-generated image qualified as a copyrightable 'work of fine arts', emphasising the creative inputs and subjective choices made by the human operator in designing the image through detailed prompts and adjustments. This decision underscores China's evolving stance on AI and IP, suggesting a willingness to recognise AI-generated works under certain conditions while highlighting the need for case-specific assessments in future disputes.[554]

This means that patent applications for AI-generated content in China must include detailed descriptions of the AI algorithms and processes used, as well as the specific technical problems they solve.[555] The human inventor must also provide evidence of their involvement in the development and implementation of the AI system. This requirement ensures that the patent system continues to reward human creativity and innovation, even as AI plays an increasingly significant role in the invention process. Furthermore, Chinese patent law also requires that the subject matter of the patent application must be within the realm of patentable technology, which excludes purely abstract ideas or mathematical algorithms without a practical application.[556]

552. Ma Junhao, *Securing AI Patents in China: The Regulatory Framework*, King & Wood Mallesons, https://www.kwm.com/cn/en/insights/latest-thinking/securing-ai-patents-in-china-the-regulatory-framework.html; World Intellectual Property Organization, *Patent Examination Guidelines 2023* (2023), https://www.wipo.int/wipolex/en/legislation/details/22371.
553. Beijing Internet Court, *Judicial Interpretation on Online Copyright Disputes* (20 Dec. 2021), https://english.bjinternetcourt.gov.cn/2021-12/20/c_492.htm.
554. Tingting Wen, *Beijing Internet Court Recognises Copyright in AI-Generated Image*, 19(3) J. of Intell. Prop. L. & Prac. (March 2024), 250–55, https://doi.org/10.1093/jiplp/jpad127; Khoon Tan et al., *China: A Landmark Court Ruling on Copyright Protection for AI-Generated Works*, Global Litigations News (8 May 2024), https://globallitigationnews.bakermckenzie.com/2024/05/08/china-a-landmark-court-ruling-on-copyright-protection-for-ai-generated-works/.
555. JPO & CNIPA, *Comparative Study on AI-Related Inventions* (2023), https://www.jpo.go.jp/news/kokusai/cn/document/ai_report_2023/cn_ai_report_en.pdf.
556. *Ibid.*

In conclusion, the current legal stance on AI-generated inventions in China reflects a cautious approach to integrating AI into the patent system. By insisting on human involvement and contribution, the Chinese legal framework aims to preserve the fundamental principles of patent law, which are designed to incentivise human ingenuity and innovation. Nevertheless, as AI technology continues to evolve, there is ongoing debate within the legal and technological communities about whether the current laws adequately address the unique challenges posed by AI. Future legislative updates and judicial interpretations will likely continue to refine the criteria for patenting AI-generated content, balancing the need to protect genuine innovations with the recognition of AI's growing role in the creative process.

6.3.6 World Intellectual Property Organization

The World Intellectual Property Organization (WIPO) plays a crucial role in the ongoing global debate regarding the patentability of AI-generated content. As the specialised agency of the United Nations (UN) responsible for the protection of IP worldwide, the organisation acknowledges the complexities involved in attributing inventorship and ownership when an invention is autonomously created by AI and has actively contributed to the global discourse through extensive research, publication of reports, and facilitating dialogue among stakeholders.

To address pressing challenges, WIPO launched the 'Conversation on IP and AI', gathering Member States, stakeholders, and experts to explore AI's impact on IP. WIPO's 'Technology Trends' series, especially the 'AI and IP' report, offers a thorough analysis of AI's influence on innovation and the IP landscape, highlighting issues like attributing inventorship and ownership for AI-generated inventions.[557] The WIPO Conversation on Intellectual Property and Frontier Technologies serves as an inclusive forum discussing frontier technologies' impact on IP rights. Over the past five years, nearly 9,000 participants from 172 countries, including Member States, academia, IP professionals, and enterprises, have joined this dialogue to bridge information gaps in this rapidly evolving field.[558] The ninth session, titled 'Training the Machines – Bytes, Rights, and the Copyright Conundrum', delved into the complex relationship between training data and IP in the context of AI and LLMs.[559]

Moreover, WIPO's role includes facilitating the harmonisation of international patent laws to ensure a cohesive approach to AI-generated content. Given the differing national laws and the varying degrees of recognition of AI as an inventor, WIPO's efforts in creating a more unified legal framework are essential. Through its Standing

557. WIPO, *WIPO Technology Trends 2019: Artificial Intelligence* (2019), https://www.wipo.int/publications/en/details.jsp?id=4386.
558. World Intellectual Property Organization, *The WIPO Conversation on Intellectual Property and Frontier Technologies*, https://www.wipo.int/about-ip/en/frontier_technologies/frontier_conversation.html (accessed on 3 Aug. 2024).
559. World Intellectual Property Organization (WIPO), *WIPO DG Tang Opens the 9th WIPO Conversation: Training AI Not Just a Challenge, but an Opportunity for New Forms of Creative Expression*, https://www.wipo.int/about-ip/en/frontier_technologies/news/2024/news_0003.html.

Committee on the Law of Patents (SCP), WIPO works on policy recommendations and harmonisation efforts that address these disparities, aiming to provide clarity and predictability for innovators and patent offices around the world. Generally, SCP examines various aspects of patents, including exceptions to patent rights, patent quality, the role of patents in health, confidentiality issues, and the impact of patents on technology transfer.[560]

In September 2023, the 8th WIPO Dialogue on GAI and Intellectual Property convened over 2,000 industry experts and global professionals from 160 nations.[561] The event focused on current developments in GAI, including the role of LLMs in stimulating AI-driven creativity, the methodologies used to train machine-learning models, and the implications of AI-generated content on IP rights. Discussions spanned from practical applications like enhancing efficiency in IP offices using AI to addressing intricate ethical and philosophical dilemmas. WIPO also highlighted unresolved issues concerning the attribution and ownership of copyright for AI-assisted creations.[562] Despite these discussions, a definitive stance on copyright, patent ownership, and authorship specific to LLMs remains unsettled.

Despite holding multi-tasked dialogues at different times in different cities by WIPO, the institution has not yet explicitly endorsed a definitive stance on the patentability of AI-generated content, as this remains a highly debated topic among its Member States. Their focus is on discussions to establish best practices. Accordingly, WIPO recognises the complexities and implications of AI in IP law, and it acknowledges that traditional IP frameworks, which typically require human inventorship or authorship, are challenged by AI's capabilities.[563] Accordingly, most jurisdictions represented within WIPO do not allow AI to be listed as an inventor or author, requiring a natural person to be designated instead.[564]

In summary, WIPO's role in the debate on the patentability of AI-generated content is multifaceted, encompassing research, policy dialogue, and international harmonisation efforts. Nonetheless, WIPO has not yet provided formal guidelines on copyright, patent ownership, or authorship for AI and LLMs like ChatGPT. Since 2018, WIPO's Standing Committee on Copyright and Related Rights has explored the impact of AI on the creative sector.[565] A 2022 report raised questions about the copyright ownership of AI-generated works and their patentability.[566] In 2023, WIPO experts

560. World Intellectual Property Organization, *Standing Committee on the Law of Patents (SCP)*, https://www.wipo.int/policy/en/scp/ (accessed 3 Aug. 2024).
561. *See supra* n. 529.
562. *Ibid.*
563. World Intellectual Property Organization (WIPO), *8th WIPO Conversation Wraps Up, Igniting Discussions on Generative AI's Impact on Intellectual Property* (2023), https://www.wipo.int/about-ip/en/frontier_technologies/news/2023/news_0002.html.
564. Ryan Abbott, *The Artificial Inventor Project*, World Intellectual Property Organization (WIPO) (18 Jun. 2019), https://www.wipo.int/wipo_magazine/en/2019/06/article_0002.html.
565. World Intellectual Property Organization, *Standing Committee on Copyright and Related Rights (SCCR)*, https://www.wipo.int/policy/en/sccr/ (accessed 2 Aug. 2024).
566. World Intellectual Property Organization, *World Intellectual Property Report 2022: The Direction of Innovation* (2022), https://www.wipo.int/edocs/pubdocs/en/wipo-pub-944-2022-en-world-intellectual-property-report-2022.pdf.

noted that AI can produce works indistinguishable from those created by humans, challenging traditional concepts of authorship.[567]

Despite its observations and monitoring, WIPO has not yet reached any conclusions on these issues, but it is committed to continuing to monitor the development of AI and its implications for IP law. Therefore, WIPO continues to facilitate discussions and studies to explore the evolving relationship between AI and IP, aiming to guide international consensus and policy development in this rapidly advancing field.

6.4 CONCLUSION

The rapid advancement of LLMs like ChatGPT has sparked complex debates around IP rights and the patentability of AI-generated content. Current legal frameworks across major jurisdictions generally require human inventorship for patent protection, creating challenges for inventions autonomously generated by AI systems. For example, US rules require human involvement for inventorship, creating uncertainties about the patentability of AI-generated inventions.[568] This means that copyright ownership is tied to the human author, who is always the first rights holder.[569]

While some countries like South Africa and Australia have taken steps to recognise AI as inventors, most nations maintain that only human inventors can be named on patent applications.[570] Other major nations, including Russia, France, Germany, Japan, South Korea, and India, have not yet issued any official guidance or ruling on the issue of AI inventorship.[571] This stance poses a challenge for AI-generated work, as identifying a human inventor or explaining the AI system's creative process may prove difficult or impossible.[572]

AI systems might generate content resembling existing works, such as songs, images, or texts, raising the potential risk of infringing on the IP rights of the original creators, especially if the AI system incorporates their works in its training data. To address this risk, users and developers of AI systems should ensure they possess the required licenses or permissions and rely on fair use or other legal exceptions

567. *See supra* n. 564.
568. Dylan Walsh, *The Legal Issues Presented by Generative AI*, MIT Sloan Management Review (28 Aug. 2023), https://mitsloan.mit.edu/ideas-made-to-matter/legal-issues-presented-generative-ai.
569. For European copyright law, *see, e.g.*, Ger. Copyright Act §7; Fr. Intellectual Property Code (IPC) Art. L111-1; Aust. Copyright Act §10(1); and for Swiss law, Copyright Act Art. 6.
570. Luis Monzon, *SA First Country in the World to Award a Patent to Invention Made by AI*, IT News Africa (3 Aug. 2021), https://www.itnewsafrica.com/2021/08/sa-first-country-in-the-world-to-award-a-patent-to-invention-made-by-ai/; Alexandra Jones, *Artificial Intelligence Can Now Be Recognised as an Inventor After Historic Australian Court Decision*, CNN News (1 Aug. 2021), https://www.abc.net.au/news/2021-08-01/historic-decision-allows-ai-to-be-recognised-as-an-inventor/100339264.
571. TechHQ, *Countries Are Divided on AI Machines That 'Invent' Things* (9 Sep. 2021), https://techhq.com/2021/09/countries-are-divided-on-ai-machines-that-invent-things-should-they-be-given-patent-rights/.
572. Francina Cantatore, *Creative Machines: AI and IP Rights in Digital Authorship and Patentable Inventions*, Faculty of Law, Centre for Professional Legal Education (2024), https://research.bond.edu.au/en/publications/creative-machines-ai-and-ip-rights-in-digital-authorship-and-pate.

applicable in their jurisdiction.[573] There should be a new theoretical framework for RAI implementation, emphasising a synergistic business-technology approach to streamline AI adoption with a focus on human-centred design and trust throughout the entire co-creation process.[574]

The issues surrounding copyright for AI-generated works are equally complex. Most jurisdictions tie copyright ownership to human authorship, raising questions about how to handle content created solely by AI systems. There are concerns about potential copyright infringement when AI models are trained on copyrighted data. As AI capabilities continue to expand, policymakers and courts are grappling with balancing the need to incentivise AI development while protecting the rights of human creators. Some argue for extending copyright protection to AI-generated works, while others contend this is unnecessary and could require fundamental changes to existing IP systems. While there are arguments in favour of copyright protection for AI-generated works, they are generally considered unconvincing. Some scholars argue that incentivising the use of AI systems does not necessitate extending copyright protection to their output.[575]

Moving forward, a coordinated global approach will likely be needed to address the challenges posed by AI to IP regimes. Organisations like WIPO facilitate international dialogues to explore these issues, but a clear consensus has yet to emerge. As AI becomes increasingly integral to innovation across industries, adapting legal and regulatory frameworks to accommodate AI-generated inventions and creative works while safeguarding human IP rights will be crucial. This will require ongoing collaboration between policymakers, legal experts, AI developers, and other stakeholders to craft nuanced solutions that foster RAI innovation while upholding the core principles of IP protection. The coming years will likely see continued evolution in this space as nations and international bodies work to strike an appropriate balance.

573. Gil Appel et al., *Generative AI Has an Intellectual Property Problem*, Harvard Business Review (7 Apr. 2023), https://hbr.org/2023/04/generative-ai-has-an-intellectual-property-problem.
574. Dian Tjondronegoro et al., *Responsible AI Implementation: A Human-Centered Framework for Accelerating the Innovation Process*, arXiv preprint arXiv:2209.07076 (2022), https://arxiv.org/ftp/arxiv/papers/2209/2209.07076.pdf.
575. Germany National Group, *Copyright in Artificially Generated Works*, AIPPI Q269 (2019), https://aippi.soutron.net/Portal/Default/en-GB/RecordView/Index/254 (accessed 3 Aug. 2024).

CHAPTER 7
ChatGPT and Healthcare Systems

7.1 INTRODUCTION

LLMs, such as ChatGPT, which are driven by advanced NLP algorithms, have significant potential to impact a wide range of industries, including healthcare. These models can aid in medical documentation, respond to patient inquiries, and enhance communication between healthcare providers and patients.[576] Specifically, ChatGPT has a wide range of applications in healthcare systems, including disease diagnosis, personalised medicine, patient education, mental health support, remote patient monitoring, drug discovery, clinical trial matching, electronic health record management, symptom evaluation, health counselling, telemedicine, online pharmacy services, and medical image analysis.[577] Nevertheless, integrating LLMs in healthcare presents regulatory challenges requiring the ethical, legal, and safe use of these technologies. This chapter primarily focuses on two key issues: (a) regulatory challenges associated with LLMs like ChatGPT in healthcare and (b) the regulation of LLMs to ensure safety, privacy, and ethical considerations in healthcare.

7.2 HEALTHCARE REGULATORY CHALLENGES IN AI GOVERNANCE

While LLMs offer significant healthcare benefits, their integration into clinical settings faces substantial regulatory challenges, necessitating careful attention to ethical, legal,

576. Leyao Wang et al., *A Systematic Review of ChatGPT and Other Conversational Large Language Models in Healthcare*, medRxiv (27 Apr. 2024), https://www.medrxiv.org/content/10.1101/2024.04.26.24306390v1.full.pdf; Ye-Jean Park et al., *Assessing the Research Landscape and Clinical Utility of Large Language Models: A Scoping Review*, 24 BMC Med. Inform. Decis. Mak., 72 (2024), https://doi.org/10.1186/s12911-024-02459-6.
577. Shiavax J. Rao et al., *ChatGPT: A Conceptual Review of Applications and Utility in the Field of Medicine*, 48 J. Med. Syst. 59 (2024). https://doi.org/10.1007/s10916-024-02075-x; Tirth Dave et al., *ChatGPT in Medicine: An Overview of Its Applications, Advantages, Limitations, Future Prospects, and Ethical Considerations, Frontiers in Artificial Intelligence*, 6 Section Medicine and Public Health (4 May 2023), https://doi.org/10.3389/frai.2023.1169595.

and secure utilisation. These challenges are multifaceted, encompassing issues such as accuracy and verifiability, data quality and privacy, transparency and explainability, bias and fairness, clinical oversight and accountability, socio-cultural impacts, and the delicate balance between innovation and regulation.

7.2.1 Accuracy and Verifiability

LLMs can assist medical professionals and researchers by generating and summarising text, correcting errors, and saving time in medical and academic writing. They enhance grammar, readability, and clarity, helping to convert manuscripts into different journal formats. Additionally, LLMs can rephrase complex information for patient-friendly communication in clinical settings.[578] Moreover, LLMs like ChatGPT can capture the vast medical knowledge base and provide personalised feedback to doctors and patients, potentially improving patient outcomes and reducing healthcare costs. By analysing large amounts of medical data, LLMs can enhance patient care and medical decision-making by providing up-to-date information and guidelines. Moreover, LLMs can make healthcare more accessible, scalable, and efficient, especially in resource-limited settings.[579]

Nonetheless, LLMs are trained on vast amounts of data, often encompassing medical literature, clinical records, and patient interactions. While this extensive training provides LLMs with a broad knowledge base, the quality and accuracy of this data can vary significantly. Inconsistent data sources, incomplete or outdated information, and inherent biases in the data can all lead to inaccuracies and errors in LLM outputs. Moreover, LLMs can generate fabricated information, perpetuate biases, present false information as truth, and replace human judgment, posing risks to patient safety, fairness, credibility, and the doctor-patient relationship.

Recent studies have investigated the diagnostic capabilities of ChatGPT-4 in the context of both common and rare diseases, including those within the field of rheumatology. In a recent study, Krusche et al. found that ChatGPT-4 outperformed rheumatologists in identifying inflammatory rheumatic diseases (IRD) in terms of sensitivity, although it did not surpass them in specificity. The overall accuracy rate of ChatGPT-4 was 71%, compared to 62% for the rheumatologists.[580] However, ChatGPT-4 demonstrated a higher false-positive rate in certain cases. In another study, researchers assessed ChatGPT-4's diagnostic accuracy for both common and rare diseases, showing that it was effective in providing accurate diagnoses across both categories. The study found that ChatGPT-4 correctly diagnosed 90% of cases,

578. Meskó, B., *The Impact of Multimodal Large Language Models on Health Care's Future*, 25 Journal of Medical Internet Research, e52865 (2023), https://doi.org/10.2196/52865.
579. *See supra* n. 200.
580. Martin Krusche et al., *Diagnostic Accuracy of a Large Language Model in Rheumatology: Comparison of Physician and ChatGPT-4*, 44 Rheumatol. Int., 303–06 (2024), https://doi.org/10.1007/s00296-023-05464-6.

including both common and rare diseases, but this accuracy was achieved only when considering the top eight diagnostic suggestions provided by the model.[581]

While ChatGPT-assisted diagnosis offers the potential for enhancing access, efficiency, and accuracy in healthcare, it also introduces significant ethical, legal, and social challenges. The limitations and risks of this technology, such as the lack of explainability, accountability, and reliability, necessitate thorough evaluation and careful consideration before it can be widely adopted.[582] These findings highlight the potential of LLMs in healthcare. However, experts warn about their limitations and stress the necessity for further research and ethical considerations before broad implementation. Additionally, all studies advised against the use of ChatGPT by non-professionals due to the risks of providing false reassurance or causing unnecessary anxiety. Therefore, ensuring accuracy and verifiability is crucial for deploying LLMs, such as ChatGPT, in healthcare settings.

Above all, before their integration into healthcare, LLMs such as ChatGPT require thorough clinical validation and ethical assessment. Users should be mindful of the limitations and potential risks of LLMs, always verifying generated content with reliable sources and human experts. It is also crucial to note that LLMs are designed to augment and assist human doctors, not to replace them, aiming to enhance the overall quality of healthcare provision.

7.2.2 Data Quality and Privacy

Data quality and privacy are critical challenges when employing LLMs like ChatGPT in healthcare settings. LLMs rely on vast amounts of text data, which may contain inaccuracies, biases, or sensitive information. Additionally, LLMs can produce text based on probabilities and patterns rather than factual evidence.[583] This context poses substantial risks to the accuracy, reliability, and trustworthiness of LLM outputs, especially in fields like biomedicine and healthcare, where rigorous quality and ethical standards are crucial. Current literature has identified several data quality and privacy issues associated with LLMs, such as ChatGPT, when utilised in healthcare settings. These include data errors and biases, sensitive data exposure, fact-based versus probabilistic outputs, fabricated information, and data protection and compliance.

LLMs rely on massive amounts of medical data for training, which may contain errors, inconsistencies, or biases. These imperfections can significantly impact the quality and reliability of LLM outputs, potentially leading to inaccurate or misleading information. Moreover, LLMs may generate hallucinations, which are false or irrelevant facts that lack support from the underlying data. Additionally, LLMs may exhibit biases stemming from the demographics, language, or diverse cultures, potentially

581. Pooja Toshniwal Paharia, *ChatGPT: A Diagnostic Sidekick for Doctors? Caution Advised for Non-Professionals,* News Medical (27 Apr. 2023), https://www.news-medical.net/news/20230427/ChatGPT-A-diagnostic-sidekick-for-doctors-Caution-advised-for-non-professionals.aspx.
582. Ruth Hailu et al., *ChatGPT-Assisted Diagnosis: Is the Future Suddenly Here?,* STAT (13 Feb. 2023), https://www.statnews.com/2023/02/13/chatgpt-assisted-diagnosis/.
583. Ilan S. Schwartz et al., *Black Box Warning: Large Language Models and the Future of Infectious Diseases Consultation,* 78 Clin. Infect. Dis. 860 (2024), https://doi.org/10.1093/cid/ciad633.

resulting in unfair or discriminatory outcomes.[584] Therefore, ensuring the quality and diversity of the training data is paramount, along with rigorous validation and monitoring of LLM outputs.

LLMs receive training on massive patient' datasets, records, and other personal information, often considered sensitive and confidential. Addressing this challenge requires implementing robust privacy and security measures, including encryption and data de-identification, to protect patients' personal information. Open-source LLMs provide cost-effectiveness and customisation benefits but carry the risk of data leakage or misuse due to their easy accessibility and modifiability by anyone. Hence, responsible and effective LLM utilisation in healthcare demands ethical guidelines, regulations, and comprehensive education for both healthcare professionals and patients.[585]

LLMs are based on probabilistic models, meaning they generate outputs based on the likelihood of occurrence rather than definitive factual evidence.[586] This probabilistic nature can pose challenges for healthcare professionals, who often rely on facts and certainty to make informed decisions. LLMs may generate grammatically correct and coherent outputs while disregarding factual accuracy or contextual relevance. Moreover, LLMs may generate outputs that are contradictory or inconsistent, both internally within a single response and when compared to previous outputs. Therefore, providing clear and transparent explanations for LLM outputs is crucial, along with verification and cross-checking against other reliable sources of information.

Gartner has identified six risks associated with ChatGPT, including fabricated and inaccurate answers, data privacy and confidentiality, model and output bias, IP and copyright risks, cyber fraud risks, and consumer protection risks.[587] Among these, the tendency to provide incorrect or fabricated information is perhaps the most common issue with LLMs, especially in healthcare settings. This situation occurs when LLMs generate text that is not supported by the underlying data. Such fabricated information can be highly misleading and even harmful, as it could alter the outcome of clinical decisions. For instance, an LLM employed to generate a literature review for a medical systematic review might introduce false or incomplete information, potentially leading to an incorrect clinical decision.

Furthermore, data privacy and confidentiality are paramount concerns with ChatGPT and other LLMs. Information entered by ChatGPT can become part of its training dataset, potentially leading to unintended disclosure in future responses. Therefore, legal and compliance leaders should establish a framework for ChatGPT use, prohibiting the entry of sensitive data into public LLMs. Nonetheless, ensuring adherence to data protection regulations remains challenging due to the inherent complexity of LLMs and the varied ways in which they are utilised.

584. *See supra* n. 311.
585. Karen O'Leary, *LLMs Get a Medical Education: A Large Language Model Designed to Give High-Quality Answers to Medical Questions Outperforms Previous Iterations: But Remains Inferior to Clinicians*, Nature Medicine (24 Jul. 2023), https://www.nature.com/articles/d41591-023-00064-0.
586. Xuming Hu et al., *Do Large Language Models Know about Facts?*, arXiv preprint arXiv:2310.05177 (8 Oct. 2023), https://arxiv.org/pdf/2310.05177.
587. *See supra* n. 334.

LLMs, including ChatGPT, must operate within the confines of applicable data protection and compliance laws like the Health Insurance Portability and Accountability Act of 1996 (HIPAA)[588] and GDPR,[589] which mandate adherence to principles, including transparency, fairness and lawfulness, data minimisation, purpose specification, storage minimisation, and user consent to protect individuals' privacy rights. Nevertheless, LLMs may struggle to provide clear explanations for their outputs and track data provenance, hindering transparency and raising legal and ethical concerns. Therefore, rigorous evaluation and verification of LLM outputs are crucial to ensure their accuracy and reliability.

7.2.3 Transparency and Explainability

LLMs like ChatGPT have significant potential to transform healthcare through applications in diagnostics, treatment, research, and patient care. Nonetheless, incorporating these advanced tools into sensitive healthcare environments necessitates addressing substantial challenges related to transparency and explainability. Given that LLMs are trained on extensive datasets, their decision-making processes can be opaque, complicating efforts to understand how they generate their conclusions. This lack of transparency hinders trust and accountability, exacerbates existing disparities, and discourages adoption and innovation, ultimately hindering their potential to revolutionise healthcare.

Transparency refers to making the model's internal processes and decision-making mechanisms accessible to users. Transparency in ML seeks to clarify the functioning of ML models for various stakeholders. This includes procedural transparency, which involves making information like code, model details, and datasets publicly available. Algorithmic transparency goes further by exposing the model's behaviour and internal workings, allowing stakeholders to understand, improve, and even challenge predictions.[590] This open access to information empowers various parties to understand, improve, and even contest the predictions made by the model.

Explainability, on the other hand, involves providing clear and interpretable reasoning for the model's outputs. This enables users to assess the validity of LLM outputs and identify potential biases or errors. While explainability aims to provide understandable reasoning for a model's behaviour, solely understanding its specific actions might not be enough for stakeholders to determine if the model is wrong or lacks the necessary information to solve the task.[591] In healthcare, where decisions can

588. Health Insurance Portability and Accountability Act of 1996 (HIPAA), Centres for Disease Control & Prevention, https://www.cdc.gov/phlp/php/resources/health-insurance-portability-and-accountability-act-of-1996-hipaa.html (accessed 2 Aug. 2024).
589. *See supra* n. 397.
590. Umang Bhatt et al., Explainable Machine Learning in Deployment, in *Proceedings of the 2020 Conference on Fairness, Accountability, and Transparency* 648 (2020), https://arxiv.org/pdf/1909.06342.pdf.
591. Umang Bhatt et al., *Uncertainty as a Form of Transparency: Measuring, Communicating, and Using Uncertainty,* in *Proceedings of the 2021 AAAI/ACM Conference on AI, Ethics, and Society* 401, 401–413 (21 Jul. 2021), https://dl.acm.org/doi/pdf/10.1145/3461702.3462571.

have life-altering consequences, clinicians, patients, and regulatory bodies need to comprehend how LLMs generate recommendations or diagnoses. Nevertheless, the 'black box' nature of these models raises concerns about accountability and reliability.

Achieving transparency and explainability in LLMs is not only a technical challenge but also raises ethical and regulatory considerations. Patients and healthcare professionals have the right to understand the basis of decisions made by these models. Moreover, regulatory frameworks may demand transparent AI systems, especially in healthcare, where accountability is paramount. Hence, researchers are actively exploring techniques to enhance the transparency and explainability of LLMs. This includes developing interpretable architectures, generating model explanations, and implementing techniques to trace model decisions back to specific input features.[592] These strategies aim to bridge the gap between the technical complexity of LLMs and the need for human-understandable outputs.

Achieving transparency and explainability in LLMs necessitates a multifaceted approach. One effective strategy involves enabling LLMs to articulate their reasoning and provide evidence through numerous techniques, such as attention visualisation and counterfactual explanations, and enhancing trust and accountability. Additionally, employing diverse training datasets curated in collaboration with healthcare professionals helps mitigate bias and ensures the accuracy of outputs. Frameworks that clearly explain LLM outputs for healthcare professionals, while incorporating human-in-the-loop (HITL) methodologies and integrating these outputs with existing clinical decision support systems, have the potential to enhance informed decision-making in medical practice. Finally, establishing transparent ethical guidelines and regulations addressing data privacy, transparency, accountability, and fairness is essential for the responsible development, deployment, and use of LLMs in healthcare.

7.2.4 Bias and Fairness

LLMs like ChatGPT have been increasingly employed in healthcare to assist with various tasks, including diagnosis, treatment planning, and patient communication. However, these models are not without challenges, particularly regarding bias and fairness. Biases inherent in LLMs can lead to inaccurate or unreliable outputs, which may result in serious consequences in healthcare settings. This raises ethical concerns and highlights the need for careful consideration when integrating these models into clinical practice.

A study by Ferrara et al. underscores the challenges and risks posed by biases in LLMs like ChatGPT. The authors examine the sources of these biases, which may originate from various factors, including the nature of the training data, model architecture, algorithmic limitations, product design, and policy decisions. They also delve into the ethical concerns arising from the unintended consequences of biased

592. AST Consulting, *Analyzing LLMs: Interpretability and Explainability*, https://astconsulting.in/artificial-intelligence/nlp-natural-language-processing/llm/analyzing-llms-interpretability-and-explainability/.

outputs produced by these models. The study highlights the necessity of a multidisciplinary, collaborative approach to developing AI systems that are more equitable, transparent, and responsible, aiming to expand their applications while minimising unintended harms.[593]

Another study by Zhang et al. found that ChatGPT and other LLMs exhibit biases reflective of their training data.[594] One of the primary sources of bias in LLMs is the training data itself. Consequently, the performance of ChatGPT and other LLMs mirrors the biases present in the available text. For example, ChatGPT is known to perpetuate stereotypes such as nurses being female and doctors being male, a bias derived from its training data. The study also emphasises the importance of having more diverse and representative training data to mitigate biases in LLMs.

Some authors propose a framework for creating reliable, trustworthy, and unbiased models as a necessary condition for their adoption in healthcare. The framework focuses on the quantification, validation, and mitigation of hallucinations in the context of healthcare.[595] To address bias and fairness challenges, researchers have proposed various other strategies too. For instance, Guidotti et al. suggested the use of debiasing techniques, such as re-sampling and re-weighting, to mitigate biases in healthcare data.[596] Additionally, Beutel et al. discussed the integration of fairness-aware ML techniques, which can play a crucial role in improving fairness by explicitly considering fairness metrics during model training.[597]

In essence, ensuring fairness and mitigating bias in LLMs is critical for developing ethical and reliable healthcare models. This requires diverse and representative training datasets, achieved through collaboration with diverse healthcare professionals and data scientists. Various debiasing techniques, like data augmentation and fairness-aware training, help identify and correct biases. Additionally, enhancing transparency and explainability through techniques like attention visualisation is crucial for addressing bias. Finally, comprehensive ethical guidelines and regulations are essential to govern the development, deployment, and use of LLMs in healthcare, addressing issues like data privacy, fairness, and accountability.

7.2.5 Clinical Oversight and Accountability

ChatGPT, as an LLM, exhibits significant proficiency in generating natural language text across various domains, including medical applications. Trained on extensive datasets that include medical literature and dialogues, ChatGPT has demonstrated

593. Shania Kennedy, *Researchers Highlight Pros and Cons of ChatGPT in Clinical Radiology*, TechTarget (1 Jun. 2023), https://www.techtarget.com/healthtechanalytics/news/366590246/Researchers-Highlight-Pros-and-Cons-of-ChatGPT-in-Clinical-Radiology.
594. *See supra* n. 249.
595. Muhammad Aurangzeb Ahmad et al., *Creating Trustworthy LLMs: Dealing with Hallucinations in Healthcare AI*, arXiv preprint arXiv:2311.01463 (26 Sep. 2023), https://arxiv.org/pdf/2311.01463.
596. Emanuele Guidotti & David Ardia, *COVID-19 Data Hub*, 5 J. Open Source Software 51, 2376 (2020), https://doi.org/10.21105/joss.02376.
597. Alex Beutel et al., Putting Fairness Principles into Practice: Challenges, Metrics, and Improvements, in *Proceedings of the 2019 AAAI/ACM Conference on AI, Ethics, and Society* 453 (2019).

capabilities in tasks such as passing medical exams, producing scientific articles, and drafting clinical reports. However, integrating ChatGPT into healthcare settings introduces significant challenges and concerns, particularly in the areas of clinical oversight and accountability.

While ChatGPT and similar LLMs have the potential to improve healthcare and enhance patients' quality of life, this potential can only be realised within a regulatory framework that emphasises the augmentation of human expertise rather than its replacement.[598] There is a risk that these models may generate inaccurate, misleading, or harmful information, which could negatively impact patient care and outcomes. Therefore, all outputs generated by ChatGPT must be thoroughly reviewed and verified by qualified clinicians before being utilised for diagnosis, treatment, or research purposes. Furthermore, the issue of liability for errors or damages resulting from ChatGPT's advice or recommendations remains unclear, particularly if such outputs are not disclosed to or consented to by patients.

ChatGPT is also not HIPAA compliant,[599] which means that it may expose sensitive patient data to unauthorised parties or use it for further training without permission. This implies that ChatGPT might use patient information processed by its language model without consent, potentially violating HIPAA rules. Such actions could lead to legal issues and harm the reputation of healthcare organisations using ChatGPT. To prevent this, it is recommended not to use ChatGPT with any electronic patient health information (ePHI) unless OpenAI agrees to a business associate agreement and ensures HIPAA compliance.

Furthermore, ChatGPT may affect the social and humanistic aspects of health care, such as the doctor-patient relationship, the quality of communication, and the trust and empathy between the parties involved.[600] ChatGPT may create a sense of detachment, impersonality, or deception, especially if the patients are not aware that they are interacting with an AI system. ChatGPT may also lack the emotional and cultural sensitivity, contextual awareness, and ethical reasoning that are essential for effective and compassionate health care. Above all, ChatGPT may pose numerous ethical challenges for its users, including the generation of misleading or false information (hallucination), the dissemination of misinformation, copyright infringement, the perpetuation of biases, data privacy issues, and challenges for sustainable development.[601]

To address these challenges, ChatGPT's outputs should respect the dignity, autonomy, and privacy of the patients, and they should be aligned with the ethical principles and standards of health care, such as beneficence, non-maleficence, and

598. *Will ChatGPT Transform Healthcare?*, 29 Nature Medicine 505–506 (2023), https://www.nature.com/articles/s41591-023-02289-5.
599. Steve Alder, *Is ChatGPT HIPAA Compliant?*, The HIPAA Journal, https://www.hipaajournal.com/is-chatgpt-hipaa-compliant/.
600. Changyu Wang et al., *Ethical Considerations of Using ChatGPT in Health Care*, 25 J. Med. Internet Res. e48009 (2023), https://doi.org/10.2196/48009.
601. Shangying Hua et al., *The Limitations and Ethical Considerations of ChatGPT*, 6 Data Intelligence 201, 201–239 (2024), https://doi.org/10.1162/dint_a_00243.

justice.[602] Moreover, establishing clear guidelines and accountability structures is essential to ensure that the use of LLMs in healthcare does not compromise patient safety or the integrity of medical practice.

7.2.6 Social and Cultural Impacts

The integration of LLMs like ChatGPT in healthcare has brought forth a myriad of social and cultural impacts that necessitate careful consideration. The introduction of LLMs has the potential to reshape the dynamics of doctor-patient relationships. Patients may find themselves interacting with AI-driven models for preliminary information, impacting the traditional rapport-building process.[603] This shift poses challenges in maintaining the humanistic aspects of healthcare, emphasising the need for further research on the emotional and psychological impact of AI interactions in medical settings.

The cultural nuances embedded in patient-doctor communication may not always be fully understood by LLMs, raising concerns about the potential for misinterpretation or insensitivity. Cultural sensitivity is a fundamental component of equitable and effective healthcare. It fosters inclusive care that honours the cultural beliefs and practices of patients, ultimately improving health outcomes for diverse populations. By adopting a cultural respect framework, healthcare providers and systems can better understand and address the needs of patients from different backgrounds, ensuring equitable access to high-quality care.[604]

Furthermore, the potential for LLMs to perpetuate biases based on their training data is a significant concern. Studies have indicated that biases present in the training data can be reflected in AI outputs, leading to biased outputs that unfairly disadvantage certain groups, often those historically marginalised.[605] Such a bias may exacerbate existing health disparities and contribute to inequities in healthcare outcomes. Addressing AI bias requires a comprehensive socio-technical approach that considers the social and technical dimensions of AI systems. This approach necessitates collaboration among experts from various fields, including engineering, social science, and community representatives. By incorporating diverse perspectives, these approaches can help develop AI systems that are fair, responsible, and aligned with societal values.[606]

602. Keymanthri, M. & Rennie, S., *ChatGPT: Legal and Ethical Challenges for Healthcare and Medical Research*, Globely News (August 2024), https://globelynews.com/world/chatgpt-ai-ethics-healthcare/.
603. John Kuhn, *AI and LLMs: The Future Of Healthcare Data Interoperability*, Forbes Tech Council (20 Jun. 2023), https://www.forbes.com/sites/forbestechcouncil/2023/06/20/ai-and-large-language-models-the-future-of-healthcare-data-interoperability/?sh=468dda0367dc.
604. US Dep't of Health & Hum. Servs., Nat'l Insts. of Health, *Cultural Respect*, NIH.gov, https://www.nih.gov/institutes-nih/nih-office-director/office-communications-public-liaison/clear-communication/cultural-respect (accessed 3 Aug. 2024).
605. Lorenzo Belenguer, *AI Bias: Exploring Discriminatory Algorithmic Decision-Making Models and the Application of Possible Machine-Centric Solutions Adapted from the Pharmaceutical Industry*, 2 AI Ethics 771 (2022), https://doi.org/10.1007/s43681-022-00138-8.
606. Reva Schwartz, *There's More to AI Bias Than Biased Data, NIST Report Highlights*, Nat'l Inst. of Standards & Tech. (3 Mar. 2022), https://www.nist.gov/news-events/news/2022/03/theres-more-ai-bias-biased-data-nist-report-highlights.

The deployment of LLMs in healthcare exacerbates existing power imbalances between patients and healthcare providers, potentially diminishing patient autonomy. Patients may not fully understand the implications of interacting with an AI system or may unknowingly share sensitive information.[607] The lack of transparency in LLM decision-making processes can hinder patient trust and make it difficult for patients to understand the rationale behind AI-generated recommendations. Therefore, it becomes essential for healthcare providers and developers to establish clear communication channels and educational resources to ensure patients are well-informed about the nature, purpose, and potential risks associated with interacting with LLMs. Additionally, patients should be informed about the use of AI in their healthcare, enabling them to make informed decisions about their involvement.

Furthermore, the potential for LLMs to alter communication styles and preferences in healthcare settings could impact the broader social fabric. The incorporation of AI-driven communication may lead to changes in patient expectations and, consequently, the delivery of healthcare services. The social implications of such shifts warrant in-depth examination to ensure that advancements in technology align with societal values and preferences.[608] The growing reliance on AI-driven communication in healthcare could reshape the patient-provider dynamic, potentially influencing patient trust and satisfaction. Above all, the integration of AI-powered communication tools may alter healthcare workflows and resource distribution, requiring careful assessment of their impact on healthcare professionals.

In conclusion, the integration of LLMs in healthcare presents a complex interplay of social and cultural considerations. While LLMs hold promise for enhancing healthcare accessibility and efficiency, they also pose challenges to maintaining humanistic care, ensuring cultural sensitivity, and addressing potential biases. To navigate these complexities effectively, a comprehensive approach is necessary, encompassing ongoing research, collaboration among diverse stakeholders, and robust ethical frameworks. Ongoing research and engagement with diverse communities are essential to evaluate the social implications of AI-facilitated communication in healthcare, ensuring equitable and inclusive healthcare delivery. By carefully considering the social and cultural dimensions of LLMs, healthcare can harness their benefits while mitigating potential risks, ensuring equitable and inclusive healthcare delivery.

7.2.7 Innovation and Regulation of LLMs like ChatGPT in Healthcare

LLMs like ChatGPT have the transformative potential to revolutionise healthcare by providing swift and accurate responses to patient queries. LLMs have the potential to reshape healthcare delivery by enhancing clinical efficiency and improving patient

607. Amy Scharf et al., *What Should Clinicians Do When a Patient's Autonomy Undermines Her Being Treated Equitably?*, 24 J. Ethics 123 (2024) https://doi.org/10.1001/amajethics.2021.97.
608. Abukari Kwame & Pammla M. Petrucka, *A Literature-Based Study of Patient-Centered Care and Communication in Nurse-Patient Interactions: Barriers, Facilitators, and the Way Forward*, 20 BMC Nurs. 158 (2021), https://doi.org/10.1186/s12912-021-00684-2.

outcomes.[609] These technologies can also improve communication in healthcare by simplifying medical language, especially for sensitive topics. Furthermore, LLMs can aid in detecting abnormalities, assist in diagnosis, and provide additional context for healthcare settings. Nevertheless, the integration of LLMs in healthcare presents significant regulatory and innovation challenges that demand meticulous consideration.

LLMs may struggle to effectively communicate their reasoning, especially when dealing with intricate medical concepts. This situation poses the risk of misinterpretation, potentially leading to devastating consequences.[610] Despite efforts to enhance interpretability, ensuring clear and accurate communication in healthcare remains a persistent challenge. The need for user-friendly interfaces and plain language outputs becomes crucial for effective interaction. To mitigate the risks associated with misinterpretation, developers must prioritise human-centric design principles, ensuring LLMs communicate their reasoning clearly and transparently. Additionally, providing users access to explanations and justifications behind LLM outputs can foster trust and confidence in their accuracy.

Many LLM applications in healthcare are in their early stages, lacking rigorous real-world testing. Concerns about their effectiveness and safety persist, emphasising the need for more robust testing and validation. Therefore, two recent studies, one conducted by Sara Monti et al. and the other by Fang Liu and Demosthenes Panagiotakos, highlight the significance of real-world scenarios, patient outcomes, and extended validation to ensure the reliability and safety of LLMs in diverse healthcare settings. They also emphasise the need for a thorough evaluation of LLMs before the widespread adoption in healthcare.[611]

Furthermore, the use of LLMs in healthcare raises concerns about competition, potential displacement of human healthcare providers, IP rights, and cybersecurity. The ownership of data used to train LLMs and the algorithms generating responses requires careful consideration. The ethical implications of these considerations should be at the forefront to ensure the responsible deployment and use of LLMs in healthcare. To address data security, ownership, and content responsibility concerns with LLMs, developers need to use robust data security measures, follow ethical data governance practices and have clear guidelines and regulations in place.[612]

609. Eli Ben-Joseph, *The Impact of Large Language Models on Healthcare*, Forbes Tech Council (20 Jun. 2023), https://www.forbes.com/sites/forbestechcouncil/2023/06/20/the-impact-of-large-languages-models-on-healthcare/.
610. University of Oxford, *Tackling the Ethical Dilemma of Responsibility in Large Language Models* (5 May 2023), https://www.ox.ac.uk/news/2023-05-05-tackling-ethical-dilemma-responsibility-large-language-models.
611. Sara Monti et al., *Randomized Controlled Trials and Real-World Data: Differences and Similarities to Untangle Literature Data*, 57 Rheumatology (Suppl. 7) vii54 (2018), https://doi.org/10.1093/rheumatology/key109; Fang Liu & Demosthenes Panagiotakos, *Real-World Data: A Brief Review of the Methods, Applications, Challenges and Opportunities*, 22 BMC Med. Res. Methodol. 287 (2022), https://doi.org/10.1186/s12874-022-01768-6.
612. Ewa Janiszewska-Kiewra et al., *Ethical Data Usage in an Era of Digital Technology and Regulation*, McKinsey & Co. (26 Aug. 2020), https://www.mckinsey.com/capabilities/mckinsey-digital/our-insights/tech-forward/ethical-data-usage-in-an-era-of-digital-technology-and-regulation.

Above all, the fragmented global regulatory landscape for LLMs in healthcare presents challenges, hindering widespread adoption. International collaboration is imperative to develop harmonised regulations that balance innovation with patient safety and privacy. Regulatory frameworks must be agile and adaptable to the rapid evolution of LLMs, ensuring a dynamic approach that aligns with the evolving technological landscape. The ongoing dialogue between regulatory bodies, healthcare professionals, technologists, and policymakers is essential for creating adaptive frameworks that balance innovation with patient safety and privacy worldwide.[613] To collaborate worldwide, global regulatory bodies should create working groups with different stakeholders, including developers, healthcare professionals, and patients.

7.3 HEALTHCARE SAFETY, PRIVACY, AND ETHICS IN AI GOVERNANCE

Integrating LLMs into healthcare presents a new frontier of opportunity and challenge. While the potential benefits of LLMs, such as personalised medicine, improved patient care, and automated tasks, are undeniable, their application in such a sensitive domain raises critical questions about safety, security, and ethics. This sub-section explores these concerns and proposes potential solutions to ensure the responsible and ethical integration of LLMs in healthcare.

One of the primary concerns surrounding LLMs in healthcare is potential harm to patients due to errors in diagnosis, treatment recommendations, or other LLM-driven decisions. These errors can stem from biases in the data used to train the LLM, limitations in its capabilities, or misinterpretations of information. Scholars highlighted the need for rigorous testing and validation of LLM-powered healthcare technologies to ensure their safety and effectiveness in clinical settings.[614] Additionally, clear guidelines and protocols are essential to define how LLMs can be used with human expertise to minimise risks and optimise patient outcomes.

Further, it is essential to evaluate the accuracy, validity, and robustness of LLMs before deploying them in healthcare settings and to monitor their performance and impact over time. Additionally, it is important to ensure that LLMs are transparent and explainable, meaning that they can provide clear and understandable reasons for their outputs and can be audited and corrected if needed. Furthermore, it is crucial to ensure that LLMs are supervised and regulated by human experts, such as clinicians, researchers, and ethicists, who can oversee their use, provide feedback, and intervene when necessary.

The use of LLMs in healthcare introduces cybersecurity challenges due to the sensitivity of patient data. The risk of data breaches and cyberattacks underscores the

613. World Health Organization, *WHO Outlines Considerations for Regulation of Artificial Intelligence for Health* (19 Oct. 2023), https://www.who.int/news/item/19-10-2023-who-outlines-considerations-for-regulation-of-artificial-intelligence-for-health.
614. Emily A. Beam et al., *Loss Aversion or Lack of Trust: Why Does Loss Framing Work to Encourage Preventative Health Behaviors?*, National Bureau of Economic Research (March 2022), https://www.nber.org/papers/w29828.

importance of implementing robust security measures. Some scholars emphasise the importance of real-world scenarios and extended validation in diverse healthcare settings to ensure the reliability and safety of LLMs.[615] Moreover, implementing stringent security protocols is essential to safeguard patient information and maintain trust in the healthcare system.

This involves implementing appropriate technical and legal measures, such as encryption, anonymisation, consent, and data governance, to safeguard the data from hackers, competitors, or other malicious actors. Additionally, it is essential to respect the data rights and preferences of the data subjects, such as patients, clinicians, and researchers, who may have different expectations and concerns regarding the use of their data by LLMs. This requires establishing clear and informed consent mechanisms, providing opt-out options, and ensuring data accountability and transparency.

Integrating LLMs into healthcare also raises ethical concerns around informed consent, patient autonomy, and potential discrimination.[616] Patients should have enough information to understand how LLMs are used in their care and be able to refuse their involvement. Furthermore, algorithms trained on biased data can perpetuate existing inequalities in healthcare, leading to discriminatory outcomes for specific patient groups. Frameworks like the Belmont Report provide ethical guidelines for research involving human subjects, and adapting these frameworks to LLM-based healthcare applications is essential.[617] Furthermore, a collaborative approach between regulatory bodies, healthcare professionals, technologists, and the wider public is imperative to establish adaptive regulations that foster innovation while upholding ethical standards.

In essence, the applications of LLMs in healthcare offer transformative potential, but the journey requires a meticulous focus on safety, security, and ethical considerations. A multidisciplinary approach that involves stakeholders across various domains is crucial to strike the right balance between innovation and responsibility. As the field evolves, ongoing research, collaboration, and the development of clear regulatory frameworks will be instrumental in realising the full benefits of LLMs in enhancing patient care while ensuring safety, security, and ethical integrity in healthcare systems. By doing so, we can ensure that LLMs are used in a safe, secure, and ethical manner and that they serve the best interests of humanity.

7.4 CONCLUSION

LLMs like ChatGPT offer transformative potential in healthcare, from improving diagnosis and treatment planning to enhancing patient education and streamlining administrative tasks. Recent studies show that LLMs can greatly improve healthcare,

---

615. Fang Liu & Demosthenes Panagiotakos, *supra* n. 611.
616. Hanzhou Li et al., *Ethics of Large Language Models in Medicine and Medical Research*, The Lancet Digit. Health e333 (2023).
617. Department of Health, Education, and Welfare; National Commission for the Protection of Human Subjects of Biomedical and Behavioral Research, *The Belmont Report: Ethical Principles and Guidelines for the Protection of Human Subjects of Research*, 81 J. Am. Coll. Dent. 4 (2014) https://doi.org/10.1017/cbo9780511550089.028.

especially in understanding clinical language for tasks like identifying entities, extracting relationships, and answering questions.[618] Nonetheless, their integration necessitates careful navigation of regulatory landscapes to ensure ethical, legal, and safe utilisation. The regulatory landscape must evolve to address critical concerns such as data privacy, the accuracy of medical information, transparency in AI decision-making, the potential for bias, and ethical considerations. By addressing these issues, the power of advanced NLP algorithms can be leveraged to create a more efficient, effective, and accessible healthcare system, benefiting both providers and patients alike.

The challenges posed by LLMs in healthcare require robust regulatory frameworks and ongoing collaboration among stakeholders, including policymakers, healthcare providers, and technology developers. This collaborative effort should focus on establishing clear guidelines for clinical validation, implementing stringent data protection measures, enhancing model transparency and explainability, and mitigating potential biases to ensure equitable care. Moreover, maintaining human oversight in AI decision-making processes will be crucial to ensure patient safety and ethical standards.

While the potential of LLMs like ChatGPT to contribute significantly to improving healthcare outcomes is substantial, the regulatory landscape remains complex and fragmented.[619] This necessitates a delicate balance between fostering innovation and ensuring patient safety. The future of AI-augmented healthcare is promising, but it demands vigilance, continuous evaluation, and adaptive regulatory approaches to ensure that technological advancements truly serve the best interests of patients and society at large.

By prioritising patient safety, upholding ethical standards, and fostering a regulatory environment that supports responsible innovation, LLMs can be effectively integrated into healthcare systems. However, this integration must be accompanied by ongoing research, rigorous testing, and continuous monitoring to address emerging challenges and optimise the benefits of these technologies in healthcare settings.

618. Nazi, Z.A., & Peng, W., *Large Language Models in Healthcare and Medical Domain: A Review*, arXiv preprint arXiv:2401.06775 (12 Dec. 2023), https://arxiv.org/abs/2401.06775.
619. *See* Ye-Jean Park et al., *supra* n. 576.

CHAPTER 8

LLMs like ChatGPT and Financial Sector

8.1 INTRODUCTION

The rise of LLMs like ChatGPT has sparked a revolution across diverse industries, including the complex world of finance. These powerful tools offer the potential to optimise processes, improve decision-making, and revolutionise customer service. Nonetheless, their integration into the financial sector also raises significant concerns encompassing the field. This chapter delves into the intricate relationship between LLMs and the financial landscape, exploring both the immense opportunities and the critical challenges associated with their application in this sensitive domain. By conducting a thorough analysis, this chapter aims to shed light on the future of LLMs in finance, paving the way for responsible and ethical integration that fosters innovation while safeguarding trust and integrity.

8.2 REGULATORY CHALLENGES OF AI ADOPTION IN THE FINANCIAL INDUSTRY

LLMs like ChatGPT offer immense potential for the financial sector by automating routine tasks, enhancing customer service, and providing personalised financial advice. Nevertheless, integrating these powerful language models into a critical and regulated domain presents unique challenges. These challenges include explainability and transparency, bias and fairness, security and data privacy, regulatory compliance and ethical considerations, and operational challenges. These challenges require careful consideration from all stakeholders, adhering to regulatory compliance and ethical considerations, and overcoming operational hurdles. Additionally, fostering collaboration between LLM developers, financial institutions, and regulatory bodies is crucial for developing responsible and ethical frameworks for LLM deployment in finance. Furthermore, ensuring the robustness and accuracy of LLM outputs is vital for building trust and confidence in their use within the financial sector.

8.2.1 Explainability and Transparency

GAI like ChatGPT has immense potential to improve the efficiency and quality of various domains, including finance. Nonetheless, they may also pose significant challenges to explainability and transparency, especially in finance, where accuracy, accountability, and trust are crucial. Explainability refers to the ability to understand how and why an AI system produces a certain output or decision.[620] Transparency refers to the ability to access and verify the data, algorithms, and processes of an AI system.[621] Both explainability and transparency are vital for ensuring the reliability, fairness, and ethics of AI systems, and for complying with regulations and standards. Moreover, the lack of explainability raises concerns about accountability, trustworthiness, and the potential for biased or unintended outcomes.

One of the main challenges for the explainability and transparency of LLMs like ChatGPT is their complexity and opacity.[622] Deep neural networks, with millions or billions of parameters, form the core of LLMs, and their internal workings remain elusive even for experts. Moreover, the training data that are often heterogeneous, unstructured, and noisy further confuses tracing information sources and assessing quality.[623] Furthermore, LLM outputs are probabilistic, dynamic, and context-dependent, evolving with input, interactions, and external factors. These characteristics of LLMs create difficulty in grasping and explaining the rationale behind their outputs and decisions. Addressing these limitations is crucial for ensuring responsible LLM development and deployment, particularly in sensitive domains like finance.

Another challenge to the explainability and transparency of LLMs like ChatGPT is their potential for bias, error, and manipulation. LLMs can inherit and amplify the bias, error, and manipulation in the data, algorithms, and development and deployment processes.[624] For example, LLMs trained on text data containing stereotypes, prejudices, and misinformation can adopt these biases and perpetuate them in their outputs and decisions, leading to unfair and inaccurate results. Similarly, limitations in LLM models, data, and methods can lead to errors and mistakes, resulting in unreliable and

620. Organisation for Economic Co-operation and Development, *OECD AI Principles*, OECD.AI, https://oecd.ai/en/dashboards/ai-principles/P7/; Nagadivya Balasubramaniam et al., Transparency and Explainability of AI Systems: Ethical Guidelines in Practice, in *Requirements Engineering: Foundation for Software Quality*, REFSQ 2022 3 (Vincenzo Gervasi & André Vogelsang eds, 2022), https://doi.org/10.1007/978-3-030-98464-9_1.
621. François Candelon et al., *AI Can Be Both Accurate and Transparent*, Harv. Bus. Rev. (12 May 2023), https://hbr.org/2023/05/ai-can-be-both-accurate-and-transparent; Kelly Churchill, *Foundations of Trustworthy AI: Governed Data and AI, AI Ethics and an Open Diverse Ecosystem*, IBM Blog, https://research.ibm.com/topics/trustworthy-ai.
622. Haiyan Zhao et al., *Explainability for Large Language Models: A Survey*, 15 ACM Transactions On Intelligent Sys. & Tech. 1, 1–38 (2024), https://arxiv.org/pdf/2309.01029.
623. Pat Lasserre, *Making Large Language Models More Explainable*, GSI Tech. (27 Mar. 2023), https://medium.com/gsi-technology/making-large-language-models-more-explainable-b8215696a659.
624. Talboy, A.N. & Fuller, E., *Challenging the Appearance of Machine Intelligence: Cognitive Bias in LLMs and Best Practices for Adoption*, arXiv preprint arXiv:2304.01358 (2023), https://arxiv.org/ftp/arxiv/papers/2304/2304.01358.pdf.

incorrect outputs that can have significant consequences.[625] Furthermore, LLMs can be vulnerable to manipulation by malicious actors who may alter, tamper, or spoof data, algorithms, and outputs to achieve harmful objectives.[626] Mitigating these risks through careful data selection, robust model development, and ethical considerations is essential to build trust in LLM technology and ensure its responsible use.

Moreover, the opacity of LLMs raises concerns about bias and fairness in the financial sector. This lack of transparency makes it difficult to identify and mitigate algorithmic bias that could unfairly disadvantage certain demographics or groups of individuals.[627] For instance, an LLM might be trained on historical financial data that reflects historical biases, leading to discriminatory outcomes in areas such as loan approvals, investment recommendations, and risk assessments. Additionally, the opacity of LLMs can make it difficult to hold them accountable for biased or unfair decisions, further undermining trust and confidence in their use within the financial sector.[628] To address these concerns, it is crucial for LLM developers to actively work towards improving explainability and transparency. Additionally, regulators must establish robust frameworks to ensure the fair and unbiased use of LLMs in the financial industry.

Above all, while LLMs offer exciting opportunities for the financial sector in areas like customer service and risk management, their lack of explainability and transparency raises significant concerns. These concerns can compromise security and privacy, violate ethical principles, and undermine customer trust. To address these challenges, it is crucial to develop and adopt standards, regulations, tools, and educational initiatives that ensure the responsible and trustworthy use of LLMs in finance. Thus, we can fully unleash the positive potential of LLMs by using them wisely, making finance more inclusive, preventing fraud, and managing risks effectively.

8.2.2 Security and Data Privacy

Integrating LLMs like ChatGPT in the financial sector raises significant data security and privacy concerns. These models, built on sophisticated deep learning architectures, can process vast amounts of sensitive information, including personal and

625. *AI Origins & Evolution: How Bias Creeps into Large Language Models*, Analytics India Mag (4 Jul. 2023), https://analyticsindiamag.com/ai-origins-evolution/how-bias-creeps-into-large-language-models/; Khan Academy, *How Do the Large Language Models Powering Khanmigo Work?*, https://support.khanacademy.org/hc/en-us/articles/13888935335309-How-do-the-Large-Language-Models-powering-Khanmigo-work-.
626. Deval Shah, *The Beginner's Guide to Hallucinations in Large Language Models*, Lakera (23 Aug. 2023), https://www.lakera.ai/blog/guide-to-hallucinations-in-large-language-models; Metabase, *6 Most Common Types of Data Bias in Data Analysis* (30 May 2023), https://www.metabase.com/blog/6-most-common-type-of-data-bias-in-data-analysis.
627. Alexandra Rizzi, *The Stories Algorithms Tell: Bias and Financial Inclusion at the Data Margins*, Ctr. for Fin. Inclusion, Accion (March 2021); Aaron Klein, *Reducing Bias in AI-Based Financial Services*, Brookings Institution (10 Jul. 2020), https://www.brookings.edu/articles/reducing-bias-in-ai-based-financial-services/.
628. *See supra* n. 623; *see* Alexandra Rizzi, *supra* n. 627.

financial data. The sheer volume and sensitivity of the data processed by LLMs create challenges in ensuring robust security measures to protect against potential cyber threats and unauthorised access. Nevertheless, security breaches in financial systems can have severe consequences, leading to financial losses, identity theft, and damage to the reputation of financial institutions.[629]

Another prime concern of LLMs like ChatGPT deployment in the financial sector is the potential for data breaches and leaks. LLMs are trained on massive datasets of text and code, often containing sensitive financial information. This data can be vulnerable to hacking attempts, insider threats, or accidental leaks, leading to significant financial losses and regulatory repercussions. The recent leak of ChatGPT's chat logs, exposing user information and prompts, exhibits its stark reminder of these vulnerabilities.[630] The need to strike a balance between leveraging the power of LLMs for financial innovation and safeguarding the privacy of individuals is a critical challenge that financial institutions must navigate.

Further security challenge lies in the vulnerability of LLMs to adversarial attacks. Malicious actors can manipulate inputs or exploit vulnerabilities in the models to generate misleading or harmful outputs. This threat could involve financial news feed manipulation to influence market behaviour, crafting targeted phishing emails, or even generating fake financial documents. Such attacks pose a significant threat to the integrity of financial markets and the security of individuals' financial data.[631] Additionally, the ability of attackers to leverage LLMs to spread misinformation and manipulate financial sentiment could have significant negative ramifications for the stability and integrity of financial markets. Therefore, developing robust defence mechanisms and fostering collaboration between LLM developers, security researchers, and financial institutions are crucial to mitigating the risks associated with adversarial attacks on LLMs in the financial sector.

The emergence of deepfake further complicates the security landscape in ChatGPT deployment in the financial sector. By exploiting AI to create realistic audio and video recordings, miscreants can use deepfake technology to mimic real people, enabling financial fraudsters to impersonate executives and authorise fraudulent

629. Keman Huang et al., *The Devastating Business Impacts of a Cyber Breach*, Harvard Business Review (May 2023), https://hbr.org/2023/05/the-devastating-business-impacts-of-a-cyber-breach; World Economic Forum, *How Does Your Industry Compare When It Comes to the Financial Impact of Cyber Threats?* (7 Mar. 2023), https://www.weforum.org/agenda/2023/03/how-does-your-industry-compare-when-it-comes-to-the-financial-impact-of-cyber-threats/.
630. Matt G. Southern, *Massive Leak of ChatGPT Credentials: Over 100,000 Accounts Affected*, Search Engine Journal (29 Aug. 2024), https://www.searchenginejournal.com/massive-leak-of-chatgpt-credentials-over-100000-accounts-affected/489801/; Statista, *Largest Data Breaches in Financial Sector Worldwide*, https://www.statista.com/statistics/1323568/largest-data-breaches-in-financial-sector-worldwide/ (accessed 4 Aug. 2024).
631. Erfan Shayegani et al., *Survey of Vulnerabilities in Large Language Models Revealed by Adversarial Attacks*, arXiv preprint arXiv:2310.10844, https://arxiv.org/abs/2310.10844; Andy Zou et al., *Universal and Transferable Adversarial Attacks on Aligned Language Models* (July 2023), https://arxiv.org/abs/2307.15043; Jiongxiao Wang et al., *Adversarial Demonstration Attacks on Large Language Models*, arXiv preprint arXiv:2305.14950 (2023), https://arxiv.org/abs/2305.14950.

transactions or manipulate financial records.[632] This increasing availability of deepfake can erode trust in financial institutions and discourage customers from engaging with LLMs for financial services. To keep LLMs like ChatGPT safe and secure in the financial sector, we need robust tools to spot and stop deepfakes alongside clear communication and training for both customers and institutions.

In conclusion, the security and data privacy challenges associated with LLMs like ChatGPT in the financial sector underscore the need for a comprehensive and proactive approach. By incorporating robust encryption, adhering to privacy regulations, conducting regular security audits, and promoting transparency, financial institutions can harness the benefits of LLMs while mitigating risks and safeguarding the privacy of individuals and organisations.[633] Promoting cooperation among stakeholders, including LLM developers, financial institutions, regulatory bodies, and cybersecurity experts, is crucial for establishing a responsible and ethical framework for LLM deployment in finance. This collaborative effort will ensure the security and privacy of financial data while unlocking the transformative potential of LLMs within the financial sector.

8.2.3 Regulatory Compliance

Integrating LLMs like ChatGPT in the financial industry presents numerous regulatory compliance challenges. Financial institutions must follow strict rules to be open, responsible, and protect customer information. Ensuring data security and implementing robust encryption measures are imperative to comply with these regulations and maintain the trust of customers in the financial sector. Nonetheless, the opaque nature of LLMs poses a challenge in meeting these regulatory requirements, as it becomes difficult to explain the decision-making processes of these complex models.[634] Additionally, inherent biases within LLMs trained on large datasets raise concerns about fair and ethical treatment of all customers, potentially leading to discriminatory outcomes. Furthermore, the rapid development and evolving nature of LLM technology outpaces regulatory frameworks, creating uncertainty for financial institutions and hindering their ability to ensure long-term compliance.

Moreover, financial institutions might be unable to comply with data protection, anti-money laundering, and other regulations due to the hardship in explaining and understanding their decision-making process. Additionally, financial institutions must ensure that their decisions are fair and do not discriminate against anyone. ChatGPT's

632. *Why Deepfake Fraud Losses Should Scare Financial Institutions*, Finextra (14 Nov. 2022), https://www.finextra.com/blogposting/23223/why-deepfake-fraud-losses-should-scare-financial-institutions; Níamh Curran, *Deepfake Fraud: The Rising Threat in Financial Crime*, Finextra (31 Oct. 2023). https://www.finextra.com/the-long-read/844/deepfake-fraud-the-rising-threat-in-financial-crime.
633. Nicolas Vidal, *How AI and LLMs Are Streamlining Financial Services*, Forbes (5 May 2023), https://www.forbes.com/sites/forbestechcouncil/2023/05/05/how-ai-and-llms-are-streamlining-financial-services/?sh=7a0374052301.
634. Rich Caruana et al., *Intelligible High-Accuracy Models in HealthCare: Predicting Pneumonia Risk and Hospital 30-day Readmission* (3 Sep. 2015), https://shahlab.stanford.edu/lib/exe/fetch.php?media=caruana-kdd2015-by-dave-no-anim.pdf.

training on human-generated content risks inheriting biases, leading to potentially flawed reasoning and discriminatory outcomes.[635] Addressing and mitigating these biases is essential to comply with anti-discrimination laws and regulations governing the financial industry. It is crucial to develop and implement robust bias detection and mitigation techniques to ensure the responsible and ethical use of AI in the financial sector. Additionally, promoting transparency and explainability in AI models is essential to build trust and confidence in the financial system.

The dynamic nature of the financial industry and evolving regulations pose additional challenges. For example, financial regulations are subject to frequent updates and amendments, and ensuring that LLMs remain compliant with these changes requires continuous monitoring and adaptation. This demands a proactive approach from financial institutions and LLM developers to stay abreast of regulatory developments and swiftly implement necessary adjustments.[636] Furthermore, the complex and multifaceted nature of financial regulations necessitates specialised domain expertise in LLM development and deployment within the financial sector. Additionally, ongoing collaboration with regulatory bodies is crucial to ensure the responsible development and alignment of LLMs with evolving regulatory landscapes.

Despite offering great potential in areas like customer support and financial advice, LLMs require careful regulation and collaboration between regulators and industry players to address data privacy, security, and ethical concerns.[637] Collaboration between regulatory bodies and industry stakeholders is essential to address the challenges associated with LLM adoption in the financial industry. Establishing clear guidelines and standards specific to LLMs deployment in finance can provide a roadmap for compliance. Regulatory bodies should engage with experts in AI and finance to develop a nuanced understanding of the implications of LLM adoption and to tailor regulations accordingly.

Additionally, the financial industry can benefit from self-regulation initiatives. Industry-led efforts to establish ethical guidelines and best practices for LLM adoption can complement existing regulatory frameworks. This proactive approach allows financial institutions to demonstrate commitment to RAI use, potentially reducing regulatory burdens.[638] Moreover, industry-wide data-sharing initiatives can facilitate the development of robust LLM models tailored to specific financial use cases. Additionally, fostering a collaborative environment where financial institutions can share best practices and lessons learned can accelerate responsible LLM adoption throughout the sector. Finally, establishing specific ethical guidelines for LLM development and deployment can help build public trust and confidence in AI-powered financial services.

---

635. *See supra* n. 112.
636. Dutta, S. et al., *Global Innovation Index 2017: Innovation Feeding the World* (Cornell Univ., INSEAD & WIPO 2017), https://tind.wipo.int/record/28218.
637. *See supra* n. 634; Wiz.ai, *Unleashing the Potential of LLMs: A New Era for Financial Services*, https://www.wiz.ai/unleashing-the-potential-of-llms-a-new-era-for-financial-services/ (accessed 4 Aug. 2024).
638. Daron Acemoglu et al., *Machine Learning: An Applied Econometric Approach*, 31 J. Econ. PERSPS. 87 (2019), https://doi.org/10.1257/jep.31.2.87.

In conclusion, deploying LLMs like ChatGPT in the financial industry introduces complex challenges related to regulatory compliance. Addressing these challenges requires a multidimensional approach involving collaboration among regulatory bodies, financial institutions, and AI experts. Financial institutions can safely adopt LLMs by adhering to clear guidelines, staying informed about changing regulations, addressing bias and data security, and maintaining openness and accountability. To remain compliant with constantly changing regulations and technology, financial institutions need to foster a culture of continuous learning and adaptation. Additionally, ongoing collaboration with regulatory bodies will be essential to ensure the responsible development and alignment of LLMs with the evolving landscape of financial regulations.

8.2.4 Ethical Considerations

LLMs like ChatGPT deployment in the financial sector raise significant ethical challenges warranting careful consideration. One primary concern revolves around data privacy and security. These models require large amounts of data for training purposes, including personal and financial information. There is a risk that this data could be compromised, leading to financial fraud or other malicious activities. Ensuring robust encryption and strict access controls becomes imperative to mitigate such risks. Utilising data minimisation techniques in ML models offers a promising way to mitigate privacy risks, enhance model fairness, and prevent unnecessary data collection.[639] Furthermore, implementing comprehensive data governance frameworks and adhering to stringent data protection regulations are crucial to fostering trust and transparency in LLM-driven financial services. Additionally, financial institutions must be prepared to address potential security vulnerabilities and cyberattacks that could exploit the vast data used by LLMs.

LLMs may inherit and amplify the bias and discrimination present in the training data, which may affect the fairness and accuracy of their outputs. For example, LLMs may generate text that is sexist, racist, or otherwise harmful to certain groups of people, or they may make decisions that favour or disadvantage some customers or stakeholders based on their characteristics or preferences.[640] This context may lead to ethical violations, legal liabilities, and reputational damages for the financial institutions that employ LLMs. Addressing bias in LLMs requires ongoing efforts in data curation, model training, and regular audits to identify and rectify potential sources of bias.[641]

639. Abigail Goldsteen, *Reduce Data Privacy Issues with Machine Learning Models*, IBM Developer, https://developer.ibm.com/blogs/data-minimization-for-machine-learning/ (accessed 4 Aug. 2024).
640. Haziqa Sajid, *8 Ethical Considerations of Large Language Models (LLM) Like GPT-4*, Unite.ai (4 Aug. 2024), https://www.unite.ai/8-ethical-considerations-of-large-language-models-llm-like-gpt-4/; Sander Schulhoff, *Pitfalls of LLMs*, Learn Prompting (6 Jul. 2024), https://learnprompting.org/docs/basics/pitfalls.
641. Isabel O. Gallegos et al., *Bias and Fairness in Large Language Models: A Survey*, Computational Linguistics 1–79 (2024), https://arxiv.org/pdf/2309.00770.

Moreover, collaborative efforts between researchers, policymakers, and industry players are essential to overcoming these challenges and driving progress towards more unbiased AI.[642]

Transparency and accountability are essential considerations in the ethical deployment of LLMs in finance. Nevertheless, LLMs often operate as 'black boxes', making it difficult to understand how they arrive at their decisions or responses.[643] This lack of transparency can erode trust in AI-powered financial services and raise concerns about fairness and accountability. Developing techniques to explain LLM decisions in a human-understandable manner is crucial to building trust and ensuring responsible use of the technology. Furthermore, implementing mechanisms for explainability and accountability in LLMs, such as interpretable algorithms and clear documentation, is crucial for fostering trust and ensuring responsible use.[644]

LLMs, while capable of generating seemingly convincing text, can also unintentionally or deliberately produce false, misleading, or harmful content. This potential of LLMs poses significant risks to users and recipients of the generated information, as LLMs may leak sensitive data, IP, or misinterpret financial data. Malicious actors can exploit these capabilities for phishing, spamming, and scamming, potentially leading to information hazards like secret disclosures, widespread confusion, and manipulated beliefs and behaviours.[645] These hazards can have detrimental consequences for both the financial sector and society at large, necessitating robust safeguards, ethical guidelines, and rigorous testing to ensure accurate and reliable LLM outputs.

Further, LLMs have the potential to automate many tasks currently performed by humans, raising concerns about job displacement in the financial sector. According to a recent study, the application of AI and robotics is likely to have a massive impact on the banking sector, potentially leading to the loss of 50% of jobs within the next five to 20 years.[646] The resulting job displacement poses pressing economic, social, and psychological challenges for the workforce, especially in developing countries where informal labourers are disproportionately affected and worsened by the current COVID-19 crisis. Hence, it is imperative to formulate meticulous public policy responses that address the multifaceted costs of job displacements and actively support affected workers in securing reemployment opportunities.

In conclusion, while LLMs like ChatGPT offer significant potential for enhancing efficiency and innovation in the financial sector, their deployment also requires careful

642. Vishesh Thakur, *Unveiling Gender Bias in Terms of Profession Across LLMs: Analyzing and Addressing Sociological Implications*, arXiv preprint arXiv:2307.09162 (2023), https://arxiv.org/pdf/2307.09162.
643. *See supra* n. 584; Chandan Singh et al., *Explaining Black Box Text Modules in Natural Language with Language Models*, arXiv preprint arXiv:2305.09863 (2023), https://arxiv.org/pdf/2305.09863.
644. *See supra* n. 623; AST Consulting, *Analyzing LLMs: Interpretability and Explainability* (27 Jul. 2023), https://astconsulting.in/artificial-intelligence/nlp-natural-language-processing/llm/analyzing-llms-interpretability-and-explainability/.
645. *See supra* n. 272; *see also supra* n. 611.
646. Osborne Jackson, *Job Displacement and Sectoral Mobility, Fed. Reserve Bank of Boston Working Paper Series No. 2021-13* (2021), https://www.bostonfed.org/publications/research-department-working-paper/2021/job-displacement-and-sectoral-mobility.aspx.

consideration of ethical challenges. These challenges encompass potential biases and discriminatory practices, the spread of misinformation and information hazards, and issues of responsibility and accountability. The financial sector needs robust rules and guidance for using LLMs ethically and responsibly. This framework should prioritise transparency and disclosure regarding LLM capabilities and limitations, emphasise the quality and reliability of generated outputs, and uphold ethical principles aligned with the broader values of the industry. By proactively addressing these ethical considerations, the financial sector can unlock the full potential of LLMs while minimising associated risks and ensuring responsible and ethical integration into diverse financial industries.

8.2.5 Operational Challenges

Operational challenges emerge as one of the primary obstacles to integrating AI into the financial sector. LLMs thrive on massive datasets of high-quality and domain-specific text, yet much financial data remains inaccessible due to confidentiality, privacy, and proprietary concerns. Furthermore, this data often presents complexities, characterised by dynamic evolution and heterogeneity, as well as potential errors, inconsistencies, and biases.[647] As a result, LLMs require meticulous design and customisation to tackle the specific characteristics and demands of financial data, encompassing aspects like data security, privacy, accuracy, completeness, and timeliness. Continuous updates and monitoring become necessary to reflect the changing landscape and trends within the financial market and environment.

The computational needs of LLMs pose significant challenges for their deployment within the financial sector. Training and running these complex models require substantial resources, with expenses growing alongside model size and complexity. For instance, training an LLM like ChatGPT requires immense computational resources, consuming 10 times the energy of its predecessor GPT-2 and demanding the equivalent of over 1,000 US households' annual electricity usage.[648] This estimation highlights the significant energy consumption by these advanced models. Additionally, efficient deployment and operation require seamless integration with existing systems and platforms, including databases, APIs, and cloud services.

Deploying LLMs in the financial sector also raises ethical and regulatory concerns stemming from their potential impact. LLMs may perpetuate biases, discrimination, manipulation, or deception, reflecting and amplifying existing prejudices, stereotypes,

647. *Ibid. See also* Itay Goldstein et al., 34(7) The Review of Financial Studies (July 2021), 3213–3225, https://doi.org/10.1093/rfs/hhab038; Lewis Evans, Big Data Fusion Model for Heterogeneous Financial Market Data (FinDf), in *Intelligent Systems and Applications* (K. Arai, S. Kapoor & R. Bhatia eds, Springer, Cham 2018), 868 Advances in Intelligent Systems and Computing, https://doi.org/10.1007/978-3-030-01054-6_75.

648. Sarah McQuate, *Q&A: UW Researcher Discusses Just How Much Energy ChatGPT Uses*, University of Washington (27 Jul. 2023), https://sph.washington.edu/faculty/newsletter/ChatGPT-AI.

or misinformation.[649] Additionally, they may pose regulatory risks related to compliance, accountability, and liability, potentially violating existing laws, rules, or standards governing the financial sector, such as data protection, consumer protection, and financial regulation.[650] Responsible and transparent development and deployment of LLMs, adhering to AI ethics principles like fairness, explainability, privacy, and security, is crucial to mitigate ethical and regulatory risks in the financial sector. Furthermore, human oversight and supervision are crucial to ensuring ethical and legal compliance, aligning with stakeholder values and interests, and promoting the responsible use of LLMs within the financial industry.

LLMs can impact the roles, skills, and behaviours of human workers and users, potentially augmenting, complementing, or replacing several tasks performed by humans. While some concerns exist regarding job displacement, AI's true potential lies in collaboration, enhancing human capabilities rather than simply replacing them.[651] AI will revolutionise how we work, creating exciting new opportunities. To make the most of this technology, LLMs need to be designed with users in mind, putting their needs, preferences, and expectations first. Furthermore, training and evaluation should occur in realistic, interactive settings with human input, fostering continuous improvement and enhanced usability. By fostering effective human-AI collaboration, we can unlock the full potential of LLMs and drive a more efficient, innovative, and ethical future for the financial industry.

In conclusion, while LLMs like ChatGPT offer significant potential for revolutionising the financial industry, their deployment presents operational hurdles that require careful consideration. These challenges encompass data access and quality, model performance and scalability, ethical and regulatory concerns, and human-AI collaboration. Addressing these challenges demands solutions and strategies like data security and privacy measures, model evaluation and validation, AI ethics and governance frameworks, and user-centric design. By addressing the above challenges, LLMs can be deployed safely and effectively in the financial sector, driving increased productivity, efficiency, and innovation in financial services and products.

8.3 CONCLUSION

This chapter discusses the potential of LLMs such as ChatGPT to revolutionise the financial sector. Despite the promise of streamlining processes and enhancing decision-making, integrating these powerful tools into such a highly regulated sector presents unique challenges including explainability, transparency, bias and fairness, data security and privacy, regulatory compliance, ethical considerations, and operational challenges. To address these challenges, several recommendations can be proposed.

649. OECD, *Enterprise ChatGPT and LLM Governance: Use Cases*, https://oecd.ai/en/catalogue/tools/grace/tool-use-cases/enterprise-chatgpt-and-llm-governance (accessed 4 Aug. 2024).
650. DataArt, *Exploring the Future of AI: Large Language Models in Finance* (3 Aug. 2024), https://www.dataart.com/blog/exploring-the-future-of-ai-large-language-models-in-finance.
651. H. James Wilson & Paul R. Daugherty, *Collaborative Intelligence: Humans and AI Are Joining Forces*, Harv. Bus. Rev. (July 2018), https://hbr.org/2018/07/collaborative-intelligence-humans-and-ai-are-joining-forces.

First, financial institutions should collaborate with AI developers and regulatory bodies to establish industry-wide standards and guidelines for LLMs in finance. This collaboration is essential to ensure transparency, accountability, and compliance. Second, it is crucial to implement ongoing education and training programs that focus on ethical considerations and bias mitigation associated with LLMs. Third, establishing oversight committees and conducting comprehensive risk assessments before deployment are recommended to address security and data privacy concerns effectively. Fourth, financial institutions should actively adapt to regulatory changes, develop clear guidelines for the ethical use of LLMs, prioritise data governance, and engage with stakeholders to address job displacement issues. By collectively implementing the above strategies, the financial industry can responsibly and ethically integrate LLMs while fostering innovation and maintaining trust and integrity.

CHAPTER 9

Legal and Regulatory Challenges in AI Governance

9.1 INTRODUCTION

AI-powered chatbots and conversational agents have become ubiquitous in today's digital landscape, revolutionising how businesses interact with customers. While these virtual entities offer unparalleled convenience, efficiency, and scalability, they also present significant regulatory challenges. As AI systems continue to advance in sophistication, it is crucial to address these challenges to ensure the ethical, safe, and transparent use of this technology.

Privacy concerns are among the most critical regulatory challenges associated with LLMs like ChatGPT. AI-powered chatbots collect vast amounts of data during interactions with users, including personal information and behavioural patterns. Specifically, ChatGPT is trained using data sourced from various platforms such as websites, posts, books, and articles, which may contain personal information. This practice is particularly concerning because content like comments, blog posts, or product reviews, which individuals may have posted online, could have been used to train ChatGPT without the explicit consent of the data subjects. This situation raises significant privacy issues and could potentially violate privacy laws.[652]

9.2 REGULATORY CHALLENGES OF LLMS LIKE ChatGPT

The emergence of LLMs such as ChatGPT has significantly transformed interactions with AI by providing exceptional capabilities in natural language understanding and generation. However, this technological advancement introduces a range of regulatory challenges. As LLMs become increasingly embedded in diverse fields, including

652. *See supra* n. 47.

customer service and content creation, they give rise to concerns related to transparency, bias and discrimination, data security, accountability and liability, and interoperability. This section aims to examine these major regulatory challenges associated with LLMs like ChatGPT and to explore potential policy solutions.

The operation of ChatGPT is marked by a significant lack of transparency, which in turn gives rise to a host of concerns.[653] This lack of transparency manifests in various aspects, such as the unclear mechanisms behind its decision-making processes, the ambiguity surrounding the data it utilises for training, and the opacity in how it generates and prioritises responses. Users often find it difficult to ascertain how and why certain outputs are produced, which can lead to distrust and scepticism. Moreover, this opacity makes it challenging to hold the system accountable, as it is not always clear whether the responses are based on factual information, biases inherent in the training data, or the underlying algorithms' interpretations. Thus, in a debate on AI held on 18 July 2023, the UN Secretary-General urged the Security Council to take a leading role in ensuring transparency, accountability, and oversight of AI systems.[654]

Given the significance of transparency in AI applications and operations, the world-renowned journal *Nature* recently emphasised that AI tools, particularly ChatGPT, pose a risk to transparent scientific practices.[655] In response, *Nature* and all Springer Nature journals have established two key guidelines for AI usage. First, research articles cannot list AI tools as authors, as AI lacks the capacity for accountability. Second, when researchers use AI tools, they must acknowledge this in the methods or acknowledgements sections. If these sections are not present, the introduction or another appropriate section should indicate the use of AI.[656]

Moreover, bias and discrimination present significant regulatory concerns for ChatGPT and other language models. ChatGPT usually receives training on extensive text data, leading to potential biases. These biases can cause unfair results in various areas, such as employment, healthcare, and criminal justice.[657] ChatGPT might show bias towards specific cultural or language groups and produce prejudiced or unsuitable responses. As AI technology progresses, we can anticipate more precise models that reduce biases, understand context better, and offer valuable assistance to researchers. The regulatory framework should mandate regular audits and assessments of AI algorithms to identify, address and rectify biased usage of ChatGPT.

Data security is another pressing challenge within the regulatory frameworks of ChatGPT and similar language models. AI chatbots can be prone to massive cyberattacks, placing user data and interactions at stake. Specifically, ChatGPT's capacity to

---

653. Carter C. Price, *ChatGPT's Work Lacks Transparency and That Is a Problem*, RAND Corporation (5 May 2023), https://www.rand.org/blog/2023/05/chatgpts-work-lacks-transparency-and-that-is-a-problem.html.
654. U.N. Secretary-General, *Secretary-General Urges Security Council to Ensure Transparency, Accountability, Oversight, in First Debate on Artificial Intelligence* (18 Jul. 2023), https://press.un.org/en/2023/sgsm21880.doc.htm.
655. Editors of Nature, *Tools Such as ChatGPT Threaten Transparent Science; Here Are Our Ground Rules for Their Use.*, 613 Nature 612 (2023), https://doi.org/10.1038/d41586-023-00191-1, https://www.nature.com/articles/d41586-023-00191-1.
656. *Ibid.*
657. *See supra* n. 112.

generate human-like text raises data privacy and security concerns, as it might inadvertently expose or misuse sensitive user data. Furthermore, people can utilise ChatGPT to create deep fakes and spread wrong information, worsening trust and integrity among users.[658] Taking robust and adequate data protection measures and preventive mechanisms is advisable to mitigate the data security issue.

Determining the accountability and liability of ChatGPT becomes increasingly complex as the technology evolves and gains widespread adoption across various industries. This complexity encompasses issues related to data ownership, responsibility for the model's output, and accountability for any negative consequences arising from ChatGPT's use. Businesses must exercise caution in their data processing activities, including the collection, storage, retention, and utilisation of data for content creation. The establishment of clear guidelines and legal frameworks is crucial to address these evolving challenges. Although there have been lawsuits involving ChatGPT and similar language models, the final judgments of most of these cases are still pending.[659] Resolving AI's responsibility and accountability for errors and mistakes may require additional time and legal deliberation.

The lack of interoperability is a significant challenge in integrating LLMs across various industries. This limitation can lead to isolated AI systems, which impedes their ability to collaborate and deliver a unified, comprehensive user experience. Interoperability is crucial for the success of systems like ChatGPT, as it enables users to connect with diverse services, thereby enhancing their experience by providing access to a broader range of features and information. This interconnected approach not only improves user interaction with the system but also facilitates better decision-making. For instance, in healthcare, interoperable data benefits patients, providers, insurers, and researchers by offering more detailed information, accurate diagnoses, equitable insurance rates, and improved patient insights.[660]

Nonetheless, AI systems developed by different organisations often employ proprietary technologies and interfaces, which may not integrate seamlessly. To address this challenge, stakeholders in the AI industry must prioritise interoperability standards and open architectures. By establishing common protocols and interfaces, AI

658. *Ibid.*

659. ChatGPT and other deep fake-creating apps witnessed numerous lawsuits, including: *Chabon v. OpenAI, Inc.*, No. 23-cv-05548 (N.D. Cal. filed 8 Sep. 2023); *J.L., C.B., K.S., et al. v. Alphabet, Inc., et al.*, No. 23-cv-03440 (N.D. Cal. filed 11 Jul. 2023); *Silverman, et al. v. OpenAI, Inc.*, No. 23-cv-03416 (N.D. Cal. filed 7 Jul. 2023); *Kadrey, et al. v. Meta Platforms, Inc.*, No. 23-cv-03417 (N.D. Cal. filed 7 Jul. 2023); *Tremblay v. OpenAI, Inc.*, No. 23-cv-03286 (N.D. Cal. filed 28 Jun. 2023); *Plaintiffs P.M., K.S. et al. v. OpenAI LP et al.*, No. 23-cv-03294 (N.D. Cal. filed 28 Jun. 2023); *Young v. NeoCortext, Inc.*, No. 23-cv-01890 (S.D. Cal. filed 3 Apr. 2023); *Young v. NeoCortext, Inc.*, No. 23-cv-01891 (S.D. Cal. filed 3 Apr. 2023); *Getty Images (US), Inc. v. Stability AI, Inc.*, No. 23-cv-00135 (D. Del. filed 3 Feb. 2023); *Andersen, et al. v. Stability AI Ltd., et al.*, No. 23-cv-00062 (N.D. Cal. filed 13 Jan. 2023); *Thomson Reuters Enterprise Centre GmbH et al. v. ROSS Intelligence Inc.*, No. 20-cv-00669 (D. Del. filed May 6, 2020). *See* The Fashion Law, *From ChatGPT to Deepfake-Creating Apps: A Running List of Key AI Lawsuits* (5 Jul. 2023), https://www.thefashionlaw.com/from-chatgpt-to-deepfake-creating-apps-a-running-list-of-key-ai-lawsuits/.

660. John Kuhn, *AI and LLMs: The Future of Healthcare Data Interoperability*, Forbes (20 Jun. 2023), https://www.forbes.com/sites/forbestechcouncil/2023/06/20/ai-and-large-language-models-the-future-of-healthcare-data-interoperability/.

models like ChatGPT can more effectively communicate and share information across platforms. This approach would enhance user experiences and promote responsible and ethical development of AI systems, enabling greater transparency, accountability, and oversight.

In conclusion, as AI chatbots continue to evolve, regulations must remain adaptable and forward-looking. This aspect requires regular updates and collaboration between policymakers, businesses, and technology experts to navigate the ever-changing landscape of AI-powered chatbots effectively. While AI-powered chatbots and conversational agents offer substantial benefits, they also bring forth regulatory challenges related to privacy, transparency, bias, security, accountability, interoperability, and adaptability. Addressing these challenges through robust and flexible regulations is essential to harness the full potential of AI chatbots while ensuring ethical and RAI deployment.

9.3 EXISTING LEGAL FRAMEWORKS ON LLMs LIKE ChatGPT GOVERNANCE

9.3.1 Introduction

LLMs like ChatGPT have emerged as powerful tools with immense potential across various sectors. Nevertheless, their deployment raises significant legal and ethical concerns, prompting the need for robust governance frameworks. Building trust is crucial for LLMs' future. Inspired by the self-regulation practices in biomedicine, developers of LLMs can achieve responsible development through transparency, open dialogue, adherence to ethical guidelines, and independent audits. By implementing these measures, they demonstrate their commitment to ethical practices and earn the trust essential for the successful advancement of LLM technology.[661] This section examines existing legal frameworks and identifies gaps and challenges in regulating LLM technology. It concludes by recommending potential pathways for developing a comprehensive and functioning governance framework for LLMs.

9.3.2 Problems with Current Legal Frameworks

LLMs such as ChatGPT represent advanced AI systems that have been trained on extensive datasets of text and code. This training enables them to generate text that closely resembles human writing, translate languages, provide informative answers to questions, and even produce a wide range of creative content. Therefore, LLMs offer diverse benefits to organisations by generating text, summarising content, providing AI assistance, generating code, analysing sentiment, and translating languages.[662]

661. Sebastian Porsdam Mann et al., *Generative AI Entails a Credit–Blame Asymmetry*, 5 Nat. Mach. Intell. 472–475 (2023), https://doi.org/10.1038/s42256-023-00653-1.
662. *See supra* n. 153.

However, despite their vast potential, concerns around bias, transparency, accountability, and misuse necessitate the development of robust legal frameworks for ethical and responsible LLM governance. While no dedicated LLM-specific framework exists other than the EU AI Act, current IP, data protection, anti-discrimination, and consumer protection laws indirectly impact their development and deployment, highlighting the need for a comprehensive legal framework that adequately addresses the unique challenges posed by this emerging technology.

Prevailing copyright and patent laws play a crucial role in safeguarding the IP rights utilised in developing LLMs like ChatGPT. These laws govern the ownership and protection of both the training data used to empower LLMs and the algorithms that underpin their functionality. Copyright protects the unique expression of ideas in the training data, theoretically ensuring that contributors receive due recognition and compensation for their work. Patent law, conversely, safeguards the innovative algorithms at the heart of LLMs, ostensibly incentivising further R&D while preventing unauthorised use. Nevertheless, the biggest question encompassing LLM outputs is: who owns the copyright of content generated by LLMs like ChatGPT?

Determining the copyright status of outputs generated by LLMs like ChatGPT is a complex and unresolved issue, involving legal, ethical, and technical considerations. One perspective argues that these outputs should be considered part of the public domain, as they are produced by algorithms trained on vast amounts of publicly available text data. According to this view, anyone could use these outputs freely, without being subject to exclusive ownership restrictions. However, this stance overlooks the potential inclusion of copyrighted materials within the training data, such as books, articles, and web pages.[663] If such copyrighted materials are present, the outputs generated by LLMs could be regarded as derivative works, which may inherit the rights and limitations of the source material, thereby complicating copyright ownership claims.

Likewise, the patentability of LLMs like ChatGPT outputs is a complex and evolving issue, as it depends on several factors, such as the type of output, the jurisdiction, and the novelty and inventiveness of the prompt engineering. While some scholars argue that the underlying algorithms and technical processes may be patentable, others contend that the outputs themselves lack the novelty and non-obviousness necessary for patent protection.[664] The US Copyright Office currently considers AI-generated works ineligible for copyright protection due to the absence of human authorship.[665] This stance is grounded in the principle that only works created by human beings qualify as original works of authorship under copyright law. Given the

663. *See supra* n. 358.
664. Ana Ramalho, *Patentability of AI-Generated Inventions: Is a Reform of the Patent System Needed?* (15 Feb. 2018), available at SSRN: https://ssrn.com/abstract=3168703 or http://dx.doi.org/10.2139/ssrn.3168703 or http://dx.doi.org/10.2139/ssrn.3168703; John Villasenor, *Patents and AI Inventions: Recent Court Rulings and Broader Policy Questions*, Brookings (25 Aug. 2023), https://www.brookings.edu/articles/patents-and-ai-inventions-recent-court-rulings-and-broader-policy-questions/.
665. US Copyright Office, *Copyright and Artificial Intelligence*, https://www.copyright.gov/ai/ (accessed 4 Aug. 2024); *see also supra* n. 374.

international variations in patent and copyright laws, there is a need for further research and dialogue among stakeholders to develop clear and consistent guidelines.

Some scholars argue that the outputs generated by LLMs like ChatGPT are the property of either their creators or their users.[666] For instance, OpenAI allows users to use ChatGPT outputs freely, including for commercial purposes but also cautions that there could be legal implications. Given that ChatGPT responses may occasionally be repetitive or contain copyrighted material, users should exercise caution and consider seeking legal advice before publication.[667] This perspective considers the design, training, and prompting of the algorithms as forms of creative input, making the outputs of original works reflect human intention. Nevertheless, concerns arise regarding the autonomy and unpredictability of LLMs, as they might generate outputs beyond intended results, potentially rendering them independent works without clear ownership.

As LLM technology continues to develop rapidly, a collaborative effort between policymakers, legal experts, and the tech industry is crucial to ensure a robust and adaptable legal framework that fosters innovation while safeguarding ethical considerations and IP rights.[668] Nonetheless, the application of both copyright and patent law to LLMs is complex and evolving. Moreover, new legal questions arise regarding the ownership of data generated by LLMs themselves, the potential for copyright infringement in creative outputs, and the international scope of IP protection. This means there is no one-size-fits-all solution, and further research and dialogue are needed among stakeholders to establish clear and consistent guidelines.[669]

Furthermore, the rapid rise of LLMs like ChatGPT has ignited concerns about their compatibility with existing data protection laws. While data protection regulations provide a foundational framework for protecting personal data, their application to LLMs presents complexities that demand further analysis and adaptation. While data protection laws aim to ensure individuals have substantial control over the processing of their data,[670] LLMs like ChatGPT may face challenges in aligning with this goal due to their reliance on processing vast amounts of data, which can include sensitive personal information. Moreover, data protection laws are designed to prevent the sharing of personal data with third parties without the individual's consent. However, maintaining this standard is challenging with LLMs like ChatGPT. For

666. Yang Liu et al., *Trustworthy LLMs: A Survey and Guideline for Evaluating Large Language Models' Alignment*, arXiv preprint arXiv:2308.05374 (2023), https://arxiv.org/pdf/2308.05374.
667. OpenAI, *Terms of Use*, https://openai.com/policies/terms-of-use/ (accessed 4 Aug. 2024).
668. Lucas Mearian, *What Are Large Language Models and How Are They Used in Generative AI?*, Computerworld (7 Feb. 2024), https://www.computerworld.com/article/3697649/what-are-large-language-models-and-how-are-they-used-in-generative-ai.html.
669. *See supra* n. 37.
670. I. van Ooijen & Helena U. Vrabec, *Does the GDPR Enhance Consumers' Control over Personal Data? An Analysis from a Behavioural Perspective*, 42 J. Consum. Pol'y 91 (2019), https://doi.org/10.1007/s10603-018-9399-7; European Union, *Rights of the Individual. European Data Protection Supervisor*, https://edps.europa.eu/data-protection/our-work/subjects/rights-individual_en; Christophe Lazaro & Daniel Le Métayer, *Control over Personal Data: True Remedy or Fairy Tale?*, 12 SCRIPTed 3 (2015) https://doi.org/10.2966/scrip.120115.3.

instance, OpenAI's privacy policy states that the company may share user inputs with third parties without obtaining explicit individual consent.[671]

In particular, OpenAI collects various user data, including personal information, and may share it with third parties. While users possess certain rights over their data, OpenAI is ultimately responsible for its management, even though there remain variations in privacy regulations across countries. Despite adherence to GDPR and CCPA regulations, user concerns about data privacy persist due to the nature of ChatGPT.[672] Upholding data protection principles such as data minimisation, purpose specification, and storage limitation remain a high priority for data protection regulations.[673] Nevertheless, the architectural designs and operational characteristics of LLMs like ChatGPT make it challenging to fully comply with these principles.

To address these challenges, a multifaceted approach is crucial. Existing data protection frameworks need adjustments to accommodate the unique data practices of LLMs. This includes providing clearer guidelines for data collection, use, sharing, and transparency. Efforts are needed to develop techniques for explaining the inner workings of LLMs, enabling a better understanding of potential biases and discriminatory outputs. Implementing robust data governance frameworks specific to LLMs can help ensure responsible data practices and mitigate risks associated with data collection, use, and sharing. Above all, staying informed about developments in this field and monitoring legal discussions and regulatory updates is crucial for navigating the evolving landscape of data protection laws in the context of LLMs.

LLMs also pose ethical and legal challenges, especially regarding the potential discrimination and bias in their outputs. If left unchecked, these biases can manifest in discriminatory outcomes across various domains, impacting hiring decisions, loan approvals, and even targeted advertising. To ensure fair and unbiased treatment for all, LLM outputs should comply with the laws prohibiting discrimination based on race, gender, and other protected characteristics. Legal frameworks and ethical guidelines are essential to mitigate these risks and ensure fair and responsible use of LLMs.

It is worth noting that several anti-discrimination laws, such as the US Title VII of the Civil Rights Act of 1964[674] and the UK's Equality Act of 2010,[675] provide a strong foundation for addressing bias in LLM outputs. These laws prohibit discrimination based on protected characteristics and require organisations to utilise AI tools to ensure fairness and non-discrimination. Additionally, regulations like the EU's GDPR and the CCPA 2018[676] offer further safeguards by granting individuals control over their data and mandating transparency in automated decision-making processes.

The constantly evolving nature of LLMs necessitates ongoing vigilance and adaptation. Consequently, LLM developers and users bear a significant responsibility

671. *See supra* n. 330.
672. *See supra* n. 47.
673. *See supra* n. 397, Art. 5.
674. *See* European Union, *supra* n. 670.
675. UK Parliament, *The Equality Act 2010* (UK 2010), https://www.legislation.gov.uk/ukpga/2010/15/contents.
676. California Department of Justice, *California Consumer Privacy Act (CCPA) 2018*, https://oag.ca.gov/privacy/ccpa.

to ensure that the outputs are ethical and unbiased.[677] This includes implementing rigorous bias detection and mitigation techniques, actively seeking diverse perspectives in training data, and fostering open dialogue about potential biases and their impacts. The growing global consensus on the need for ethical and RAI development emphasises the importance of collaboration between policymakers, developers, and users. By working together and leveraging existing legal frameworks and emerging ethical guidelines, we can ensure that LLMs fulfil their potential to benefit society while mitigating the risks of bias and discrimination.

Furthermore, the use of LLMs in marketing and advertising may present several challenges and risks to consumer protection laws. For instance, LLMs might generate false or misleading claims about products or services, such as by exaggerating their benefits, omitting critical information, or making unsubstantiated comparisons.[678] LLMs may also generate fake or biased reviews, testimonials, or endorsements, affecting consumer trust and credibility.[679] LLMs may also violate consumer privacy by collecting, processing, or sharing personal data without consent or disclosure.[680] Therefore, integrating LLMs into marketing or advertising should comply with the relevant consumer protection laws and ethical standards and be transparent, accountable, and responsible for their outputs and impacts.

Consumer protection laws aim to prevent businesses from engaging in deceptive, fraudulent, or unfair practices that may harm consumers or violate their rights. These laws encompass various aspects of the economy, including product safety, warranties, contracts, antitrust, privacy, and finance.[681] Enforcement of these laws is a collaborative effort involving US federal agencies like the Federal Trade Commission (FTC) and the Consumer Financial Protection Bureau (CFPB), state agencies, private lawsuits, and class actions.[682] Consumer protection laws are particularly relevant for LLMs used in marketing or advertising, as these models may generate or analyse content that could influence consumer behaviour or decision-making.

In essence, LLMs are influential tools with vast potential, but their deployment necessitates careful consideration of legal and ethical implications. Existing legal frameworks are inadequate to address the unique challenges posed by this technology. A comprehensive and efficient LLM governance framework is crucial to ensure responsible and ethical development and deployment of these models, maximising their benefits while minimising potential harms. This framework must be developed through collaboration between legal experts, technologists, policymakers, and other stakeholders, ensuring a future where LLMs contribute positively to society.

677. Jakob Mökander et al., *Auditing Large Language Models: A Three-Layered Approach*, AI Ethics (2023), https://doi.org/10.1007/s43681-023-00289-2.
678. *See supra* n. 670.
679. Google Cloud, *Large Language Models Powered by World-Class Google AI*, https://cloud.google.com/ai/llms?hl=en (accessed 4 Aug. 2024).
680. Nvidia, *Large Language Models*, https://www.nvidia.com/en-us/glossary/data-science/large-language-models/ (accessed 4 Aug. 2024).
681. LII Legal Information Institute, *Consumer Protection Laws*, Cornell Law School, https://www.law.cornell.edu/wex/consumer_protection_laws.
682. Federal Trade Commission, *Truth in Advertising*, https://www.ftc.gov/news-events/topics/truth-advertising (accessed 4 Aug. 2024).

9.4 ADDRESSING REGULATORY GAPS IN AI GOVERNANCE

9.4.1 Introduction

The rapid advancement of LLMs like ChatGPT has ushered in a new era, transforming the way we live, work, and interact. As LLM technologies permeate various aspects of society, from healthcare to finance and beyond, it becomes imperative to assess the existing regulatory landscape and identify gaps that may impede the responsible development and deployment of AI systems. Regulatory frameworks must evolve to keep pace with these technological advancements, ensuring ethical practices, accountability, and the protection of individual rights. Several challenges and regulatory gaps have emerged, highlighting the need for comprehensive policy options to govern the AI-powered new world system.

9.4.2 Specific Regulatory Gaps in AI Governance

As AI systems become more intricate over time, stakeholders, including developers, regulators, and end-users, face numerous challenges regarding their governance. AI governance refers to a system of rules, practices, and tools which ensures the ethical and responsible use of AI technology aligning with organisational goals, legal requirements, and ethical principles.[683] Nevertheless, the current state of AI governance is fragmented, inconsistent, and inadequate to address the complex and dynamic issues raised by AI. This sub-section discusses some specific regulatory gaps in AI governance, including: (a) the lack of standardised definitions and classifications for AI, (b) the lack of transparency, (c) data security and privacy, (d) liability and responsibility challenges, and (e) copyright and patent rights issues. This sub-section also prescribes suitable policy options in response to the regulatory gaps in AI governance.

9.4.2.1 Lack of Standardised Definitions and Classifications

AI encompasses a wide spectrum of systems under the expansive umbrella of AI.[684] One notable regulatory gap in the field of AI governance pertains to the absence of standardised definitions and classifications for AI systems. Standardising means making things of the same type conform to a set of shared characteristics, essentially creating uniformity within a category. For example, the Cambridge Dictionary defines 'standardise' as making things of the same type have consistent basic features.[685] Nonetheless, the lack of a universally accepted definition and taxonomy presents a significant challenge to the development of targeted and effective regulations.

683. Matti Mäntymäki et al., *Defining Organizational AI Governance*, 2 AI Ethics 603–609 (2022) https://doi.org/10.1007/s43681-022-00143-x.
684. https://yjolt.org/sites/default/files/21_yale_j.l._tech._106_0.pdf.
685. Cambridge Dictionary, *Standardizing*, https://dictionary.cambridge.org/dictionary/english/standardizing (accessed 4 Aug. 2024).

The ambiguity concerning the definition and taxonomy of AI also makes it difficult to tailor regulations to address the unique challenges of each technology, potentially overregulating some while leaving others dangerously under-scrutinised. The consequences of this gap are far-reaching. Without a clear and shared understanding of what constitutes different types of AI technologies, regulators face difficulties in crafting policies that can adequately address the diverse and rapidly evolving landscape of AI applications.[686] This regulatory gap also hinders the establishment of a cohesive and universally applicable framework for overseeing AI development and deployment. A self-driving car, for instance, poses vastly different concerns than a facial recognition system, yet both fall under the ambiguous umbrella of AI. This ambiguity underscores the need for a common language and baseline framework to navigate the regulatory landscape effectively.

Addressing the lack of standardised definitions and classifications for AI is crucial for the responsible development and deployment of AI technologies. Despite lacking a universal definition of AI, the 'OECD Framework for the Classification of AI Systems: A Tool for Effective AI Policies' as a step in the right direction, provides a comprehensive approach to categorising AI systems, offering a foundation for future collaborations among governments, industry players, and academia to navigate the complex landscape of AI governance.[687] This framework categorises AI systems across five key dimensions (people and planet, economic context, data and input, AI model, task and output), enabling policymakers and stakeholders to assess their risks and opportunities.[688] By providing a common language and baseline framework for registries, regulations, and risk management, the Organisation for Economic Co-operation and Development (OECD) Framework fosters collaboration among governments, industry, and academia, paving the way for RAI development.

9.4.2.2 Lack of Transparency

Transparency in AI-generated decisions is essential for accountability and for identifying and addressing potential biases. The ability to scrutinise the decision-making process is crucial for ensuring fairness and minimising harm caused by AI systems. Without transparency, stakeholders face challenges in comprehending the inner workings of AI systems, hindering the responsible development and deployment of this transformative technology. Specifically, the lack of transparency hinders RAI development and deployment and raises ethical concerns in critical areas like healthcare or

686. Naveen Joshi, *7 Types Of Artificial Intelligence*, Forbes (19 Jun. 2019), https://www.forbes.com/sites/cognitiveworld/2019/06/19/7-types-of-artificial-intelligence/?sh=11874a93233e; Coursera, *What Is Artificial Intelligence*, https://www.coursera.org/articles/what-is-artificial-intelligence (accessed 4 Aug. 2024); Michael Hill, *7 Types of Artificial Intelligence and How They Work?*, Tech Research Online (5 Oct. 2020), https://techresearchonline.com/blog/types-of-artificial-intelligence/.
687. OECD, *OECD Framework for the Classification of AI Systems: A Tool for Effective AI Policies*, https://oecd.ai/en/classification (accessed 4 Aug. 2024).
688. OECD, *The OECD Framework for the Classification of AI Systems* (2022), https://wp.oecd.ai/app/uploads/2022/02/Classification-2-pager-1.pdf.

criminal justice systems. Transparency not only fosters accountability but also helps identify and rectify biases or unintended consequences that may arise in AI-generated decisions.[689]

Therefore, developers, regulators, and end-users should have access to clear information about how these systems operate and make decisions. Moreover, policies should mandate transparency requirements, enabling individuals to understand and contest AI-generated decisions. In fields like predictive policing, where AI algorithms forecast crime, transparency is vital.[690] It builds public trust by addressing potential bias and discrimination concerns. It empowers developers to constantly improve algorithms, fostering a cycle of accountability and advancement.[691] Thus, the EU's GDPR further underscores transparency as a fundamental right, allowing individuals to understand and contest decisions made by AI systems.[692] By integrating transparency mandates into AI governance policies, regulators can pave the way for responsible and ethical use of this powerful technology.

To address the lack of transparency, it is essential for policies to mandate transparency requirements. These mandates empower individuals to comprehend and contest decisions made by AI systems, thereby reinforcing accountability.[693] This becomes especially critical in sectors like predictive policing, where AI algorithms forecast crime. Transparent algorithms not only build public trust by addressing concerns related to bias and discrimination but also provide developers with valuable insights for continuous improvement.

9.4.2.3 Data Security and Privacy Issues

While transparency is essential, the next critical frontier in LLM governance lies in data security and privacy. Existing data protection laws like GDPR and CCPA offer valuable safeguards, but their application to AI-specific scenarios, particularly those involving LLMs, remains ambiguous. This ambiguity stems from the unique nature of LLMs, which infer and generate information, potentially revealing sensitive details not explicitly provided in the training data. For example, the GDPR defines personal data as any information relating to an identified or identifiable natural person yet remains silent about the identifiability of personal data or what constitutes inference.[694] Similarly, while the CCPA empowers consumers to access, delete, and opt out of the sale of their

689. Nicholas Diakopoulos, *Algorithmic Accountability: Journalistic Investigation of Computational Power Structures*, 3 Digital Journalism 398 (2014), https://doi.org/10.1080/21670811.2014.976411.
690. ProPublica, *Machine Bias: Risk Assessments in Criminal Sentencing* (23 May 2016), https://www.propublica.org/article/machine-bias-risk-assessments-in-criminal-sentencing.
691. Bryce Goodman & Seth Flaxman, *European Union Regulations on Algorithmic Decision-Making and a 'Right to Explanation'*, 38 AI Mag. 50 (2017), https://doi.org/10.1609/aimag.v38i3.2741.
692. *See supra* n. 397.
693. Hagendorff, T., *The Ethics of AI Ethics: An Evaluation of Guidelines*, 30 Minds & Machines 99 (2020), https://doi.org/10.1007/s11023-020-09517-8, https://arxiv.org/ftp/arxiv/papers/1903/1903.03425.pdf.
694. Nir Kshetri, *Cybercrime and Privacy Threats of Large Language Models*, 25 IT Prof. 9, 9–13 (May–June 2023), https://doi.org/10.1109/MITP.2023.3275489.

personal information, it offers no guidance on the issue of data generation or synthesis by AI systems.[695] Addressing these challenges requires a multifaceted approach:

- First, existing data protection frameworks need clarification, with specific guidance on how they apply to inferred data and AI-generated information.
- Second, technical advancements like 'privacy-enhancing computation' can enable secure data analysis while minimising privacy risks.
- Third, industry-wide standards and best practices for LLM development and deployment should be established, promoting responsible data handling and user privacy.
- Finally, international collaboration is crucial to harmonise data protection laws and ensure consistent, effective regulation across borders. Only by addressing these data security and privacy concerns can we ensure responsible and ethical development and deployment of LLMs, paving the way for a future where these powerful tools contribute positively to society.

9.4.2.4 Liability and Responsibility Issues

LLM deployment across industries introduces substantial liability and responsibility challenges as these AI systems become increasingly sophisticated and autonomous.[696] The intricate nature of LLMs often makes it difficult to pinpoint responsibility when their actions lead to undesirable outcomes. Another aspect of the liability and responsibility challenges of LLMs is the potential impact of their outputs on human rights and dignity. LLMs can generate content that may infringe on the rights of individuals or groups, such as privacy, freedom of expression, or non-discrimination. For example, LLMs may produce harmful content, such as hate speech, misinformation, or plagiarism, that could violate the rights of others or undermine the credibility of sources.[697] Moreover, LLMs may also affect the dignity and autonomy of human users, who may become dependent on or influenced by the LLMs' suggestions or decisions.

Therefore, it is crucial to ensure that LLMs respect human rights and dignity while empowering users with awareness of their limitations and risks. Existing legal frameworks often struggle to unravel the intricate web of LLM operations, leaving questions of liability unresolved.[698] Addressing this challenge requires a paradigm shift in legal thinking.[699] Ad hoc adjustments to existing negligence or product liability laws

695. *See supra* n. 610.
696. Vishnu Pamula, *An Introduction to LLMOps: Operationalizing and Managing Large Language Models, Tech Community,* Microsoft (27 Aug. 2023), https://techcommunity.microsoft.com/t5/ai-machine-learning-blog/an-introduction-to-llmops-operationalizing-and-managing-large/ba-p/3910996.
697. *See supra* n. 611.
698. Zhongxiang Sun, *A Short Survey of Viewing Large Language Models in Legal Aspect,* arXiv preprint arXiv:2303.09136 (16 Mar. 2023), https://arxiv.org/pdf/2303.09136.
699. Kingston, J.K.C., Artificial Intelligence and Legal Liability, in Research and Development, in *Intelligent Systems XXXIII: Incorporating Applications and Innovations in Intelligent Systems* XXIV 33, 269–279 (Springer Int'l Publishing 2016), https://arxiv.org/ftp/arxiv/papers/1802/1802.07782.pdf.

may offer temporary remedies but lack the necessary granularity to effectively address LLM-specific challenges. Instead, we need new, comprehensive legal frameworks that acknowledge the unique capabilities and limitations of these powerful systems. This could involve, for example, stricter product liability measures for AI systems, exploring avenues like strict liability for demonstrably harmful consequences, or even establishing dedicated LLM-specific insurance schemes.[700]

As these technologies advance, it is also crucial to re-evaluate traditional liability principles and develop new legal frameworks that precisely account for unique characteristics and challenges presented by LLMs.[701] Another potential approach to address LLM liability and responsibility challenges is human-centric, emphasising human oversight and accountability. This technique involves the ability of users or operators to monitor, intervene, or override LLM outputs.[702]

Moreover, by implementing mechanisms like audits, reviews, and feedback loops, we can mitigate LLM risks, address potential harms, and foster trust in these powerful technologies. Some other policy measures may include implementing stricter product liability for AI harm, creating new liability frameworks like strict liability or AI-specific insurance schemes, and formulating ethical and technical standards like transparency guidelines and XAI practices. All these measures can play a role in preventing or mitigating AI-related harm.[703]

9.4.2.5 Copyright and Patent Rights Issues

The integration of LLMs across industries raises significant copyright and patent rights issues, reflecting the challenges in balancing innovation with IP protection. As LLMs increasingly contribute to content creation, there are concerns about copyright ownership, particularly in instances where generated text closely resembles existing copyrighted works. Additionally, patenting aspects of LLMs, such as novel algorithms or architectures, introduce complexities in determining inventiveness and prior art-work. A recent study introduced a method called EmbMarker, which serves as an embedding watermark designed to protect the copyright of LLMs in the context of

700. Neel Guha et al., A Collaboratively Built Benchmark for Measuring Legal Reasoning in Large Language Models, in *Advances in Neural Information Processing Systems*, Vol. 36 (2023), https://arxiv.org/abs/2308.11462.
701. Brent Daniel Mittelstadt et al., *The Ethics of Algorithms: Mapping the Debate*, 3 Big Data & Society 1 (2016), https://doi.org/10.1177/2053951716679679.
702. Mo Aboobakar, *Large Language Models: The Missing Link in Corporate Intelligence*, Deloitte (UK) (23 Aug. 2023), https://www.deloitte.com/uk/en/Industries/technology/blogs/2023/large-language-models-the-missing-link-in-corporate-intelligence.html; Jon Burg, *The 5 Challenges Posed by LLMs for Service Leaders*, TechSee Blog (2 Aug. 2022), https://techsee.com/blog/the-5-challenges-llms-pose-to-service-leaders/.
703. Heather Fraser & Owen Daniels, *Understanding AI Harms: An Overview, Center for Security and Emerging Technology*, Georgetown University, https://cset.georgetown.edu/article/understanding-ai-harms-an-overview/ (accessed 4 Aug. 2024); *Policy Supplement: Managing AI Risks in an Era of Rapid Progress, Managing AI Risks*, https://managing-ai-risks.com/policy_supplement.pdf (accessed 4 Aug. 2024). OECD, *An Overview of National AI Strategies and Policies*, https://goingdigital.oecd.org/.

Embedding as a Service (EaaS). EmbMarker achieves this by embedding backdoors into the model's embeddings, effectively serving as a watermark to safeguard IP.[704]

However, LLMs have revolutionised the field of patent monetisation by making it easier for inventors and businesses to conduct extensive patent analysis, identify licensing opportunities, and evaluate the competitive landscape.[705] Striking a balance between fostering innovation and respecting IP rights is crucial for the responsible development and deployment of LLMs in various industries. Balancing these concerns requires a multi-pronged approach: standardised data licensing for fair compensation,[706] open-source LLM initiatives for collaboration,[707] and evolving legal frameworks with new copyright exceptions or clearer patentability guidelines.[708]

In summary, LLM integration poses intricate challenges for copyright and patent rights, necessitating sophisticated legal frameworks. Concerns about copyright ownership, especially when LLM's content resembles existing works, underscore the need for nuanced approaches. The EmbMarker method, from a recent study, showcases dynamic strategies for addressing copyright in LLMs. LLMs transform patent monetisation, offering advanced capabilities for analysis and evaluation. The multifaceted approach, with standardised data licensing and open-source initiatives, ensures responsible LLM development. Balancing innovation with IP rights is crucial for navigating this complex landscape.

9.4.3 Policy Options for LLMs like ChatGPT Governance

9.4.3.1 Role of Education and Public Awareness

The evolution of LLMs like ChatGPT presents both immense opportunities and unprecedented challenges. Nonetheless, the immense potential of these models is accompanied by equally significant ethical concerns, raising pressing questions about their regulation and governance. In navigating this complex landscape, education and public awareness emerge as crucial cornerstones for fostering responsible and effective frameworks. Educating the public about the capabilities and limitations of LLMs is essential for building trust and mitigating potential harm. This involves demystifying

704. Wenjun Peng et al., Are You Copying My Model? Protecting the Copyright of Large Language Models for EaaS via Backdoor Watermark, in *Proceedings of the 61st Annual Meeting of the Association for Computational Linguistics* 7653, 7653–7668 (Jingwei Yi et al., eds, 2023), https://arxiv.org/abs/2305.10036.
705. XLScout, *Demystifying Patent Monetization with LLMs & Generative AI* (27 Jul. 2023), https://xlscout.ai/demystifying-patent-monetization-with-llms-generative-ai (accessed 7 Aug. 2024).
706. Misha Benjamin et al., *Towards Standardization of Data Licenses: The Montreal Data License*, arXiv Preprint arXiv:1903.12262 (2019), https://arxiv.org/abs/1903.12262.
707. *Ibid.*
708. Council of Europe, Ad hoc Committee on Artificial Intelligence (CAHAI), *A Legal Framework for AI Systems* (2021), https://edoc.coe.int/en/artificial-intelligence/9648-a-legal-framework-for-ai-systems.html; European Commission, *AI Act*, https://digital-strategy.ec.europa.eu/en/policies/european-approach-artificial-intelligence.

the technology, dispelling myths surrounding its sentience or consciousness, and highlighting its inherent biases and susceptibility to manipulation.[709]

LLMs like ChatGPT lack sentience or consciousness. They operate by identifying and replicating patterns in the vast amounts of data they were trained on, producing text without any genuine understanding or intentionality. This distinction is crucial for public awareness, as it helps demystify the nature of these models and prevents misconceptions about their abilities.[710] By educating the public on the true nature of LLMs, we can foster a more accurate understanding of their functionalities and limitations, ensuring that people do not attribute human-like thought processes to these advanced, yet fundamentally non-sentient, tools. Initiatives like educational workshops, online resources, and media campaigns can play a vital role in disseminating accurate information and fostering a culture of digital literacy.

Furthermore, educating policymakers and regulators about LLMs like ChatGPT is crucial for creating effective regulations, requiring ongoing collaboration between the tech industry, academia, and government bodies. The UK's 2023 White Paper on GAI exemplifies this approach, advocating for a flexible regulatory framework that can adapt to rapid AI advancements. The establishment of a 'Foundation Model Taskforce' reflects the UK's commitment to balancing the benefits and risks of AI through informed regulation.[711] Similarly, Google emphasises the importance of balanced, fact-based analyses that include diverse perspectives, ensuring that AI regulations are both responsible and adaptable to the evolving nature of the technology.[712]

Raising public awareness about the societal implications of LLMs, such as ChatGPT, is vital for promoting responsible governance and ensuring informed democratic participation. Public discourse can significantly impact several key areas, including the potential for job displacement, the risks of algorithmic bias, and concerns regarding privacy erosion. To address job displacement challenges, it is essential to foster open discussions and establish platforms that support workers in reskilling and transitioning to new roles.[713] Developing legal and ethical frameworks that incorporate public input can contribute to the creation of fairer and more transparent AI systems while reducing algorithmic bias.[714] Moreover, public forums and open dialogues are

709. Stefan E. Huber et al., *Leveraging the Potential of Large Language Models in Education Through Playful and Game-Based Learning*, 36 Educ. Psychol. Rev. 25 (2024), https://doi.org/10.1007/s10648-024-09868-z.
710. Solenix, *Exploring AI Challenges: Common Limitations of Large Language Models Such as Those Used in AI Systems* (5 Oct. 2023), https://solenix.ch/blog/2023-10-05/exploring-ai-challenges-common-limitations-large-language-models-such-those-used.
711. Alex Kirkhope et al., *The UK Approach to Generative AI: Taking an 'LLM' in AI Regulation*, Shoosmiths (2024), https://www.shoosmiths.com/insights/articles/the-uk-approach-to-generative-ai-taking-an-llm-in-ai-regulation.
712. Google, *Building a Responsible Regulatory Framework for AI*, https://ai.google/static/documents/building-a-responsible-regulatory-framework-for-ai.pdf (accessed 7 Aug. 2024).
713. David Elliott, *3 Important Considerations for Leaders as Large Language Models Transform Business*, World Economic Forum (8 Jan. 2024), https://www.weforum.org/agenda/2024/01/large-language-models-future-jobs/.
714. Sonia M. Gipson Rankin, *Mitigating Algorithmic Bias: Strategies for Addressing Discrimination in Data*, American Bar Association scitechlawyer.org (2024), https://digitalrepository.unm.edu/cgi/viewcontent.cgi?article=1959&context=law_facultyscholarship.

crucial for making privacy considerations central to the development and governance of these technologies.[715]

In conclusion, the governance of LLMs like ChatGPT hinges on a multifaceted approach that prioritises education, public awareness, and informed policymaking. By demystifying the technology and communicating its limitations and potential risks, we can build a foundation of trust and digital literacy that empowers the public to engage with these tools responsibly. Additionally, ongoing collaboration between the tech industry, academia, and government is essential for crafting adaptable and effective regulations that keep pace with AI advancements. Moreover, fostering public discourse on the broader societal implications of LLMs ensures that the development and governance of these technologies are inclusive, ethical, and aligned with democratic values. Through these combined efforts, we can navigate the challenges and opportunities presented by LLMs in a way that maximises their benefits while minimising potential harm.

9.4.3.2 Accountability and Liability

The governance of LLMs like ChatGPT necessitates a robust framework for maintaining accountability and liability, given the potential impact and influence these models wield in various domains. Accountability is a key principle in ethical AI governance, ensuring that developers, deployers, and users are answerable for the actions and decisions made by LLMs. To establish accountability, it is imperative to define clear lines of responsibility and articulate the roles of different stakeholders in the development and deployment process. Many studies emphasise the importance of establishing transparent mechanisms for accountability in AI systems.[716]

Liability becomes a critical consideration when addressing the consequences of actions taken by LLMs. In the event of errors, biases, or unintended outcomes, understanding who is liable for the resultant harm is essential. Legal frameworks need to adapt to the challenges posed by LLMs, and lawmakers must clarify liability issues to provide a legal basis for holding individuals or entities accountable. This involves considering traditional notions of product liability and negligence and exploring novel approaches that consider the unique characteristics of AI systems. The works of Diakopoulos highlight the need for accountability in algorithmic decision-making and the challenges associated with attributing liability in complex AI systems.[717]

---

715. *See supra* n. 714.
716. Luciano Floridi et al., *AI4People: An Ethical Framework for a Good AI Society: Opportunities, Risks, Principles, and Recommendations*, 28 Minds & Machines 689 (2018), https://doi.org/10.1007/s11023-018-9482-5; Williams, R. et al., *From Transparency to Accountability of Intelligent Systems: Moving Beyond Aspirations*, Data & Policy, at e7 (2022), https://www.cambridge.org/core/journals/data-and-policy/article/from-transparency-to-accountability-of-intelligent-systems-moving-beyond-aspirations/E412FF94EC2A293985D414D80415F4AA.
717. Nicholas Diakopoulos, *Algorithmic Accountability, Digital Journalism*, Digital Journalism (2014), 10.1080/21670811.2014.976411; Nick Diakopoulos, *Accountability in Algorithmic Decision Making*, 59 Comm. ACM 56 (2016), https://doi.org/10.1145/2844110, https://acmwebvm01.acm.org/magazines/2016/2/197421-accountability-in-algorithmic-decision-making/fulltext.

Moreover, maintaining accountability and liability involves continuous monitoring and auditing of LLMs throughout their lifecycle. Regular assessments can help identify and rectify biases, errors, or ethical concerns that may emerge over time. Independent auditing bodies, collaborations between academia and industry, and the development of standardised evaluation protocols contribute to effective oversight. The Global Partnership on Artificial Intelligence's (GPAI's) guidelines on RAI development emphasises the importance of audits as a means of ensuring accountability and transparency in AI systems.[718]

In addition, fostering a culture of responsible development and deployment of LLMs requires incentives and disincentives. Encouraging ethical behaviour through positive reinforcement, such as certification programs for RAI development, can complement legal measures.[719] Simultaneously, imposing consequences for unethical practices, such as fines or restrictions, serves as a deterrent. Balancing incentives and disincentives is crucial for promoting accountability and ensuring that the development and deployment of LLMs align with ethical and societal norms.

In conclusion, accountability and liability are integral components of effective governance for LLMs like ChatGPT. The establishment of clear responsibility, legal frameworks, continuous monitoring, and a balance of incentives and disincentives contribute to a governance structure that ensures the ethical development and deployment of LLMs. As AI technology continues to advance, it is essential to adapt and refine these governance mechanisms to address emerging challenges and complexities.

9.4.3.3 Global Cooperation and Standardisation

The governance of LLMs necessitates a global approach that emphasises cooperation and standardisation. In the absence of consistent international guidelines, the development and deployment of LLMs may lead to fragmented regulatory landscapes and ethical standards. Global cooperation is essential to foster collaboration between nations, organisations, and researchers, ensuring a unified and comprehensive governance framework. Initiatives like the GPAI bridge the gap between stakeholders and promote collaborative ethical frameworks to tackle AI's global challenges.[720]

Standardisation plays a crucial role in achieving harmonised governance for LLMs. Establishing common standards helps create a level playing field, promotes interoperability, and facilitates the exchange of best practices. Organisations like the ISO can contribute by developing international standards for the ethical development,

718. OECD, *Global Partnership on Artificial Intelligence* (June 2020), https://www.oecd.org/en/about/programmes/global-partnership-on-artificial-intelligence.html.
719. It is worth noting that several organisations offer certification programmes in RAI development targeted at researchers, developers, and policymakers. Among others, these include the Microsoft Certified: Azure AI Engineer Associate, the Intel® Edge AI Certification, Nvidia's Jetson AI Courses and Certifications, as well as programmes from CITI and the Certified Artificial Intelligence Scientist (CAIS) initiative.
720. OECD, *Global Partnership on Artificial Intelligence (GPAI)*, https://oecd.ai/en/gpai (accessed 8 Aug. 2024).

deployment and use of LLMs.[721] These standards can cover many aspects like transparency, accountability, and bias mitigation, providing a shared foundation for developers, regulators, and users across the globe.

A global perspective on LLM governance requires acknowledging and respecting cultural and contextual differences. Standardisation efforts should be inclusive and consider diverse perspectives to avoid imposing a one-size-fits-all approach. Engaging with stakeholders from various regions and backgrounds ensures that ethical guidelines are culturally sensitive and reflective of different societal values.[722] This inclusivity is crucial for fostering a truly global governance framework that respects the diversity of perspectives on AI ethics.

International collaborations can extend beyond the establishment of standards to include joint research endeavours and knowledge-sharing initiatives. Collaborative research projects can help address the technical challenges associated with LLMs and contribute to a shared pool of knowledge. Open dialogues between researchers, industry professionals, and policymakers from different countries can lead to the development of governance models that are adaptable and relevant to diverse contexts. Platforms like the OpenAI Research Collaborations exemplify the potential for international cooperation in advancing R&D in AI.[723]

In conclusion, global cooperation and standardisation are integral components of effective governance for LLMs like ChatGPT. By fostering collaboration, establishing international standards, respecting cultural differences, and promoting joint research initiatives, the global community can work towards a harmonised and ethical approach to LLM development and deployment. As LLMs like ChatGPT continue to advance, a collective and inclusive effort is crucial to address the challenges and opportunities presented by LLMs on a global scale.

9.4.3.4 Adopting AI Laws and Policies

The governance of LLMs like ChatGPT requires the establishment of robust AI laws and policies to ensure their ethical development and deployment across industries. While existing legal frameworks may provide a foundation, specific regulations tailored to the unique characteristics of LLMs are imperative. Legislative bodies need to adapt to the rapid advancements in AI technology and enact laws to address issues such as transparency, accountability, and bias mitigation. Initiatives like the EU's new AI Act

721. https://www.iso.org/publication/PUB100011.html.
722. Lisa Häberlein & Philipp Hövel, Importance and Necessity of Stakeholder Engagement, in *Ethics and Responsible Research and Innovation in Practice* 27, 27 (Eduardo González-Esteban et al., eds, 2023), https://doi.org/10.1007/978-3-031-33177-0_3.
723. OpenAI, *OpenAI & Los Alamos National Laboratory Work Together* (21 Dec. 2023), https://openai.com/index/openai-and-los-alamos-national-laboratory-work-together/; AI Tool Advisor, *OpenAI's Collaborative Efforts: Partnering with Other Organizations for AI Research and Development* (21 Mar. 2023), https://www.aitooladvisor.com/2023/03/21/openais-collaborative-efforts-partnering-with-other-organizations-for-ai-research-and-development/.

represent steps toward creating a legal framework that sets standards for AI applications, including LLMs.[724]

Transparency is a key aspect of effective AI laws and policies. AI regulations should mandate that developers disclose information about the functioning, decision-making processes, and potential biases of LLMs. This ensures that users and other stakeholders have a clear understanding of how these models operate and make decisions. Transparency requirements can enhance accountability and contribute to building trust between developers, regulators, and the public. As proposed by the EU, the right to obtain an explanation of decisions made by AI systems is a crucial element to empower individuals and ensure transparency.[725]

Another crucial aspect of AI laws and policies is accountability, which involves specifying responsibilities and liabilities for various stakeholders throughout the AI lifecycle, from development to deployment. Clear guidelines are essential to address potential issues such as algorithmic errors, biases leading to discriminatory outcomes, and unforeseen negative impacts. Legal frameworks should outline mechanisms for holding developers, deployers, and users accountable for the ethical implications of LLMs. Developing effective accountability measures aligns with principles advocated by several studies, which emphasise the importance of assigning responsibility for AI systems' actions.[726]

Furthermore, AI laws should include provisions for ongoing monitoring, auditing, and updating of LLMs. Regular assessments are necessary to identify and rectify biases, errors, or ethical concerns that may arise over time. Auditing mechanisms ensure that LLMs remain in compliance with evolving ethical standards and legal requirements.[727] Incorporating flexibility in AI laws to accommodate advancements in technology and emerging ethical considerations is essential for creating a regulatory framework that can adapt to the dynamic nature of LLMs.

Finally, the governance of LLMs like ChatGPT requires the adoption of AI laws and policies that specifically address the unique challenges posed by these advanced language models. Transparency, accountability, ongoing monitoring, and adaptability should be key pillars of such legal frameworks to ensure responsible development and deployment. By enacting and continuously refining AI laws, policymakers can contribute to a regulatory environment that fosters innovation while upholding ethical standards.

724. *See supra* n. 58.
725. *Ibid.*
726. Luciano Floridi & Jeremy Cowls, *A Unified Framework of Five Principles for AI in Society*, 1 Harv. Data Sci. Rev. 1 (2019), https://doi.org/10.1162/99608f92.8cd550d1; Bryson, J. & Winfield, A., *Standardizing Ethical Design for Artificial Intelligence and Autonomous Systems*, 50(5) Computer, at 116 (May 2017), https://doi.org/10.1109/MC.2017.154.
727. *See supra* n. 678; Donovan, *How to Audit Your LLMs to Build Trusted AI*, Medium (13 Feb. 2024), https://medium.com/@donovan_10342/how-to-audit-your-llms-to-build-trusted-ai-56f3e56dc420.

9.4.3.5 *Ensuring Ethical AI Practices*

LLMs like ChatGPT have become transformative tools, weaving their magic into everything from generating creative content to translating languages. Nevertheless, their immense potential is intertwined with ethical concerns, demanding a paradigm shift towards ethical AI practices. Therefore, ethical guidelines are crucial to guide developers, researchers, and organisations in the responsible development and deployment of LLMs. Ensuring ethical AI practices for LLMs necessitates a multifaceted approach that prioritises fairness, transparency, and accountability.

Transparency is a foundational principle for ethical AI practices, particularly in the context of LLMs. Developers should provide clear information about the capabilities, limitations, and decision-making processes of these models. OpenAI, the organisation behind ChatGPT, has recognised the importance of transparency and has taken steps to share information about its models and development processes with the public.[728] This commitment to transparency is a positive step toward building trust and ensuring that users are informed about the functioning of LLMs.

Fairness is another critical aspect of ethical AI practices. LLMs can inadvertently perpetuate biases present in the training data, leading to unfair outcomes. To address this, ethical guidelines should include measures for identifying and mitigating biases in LLMs. Many researchers advocate for standardising ethical design to ensure fairness and prevent discriminatory impacts in AI and autonomous systems.[729] Adopting such principles in the governance of LLMs contributes to the ethical development of these models. Additionally, continuous monitoring and updating of these guidelines are essential to adapt to evolving societal norms and technological advancements. Engaging diverse stakeholders in the creation and review of ethical standards can further enhance the inclusivity and robustness of AI systems.

Furthermore, accountability is essential to hold stakeholders responsible for the ethical implications of LLMs. Ethical guidelines should outline mechanisms for addressing errors, biases, and unintended consequences. Developers and organisations deploying LLMs must be held accountable for the societal impact of their creations. With the growth of organisations and society over time, we must continually evolve our approach to RAI. This involves fostering open dialogue and collaboration among stakeholders, including businesses, governments, non-governmental organisations (NGOs), and academic researchers. By engaging with AI responsibly, we can ensure it benefits society and fulfils its promise of a better future.[730] Additionally, incorporating user feedback and involving affected communities in the development process contributes to a more inclusive and accountable approach.

In conclusion, ensuring ethical AI practices is fundamental to the governance of LLMs like ChatGPT. Ethical guidelines that prioritise transparency, fairness, and

728. OpenAI, *How OpenAI Is Approaching 2024 Worldwide Elections* (15 Jan. 2024), https://openai.com/index/how-openai-is-approaching-2024-worldwide-elections/.
729. *See* Luciano Floridi et al., *supra* n. 716; *see also supra* n. 37.
730. Microsoft, *Putting Principles into Practice: How We Approach Responsible AI at Microsoft*, https://www.microsoft.com/cms/api/am/binary/RE4pKH5 (accessed 8 Aug. 2024).

accountability provide a framework for responsible development and deployment. By aligning with established principles and fostering transparency and inclusivity, the governance of LLMs can contribute to the ethical advancement of AI technologies.

9.5 CONCLUSION

As we transition into an increasingly AI-driven global landscape, the task of addressing regulatory gaps and crafting effective policy frameworks becomes a pressing priority. The rapid advancement of AI demands a well-rounded approach that encompasses standardised definitions, ethical guidelines, and robust accountability mechanisms. Policymakers must strive to establish a comprehensive regulatory environment that not only encourages RAI innovation but also ensures its deployment aligns with societal values. This entails the creation of policies that are not only technically sound but also ethically grounded, aiming to mitigate risks while fostering opportunities for growth and development.

In achieving this goal, the importance of collaboration cannot be overstated. A multifaceted approach involving governments, industry leaders, academic institutions, and civil society is crucial for crafting a regulatory landscape that is both inclusive and effective. Global cooperation is essential to ensure that AI technologies are developed and deployed in a manner that benefits all, rather than exacerbating existing inequalities. Public awareness and engagement also play a pivotal role in this process, as an informed populace can contribute to and support policies that reflect the collective interest. By working together across sectors and borders, we can build a regulatory framework that maximises the potential of AI while safeguarding against its inherent risks, ensuring a future that is equitable and just for all.

CHAPTER 10

Cross-Border Regulatory Challenges in AI Governance

10.1 INTRODUCTION

The widespread adoption of AI technologies has driven significant advancements in various fields, from healthcare to finance, education and business. As AI continues to evolve, it fosters an increasingly interconnected global landscape, presenting distinct challenges for regulation and governance. Establishing effective governance mechanisms that ensure the responsible and beneficial use of AI is crucial. This context requires a coordinated and adaptable regulatory approach that transcends national borders, recognising the international nature of AI technologies. Given this context in view, this chapter aims to unravel the intricate challenges faced by policymakers in achieving effective AI governance on a global scale, illuminating the complexities inherent in the borderless nature of AI innovation.

10.2 CROSS-BORDER REGULATORY CHALLENGES IN AI GOVERNANCE

AI is a rapidly evolving technology that has the potential to transform various aspects of human society, such as the economy, education, healthcare, law, and security. Nonetheless, AI also poses significant ethical, social, and legal challenges that require appropriate regulation and governance to ensure its responsible and beneficial use. Different countries and regions have different approaches and perspectives on how to regulate and govern AI, which can create conflicts and inconsistencies in the global regulatory landscape.[731] For instance, the EU has taken a risk-based approach that

731. Patricia Gomes Rêgo de Almeida et al., *Artificial Intelligence Regulation: A Framework for Governance*, 23 Ethics Info. Tech. 505 (2021), https://doi.org/10.1007/s10676-021-09593-z.

classifies AI systems into four categories: (a) unacceptable, (b) high risk, (c) limited risk, and (d) minimal risk.[732] In contrast, the US has adopted a more flexible and sector-specific approach, relying on existing laws and regulations to address AI-related issues.[733] China has issued various guidelines and standards emphasising the ethical and social values of AI, including fairness, transparency, accountability, and human dignity.[734]

These divergent approaches may create inconsistencies and uncertainties for AI developers and users who operate across borders and may hinder the global interoperability and innovation of AI. Therefore, there is a need for harmonisation and coordination of AI regulation and governance across borders, to foster trust, cooperation, and innovation in the field. Nevertheless, AI governance is not uniform or consistent across different countries and regions, which creates regulatory challenges and uncertainties for businesses, organisations, and individuals that operate or interact with AI systems in a global context.[735] This situation presents several regulatory challenges that require thorough investigation. These challenges include the absence of a common definition and understanding of AI, the lack of global consensus and coordination, inadequate and ineffective regulatory mechanisms and institutions, the absence of standardised regulations across different jurisdictions, concerns regarding privacy and data protection, and issues related to transparency and accountability in AI systems.

10.2.1 Lack of a Common Definition and Understanding

One of the main challenges in cross-border AI governance is the lack of a common definition and understanding of what AI is and what it can do. The term 'AI' encompasses a wide range of fields, including computer science, data analytics, hardware/software engineering, linguistics, neuroscience, philosophy, and psychology.[736] Moreover, AI systems include a broad range of technologies, such as ML, deep learning, and NLP.[737] In business, AI encompasses technologies like ML and deep

732. European AI Alliance, *The EU AI Act's Risk-Based Approach to High-Risk Systems and What They Mean for Users*, Futurium (2023), https://futurium.ec.europa.eu/en/european-ai-alliance/document/eu-ai-acts-risk-based-approach-high-risk-systems-and-what-they-mean-users.
733. Exec. Off. of the President, *Guidance for Regulation of Artificial Intelligence Applications* (2020), https://www.whitehouse.gov/wp-content/uploads/2020/01/Draft-OMB-Memo-on-Regulation-of-AI-1-7-19.pdf; Alex Engler, *The EU and U.S. Diverge on AI Regulation: A Transatlantic Comparison and Steps to Alignment, Brookings Institution* (9 Sep. 2021), https://www.brookings.edu/articles/the-eu-and-us-diverge-on-ai-regulation-a-transatlantic-comparison-and-steps-to-alignment/.
734. Junhua Zhu, *AI Ethics with Chinese Characteristics? Concerns and Preferred Solutions in Chinese Academia*, 39 AI & Soc'y 1261 (2024), https://doi.org/10.1007/s00146-022-01578-w; Huw Roberts et al., *The Chinese Approach to Artificial Intelligence: An Analysis of Policy, Ethics, and Regulation*, 36 AI & Soc'y 59 (2021), https://doi.org/10.1007/s00146-020-00992-2.
735. IBM, *What Is AI Governance?*, https://www.ibm.com/topics/ai-governance.
736. Google Cloud, *What Is Artificial Intelligence?*, https://cloud.google.com/learn/what-is-artificial-intelligence.
737. Nicola Jones, *AI Now Beats Humans at Basic Tasks: New Benchmarks Are Needed, Says Major Report*, Nature 628, 700–701 (2024), https://doi.org/10.1038/d41586-024-01087-4.

learning for tasks such as data analysis, predictions, object categorisation, NLP, recommendations, and intelligent data retrieval.[738]

The dynamic and rapidly evolving nature of AI technologies further complicates cross-border AI governance, as these advancements continuously introduce new and complex challenges.[739] The rapid pace of AI innovation often exceeds the development of regulatory frameworks, making it challenging for governance structures to keep pace with emerging capabilities and potential risks. This challenge is amplified by the inherently global and interconnected nature of AI development and deployment, requiring international cooperation and coordination to address the diverse and evolving landscape of AI technologies. Furthermore, the lack of shared ethical frameworks and cultural nuances around AI further complicates the task of crafting effective governance solutions. Additionally, the potential for malicious actors to exploit vulnerabilities in AI systems necessitates robust international cybersecurity measures.[740]

The global AI landscape is further complicated by power imbalances and geopolitical tensions. The fierce competition between the US and China, vying for dominance in this critical domain, casts a long shadow over governance efforts.[741] Their differing values and strategic objectives make consensus-building on crucial issues like data privacy and ethical standards a formidable challenge. Smaller nations risk being caught in the crossfire, their voices overshadowed by the giants, raising concerns about equitable representation and a fair playing field. Moreover, the potential weaponisation of AI adds another layer of complexity, blurring the lines between civilian and military applications and fuelling a dangerous arms race.[742] These intricate challenges necessitate a multi-pronged approach, fostering collaboration between governments, industry leaders, and researchers to navigate the ever-shifting landscape of AI and ensure its responsible development and deployment.

10.2.2 Lack of Global Consensus and Coordination

Another challenge lies in the lack of global consensus and coordination on AI governance principles and norms, potentially resulting in conflicts and regulatory

738. *See supra* n. 737.
739. MIT Open Courseware, *AI Strategies and Roadmap*, https://professional.mit.edu/course-catalog/ai-strategies-and-roadmap-systems-engineering-approach-ai-development-and-deployment (accessed 8 Aug. 2024); Nir Kaldero, *Beyond Innovation: Overcoming Challenges in Developing and Deploying AI Models*, Forbes Tech Council (6 Jan. 2023), https://www.forbes.com/sites/forbestechcouncil/2023/01/06/beyond-innovation-overcoming-challenges-in-developing-and-deploying-ai-models/.
740. *See supra* n. 279; Pradeep Paraman & Sanmugam Anamalah, *Ethical Artificial Intelligence Framework for a Good AI Society: Principles, Opportunities, and Perils*, 38 AI & Soc'y 595 (2023), https://doi.org/10.1007/s00146-022-01458-3; *see also supra* n. 727.
741. Goldman Sachs, *The Generative World Order: AI, Geopolitics, and Power* (14 Dec. 2023), https://www.goldmansachs.com/insights/articles/the-generative-world-order-ai-geopolitics-and-power.html.
742. *Ibid.*

gaps.[743] While initiatives like the OECD Principles on AI and the UN Secretary-General's Roadmap for Digital Cooperation exist,[744] they are non-binding and voluntary, failing to address the specific and complex issues arising from cross-border AI. Moreover, these frameworks fall short of addressing the specific and complex issues arising from cross-border AI applications. The absence of a unified approach may lead to conflicts and regulatory gaps, hindering effective governance.

Divergent priorities and interests among different actors and regions further complicate matters, encompassing competitiveness, security, human rights, and social welfare. For instance, the strategic rivalry between the US and China over AI leadership could influence their willingness and ability to cooperate and compromise on governance issues.[745] Both countries compete for AI leadership, which could influence their willingness and ability to cooperate on governance issues. Nonetheless, while competition drives innovation, it also poses challenges in harmonising AI policies and norms on a global scale. Navigating geopolitical tensions to find common ground on AI governance is a delicate balancing act. Addressing shared challenges requires cooperation and compromise, but strategic interests can impede progress.

The EU faces its own set of challenges. The EU grapples with the challenge of balancing economic and innovation objectives with its values and principles of human-centric and trustworthy AI, potentially limiting compatibility and alignment with other regions.[746] Balancing economic objectives and innovation with values like human-centric and trustworthy AI is no easy feat. The EU's strategy for AI focuses on excellence and trust, to enhance research and industrial capabilities while safeguarding safety and fundamental rights.[747] Nevertheless, this commitment may limit compatibility and alignment with other regions that prioritise economic growth and technological advancement. Consequently, striking the right balance between innovation and ethical considerations remains a critical challenge for the EU and other jurisdictions.[748]

743. Siddharth Chatterjee, *UN Resident Coordinator in China, International Artificial Intelligence and Governance Forum 2022*, United Nations Office for Coordination of Humanitarian Affairs (UNOCHA) (09 Dec. 2022), https://china.un.org/en/210705-international-artificial-intelligence-and-governance-forum-2022; Lewis Ho, *Exploring Institutions for Global AI Governance*, DeepMind (11 Jul. 2023), https://deepmind.google/discover/blog/exploring-institutions-for-global-ai-governance.

744. United Nations, *Secretary-General's Roadmap for Digital Cooperation*, https://www.un.org/en/content/digital-cooperation-roadmap/ (accessed on 8 Aug. 2024).

745. Pedro Ferreira, *The Great Wall of Algorithms: U.S.-China Relations and the Future of Global AI Governance*, Finance Magnates (17 Nov. 2023), https://www.financemagnates.com/fintech/the-great-wall-of-algorithms-us-china-relations-and-the-future-of-global-ai-governance/.

746. *See* European Commission, *supra* n. 708; European Commission, *European Approach to Artificial Intelligence* (July 2021), https://digital-strategy.ec.europa.eu/en/policies/european-approach-artificial-intelligence.

747. *Ibid.*

748. United Nations Regional Information Centre for Western Europe, *AI: Transformative Power and Governance Challenges*, UNRIC, https://unric.org/en/ai-transformative-power-and-governance-challenges/; UNRIC, *UNBT Event: The Governance Challenges of Artificial Intelligence*, UNU-CRIS (8 Aug. 2024), https://unric.org/en/unbt-event-the-governance-challenges-of-artificial-intelligence-unu-cris/.

10.2.3 Lack of Adequate and Effective Mechanisms and Institutions

The absence of robust mechanisms and institutions poses a significant challenge to cross-border AI governance. Therefore, the third challenge lies in the lack of adequate and effective mechanisms and institutions for cross-border AI governance, resulting in regulatory fragmentation, duplication, and enforcement difficulties.[749] Successful cross-border AI governance requires not only harmonised and consistent rules and standards but also effective platforms and processes for dialogue, cooperation, and coordination among governments, international organisations, the private sector, civil society, and academia. The current global AI governance architecture remains nascent and fragmented, with numerous actors and initiatives - such as the UN, the OECD, the EU, the G7, the G20, the GPAI, the IEEE, and more - operating at different levels and domains.[750] Their mandates, scopes, and objectives often diverge, hindering effective coordination.

Indeed, the landscape of global AI governance is currently in its nascent stage, characterised by a multitude of actors and initiatives operating across various domains. Unfortunately, this fragmentation leads to a lack of coherence; these entities focus on diverse aspects of AI, ranging from both ethics and safety to technical standards, but their efforts are not always well-connected. Therefore, a cohesive approach is imperative to address the interconnected challenges posed by cross-border AI. A lack of coordination might lead to duplicating efforts and missing opportunities for effective regulation and enforcement.[751]

Even when mechanisms and institutions exist, they may lack the necessary authority, resources, and legitimacy. Monitoring cross-border AI activities, enforcing rules, and resolving disputes require robust institutions. Nonetheless, the existing mechanisms and institutions often lack the necessary capabilities. Policymakers must take proactive steps to strengthen these bodies, equip them with adequate resources, and grant them authority extending beyond national borders. To address the above challenges, we need harmonised rules, consistent standards, and collaborative platforms that facilitate dialogue and cooperation among governments, private sectors, civil society, and academia. By adopting a unified and harmonised policy measure, we can effectively address the impact of AI on a global scale.

---

749. Joshua P. Meltzer & Cameron F. Kerry, *Strengthening International Cooperation on Artificial Intelligence*, Brookings (17 Feb. 2021), https://www.brookings.edu/articles/strengthening-international-cooperation-on-artificial-intelligence/; Frank Schweitzer et al., *The Rise of Artificial Intelligence, Big Data, and the Next Generation of International Rules Governing Cross-Border Data Flows and Digital Trade*, 1 Global Trade L.J. 14 (March–April 2024) [Part 1]; 1 Global Trade L.J. 14 (May–June 2024) [Part 2].
750. Lewin Schmitt, *Mapping Global AI Governance: A Nascent Regime in a Fragmented Landscape*, 2 Ai Ethics 303 (2022), https://doi.org/10.1007/s43681-021-00083-y; Paul Cihon, Michael M. Maas & Laura Kemp, *Fragmentation and the Future: Investigating Architectures for International AI Governance*, 11 Global Policy 545 (2020), https://doi.org/10.1111/1758-5899.12890, https://papers.ssrn.com/sol3/papers.cfm?abstract_id=3756927; Peter Cihon, *Fragmentation and the Future: Investigating Architectures for International AI Governance*, 11 Global Policy 5 (2020), https://onlinelibrary.wiley.com/doi/pdf/10.1111/1758-5899.12890.
751. *See* Lewin Schmitt, *supra* n. 750.

10.2.4 Lack of Standardised Regulations Across Different Jurisdictions

Another significant challenge revolves around the lack of standardised regulations across different jurisdictions, leading to a fragmented landscape that hinders the effective oversight of AI systems.[752] For instance, some countries prioritise privacy protection, while others focus on innovation and economic growth. Some international standards have been developed to provide a framework for AI management systems, but their adoption and implementation vary across countries and sectors.[753] This divergence complicates cross-border AI deployment. Therefore, there is a need for more coordination and harmonisation of AI regulations and standards at the global level. Moreover, since AI applications transcend geographical boundaries, regulatory misalignments can impede the seamless deployment and utilisation of these technologies on a global scale.

Although international standards exist (such as ISO/IEC 27001 for information security), their adoption varies.[754] Some countries actively implement them, while others lag behind.[755] Sectors like healthcare, finance, and transportation may interpret and apply AI regulations differently. This inconsistency affects global AI development. To address this challenge, collaborative efforts are essential.[756] Nations must work together to establish common principles and standards for AI governance. Harmonisation involves aligning regulations, certification processes, and evaluation criteria. The goal is to create a level playing field for AI developers and users worldwide.

Initiatives like the GPAI[757] and the OECD AI Principles[758] aim to foster international cooperation in crafting guidelines that promote ethical and RAI development. ISO/IEC 27001 is one of the most widely recognised standards for information security management systems (ISMSs).[759] It defines requirements for organisations to implement an effective ISMS. ISO/IEC 27000 provides an overview and vocabulary of information security management. While organisations can implement the standard without seeking formal certification, they may choose to do so to demonstrate compliance with best practices and principles. Notably, the ISO/IEC 27001 standard

752. ISO/IEC 23053:2022, *Framework for Artificial Intelligence (AI) Systems Using Machine Learning (ML)* (1st edn, 2022), https://www.iso.org/standard/74438.html.
753. Ken Huang et al., AI Regulations, in *Generative AI Security* 31, 34 (Ken Huang et al., eds, Springer 2024), https://doi.org/10.1007/978-3-031-54252-7_3.
754. Frank Cremer et al., *Cyber Risk and Cybersecurity: A Systematic Review of Data Availability*, 47 Geneva Pap. Risk Insur. Issues Pract. 698 (2022), https://doi.org/10.1057/s41288-022-00266-6.
755. Linda Darling-Hammond et al., *Implications for Educational Practice of the Science of Learning and Development*, 24 Applied Dev. Sci. 97 (2020), https://doi.org/10.1080/10888691.2018.1537791.
756. McKinsey & Co., *Transforming Healthcare with AI: The Impact on the Workforce and Organizations* (2024), https://www.mckinsey.com/industries/healthcare/our-insights/transforming-healthcare-with-ai.
757. *Global Partnership on Artificial Intelligence* (15 Jun. 2020), https://gpai.ai/.
758. OECD, *AI Principles Overview* (2021), https://oecd.ai/en/ai-principles.
759. ISO/IEC 27001:2022, *Information Security, Cybersecurity and Privacy Protection – Information Security Management Systems: Requirements* (3rd edn, 2022), https://www.iso.org/standard/27001.

has been revised to improve cybersecurity and data protection. The transition period for certification to the revised standard ends in autumn 2025.[760]

10.2.5 Privacy and Data Protection Challenges

Privacy and data protection concerns pose another regulatory hurdle in cross-border AI governance. AI systems often rely on vast amounts of data for training and decision-making processes, leading to potential privacy breaches and unauthorised access.[761] Some of the major data privacy risks and challenges related to AI include re-identification and deanonymisation, discrimination and bias, opacity and secrecy of profiling, data exploitation, and prediction. To protect privacy in an AI-driven world, it is essential to ensure that AI systems are transparent, accountable, and respectful of human rights.[762] Striking a balance between enabling the benefits of AI and safeguarding individual privacy requires ongoing collaboration and dialogue among nations. While the regulator could update codes of practice to adapt to technological advancements, the fast-paced evolution of technology might pose a challenge for both the regulator and covered entities to keep pace.[763]

The evolving nature of technology adds complexity to the regulatory landscape, as the rapid pace of technological advancement outpaces the ability of regulators to keep pace.[764] While regulators can update codes of practice and guidelines to adapt to emerging technologies, such efforts may struggle to keep up with the dynamic nature of AI development. Moreover, the diverse interpretations and applications of AI regulations across different sectors and jurisdictions further complicate efforts to address privacy and data protection challenges.

Protecting privacy in the context of AI necessitates ensuring transparency, accountability, and respect for human rights in the design and deployment of AI systems.[765] Achieving this balance requires ongoing collaboration and dialogue among nations to develop effective regulatory frameworks that mitigate privacy risks while

760. A-LIGN, *ISO 27001 Transition: What Now?* (8 Aug. 2024), https://www.a-lign.com/articles/iso-27001-transition; Protiviti Consulting, Inc., *ISO 27001: 2022 – Key Changes and Approaches to Transition* (2022), https://www.protiviti.com/us-en/whitepaper/iso-27001-2022-key-changes-and-approaches-transition.
761. Cameron F. Kerry, *Protecting Privacy in an AI-Driven World*, Brookings (10 Feb. 2020), https://www.brookings.edu/articles/protecting-privacy-in-an-ai-driven-world/; Hafiz Sheikh Adnan Ahmed, *Challenges of AI and Data Privacy: And How to Solve Them*, ISACA (2021), https://www.isaca.org/resources/news-and-trends/newsletters/atisaca/2021/volume-32/challenges-of-ai-and-data-privacy-and-how-to-solve-them.
762. Lee Tiedrich et al., *The AI Data Challenge: How Do We Protect Privacy and Other Fundamental Rights in an AI-Driven World?* (19 Oct. 2023), https://oecd.ai/en/wonk/the-ai-data-challenge-how-do-we-protect-privacy-and-other-fundamental-rights-in-an-ai-driven-world.
763. Bernd Carsten Stahl et al., *A European Agency for Artificial Intelligence: Protecting Fundamental Rights and Ethical Values*, 45 Comput. L. & Sec. Rev. 105661 (2022), https://doi.org/10.1016/j.clsr.2022.105661.
764. Pablo Rozas et al., *Genetically Modified Organisms: Adapting Regulatory Frameworks for Evolving Genome Editing Technologies*, 55 Biol. Res. 31 (2022), https://doi.org/10.1186/s40659-022-00399-x.
765. Jianlong Zhou & Fang Chen, *AI Ethics: From Principles to Practice*, 38 AI & Soc'y 2693 (2023), https://doi.org/10.1007/s00146-022-01602-z.

enabling innovation. Therefore, a coordinated approach involving policymakers, industry stakeholders, and civil society is necessary to develop agile regulatory frameworks that can effectively address the evolving privacy concerns associated with AI.

Furthermore, cross-border data flows and international collaborations in AI R&D raise questions about jurisdictional authority, data sovereignty, and regulatory harmonisation. For example, when people use AI-powered apps from other countries on their mobile devices, it can involve data transfers across international borders, which may trigger various regulations depending on the jurisdiction. As a result, this increased usage of AI in foreign apps has led to a significant increase in the number of users from other countries, with an average increase of over ten times.[766]

The lack of uniformity in privacy laws and regulations across jurisdictions further complicates efforts to ensure consistent protection of individuals' data privacy rights. Moreover, differing cultural norms and societal expectations regarding privacy add another layer of complexity to cross-border AI governance.[767] Addressing these challenges also requires international cooperation and the development of interoperable frameworks that respect diverse legal, cultural, and ethical considerations.

10.2.6 Transparency and Accountability in AI Systems

Despite privacy concerns, maintaining transparency and accountability in AI systems across borders is another major concern. Many AI algorithms operate as 'black boxes', making it difficult to understand the decision-making processes and potential biases embedded within them. Establishing a regulatory framework that mandates transparency and accountability in AI development can mitigate risks associated with biased algorithms and ensure responsible deployment. The 'AI Ethics Impact Assessment Toolkit' proposed by the European Commission represents one attempt to address this challenge by providing a structured approach to evaluating the ethical implications of AI systems.[768]

The best way for companies to prepare for AI regulation is through a RAI initiative that stresses accountability, transparency, privacy and security, and fairness and inclusiveness in how they develop and deploy algorithms. RAI is not only a compliance matter but also an enabler and an engine for innovation that improves the performance and feedback cycle of AI. The Boston Consulting Group (BCG) suggests five ways to implement RAI: (a) engage the chief executive officer (CEO), (b) assess the AI maturity, (c) prioritise the use cases, (d) leverage third-party tools, and (e) monitor

766. Ruiqi Sun & Daniel Trefler, *The Impact of AI and Cross-Border Data Regulation on International Trade in Digital Services: A Large Language Model*, Nat'l Bureau of Econ. Research, Working Paper No. 31925 (2023), https://www.nber.org/papers/w31925.
767. Bellovin, S.M. et al., *Privacy and Synthetic Datasets* (20 Aug. 2018) (unpublished manuscript), https://ssrn.com/abstract=3255766 or http://dx.doi.org/10.2139/ssrn.3255766.
768. Mauritz Kop, *AI Impact Assessment & Code of Conduct*, Futurium (29 May 2019), https://futurium.ec.europa.eu/en/european-ai-alliance/best-practices/ai-impact-assessment-code-conduct.

the regulatory landscape.[769] By proactively integrating these principles, companies cannot only comply with regulations but also unlock the full potential of AI while building trust with stakeholders.

Indeed, cross-border AI governance is a complex and challenging issue that requires a holistic and collaborative approach among various actors and regions. By addressing the regulatory challenges and pursuing possible solutions, cross-border AI governance can ensure the beneficial and responsible use of AI for the common good of humanity. Nevertheless, there is no one-size-fits-all solution, and each approach may have its advantages and disadvantages. Therefore, conducting further research and analysis on this topic is crucial. Additionally, continuous and collaborative learning and adaptation are essential to identifying the most appropriate and effective strategies for regulating and governing AI on a global scale.

To address this challenge, there have been various efforts to harmonise and coordinate the regulatory and governance frameworks for AI at the international level. For example, some intergovernmental and standards organisations, such as the OECD, the EU, the UN, and the IEEE, have developed guidelines, principles, and recommendations for ethical and trustworthy AI, based on common values and goals. These initiatives aim to provide a shared vision and direction for AI regulation and governance, as well as to foster dialogue and collaboration among different stakeholders and jurisdictions. Nonetheless, these efforts are not binding or enforceable, and they may not reflect the diversity and complexity of the AI landscape and its impacts.

Therefore, there is still a need for more concrete and specific actions and mechanisms to implement and monitor the compliance and effectiveness of the international regulatory and governance frameworks for AI. Some possible actions and mechanisms could enhance the harmonisation and coordination of AI regulation and governance across borders (*see* Table 10.1).

Table 10.1 Mechanisms for Cross-Border AI Governance and Coordination

Creating international forums and working groups: Establishing forums and working groups dedicated to AI policy development will help unify efforts across borders. These platforms can facilitate collaboration and the exchange of ideas among diverse stakeholders.
Formulating multilateral agreements: Developing treaties or agreements on AI governance principles and standards can provide a cohesive framework for international cooperation. Such agreements would align diverse regulatory approaches and foster consistency.
Designing shared frameworks for risk assessment: Creating shared frameworks for assessing AI risks and impacts will enable countries to evaluate AI technologies consistently. This approach helps in identifying and mitigating potential risks effectively.

769. Boston Consulting Group, *Responsible AI* (21 Sep. 2023), https://www.bcg.com/capabilities/artificial-intelligence/responsible-ai.

Implementing cross-border information sharing: Establishing mechanisms for sharing information about AI incidents and best practices can enhance collective knowledge and response strategies. This promotes transparency and learning from experiences worldwide.
Encouraging national and international collaboration: Fostering collaboration between national AI ethics committees and international regulatory bodies can harmonise ethical standards. This cooperation ensures that diverse perspectives are integrated into AI governance.
Promoting common technical standards: Adopting common technical standards and interoperability protocols for AI systems will facilitate seamless integration across borders. Standardisation supports compatibility and enhances the functionality of AI technologies.
Supporting joint research initiatives: Encouraging collaborative research on AI safety and ethics between countries can advance the understanding of AI's implications. Joint efforts can lead to more robust and globally applicable solutions.
Facilitating expertise exchange: Implementing capacity-building programs and facilitating the exchange of expertise will strengthen global AI governance capabilities. Sharing knowledge and resources helps in building robust regulatory frameworks.
Harmonising definitions and taxonomies: Developing consistent definitions and taxonomies related to AI technologies and applications will provide clarity. Harmonisation ensures that stakeholders have a common understanding of AI concepts.
Establishing international dispute resolution mechanisms: Creating mechanisms for resolving AI-related conflicts can provide structured processes for addressing disputes. These mechanisms will help in enforcing agreements and maintaining international cooperation.

Source: Author's Own Creation.

10.3 INTERNATIONAL INITIATIVES TO ADDRESS GLOBAL AI CHALLENGES

10.3.1 International Collaborations

AI is advancing at an unprecedented pace, transcending national boundaries and presenting a multitude of challenges that necessitate coordinated global efforts. International collaborations play a pivotal role in addressing these challenges. Organisations such as the UN, the OECD, and the WEF have initiated dialogues and partnerships to foster cooperation among nations in developing ethical frameworks and guidelines for AI. The UN, through its specialised agencies like the International Telecommunication Union (ITU), is actively working towards establishing a global approach to AI governance. The ITU's Focus Group on AI for Health is an example of collaborative efforts to leverage AI to address global health challenges.[770]

770. The FG-AI4H, a collaborative venture between the ITU and the WHO, is dedicated to developing a standardized evaluation system for AI-driven healthcare applications. This framework aims to

Furthermore, the Focus Group on Artificial Intelligence for Health (FG-AI4H) is a partnership between the ITU and the World Health Organization (WHO). Established in 2018 by ITU-T Study Group 16, the group aims to create a standardised assessment framework for evaluating AI-based methods in health, including diagnosis, triage, or treatment decisions. The FG-AI4H stands as an exemplary collaborative effort, leveraging AI to address global health challenges.[771] Moreover, its work also focuses on developing a benchmarking framework for international standards and guiding the creation of policies to ensure the safe and appropriate use of AI in the health sector. So far, the FG-AI4H has delivered 35 outputs, organised around four pillars of AI for health: (1) ethics, (2) regulations, (3) technology, and (4) clinical evaluation and use cases. Additionally, the group has produced tailored outputs to meet specific needs.[772]

The OECD AI Principles are guidelines that advocate for the use of innovative, trustworthy AI that respects human rights and democratic values. Adopted in May 2019 by OECD member countries through the OECD Council Recommendation on Artificial Intelligence, these principles aim to shape a human-centric approach to trustworthy AI.[773] They establish standards that are practical, and flexible, and cover values-based, system-based, and policy-based aspects of trustworthy AI.

The principles underscore the importance of human-centric values, transparency, and accountability in AI development and deployment. They recognise the necessity for inclusive growth, sustainable development, and well-being, emphasising fairness, robustness, security, and safety in AI systems. Providing recommendations for policymakers, the principles advocate for investing in AI R&D, fostering a digital ecosystem for AI, creating an enabling policy environment, building human capacity, preparing for labour market transitions, and promoting international cooperation for trustworthy AI.[774] Serving as an international reference point, the OECD AI Principles emphasise human-centric values, transparency, and accountability in establishing trustworthy AI.

The WEF's AI Governance Alliance (AIGA) has recently released three new reports on advanced AI. The reports focus on GAI Governance, unlocking its value, and a framework for RAI development and deployment.[775] The alliance brings together governments, businesses, and experts to shape RAI development applications and governance and ensure equitable distribution and enhanced access to this path-departing technology worldwide. AIGA is calling upon experts from various sectors to address several key areas, including improving data quality and availability across

assess the efficacy of AI technologies in areas such as diagnosis, patient prioritization, and treatment planning. *See* International Telecommunication Union (ITU), *Focus Group on Artificial Intelligence for Health* (2018), https://www.itu.int/en/ITU-T/focusgroups/ai4h/Pages/default.aspx.

771. *Ibid.*
772. *Ibid.*
773. OECD, *Artificial Intelligence*, https://www.oecd.org/digital/artificial-intelligence/ (accessed 8 Aug. 2024).
774. *See supra* n. 759.
775. World Economic Forum, *AI Governance Alliance Calls for Inclusive Access to Advanced Artificial Intelligence* (18 Jan. 2024), https://www.weforum.org/press/2024/01/ai-governance-alliance-calls-for-inclusive-access-to-advanced-artificial-intelligence/.

nations, boosting access to computational resources, and adapting foundation models to suit local needs and challenges.[776]

The reports offer recommendations on building safe systems and technologies, ensuring responsible applications and transformation, and advancing resilient governance and regulation. The alliance aims to create equitable access to AI, which holds the potential to address global challenges but also poses risks of widening existing digital divides or creating new ones.[777] The alliance's efforts are commendable, and it is heartening to see governments, businesses, and experts coming together to shape RAI development applications and governance. The recommendations made by the alliance are crucial to ensure that AI is developed and deployed responsibly and that its benefits are accessible to all.

Besides, the Information Technology Industry Council (ITI) has released globally applicable AI policy proposals in five key areas: innovation and investment, facilitating public understanding and trust, ensuring security and privacy, approaches to regulation, and global engagement.[778] These recommendations offer a comprehensive framework for government, industry, and stakeholder collaboration on AI.[779] The report emphasises the crucial need for international cooperation and jurisdictional interoperability to ensure that global AI systems are ethically sound, robust, and trustworthy. It also recommends that governments take steps to ensure a skilled and diverse workforce, invest in R&D, utilise publicly accessible data, and prioritise and improve the transparency of AI-enabled information and communications technology (ICT) procurement processes. These measures aim to leverage the technology for the benefit of diverse groups within society.

In addition, governments worldwide can play a vital role in facilitating dialogues about AI between companies that use and develop the technology and the communities they impact. Governments should encourage a responsible design approach and promote the development of AI systems that are meaningfully explainable. Cybersecurity and privacy are foundational to trustworthy AI systems, and policymakers must consider the cybersecurity implications of AI systems, ensuring that users trust that their personal and sensitive data is protected and handled appropriately. Moreover, governments considering regulating AI should do so in a way that focuses on responding effectively to specific harms while allowing for advancements in technology and innovation.[780]

In essence, the rapid growth of AI demands a coordinated global response. Fortunately, international collaborations led by organisations such as the UN, OECD, WEF, and ITU offer promising pathways for addressing this complex challenge. By

776. *Ibid.*
777. *Ibid.*
778. Information Technology Industry Council, *Global AI Principles* (23 Mar. 2021), https://www.itic.org/documents/artificial-intelligence/ITI_GlobalAIPrinciples_032321_v3.pdf.
779. New ITI Global AI Policy Recommendations Promote Government, *Industry, and Stakeholder Collaboration on AI*, ITI (24 Mar. 2021), https://www.itic.org/news-events/news-releases/new-iti-global-ai-policy-recommendations-promote-government-industry-and-stakeholder-collaboration-on-ai.
780. *See supra* n. 778.

promoting open dialogue, establishing ethical frameworks, and developing standardised assessment tools, these initiatives aim to facilitate the development of trustworthy AI applications that benefit everyone. The emphasis on human-centric values, transparency, and inclusivity must be a universal call, encouraging governments, businesses, and experts to work together in ensuring equitable access and responsible advancement of this transformative technology. Only through united global efforts can we harness AI's potential for good, bridging divides and fostering inclusive progress toward a brighter future.

10.3.2 International Standards

The rapid advancement and widespread implementation of AI offer promising opportunities but also bring substantial global challenges. Effectively addressing these challenges demands collaborative efforts through the establishment of international standards and regulatory frameworks. However, navigating the intricate and evolving landscape of AI governance requires a deep understanding of current frameworks and ongoing initiatives.

The fragmented landscape of AI regulations across countries creates several challenges. Inconsistent data privacy laws, varying levels of transparency and accountability requirements, and differing definitions of 'high-risk' AI applications hinder innovation and create legal uncertainties for businesses operating globally.[781] For instance, the EU's GDPR sets stringent data privacy standards, while other regions like the US have fewer comprehensive frameworks. This lack of harmonisation can also hinder the development of global AI solutions and limit their potential benefits.

While international standards provide a high-level framework, regional initiatives are addressing AI governance from different perspectives. The EU's AI Act aims to establish a comprehensive regulatory framework for high-risk AI applications.[782] Similarly, China's New Generation Artificial Intelligence Development Plan outlines its aspirations for AI leadership and regulatory pathways for specific sectors.[783] These regional initiatives, while fostering innovation within their respective jurisdictions, necessitate ongoing dialogue and collaboration to ensure global coherence and avoid further fragmentation.

781. World Economic Forum, *The Global Risks Report 2023 18th Edition, World Economic Forum* (2023), https://www3.weforum.org/docs/WEF_Global_Risks_Report_2023.pdf; European Commission, *White Paper on Artificial Intelligence: A European Approach to Excellence and Trust* (2020), https://commission.europa.eu/publications/white-paper-artificial-intelligence-european-approach-excellence-and-trust_en; Council of Europe, *Council of Europe and Artificial Intelligence*, https://www.coe.int/en/web/portal.
782. *See supra* n. 366.
783. China Aerospace Studies Institute, *In Their Own Words: New Generation Artificial Intelligence Development Plan*, US Air Force (3 Feb. 2021), https://www.airuniversity.af.edu/CASI/Display/Article/2521258/in-their-own-words-new-generation-artificial-intelligence-development-plan/; New America, *China's New Generation of Artificial Intelligence Development Plan (2017) (Full Translation)* (20 Jul. 2017), https://www.newamerica.org/cybersecurity-initiative/digichina/blog/full-translation-chinas-new-generation-artificial-intelligence-development-plan-2017/.

Thus, finding the right balance between fostering innovation and implementing necessary regulations is crucial. Overly restrictive regulations can stifle innovation, while insufficient regulation can lead to harmful consequences. The challenge lies in developing flexible and adaptable frameworks that can evolve alongside the rapid pace of technological development. In such a context, regulatory sandboxes act as testing grounds for new AI ideas, allowing responsible exploration and advancement. Additionally, regulatory sandboxes can facilitate dialogue between regulators and industry players to develop effective and agile regulatory frameworks.[784]

It is worth mentioning that the increasing use of AI requires the collection and analysis of vast amounts of data. This context raises concerns about data privacy and the potential for misuse of personal information. International standards and regulations need to ensure that data is collected, used, and stored responsibly, respecting individual privacy rights. The EU GDPR represents a significant step in this direction, but the harmonisation of data privacy regulations across different jurisdictions remains a complex issue. Collaborative efforts between governments and international organisations are needed to develop a global framework for data governance that facilitates responsible data flows while protecting individual privacy.

The pervasive integration of AI into sophisticated applications is often accompanied by a lack of transparency in many AI models, which hinders our ability to comprehend and rely on their outputs. To foster trust and public acceptance, AI systems must be transparent and explainable. While initiatives like XAI are actively developing methods to increase the transparency of AI systems, regulatory frameworks must incentivise and mandate explainability in specific applications.[785] Understanding the underlying reasoning behind AI model decisions is crucial, prompting the emergence of XAI techniques designed to enhance trust in these models.[786] XAI encompasses methods and procedures that enable human users to comprehend and trust the outcomes generated by ML algorithms.[787] Consequently, XAI has gained significant attention as a research topic within the AI field in recent years.

Addressing global AI challenges requires maintaining and implementing fitting international standards and regulatory approaches. To this end, it is essential to assess national approaches to AI governance, engage in critical discussions on GAI, and promote international cooperation and coordination. This approach might prevent fragmentation in AI governance and regulation, ensuring the ethical soundness, robustness, and trustworthiness of global AI systems. Crucially, international cooperation and jurisdictional interoperability are necessary for this to succeed. Additionally,

784. European Commission, *First Regulatory Sandbox on Artificial Intelligence Presented*, https://digital-strategy.ec.europa.eu/en/news/first-regulatory-sandbox-artificial-intelligence-presented; OECD, *Regulatory Sandboxes in Artificial Intelligence* (2020), https://www.oecd.org/en/publications/2023/07/regulatory-sandboxes-in-artificial-intelligence_a44aae4f.html.
785. Giulia Vilone & Luca Longo, *Notions of Explainability and Evaluation Approaches for Explainable Artificial Intelligence*, 76 Information Fusion 89 (2021), https://doi.org/10.1016/j.inffus.2021.05.009.
786. Sajid Ali et al., *Explainable Artificial Intelligence (XAI): What We Know and What Is Left to Attain Trustworthy Artificial Intelligence*, 99 Information Fusion 101805 (2023), https://doi.org/10.1016/j.inffus.2023.101805.
787. IBM, *What Is Explainable AI*, https://www.ibm.com/topics/explainable-ai.

emphasising the importance of education and cultivating local expertise is vital for effectively establishing and navigating AI ecosystems.[788]

Addressing cross-border AI regulatory challenges demands global collaboration through international organisations like the UN, World Trade Organization (WTO), and OECD, alongside regional and bilateral cooperation, to develop harmonised standards and ensure responsible, ethical AI development and use worldwide. Notably, international standards for AI are being developed to ensure uniform global adoption of AI technologies. The ISO and the IEEE play a pivotal role in developing these standards.[789] Moreover, standards created by ISO/IEC and IEEE are essential for ensuring that global AI systems are ethically responsible, reliable, and trustworthy.[790] Further, industry experts have identified leading practices for in-depth assessment of AI risk assessment methodologies and their role in AI regulation.[791] These practices include categorising risks based on the application, not just the AI technology features.

While international standards and regulatory approaches are crucial for addressing the vast challenges posed by AI on a global scale, a truly effective solution demands more than just uniformity. Ultimately, navigating the complex landscape of AI governance requires a collective effort. By working together, stakeholders from government, industry, and academia can ensure AI will benefit all, shaping a future, where innovation flourishes alongside responsible governance. This is not just an opportunity but a responsibility we must embrace collectively.

10.4 CONCLUSION

The global reach of AI necessitates a coordinated approach to governance. As highlighted throughout this chapter, the intricate challenges posed by cross-border AI governance demand solutions that transcend national borders. While diverse initiatives like the OECD AI Principles and the UN Secretary-General's Roadmap for Digital Cooperation offer valuable guidance,[792] their non-binding nature underscores the need for more robust frameworks. Addressing the lack of harmonised regulations, standardised data privacy measures, and transparent accountability mechanisms requires international collaboration and a shared commitment to ethical and RAI development.

The path forward demands a multifaceted approach. Collaborative efforts led by international organisations, governments, and industry leaders are crucial to establish

788. AI Governance Alliance, *Generative AI Governance: Shaping a Collective Global Future*, World Economic Forum (January 2024), https://www3.weforum.org/docs/WEF_Generative_AI_Governance_2024.pdf.
789. IEC Editorial Team, *International Standards: Key Tools for Regulation and Trade in AI*, International Electrotechnical Commission (7 Jul. 2023), https://www.iec.ch/blog/international-standards-key-tools-regulation-and-trade-ai; World Standards Cooperation (WSC), *AI and Standards, World Standards Cooperation* (8 Aug. 2024), https://www.worldstandardscooperation.org/ai-and-standards/.
790. *Ibid.*
791. OECD, *Tools for Trustworthy AI*, https://www.oecd.org/science/tools-for-trustworthy-ai-008232ec-en.htm; World Economic Forum, *Centre for the Fourth Industrial Revolution*, https://centres.weforum.org/centre-for-the-fourth-industrial-revolution/home.
792. *See supra* n. 745.

common ground and develop adaptable frameworks that can keep pace with the dynamic nature of AI. Fostering open dialogue, exchanging best practices, and promoting inclusive participation from diverse stakeholders are essential steps. By prioritising human-centric values, transparency, and accountability, we can harness the immense potential of AI while mitigating its risks, ensuring its responsible development and deployment for the benefit of all. Through concerted global efforts, we can navigate the complexities of cross-border AI governance and unlock a future where AI serves as a powerful tool for progress and shared prosperity.

CHAPTER 11
Future Policy Directions for AI Governance

11.1 INTRODUCTION

AI is rapidly transforming various aspects of society from clinical decision support systems to policing algorithms and personalised content filtering. As AI applications become increasingly widespread, governments around the world face the crucial challenge of managing the scale and pace of socio-technical transitions that result from this technological advancement. While AI offers economic efficiency and improved quality of life, it also introduces unexpected consequences and risks. Thus, the governance of AI is an underdeveloped area that demands attention to maximise benefits while minimising adverse effects.[793]

Understanding these trends and challenges helps policymakers, regulators, and stakeholders adapt and develop effective governance frameworks to address potential risks and harness the benefits of AI responsibly. As AI evolves, so do the challenges associated with its development and deployment. This chapter explores the emerging trends and future challenges in AI governance, followed by valuable recommendations for effective and adaptable regulatory frameworks for AI.

11.2 EMERGING TRENDS IN AI GOVERNANCE

The rapid advancement of LLMs like ChatGPT has ignited an urgent debate over their regulation and governance.[794] While their potential to revolutionise industries is undeniable, their capabilities also raise complex questions regarding bias, accountability, and control in the era of AI-generated content.[795] The conversation about LLM governance extends beyond technical concerns. Ethical considerations surrounding

793. Araz Taeihagh, *Governance of Artificial Intelligence*, 40 Pol'y & Soc'y 137 (2021), https://doi.org/10.1080/14494035.2021.1928377.
794. *See supra* n. 38.
795. *See supra* n. 121.

data privacy, explainability of decisions, and potential for misuse are paramount.[796] Governments, tech companies, and civil society organisations are actively developing frameworks and standards to ensure responsible LLM development and deployment.[797]

Therefore, collaboration and international harmonisation are crucial to navigating the complex landscape of LLM governance, ensuring both innovation and societal well-being in the face of this rapidly evolving technology. Understanding these emerging trends is vital for shaping a future where LLMs benefit humanity without exacerbating existing inequalities or compromising fundamental rights. Accordingly, this sub-section delves into the emerging trends in LLM governance, exploring how stakeholders grapple with these challenges and shape the future of this powerful technology.

11.2.1 From Hype to Reality: Rise of AI Across Industries

The transition from hype to reality marks a pivotal moment in the rise of LLMs like ChatGPT across industries. Initially, there was a surge of excitement and speculation surrounding the potential of LLMs to revolutionise various sectors, fuelled by impressive demonstrations of their capabilities in NLP tasks. Nonetheless, as these models have become more widely adopted and integrated into real-world applications, the focus has shifted towards understanding their practical implications, challenges, and opportunities.[798] This shift reflects a growing recognition that the true value of LLMs lies not in their mere existence, but in their responsible and effective deployment to address specific industry needs.[799]

One key aspect of the rise of LLMs across industries is their ability to streamline and enhance communication and interaction processes. ChatGPT, for instance, has demonstrated remarkable proficiency in generating human-like text responses, enabling more natural and engaging interactions between humans and machines. ChatGPT offers users the ability to tailor interactions by specifying desired length, format, detail level, and language style.[800] This flexibility allows users to guide the conversation towards their specific needs. Moreover, ChatGPT possesses the ability to perceive, listen, and speak, and it can generate visual representations through verbal descriptions.[801]

Nevertheless, it is important to clarify that ChatGPT does not possess the ability to 'see' or 'hear' in the traditional sense. While it can process and respond to text-based

796. *See supra* n. 328.
797. European Commission, Proposal for a Regulation of the European Parliament and of the Council on the European Union Agency for Criminal Justice Cooperation (Eurojust) and Repealing Regulation (EU) No. 141/2014 (21 Apr. 2021), https://eur-lex.europa.eu/legal-content/EN/TXT/HTML/?uri=CELEX:52021PC0206.
798. *See supra* n. 99.
799. Jared Kaplan et al., *Scaling Laws for Neural Language Models*, arXiv (23 Jan. 2020), https://arxiv.org/pdf/2001.08361.
800. *See* OpenAI, *supra* n. 167.
801. *Ibid.*

prompts, it lacks the sensory capabilities and physical embodiment necessary for true sight and sound perception. Additionally, while ChatGPT can generate text descriptions of images, it cannot directly create visual content itself.

Additionally, LLMs like ChatGPT have proven to be invaluable tools for automating and augmenting a wide range of tasks that involve language understanding and generation.[802] From text summarisation and sentiment analysis to language translation and content generation, these models have the potential to significantly boost efficiency, productivity, and innovation across diverse domains. For example, in the legal industry, LLMs can assist lawyers in drafting legal documents, conducting legal research, and analysing case law, thereby improving the speed and accuracy of legal processes.

Nonetheless, ethical concerns surrounding potential bias in legal documents, explainability of decisions, and potential misuse by malicious actors highlight the need for responsible development and deployment of LLMs in sensitive domains. Continuous collaboration between legal professionals, AI developers, and policymakers is crucial to ensure that LLMs enhance the legal system while adhering to ethical principles and upholding fundamental rights.[803]

The evolution from hype to practical application in the proliferation of LLMs like ChatGPT across diverse sectors reflects the maturity of AI technology and its seamless integration into daily operations. While these models promise significant benefits in improving communication, streamlining tasks, and fostering innovation, their widespread usage poses ethical, social, and technical dilemmas demanding thoughtful scrutiny and proactive solutions. Addressing these issues with responsibility and collaboration enables us to leverage the transformative potential of LLMs for forging a more inclusive, sustainable, and human-centred future. Nonetheless, the broad adoption of LLMs also underscores the necessity of confronting ethical, social, and technical hurdles to ensure their deployment is fair and equitable.

11.2.2 Challenges of Integrating AI Across Diverse Fields

One of the primary concerns is the potential for biases and inaccuracies in LLM-generated outputs, which can perpetuate or amplify existing societal biases present in the training data.[804] Addressing bias in LLMs requires robust data pre-processing techniques, bias detection mechanisms, and ongoing monitoring and evaluation (M&E) to mitigate harmful impacts on marginalised communities. Additionally, the opaque nature of LLM decision-making processes can raise concerns about accountability and explainability.[805] Additionally, understanding how LLMs arrive at their outputs is crucial for building trust and ensuring that they are not used for discriminatory purposes. Addressing this challenge requires advancements in interpretable AI

802. *See supra* n. 99.
803. *See supra* n. 328.
804. *Ibid.*
805. *See supra* n. 121.

techniques and the development of clear guidelines for responsible LLM development and deployment.

Additionally, the rise of LLMs across industries has implications for workforce dynamics and job displacement as automation technologies increasingly encroach upon tasks traditionally performed by humans. While LLMs have the potential to augment human capabilities and create new opportunities for skilled workers, they also pose challenges related to job displacement, skills gaps, and the need for reskilling and upskilling initiatives to ensure a smooth transition to the AI-driven economy.[806] This landscape also necessitates proactive measures from policymakers, educators, and businesses to prepare individuals for the evolving job landscape, fostering lifelong learning and adaptability to ensure that the benefits of LLMs are distributed equitably and contribute to a more inclusive and prosperous future for all.

Furthermore, there are concerns about the environmental footprint of training and deploying large-scale LLMs, which consume significant computational resources and energy.[807] The carbon footprint of training a single LLM model can be substantial, leading to calls for more sustainable practices in AI R&D. Efforts to develop more energy-efficient algorithms, optimise model architectures, and explore alternative training methodologies are essential for reducing the environmental impact of LLMs.[808] Additionally, the potential for LLMs to exacerbate existing social inequalities through biased outputs or amplifying misinformation necessitates responsible development practices.

LLMs have also the potential to inadvertently disclose sensitive or personal information, including details like names, addresses, passwords, or personal opinions.[809] These disclosures pose serious threats to the confidentiality and integrity of the data, leaving users vulnerable to identity theft, fraudulent activities, or discriminatory practices. LLMs could keep user data longer than required or without consent, breaking the provisions of data protection regulations and user consent by increasing the risk of data breaches or unauthorised access.[810] Furthermore, sharing user data with third parties, such as developers, researchers, or advertisers, without adequate safeguards or

806. World Economic Forum, *Reskilling Revolution* (2023), https://widgets.weforum.org/reskillingrevolution/index.html; Pablo Illanes et al., *Retraining and Reskilling Workers in the Age of Automation*, McKinsey & Co. (January 2018), https://www.mckinsey.com/featured-insights/future-of-work/retraining-and-reskilling-workers-in-the-age-of-automation; https://www.weforum.org/agenda/2024/01/davos-2024-6-innovative-ideas-for-reskilling-upskilling-and-building-a-future-ready-workforce/; Sagar Goel et al., *6 Strategies to Upskill Your Workforce*, Harv. Bus. Rev. (25 Apr. 2022), https://hbr.org/2022/04/6-strategies-to-upskill-your-workforce.
807. Peter Szarmes & Gábor Élő, *Sustainability of Large AI Models: Balancing Environmental and Social Impact with Technology and Regulations*, 107 Chem. Eng'g Transactions 103 (2023), https://www.cetjournal.it/cet/23/107/018.pdf.
808. Tianyu Ding et al., *The Efficiency Spectrum of Large Language Models: An Algorithmic Survey*, arXiv preprint arXiv:2312.00678 (2023), https://arxiv.org/html/2312.00678v1.
809. *See supra* n. 345.
810. Mark Hinkle, *LLMs and Data Privacy: Navigating the New Frontiers of AI*, The New Stack (27 Sep. 2023), https://thenewstack.io/llms-and-data-privacy-navigating-the-new-frontiers-of-ai/.

transparency undermines user trust and autonomy, potentially causing conflicts of interest or ethical dilemmas.[811]

Moreover, the expanding field of AI is facing a significant talent gap, with demand for skilled professionals far exceeding the current supply. A McKinsey survey found that just 10% of global data scientists possess the necessary skills to work with emerging AI technology.[812] Another recent study indicates that only 1 out of every 10 workers worldwide possesses the desired AI skills.[813] This highlights a significant skills gap that could hinder the adoption and responsible development of AI technologies. As AI technologies become increasingly integral to various industries, the need for individuals proficient in ML, data science, and AI research continues to rise.

This talent shortage poses challenges for organisations seeking to implement AI solutions effectively and innovate in this rapidly evolving landscape. Additionally, the scarcity of AI talent could hinder economic growth and technological advancement, further underscoring the urgency of addressing this gap. Efforts to bridge the AI talent divide include educational initiatives, workforce development programs, and collaborations between academia and industry to cultivate a pipeline of skilled AI professionals.

The widespread use of LLMs has also sparked significant social and ethical concerns.[814] Key issues include generating harmful content (e.g., hate speech, deepfakes), disrupting the economy and labour market, creating an achievement gap (e.g., for students or artists), and raising questions of responsibility and authorship.[815] This harmful content often reflects biases, stereotypes, and misinformation from the training data, potentially confusing, deceiving, or manipulating users. Additionally, LLMs can be misused for malicious purposes like cyberattacks, propaganda, and fraud.[816] Furthermore, their ability to produce false or misleading information, and their potential to cause human-computer interaction harms like addiction or loss of agency, necessitates careful consideration and regulation to ensure their ethical and beneficial use.

In conclusion, integrating AI, particularly LLMs, across diverse fields presents a multifaceted set of challenges that require coordinated and proactive efforts to address.

811. Privacy Analytics, *Will ChatGPT Put Data Sharing at Risk?*, Privacy Analytics (26 May 2023), https://privacy-analytics.com/resources/articles/will-chatgpt-put-data-sharing-at-risk/.

812. Flavia Cristian, *The AI Talent Shortage: Outsourcing or In-house Development*, Craftworks.AI (27 Feb. 2023), https://www.craftworks.ai/post/the-ai-talent-shortage-outsourcing-or-in-house-development;https://itechindia.co/blog/building-ai-solutions-in-house-vs-outsourcing-ai-development/.

813. Goh Chiew Tong, *Workers Want to Embrace A.I.: But Only 1 in 10 Say Their Jobs Involve Related Skills, Salesforce Says*, CNBC (18 May 2023), https://www.cnbc.com/2023/05/19/only-1-in-10-workers-have-skills-related-to-ai-salesforce.html; Salesforce.com, *New Study Reveals Only 1 in 10 Global Workers Have In-Demand AI Skills* (6 Mar. 2023), https://www.salesforce.com/news/stories/digital-skills-based-experience/.

814. *See supra* n. 329.

815. Alex Tamkin et al., *Understanding the Capabilities, Limitations, and Societal Impact of Large Language Models*, arXiv preprint arXiv:2102.02503 (2021), https://nlp.stanford.edu/pubs/tamkin2021understanding.pdf.

816. Zhiheng Xi et al., Safety and Ethical Concerns of Large Language Models, in *Proceedings of the 22nd Chinese National Conference on Computational Linguistics* 9, 9–16 (Volume 4: Tutorial Abstracts, 2023), https://aclanthology.org/2023.ccl-4.2.pdf.

From mitigating biases and ensuring accountability to navigating workforce implications and environmental impacts, the path forward demands robust frameworks for RAI development and deployment. The pressing need for talent development, along with the ethical concerns surrounding data privacy and misuse, underscores the importance of fostering collaboration among policymakers, researchers, educators, and civil society. By prioritising inclusivity, sustainability, and transparency, we can harness the transformative potential of AI while safeguarding the interests of all stakeholders, ultimately contributing to a more equitable and prosperous future.

11.2.3 Global Initiatives to AI Regulations

Global initiatives for AI regulations have gained significant momentum in recent years as countries recognise the importance of governing AI systems. With the rapid advancement and widespread adoption of AI technologies across various sectors, there is a growing consensus on the need for comprehensive frameworks to address the ethical, social, and legal implications of AI deployment.[817] From the EU's groundbreaking AI Act 2024[818] and the US's AI Policy[819] to China's national guidelines[820] and initiatives by international organisations like the OECD AI initiatives,[821] these efforts aim to ensure AI benefits all of humanity, fostering innovation while mitigating risks and upholding fundamental rights. As nations grapple with the complexities of AI governance, collaboration and coordination on an international scale have become increasingly essential to foster innovation while safeguarding individual privacy, safety, and societal well-being. This exploration will delve into the key trends shaping this dynamic field, examining the diverse approaches, challenges, and opportunities that lie ahead in regulating AI for a responsible and equitable future.

To begin with, the EU's journey toward the AI Act started in 2018 with initial drafts, followed by more concrete drafting in 2020. The official proposal was released in April 2021, initiating a legislative process that involved the Council, the Parliament, and the Commission. The Council adopted its position in December 2022, allowing for the start of negotiations with the Parliament. After three days of marathon talks, the two co-legislators reached a provisional agreement on the AI Act in December 2023.

817. Matti Mäntymäki et al., *Putting AI Ethics into Practice: The Hourglass Model of Organizational AI Governance*, arXiv:2206.00335 (2022), https://doi.org/10.48550/arXiv.2206.00335.
818. Council of the European Union, *Press Release, Artificial Intelligence Act: Council and Parliament Strike a Deal on the First Worldwide Rules for AI* (2 Feb. 2024), https://www.consilium.europa.eu/en/press/press-releases/2023/12/09/artificial-intelligence-act-council-and-parliament-strike-a-deal-on-the-first-worldwide-rules-for-ai/.
819. US Dep't of State, *Artificial Intelligence*, https://www.state.gov/artificial-intelligence/ (accessed 9 Aug. 2024).
820. Yan Luo et al., *China Proposes Draft Measures to Regulate Generative AI*, Inside Privacy Inc. (August 2024), https://www.insideprivacy.com/artificial-intelligence/china-proposes-draft-measures-to-regulate-generative-ai/.
821. The OECD AI initiatives comprise policies, data, and analysis designed to assist nations and stakeholders in developing trustworthy AI aligned with the OECD AI Principles. The OECD.AI Policy Observatory serves as a platform offering access to more than 900 national AI policies and initiatives from 69 countries. It also provides real-time data, tools, and a blog dedicated to AI policy discussions. For details, *see supra* n. 771.

The European Parliament adopted the AI Act 2024 on 13 March 2024, which is recognised as the world's first comprehensive and horizontal legal framework for AI.[822]

Undoubtedly, the EU Artificial Intelligence Act (EU AI Act) is landmark legislation governing the development and usage of AI systems within the EU and beyond. It aims to ensure the safety, trustworthiness, and adherence to fundamental rights and values, additionally fostering competitiveness in the EU's AI sector. Adopting a risk-based approach, the Act categorises AI systems into four levels: unacceptable, high, limited, and minimal. Unacceptable-risk AI systems, such as those that manipulate human behaviour or exploit vulnerabilities, are prohibited. High-risk AI systems are subjected to stringent requirements, including transparency, human oversight, and data quality standards. Limited-risk AI systems must adhere to transparency obligations, such as notifying users when interacting with an AI system. Minimal-risk AI systems are largely exempt from regulation but are encouraged to adhere to voluntary codes of conduct.[823]

On the other hand, the US AI policy consists of principles, actions, and initiatives intended to position the US as a leader in embracing the potential and addressing the challenges of AI. It encompasses diverse aspects of AI advancement and applications, including safety, security, privacy, fairness, civil rights, innovation, competition, and global leadership. The policy draws upon the OECD Recommendation on Artificial Intelligence,[824] which the US adopted in 2019, as a foundation for fostering trustworthy AI practices.[825] Implementation of the policy occurs through executive orders, legislation, regulations, and guidance issued by various federal departments and agencies.

The US AI policy landscape is evolving and fragmented initiatives, lacking a single comprehensive law like the EU's AI Act. Nevertheless, several key initiatives and documents shape the country's approach to AI governance. Among other things, the US's initiatives for AI governance include Executive Order on Promoting the Use of Trustworthy Artificial Intelligence in the Federal Government (2020),[826] Executive Order on Advancing Racial Equity and Support for Underserved Communities Through the Federal Government (2021),[827] proposed Algorithmic Justice League Act of 2023,[828] and Artificial Intelligence Applications Act of 2023.[829]

While the recent Executive Order emphasises safety, security, and trustworthy development, it lacks teeth and relies on voluntary industry commitments. Efforts like

822. *See supra* n. 487.
823. *See supra* n. 366.
824. *See supra* n. 775.
825. OECD, *Recommendation on Artificial Intelligence*, OECD Legal Instruments (22 May 2019), https://oecd.ai/en/assets/files/OECD-LEGAL-0449-en.pdf.
826. Promoting the Use of Trustworthy Artificial Intelligence in the Federal Government, 85 Fed. Reg. 80,592 (8 Dec. 2020) (to be codified at 48 C.F.R. pts 1, 2, 39).
827. The White House, *Executive Order on Advancing Racial Equity and Support for Underserved Communities Through the Federal Government* (20 Jan. 2021), https://www.whitehouse.gov/briefing-room/presidential-actions/2023/02/16/executive-order-on-further-advancing-racial-equity-and-support-for-underserved-communities-through-the-federal-government/.
828. Algorithmic Justice and Online Platform Transparency Act, S. 2325, 118th Cong. (2023), https://www.congress.gov/bill/118th-congress/senate-bill/2325.
829. Artificial Intelligence Advancement Act of 2023, S. 3050, 118th Cong. (2023), https://www.congress.gov/118/bills/s3050/BILLS-118s3050is.pdf.

the Blueprint for an AI Bill of Rights address ethical principles,[830] but their implementation is uncertain. It is noteworthy that the Blueprint for an AI Bill of Rights comprises five principles and related practices aimed at directing the creation, utilisation, and implementation of automated systems to safeguard the rights of the American people in the era of AI. These principles encompass ensuring the safety and efficacy of systems, safeguarding against algorithmic discrimination, protecting data privacy, providing notice and explanation, and incorporating human alternatives, considerations, and fallbacks.[831]

Apart from the above, the AI Safety Institute (AISI) plays a crucial role in ensuring that AI aligns with human values and serves positive purposes. The term 'AISI' refers to various organisations worldwide dedicated to the responsible development and implementation of AI. These institutes engage in research, establish standards, and offer guidance to mitigate risks and maximise AI's societal benefits. One example is the US Artificial Intelligence Safety Institute (USAISI), inaugurated at the NIST in 2024.[832] Comprising over 200 stakeholders from diverse backgrounds, including academia, industry, government, and civil society, the USAISI collaborates on crafting evidence-based guidelines and standards for AI measurement and policy.[833] With a focus on preventing unforeseen consequences of rapid AI advancements, the USAISI endeavours to safeguard both the US and humanity.

However, ongoing debates about data privacy regulations in the US are marked by the absence of a federal standard and a fragmented landscape across individual states. As a result, the future of US AI policy depends on effectively navigating these complexities and promoting innovation while managing associated risks. This will require a collaborative approach involving government, industry, and civil society.

Other than the US, there remains an AISI in the UK, established by the UK government in 2023, which aims to minimise the potential for surprise and harm from advanced AI.[834] Focused on public interest, it works to develop the socio-technical infrastructure needed to understand and manage AI risks effectively. Through fundamental research and collaboration with experts, the Institute seeks to establish ethical frameworks, standardised assessment tools, and responsible governance practices. This effort is documented in the GOV.UK publications, which aim to guide the development and deployment of AI in a way that benefits all of humanity.

The AISI faces challenges in keeping pace with the rapid evolution of AI technologies, ensuring interdisciplinary collaboration, addressing ethical concerns, maintaining transparency, and navigating regulatory complexities. Nonetheless, it

830. Executive Office of the President, *Blueprint for an AI Bill of Rights* (10 Feb. 2022), https://www.whitehouse.gov/ostp/ai-bill-of-rights/what-is-the-blueprint-for-an-ai-bill-of-rights/.
831. *Ibid.*
832. US Artificial Intelligence Safety Institute, *U.S. Artificial Intelligence Safety Institute*, National Institute of Standards and Technology, https://www.nist.gov/ (accessed 9 Aug. 2024).
833. *Ibid.*
834. Dep't for Sci., Innovation & Tech., *Introducing the AI Safety Institute* (17 Jan. 2024), https://www.gov.uk/government/publications/ai-safety-institute-overview/introducing-the-ai-safety-institute.

holds prospects in fostering international cooperation, leveraging emerging technologies such as XAI and federated learning, promoting knowledge-sharing, advocating for robust guidelines and standards, and shaping a future where AI benefits society while minimising risks.[835] Ultimately, the AISI's success hinges on its ability to navigate these challenges and leverage its unique position to guide the responsible development of AI for a safer and more beneficial future.

China has been at the forefront of AI governance initiatives, implementing various strategies and policies to advance its AI capabilities while addressing ethical and societal concerns. China's approach to AI governance stands out for its ambitious and centralised initiatives. One of the key initiatives is the New Generation Artificial Intelligence Development Plan, launched by the Chinese government in 2017.[836] This plan outlines China's strategic goals and investments in AI research, development, and deployment, aiming to position China as a global leader in AI technology by 2030.[837] Additionally, China has introduced the Governance Principles for a New Generation of Artificial Intelligence, which emphasises the importance of ethical AI development and responsible use.[838] These principles aim to guide the development and application of AI technologies in China, promoting transparency, accountability, and fairness.

Furthermore, China has established various regulatory frameworks and guidelines to govern AI development and deployment. The Cybersecurity Law, implemented in 2017, includes provisions related to AI security and data protection, requiring AI developers and users to comply with cybersecurity standards and protect user privacy.[839] Additionally, the National Standardisation Committee for Artificial Intelligence, launched in 2019, is responsible for developing national standards and guidelines for AI technologies, ensuring interoperability, safety, and reliability.[840] These initiatives demonstrate China's commitment to fostering innovation and ensuring the ethical and responsible use of AI technologies.

Nonetheless, there exist substantial challenges and concerns in the field of AI applications and deployments. For instance, the centralised nature of Chinese AI

835. *See supra* n. 834; *see infra* n. 836.
836. *See supra* n. 785.
837. Owen Churchill, *China's AI Dreams*, Nature (17 Jan. 2018), https://www.nature.com/articles/d41586-018-00539-y.; Huw Roberts et al., *The Chinese Approach to Artificial Intelligence: An Analysis of Policy, Ethics, and Regulation*, 36 AI & Soc'y 59 (2021), https://doi.org/10.1007/s00146-020-00992-2.
838. Laney Zhang, *China: AI Governance Principles Released*, Library of Congress (9 Sep. 2019), https://www.loc.gov/item/global-legal-monitor/2019-09-09/china-ai-governance-principles-released/.
839. Rogier Creemers et al., *Translation: Cybersecurity Law of the People's Republic of China*, Stanford University (29 Jun. 2018), https://digichina.stanford.edu/work/translation-cybersecurity-law-of-the-peoples-republic-of-china-effective-june-1-2017/; Grace Pyo, *An Alternate Vision: China's Cybersecurity Law and Its Implementation in the Chinese Courts*, 60 Colum. J. Transnat'l L. 1 (2021), https://ssrn.com/abstract=4101377.
840. Big Data Security Standards Special Working Group of the National Information Security Standardization Technical Committee, *Artificial Intelligence Security Standardization White Paper* (Center for Security and Emerging Technology, Georgetown University 2019), https://cset.georgetown.edu/publication/artificial-intelligence-security-standardization-white-paper-2019-edition/; *see infra* n. 837.

initiatives, strategies and regulations raises questions about transparency and accountability. Critics argue that a lack of independent oversight and public participation can hinder effective governance.[841] Overall, China's AI governance initiatives represent a significant effort to regulate and guide the development of this powerful technology. Nonetheless, addressing transparency, accountability, and potential bias remains crucial for ensuring responsible and equitable AI development in China.

Above all, there is no definitive ranking of the countries or regions with the most advanced or comprehensive AI regulations, as different jurisdictions have varying approaches and priorities. Some, for example, prioritise data privacy, while others focus on algorithmic fairness.[842] Several other countries and regions are also actively involved in enacting new AI laws, proposing AI regulations, or developing policies and initiatives to promote or govern AI development. These include Australia, Brazil, Canada, India, Israel, Japan, New Zealand, Saudi Arabia, Singapore, South Korea, and the United Arab Emirates (UAE).[843] Canada is developing a comprehensive AI Act addressing various aspects like data privacy and algorithmic bias,[844] while Singapore has implemented a 'Model AI Governance Framework' outlining guidelines for RAI development.[845] It is important to note that this list is not exhaustive, and many other countries are also involved in shaping the future of AI governance.

11.2.4 Data Governance Integration

Since LLMs like ChatGPT continue to grow and become more integrated into various sectors, relevant organisations will become intrinsically linked to ensuring RAI practices through data governance. This convergence necessitates a focus on several key areas, including data privacy to ensure user trust, compliance with evolving regulations, data quality management to avoid biased AI outputs, data lineage to track the origin and flow of information, and robust metadata creation to improve data understandability for both humans and AI systems.[846] Data lineage refers to the tracking of

---

841. Zeyi Yang, *Four Things to Know about China's New AI Rules in 2024*, MIT Tech. Rev. (17 Jan. 2024), https://www.technologyreview.com/2024/01/17/1086704/china-ai-regulation-changes-2024/; Adam Au, *China vs US Approaches to AI Governance*, The Diplomat (10 Oct. 2023), https://thediplomat.com/2023/10/china-vs-us-approaches-to-ai-governance/.
842. Benedikt Kohn & Fritz-Ulli Pieper, *AI: Are We Getting the Balance Between Regulation and Innovation Right? AI Regulation Around the World*, Taylor Wessing (9 May 2023), https://www.taylorwessing.com/en/interface/2023/ai---are-we-getting-the-balance-between-regulation-and-innovation-right/ai-regulation-around-the-world.
843. International Association of Privacy Professionals, *Global AI Legislation Tracker* (2024), https://iapp.org/media/pdf/resource_center/global_ai_legislation_tracker.pdf.
844. Innovation, Science and Economic Development Canada, *Artificial Intelligence and Data Act (AIDA) Companion Document*, https://ised-isde.canada.ca/site/innovation-better-canada/en/artificial-intelligence-and-data-act-aida-companion-document.
845. Infocomm Media Development Authority, *Model AI Governance Framework 2024: Press Release* (July 2024), https://www.imda.gov.sg/resources/press-releases-factsheets-and-speeches/press-releases/2024/public-consult-model-ai-governance-framework-genai; Singapore Personal Data Protection Commission (PDPC), *A Model AI Governance Framework* (21 Jan 2020), https://www.pdpc.gov.sg/help-and-resources/2020/01/model-ai-governance-framework.
846. IBM, *What Is Data Governance?*, https://www.ibm.com/topics/data-governance (accessed 9 Aug. 2024).

data movement throughout its journey, offering insights into its origin, transformations, and eventual placement within the data pipeline.[847]

By organising data with clear and structured metadata frameworks, companies can unlock its full potential. These frameworks make it easier to find, categorise, and analyse information, boosting agility and understanding, especially as AI and ML become crucial business tools.[848] Overall, the synergy between AI governance and data governance is essential for responsible and effective AI implementation, addressing ethical concerns, mitigating risks, and maximising the benefits of AI technologies in a data-driven world.

Considering the above contexts, organisations are placing a strong emphasis on data privacy, ensuring compliance with regulations such as GDPR and CCPA to safeguard sensitive information and maintain trust with users. Additionally, there is a growing focus on data quality management to ensure the accuracy, reliability, and consistency of data inputs for AI systems, thereby improving decision-making processes. Informed decisions, powered by clean data, pave the way for organisational success. Implementing effective data quality practices is crucial in reaching all these objectives.[849]

Meanwhile, the EU has taken a significant step towards integrated data governance with the recently adopted AI Act.[850] Specifically, this groundbreaking regulation acts as a cornerstone for integrating robust data governance practices within the bloc. Much like the GDPR's focus on privacy, the AI Act strives to establish a global precedent for AI regulation. Through its emphasis on transparency, accountability, and risk management, the EU AI Act compels adherence to data protection principles, quality management systems, human oversight, and cybersecurity.[851] It mandates a risk-based classification system for AI systems, with stricter requirements for higher-risk models. Furthermore, the Act promotes RAI deployment across diverse sectors like healthcare, finance, and energy, solidifying Europe's position as a leader in trustworthy AI development.

11.2.5 Ethics and Responsibility

As AI becomes more integrated into our daily routines, there is a growing focus on discussions regarding its ethical implications, responsibilities, and risk mitigation strategies. What was once confined to advanced STEM research has now permeated various sectors, including healthcare, finance, retail, and manufacturing. AI holds the promise of improving efficiency, cutting costs, and accelerating R&D efforts. Nonetheless, this transformative technology also raises concerns regarding potential societal

847. IBM, *Data Lineage*, https://www.ibm.com/topics/data-lineage (accessed 9 Aug. 2024).
848. Deasie, *Metadata Frameworks: Transforming Data Governance in the AI Era* (2024), https://www.deasie.com/post/metadata-frameworks-transforming-data-governance-in-the-ai-era.
849. Cem Dilmegani, *Data Quality Assurance: Importance & Best Practices in 2024*, AIMultiple (23 Jun. 2024), https://research.aimultiple.com/data-quality-assurance/.
850. Council of the European Union, *Council Conclusions on EU Digital Diplomacy*, ST 5662/24 INIT (14 Feb. 2024), https://data.consilium.europa.eu/doc/document/ST-5662-2024-INIT/en/pdf.
851. *See supra* n. 58, Art. 17.

harm, biases, and the need for transparency. With global expenditures on AI projected to reach USD 110 billion annually by 2024,[852] it is imperative to strike a delicate balance between harnessing its benefits and addressing associated risks.

As AI algorithms heavily rely on training data, the resulting AI system can perpetuate discriminatory practices, if these datasets are imbalanced or skewed. For instance, an AI-powered recruitment tool trained on biased resumes might disadvantage certain demographics in the job selection process, leading to unintended consequences such as underrepresentation or exclusion.[853] To mitigate this risk, fostering RAI development practices that emphasise fairness and inclusivity in data collection and algorithm design is crucial. Ongoing monitoring and auditing of AI systems post-deployment can help identify and address biases, ensuring that AI technologies contribute positively to societal advancement without reinforcing harmful stereotypes or inequalities.

Another crucial aspect of AI governance is ensuring a balance between leveraging AI benefits and mitigating potential risks, such as data privacy concerns, security breaches, job displacement, and ethical issues related to autonomous AI decision-making. Collaborative efforts between regulatory bodies and industry stakeholders are essential to developing comprehensive AI governance policies that foster innovation and competitiveness while addressing these challenges.[854] Implementing RAI practices is key for organisations to reduce risks and establish trust in AI technologies by ensuring transparency, fairness, and accountability in AI systems. Waiting for AI regulations to mature is not a viable approach. Instead, proactively establishing robust AI governance programs and policies is essential for effectively managing AI governance, data usage, and ethical practices. This proactive stance ensures compliance and mitigates risks as AI continues to shape industries and societies.[855]

In essence, the ethical landscape of AI is constantly shifting. While data privacy and bias are pressing concerns today, future dilemmas loom on the horizon. AI's potential for persuasion, human enhancement, autonomous weaponry, and even artificial general intelligence raises new ethical questions. To navigate these complexities, continuous conversation, collaboration across disciplines, and strong governance

852. ITPRO, *Worldwide AI Spending Expected to Reach $110 Billion in 2024* (25 Aug. 2020), https://www.itpro.com/technology/artificial-intelligence-ai/356880/worldwide-ai-spending-expected-to-reach-110b-in-2024.
853. World Economic Forum, *Why AI Bias May Be Easier to Fix Than Humanity's* (30 Jun. 2023), https://www.weforum.org/agenda/2023/06/why-ai-bias-may-be-easier-to-fix-than-humanity-s/.
854. Digital Regulation Platform, *Collaborative Approaches to Policy Implementation for Digital Transformation* (1 Sep. 2020), https://digitalregulation.org/collaborative-approaches-to-policy-implementation-for-digital-transformation/.
855. Christina Pazzanese, *Ethical Concerns Mount as AI Takes Bigger Decision-Making Role*, Harv. Gazette (26 Oct. 2020), https://news.harvard.edu/gazette/story/2020/10/ethical-concerns-mount-as-ai-takes-bigger-decision-making-role/; Cointelegraph, *What Is AI Governance?* Cointelegraph (August 2024), https://cointelegraph.com/explained/what-is-ai-governance; Shelby Hiter, *AI Policy and Governance: What You Need to Know*, EWeek (9 Aug. 2024), https://www.eweek.com/artificial-intelligence/ai-policy-and-governance/.

structures are essential.[856] Researchers, policymakers, and industry leaders must join forces to guarantee AI serves humanity as a force for good by minimising potential risks. Public awareness and involvement in AI ethics discussions are vital for informed AI adoption and promoting ethical practices.[857] Educating the public empowers stakeholders to contribute to policy development and advocate for the ethical use of AI. This collaborative effort, along with ongoing dialogues on balancing benefits and risks, will lead to robust and inclusive AI governance frameworks, prioritising innovation, and societal well-being.

11.3 FUTURE AI CHALLENGES

As the world rapidly advances technologically, navigating the future demands of AI confronts multifaceted challenges. Ethical dilemmas surrounding AI concerns about privacy, and data security require holistic solutions. Climate change looms large, necessitating urgent global cooperation to mitigate its effects. The ongoing pursuit of sustainable energy, equitable access to healthcare, and social justice remains a priority. To tackle these complexities, we need innovative solutions, unwavering resilience, and a collective commitment to building a better future.

Addressing future challenges in AI involves overcoming integration hurdles, democratising AI development, ensuring continuous adaptation of AI systems, and managing the transformation of the workforce through reskilling initiatives. Collaboration among stakeholders, including governments, industry leaders, researchers, and civil society, is crucial.[858] Together, they can develop robust regulatory frameworks and ethical guidelines that foster RAI innovation and promote inclusive practices. By harnessing the transformative potential of AI while addressing societal, ethical, and technological complexities, a collaborative approach can pave the way for a more sustainable and equitable future.[859] However, this section delves into a few major future challenges of AI, including challenges in AI integration, ensuring trustworthy and RAI, balancing innovation, and regulation, fostering international collaboration, and establishing international regulatory standards.

11.3.1 AI Integration Challenges

One of the significant challenges in AI integration is democratising access to AI technologies and tools. Traditionally, AI development has been dominated by large tech companies and research institutions due to the high cost of resources, computing power, and expertise required. Nonetheless, there is a growing need to make AI more

856. World Health Organization, *WHO Releases AI Ethics and Governance Guidance for Large Multi-Modal Models* (18 Jan. 2024), https://www.who.int/news/item/18-01-2024-who-releases-ai-ethics-and-governance-guidance-for-large-multi-modal-models.
857. *Ibid.*
858. OECD, *Recommendation of the Council on Artificial Intelligence*, OECD/LEGAL/0449, https://oecd.ai/en/assets/files/OECD-LEGAL-0449-en.pdf.
859. United Nations Educational, Scientific and Cultural Organization, *Recommendation on the Ethics of Artificial Intelligence* (2021), https://unesdoc.unesco.org/ark:/48223/pf0000380455.

accessible to smaller businesses, startups, researchers, and developers to spur innovation and democratise its benefits across industries. AI democratisation refers to making AI technologies, tools, and capabilities accessible and usable by a broader and more diverse group of people. By lowering entry barriers to AI adoption, organisations and individuals without extensive technical expertise can leverage AI for specific needs.

The increasing attention paid to Findable, Accessible, Interoperable, and Reusable (FAIR) data-sharing principles highlights the continued significance of data democratisation.[860] This concept is also evident in conversations about AI democratisation, which focuses on key areas like broadening access to AI use, facilitating participation in AI development, ensuring equitable distribution of AI benefits, and enhancing transparency and inclusivity in AI governance.[861] Moreover, aligning FAIR data principles with AI democratisation initiatives helps create a more open and collaborative environment, fostering innovation and accountability. As data and AI become more integral to society, these efforts are crucial in preventing the monopolisation of resources and knowledge, ensuring that technological advancements benefit all members of society.

Although major tech companies hold the potential to bolster core principles like accountability in global AI governance, their absence of clear authority impedes true democratisation.[862] To overcome this, collaboration is crucial among diverse stakeholders, including governments, researchers, and civil society. Favourably, efforts are being made to develop user-friendly AI platforms, open-source AI frameworks, and cloud-based AI services that can lower barriers to entry and empower a broader range of stakeholders to leverage AI capabilities.

11.3.2 Ensuring Trustworthy and RAI

Ensuring trustworthy and RAI is critical to harnessing its full potential while addressing potential harms. Future AI challenges in this regard involve a range of ethical, technical, and regulatory considerations that demand collaboration from various stakeholders. A key challenge is mitigating AI bias and ensuring fairness in AI systems. LLMs may exhibit biases across various dimensions, including gender, socioeconomic status, race, linguistic background, and ability. These biases can originate from multiple stages of the ML process, encompassing data acquisition, algorithmic development, and user engagement.[863] Addressing this challenge involves developing bias detection and mitigation techniques, promoting diversity in AI development teams,

860. Christophe Dessimoz & Paul D. Thomas, *AI and the Democratization of Knowledge*, 11 Sci. Data 268 (2024), https://doi.org/10.1038/s41597-024-03099-1.
861. Elizabeth Seger et al., Democratising AI: Multiple Meanings, Goals, and Methods, in *Proceedings of the 2023 AAAI/ACM Conference on AI, Ethics, and Society* 715, 715–722 (2023), https://arxiv.org/abs/2303.12642.
862. Eva Erman & Markus Furendal, *The Democratization of Global AI Governance and the Role of Tech Companies*, 6 Nat. Mach. Intell. 246 (2024), https://doi.org/10.1038/s42256-024-00811-z.
863. Vithya Yogarajan et al., *Tackling Bias in Pre-Trained Language Models: Current Trends and Under-Represented Societies*, arXiv Preprint arXiv:2312.01509 (2023), https://arxiv.org/pdf/2312.01509.

and establishing fairness-aware AI frameworks.[864] Regular audits and human oversight can also be integrated into these frameworks to identify and mitigate potential biases.[865]

Another critical challenge in ensuring trustworthy AI lies in achieving transparency and explainability. As AI systems become more complex and opaque, understanding their decision-making processes becomes crucial for building trust and accountability. Methods such as XAI aim to provide insights into AI model behaviour and decision logic, enabling stakeholders to understand, validate, and interpret AI-driven outcomes.[866] Enhancing transparency and explainability can also help address concerns related to AI's impact on privacy, autonomy, and human rights. Further research into interpretable AI models and fostering open-source development practices can illuminate internal AI decision-making processes. Additionally, regulatory frameworks mandating explainability for high-stakes AI applications, such as those in loan approvals or criminal justice, are crucial in addressing this challenge.

Ensuring data privacy and security is likely to remain a major challenge in AI governance, both now and in the foreseeable future. As AI heavily relies on vast amounts of data, this necessitates robust privacy and security practices to collect, store, and ethically use user data. Data breaches can have serious ramifications, such as financial losses, identity theft, discrimination due to biased algorithms, loss of anonymity, and unauthorised exploitation of personal information. To address these challenges, a comprehensive approach is essential, including the adoption of robust data governance frameworks that emphasise user consent, data minimisation, and secure storage practices.[867]

Additionally, implementing encryption and anonymisation techniques serves to further safeguard sensitive information. Organisations like OWASP and ISACA play a crucial role in promoting rigorous safeguards such as data enclaves and a heightened focus on accountability.[868] These measures, aligned with established privacy principles

---

864. Solon Barocas & Andrew D. Selbst, *Big Data's Disparate Impact*, 104 Calif. L. Rev. 671 (2016), https://www.cs.yale.edu/homes/jf/BarocasSelbst.pdf; Joy Buolamwini & Timnit Gebru, Gender Shades: Intersectional Accuracy Disparities in Commercial Gender Classification, in *Proceedings of the 1st NeurIPS Conference on Fairness, Accountability and Transparency (FAT '18)** 77, 77–91 (Vol. 81, 2018), https://proceedings.mlr.press/v81/buolamwini18a.html.
865. Nick Bostrom, *Superintelligence* (Oxford Univ. Press 2014).
866. Zachary C. Lipton, *The Mythos of Model Interpretability: In Machine Learning, the Concept of Interpretability Is Both Important and Slippery*, 16 Queue 31 (2018), https://arxiv.org/pdf/1606.03490; Amina Adadi, *Peeking Inside the Black-Box: A Survey on Explainable Artificial Intelligence (XAI)*, 6 IEEE Access 52138 (2018), https://ieeexplore.ieee.org/stamp/stamp.jsp?tp=&arnumber=8466590.
867. Brent Daniel Mittelstadt et al., *The Ethics of Algorithms: Mapping the Debate*, 3 Big Data & Society 1 (2016), https://doi.org/10.1177/2053951716679679.
868. OWASP provides a list of the top 10 data security risks, emphasizing the need for robust data security measures, while ISACA offers insights into data centre systems security and the complexity of simplifying data security measures. For details, *see* OWASP Foundation, *OWASP Data Security Top 10*, https://owasp.org/www-project-data-security-top-10/ (accessed 9 Aug. 2024); Ravi Shankar Vemuri, *A Five-Layer View of Data Center Systems Security*, 2 ISACA J. (2022), https://www.isaca.org/resources/isaca-journal/issues/2022/volume-2/a-five-layer-view-of-data-center-systems-securit; Ved Prakash, *The Complexity Conundrum: Simplifying Data Security*, ISACA (11 Aug. 2021), https://www.isaca.org/resources/news-and-trends/isaca-now-blog/2021/the-complexity-conundrum-simplifying-data-security.

outlined in frameworks like GDPR and ISO 31700, are pivotal in upholding data integrity and individual privacy in the era of AI.[869]

Effective collaboration between humans and AI systems is another major challenge for the future of AI. This challenge involves designing AI systems that complement human capabilities, enhance productivity, and support human decision-making instead of replacing human workers. Hence, it is imperative to design AI systems that can collaborate effectively with humans, offering support and valuable insights while respecting human intuition and ethical considerations. Ongoing research in human-AI interaction encompasses various areas such as enhancing the transparency of AI decision-making processes,[870] ensuring the inclusivity and benefits of AI systems across diverse populations[871] and building trust through XAI that can elucidate its reasoning in a comprehensible manner for users.[872] These endeavours are aimed at shaping a future where AI not only enhances human capabilities but also aligns with our ethical values and societal norms.

While AI has the promise of creating new job opportunities, it also poses a risk of displacing current jobs. To navigate these challenges, a concerted effort towards education and retraining is essential. Equipping individuals with the skills needed for the evolving job landscape is crucial.[873] Furthermore, open dialogue and strategic foresight are critical in managing AI's societal impact and fostering a fair transition. Incorporating ethical frameworks into the deployment of AI in critical sectors such as healthcare, education, and social services is also vital to minimise associated risks.[874] Additionally, there is a growing need for global cooperation to establish standards and regulations that guide the ethical use of AI, ensuring that its benefits are distributed equitably, and its challenges are addressed collaboratively. Finally, fostering a culture of continuous learning and adaptability among the workforce is important, as the dynamic nature of AI will continually reshape job roles and industry demands.

11.3.3 Balancing Innovation and Regulation

The intersection of innovation and regulation within the AI landscape presents a nuanced dynamic of progress and precaution. AI holds immense potential to transform various sectors such as healthcare, transportation, finance, business, education, and

869. The GDPR outlines seven main principles for data protection, including lawfulness, fairness, transparency, and accountability. Whereas the ISO 31700-1:2023 establishes high-level requirements for privacy by design to protect privacy throughout the lifecycle of a consumer product. For details, please *see supra* n. 397; ISO 31700-1:2023, *Consumer Protection: Privacy by Design for Consumer Goods and Services*, ISO (2023), https://www.iso.org/standard/84977.html.
870. Carlo Reverberi et al., *Experimental Evidence of Effective Human–AI Collaboration in Medical Decision-Making*, 12 Sci. Rep. 14952 (2022), https://doi.org/10.1038/s41598-022-18751-2.
871. Interaction Design Foundation, *What Is Human-Centered AI (HCAI)?*, https://www.interaction-design.org/literature/topics/human-centered-ai.
872. *See supra* n. 789.
873. *See* Pablo Illanes et al., *supra* n. 806.
874. *See* Pradeep Paraman & Sanmugam Anamalah, *supra* n. 740; Laura Arbelaez Ossa et al., *Integrating Ethics in AI Development: A Qualitative Study*, 25 BMC Med. Ethics 10 (2024), https://doi.org/10.1186/s12910-023-01000-0.

more. AI-driven diagnostic tools can revolutionise healthcare by enabling faster and more accurate diagnoses, while AI can optimise energy consumption in smart cities, contributing to sustainability efforts. Moreover, AI impacts society by automating tasks, generating valuable insights, and enhancing decision-making processes, all of which contribute to societal advancement and the overall improvement of quality of life.[875]

Regulation plays a vital role in ensuring the responsible advancement and implementation of AI systems. It establishes rules that safeguard individual rights, promote transparency, and enforce accountability in AI operations. For instance, the EU GDPR within the EU serves as a notable example of how regulations can set standards for the ethical handling of personal data by AI systems, emphasising the significance of consent and the right to explanation.[876] Furthermore, regulations are essential for preventing monopolistic behaviours and encouraging fair competition, which are crucial elements in nurturing a strong AI environment.[877] These measures contribute to striking a balance between fostering innovation and upholding ethical standards, ultimately ensuring that AI advancements benefit society as a whole.

Nevertheless, overly stringent regulations can act as impediments to innovation, deterring start-ups and investment in AI R&D. Striking a delicate balance between ensuring accountability and fostering innovation is crucial. Collaborative efforts between policymakers, industry experts, and researchers are vital to developing regulatory frameworks that promote RAI deployment while encouraging continued innovation and investment in AI technologies.[878] Implementing regulatory 'sandbox' environments could facilitate innovation by allowing AI developers to test new technologies under regulatory supervision, mitigating compliance burdens.[879]

The consequences of tipping the balance in either direction can be significant. Moreover, overregulation could lead to a situation where AI innovations are stifled due to excessive bureaucratic hurdles and compliance burdens, discouraging the development of breakthrough technologies. This could also result in a competitive disadvantage for regions that impose stringent regulations, as companies may choose to operate in jurisdictions with more favourable regulatory environments. Conversely, underregulation may create a scenario where unethical AI practices go unchecked, leading to societal backlash and calls for stricter oversight, thereby highlighting the importance of finding a balanced regulatory approach.

---

875. Kalina Bryant, *How AI Is Impacting Society and Shaping the Future*, Forbes (13 Dec. 2023), https://www.forbes.com/sites/kalinabryant/2023/12/13/how-ai-is-impacting-society-and-shaping-the-future/?sh=76dbe52c2f92.
876. Ben Wolford, *What Is GDPR, the EU's New Data Protection Law?* GDPR.eu, https://gdpr.eu/what-is-gdpr/ (accessed 9 Aug. 2024).
877. John Doe, *AI Is Too Important to Be Monopolised*, Fin. Times (9 Aug. 2024), https://www.ft.com/content/1fda45a2-43e0-4c10-b5fb-b6097e3f5c56; Open Markets Institute, *AI in the Public Interest: Confronting the Monopoly Threat* (2023), https://www.openmarketsinstitute.org/publications/report-ai-in-the-public-interest-confronting-the-monopoly-threat.
878. European Commission, Communication from the Commission to the European Parliament, the Council, the European Economic and Social Committee and the Committee of the Regions, COM (2023) 638 final (17 Oct. 2023).
879. OECD, *Regulatory Sandboxes in Artificial Intelligence* (2023), https://www.oecd-ilibrary.org/science-and-technology/regulatory-sandboxes-in-artificial-intelligence_8f80a0e6-en.

Furthermore, regulatory bodies should actively engage with AI experts, industry stakeholders, and civil society to gather diverse perspectives and insights when formulating AI policies.[880] This collaborative approach can lead to more informed and balanced regulations that address the needs of various stakeholders while promoting innovation and ethical AI practices. This inclusive strategy ensures that the policies are well-rounded, considerate of various implications, and can effectively guide the ethical development and deployment of AI technologies. Additionally, continuous M&E of regulatory frameworks are essential to ensure their effectiveness and relevance in a rapidly evolving AI landscape, allowing for timely adjustments and improvements as needed.

In conclusion, achieving a harmonious balance between innovation and regulation in AI governance is paramount. It requires foresight, adaptability, and a commitment to ethical principles. By collaboratively navigating this intricate landscape, we can ensure that AI serves as a force for good, enhancing human capabilities while safeguarding societal values. The future of AI governance hinges on our ability to maintain this equilibrium, fostering innovation while safeguarding the public interest.

11.3.4 Fostering International Collaboration

Fostering international collaboration in AI governance is crucial due to the complex and multifaceted nature of AI-related challenges. AI technologies are rapidly evolving and have the potential to impact various aspects of society, including ethics, privacy, security, and economic development. Therefore, a coordinated global effort is necessary to address these challenges effectively and ensure that AI development and deployment benefit humanity.[881] Nonetheless, achieving such collaboration is not without its challenges.

Furthermore, differences in legal systems across countries can also pose challenges to international collaboration in AI governance. Legal frameworks related to AI vary widely, ranging from strict regulations to more flexible approaches.[882] Some nations may prioritise innovation and economic growth, while others may emphasise privacy, transparency, and human rights. The US and China, for example, have different approaches to AI governance. The US focuses on mitigating risks through 'red teaming' (testing for vulnerabilities) while China emphasises adherence to its values.[883] Harmonising these legal frameworks to ensure consistent AI governance practices globally requires extensive coordination and negotiation among nations with diverse legal traditions and philosophies. Bridging the gaps between different priorities

880. *See supra* n. 713.
881. *See supra* n. 790.
882. Corinne Cath, *Governing Artificial Intelligence: Ethical, Legal and Technical Opportunities and Challenges*, 376 Philosophical Transactions of the Royal Society A, 20180080 (2018), http://dx.doi.org/10.1098/rsta.2018.0080.
883. Courtney Lang, *AI Governance on a Global Stage: Key Themes from the Biggest Week in AI Policy*, Atlantic Council (16 Nov. 2023), https://www.atlanticcouncil.org/blogs/geotech-cues/ai-governance-on-a-global-stage-key-themes-from-the-biggest-week-in-ai-policy/.

and legal systems is also crucial to avoid a fragmented approach to AI development and deployment.

Despite challenges like differing national priorities and legal systems, international collaboration is essential for creating strong AI governance frameworks. By sharing best practices and resources, nations can work together to ensure AI is developed safely, ethically, and for everyone's benefit. Collaboration also levels the playing field, preventing any one country from gaining an unfair advantage through weak regulations.

To achieve this, various organisations like the OECD, Council of Europe's AI committee, and IEEE are establishing international AI principles focused on ethics, transparency, and human rights. Coordination is underway at various levels, including but not limited to the following: the Council of Europe's Committee on AI, OECD's Working Party on Artificial Intelligence Governance, African Union High Level Panel on Emerging Technologies (APET) the Association of Southeast Asian Nations (ASEAN) workshops, G7's Hiroshima Process on GAI, UN's High-Level Advisory Body on AI, and the WEF's AIGA.[884]

Another strategy is to encourage the development of international standards. These standards play a crucial role in fostering collaboration and ensuring consistency across borders. While achieving complete harmonisation might be unrealistic, international standards can create a level playing field for businesses operating across borders and facilitate collaboration on R&D. The NIST AI Risk Management Framework (AI RMF) incorporates an AI governance framework that aims to better manage AI-driven risks for individuals, organisations, and society by incorporating trustworthiness considerations in the design, development, usage, and evaluation of AI products, services, and systems.[885]

Moreover, the International Electrotechnical Commission (IEC) and the ISO have jointly developed a series of standards covering the entire AI ecosystem, including terminology, governance, risk management, cybersecurity, and ethical considerations to create a common foundation for AI practices globally.[886] Furthermore, the ISO/IEC 38505-1:2017 standard, while not specific to AI, offers guiding principles for data governance, including guidelines on data classification.[887] It complements existing standards on IT governance (ISO/IEC 38500). Organisations can use these guidelines to maintain oversight of their data portfolio, essential for effective AI governance, as AI systems rely heavily on high-quality, well-governed data.

Above all, fostering international collaboration in AI governance necessitates a delicate balancing act. Countries must acknowledge their unique contexts, which

884. *See supra* n. 790.
885. National Institute of Standards and Technology, *AI Risk Management Framework* (26 Jul. 2024), https://www.nist.gov/itl/ai-risk-management-framework; US Dep't of Commerce, Nat'l Inst. of Standards & Tech., *Artificial Intelligence Risk Management Framework (AI RMF 1.0)* (January 2023), https://www.nist.gov/itl/ai-risk-management-framework.
886. *See supra* n. 791.
887. International Organization for Standardization & International Electrotechnical Commission, *ISO/IEC TS 38505-3:2021, Information Technology: Governance of Data – Guidelines for Data Classification* (2021), https://aistandardshub.org/ai-standards/information-technology-governance-of-data-guidelines-for-data-classification.

include national priorities, legal systems, and cultural values while working towards a shared vision for RAI development.[888] International forums and conferences serve this purpose by bringing together policymakers, researchers, industry leaders, and civil society representatives from different countries to share insights, best practices, and collaborative strategies. These platforms, like those offered by the OECD[889] and UNESCO,[890] facilitate knowledge exchange, mutual learning, and the development of more robust and inclusive approaches to AI governance on a global scale.[891] Ultimately, ongoing dialogue, cooperation, and coordination among stakeholders worldwide are crucial to addressing the complexities and challenges posed by AI technologies in our interconnected world.

11.3.5 Setting International Regulatory Standards

As AI technologies continue to evolve and permeate various sectors of society, the need for international regulatory standards becomes increasingly apparent. Setting these standards is crucial for addressing potential risks associated with AI deployment and ensuring its responsible development. One of the primary areas of focus for regulatory frameworks is data privacy. With AI systems often relying on vast amounts of data, there is a growing concern about how this data is collected, stored, processed, and used. Regulations like the EU GDPR[892] and the US's CCPA[893] establish high standards for data collection, storage, and use, while also setting guidelines and rules to safeguard individuals' privacy rights in the age of AI.

Another critical aspect of regulatory standards is addressing algorithmic bias. AI algorithms can inadvertently reflect biases present in the data they are trained on, leading to discriminatory outcomes. This can lead to discriminatory outcomes in areas like loan approvals, facial recognition, and job recruitment. To mitigate bias in AI systems, standards should focus on fairness, transparency, and accountability. Standards should require developers to employ techniques for bias detection and mitigation during AI development and deployment.[894] Further, standards should address the role of human oversight in AI decision-making processes and ensure mechanisms for redressal in case of biased outcomes.[895] Organisations like the Algorithmic Justice League advocate for fairness in AI and highlight the importance of auditing algorithms

888. Brookings Institution, *AI Governance*, https://www.brookings.edu/tags/ai-governance/ (accessed 9 Aug. 2024).
889. OECD Working Party and Network of Experts on AI (February 2020 to March 2022), https://oecd.ai/en/network-of-experts.
890. *See supra* n. 279.
891. Haim Ravia & Dotan Hammer, *International Collaborations Seek to Establish a Framework for the Use of AI*, Pearl Cohen (30 Oct. 2023), https://www.pearlcohen.com/international-collaborations-seek-to-establish-a-framework-for-the-use-of-ai/.
892. *See supra* n. 397.
893. *See supra* n. 677.
894. Boris Ruf & Marcin Detyniecki, *Explaining How Your AI System Is Fair*, arXiv:2105.00667 (2021), https://arxiv.org/abs/2105.00667.
895. Michele Loi, *Investigative Journalism and Algorithmic Fairness*, Algorithm Watch (20 Apr. 2023), https://algorithmwatch.org/en/investigative-journalism-and-algorithmic-fairness/.

for bias and discrimination.[896] Since 2018, ISO has been engaged in ongoing efforts to standardise AI.[897]

Moreover, specific sectors such as healthcare and finance require tailored regulatory frameworks for AI. AI is transforming healthcare finance by streamlining processes and offering personalised solutions. Hospitals are using AI to optimise their financial systems, including governance, revenue raising, pooling resources, and strategic purchasing.[898] This allows them to manage their revenue cycle more effectively, maximise investment returns, and extract valuable financial insights.[899] Additionally, AI models can analyse patient data to predict and prevent insurance claim denials, automate billing processes, and even suggest personalised financial solutions for patients. Nonetheless, regulatory standards must address issues related to patient data privacy, medical ethics, and the reliability of AI-driven medical decisions. Organisations like the WHO[900] and the International Medical Informatics Association (IMIA)[901] work on guidelines and standards for AI in healthcare to ensure safe and ethical practices globally.

Similarly, in the finance sector, AI is becoming more prevalent in critical tasks, such as analysing vast datasets of financial transactions to identify patterns of fraudulent activity in real-time. For instance, AI-powered fraud detection systems can analyse customer behaviour and spending patterns to flag suspicious transactions, potentially saving financial institutions millions of dollars annually. Additionally, AI is used to optimise risk assessment models, allowing for more accurate credit scoring and personalised investment strategies tailored to individual risk profiles.

Regulatory bodies like the Financial Stability Board (FSB)[902] and the International Organization of Securities Commissions (IOSCO)[903] are actively involved in formulating standards to regulate AI applications in finance. These standards are designed to uphold stability, transparency, and consumer protection while encouraging innovation and efficiency within financial services. As AI continues to evolve and integrate into critical sectors, the need for robust standards and guidelines becomes increasingly paramount to ensure responsible and effective use, highlighting the importance of ongoing regulatory oversight and industry collaboration.

896. *See supra* n. 323.
897. Thomas Zielke, Is Artificial Intelligence Ready for Standardization?, in *Systems, Software and Services Process Improvement* 237, 238 (M. Yilmaz et al., eds, 2020), https://doi.org/10.1007/978-3-030-56441-4_19.
898. Maryam Ramezani et al., *The Application of Artificial Intelligence in Health Financing: A Scoping Review*, 21 Cost Effectiveness & Resource Allocation 83 (2023), https://doi.org/10.1186/s12962-023-00492-2.
899. Optum, *Three Ways AI Is Helping Hospitals Transform Their Financial Health* (2023), https://www.optum.com/content/dam/optum3/optum/en/resources/PDFs/3-ways-ai-helps-hospitals-transform-financial-health.pdf.
900. World Health Org., *WHO Calls for Safe and Ethical AI for Health* (16 May 2023), https://www.who.int/news/item/16-05-2023-who-calls-for-safe-and-ethical-ai-for-health.
901. International Medical Informatics Association, *Welcome to IMIA*, https://imia-medinfo.org/wp/ (accessed 9 Aug. 2024).
902. Financial Stability Board, https://www.fsb.org (accessed 9 Aug. 2024).
903. International Organization of Securities Commissions, *About IOSCO*, https://www.iosco.org/ (accessed 9 Aug. 2024).

To strike a balance between promoting innovation and managing risks effectively, regulatory sandboxes have emerged as a valuable tool in various jurisdictions. Regulatory sandboxes are crucial tools that allow businesses to test new products, services, or business models under regulatory supervision, creating a controlled testing environment. This not only encourages innovation but also helps regulators understand emerging technologies and supports consumer choice in the long run.[904] For their effective use, regulatory sandboxes must be backed by a strong legal framework to prevent misuse. They are increasingly embraced by progressive financial regulators to adapt to rapid technological changes in the financial sector. This technical guide is designed to aid financial regulators in evaluating the suitability of a sandbox within their regulatory framework, guiding its design and implementation to address challenges posed by technological innovation.

Examples of regulatory sandboxes include the Monetary Authority of Singapore's FinTech Regulatory Sandbox and the Financial Conduct Authority's (FCA's) Sandbox in the United Kingdom.[905] These initiatives provide a structured framework for collaboration between regulators, industry players, and technology innovators, fostering a dynamic ecosystem for RAI development and implementation in the financial sector. The feedback and insights gained from regulatory sandbox experiments contribute to refining regulatory guidelines and promoting best practices in AI governance within the finance industry and beyond.

In conclusion, setting international regulatory standards for AI is a complex yet essential endeavour. By addressing key areas such as data privacy, algorithmic bias, sector-specific regulations, and leveraging regulatory sandboxes, global stakeholders can foster RAI development while ensuring compliance with ethical, legal, and societal norms. Collaborative efforts among governments, regulatory bodies, industry players, and civil society organisations are crucial to creating a harmonised and effective regulatory framework that supports innovation, protects rights, and builds trust in AI technologies.

11.4 RECOMMENDATIONS FOR ADAPTABLE AI FRAMEWORKS

In navigating the complex landscape of AI governance, crafting robust regulatory frameworks is paramount. These frameworks should be multifaceted, grounded in core ethical principles, and centred on a human-centric perspective. They should prioritise transparency, human oversight, and explainability while adopting a risk-based approach to effectively manage AI-related risks. Algorithmic impact assessments (AIAs) and a sectoral approach may be crucial for tailoring regulations to specific industry

904. European Parliament, *Artificial Intelligence Act and Regulatory Sandboxes*, https://www.europarl.europa.eu/RegData/etudes/BRIE/2022/733544/EPRS_BRI(2022)733544_EN.pdf (accessed 10 Aug. 2024).
905. Monetary Authority of Singapore (MAS), *FinTech Regulatory Sandbox*, https://www.mas.gov.sg/development/fintech/sandbox#:~:text=The%20FinTech%20Regulatory%20Sandbox%20guidelines,to%20be%20furnished%20to%20MAS; FCA, *Regulatory Sandbox*, https://www.fca.org.uk/firms/innovation/regulatory-sandbox.

needs, while regulatory sandboxes may offer controlled environments for testing and innovation.

Public participation, coupled with AI education and awareness initiatives, could ensure inclusive policymaking regarding AI, fostering a knowledge-based society. A well-harmonised, agile regulatory framework, coupled with ongoing monitoring, upskilling, and robust enforcement, is essential for fostering RAI development in the face of rapidly evolving technologies. Investing in R&D may further strengthen regulatory capabilities, creating a holistic ecosystem conducive to the ethical, accountable, and beneficial deployment of AI technologies. Let us delve into all aspects in detail.

Public participation, coupled with AI education and awareness initiatives, could ensure inclusive policymaking regarding AI, fostering a knowledge-based society. A well-harmonised, agile regulatory framework, coupled with ongoing monitoring, upskilling, and robust enforcement, is essential for fostering RAI development in the face of rapidly evolving technologies. Investing in R&D may further strengthen regulatory capabilities, creating a holistic ecosystem conducive to the ethical, accountable, and beneficial deployment of AI technologies.

11.4.1 Ethical Principles

Integrating ethical principles into regulatory frameworks is crucial for establishing RAI practices. This involves considering factors such as fairness, privacy, accountability, and human rights when formulating policies related to AI technologies.[906] One effective approach is to mandate ethical impact assessments (EIAs) for AI systems, akin to environmental impact assessments, to thoroughly evaluate potential ethical implications across various domains.[907] Frameworks like the AI Impact Assessment (AIIA) developed by the AI Now Institute offer comprehensive methodologies for conducting ethical evaluations in AI projects.[908]

By grounding AI regulations in core ethical principles such as fairness, accountability, transparency, and human well-being, regulatory frameworks can foster trust among stakeholders and promote the development of AI systems that align with societal values and norms.[909] This ensures AI is deployed responsibly and ethically, maximising its benefits for society. Recognising the potential ethical challenges of AI, UNESCO adopted the 'Recommendation on the Ethics of Artificial Intelligence' in 2021. This globally recognised framework sets the stage for RAI development by emphasising core principles such as respect for human rights, transparency, fairness, and the importance of maintaining human oversight in AI systems.[910]

906. *See supra* n. 279.
907. Dillon Reisman et al., *Algorithmic Impact Assessments: A Practical Framework for Public Agency Accountability*, AI Now Institute (9 Apr. 2018), https://ainowinstitute.org/publication/algorithmic-impact-assessments-report-2.
908. Kate Crawford et al., *AI Now 2019 Report*, AI Now Institute at New York University (2019), https://ainowinstitute.org/wp-content/uploads/2023/04/AI_Now_2019_Report.pdf.
909. *See supra* n. 279.
910. *Ibid.*

To translate these principles into actionable measures, EIAs can be employed throughout the AI lifecycle, similar to how environmental impact assessments are used.[911] EIAs evaluate potential ethical concerns across various domains, including fairness, transparency, the role of human oversight, and potential societal impacts. This process ensures that AI development aligns with established ethical principles.[912] Additionally, EIAs promote transparency by making information about AI systems publicly available, fostering trust and public understanding. By integrating ethical principles into regulatory frameworks and conducting thorough EIAs, we can steer AI development responsibly. This fosters inclusive growth, sustainable development, and human well-being. However, navigating the complex landscape of AI governance necessitates ongoing collaboration, multidisciplinary dialogue, and ethical stewardship from all stakeholders involved.[913]

11.4.2 Human-Centric Approach

In navigating the complexities of AI governance, a human-centric approach is paramount. This approach prioritises human well-being and societal needs, ensuring AI development serves humanity and avoids potential harm. Initiatives such as the IEEE Global Initiative for Ethical Considerations in Artificial Intelligence and Autonomous Systems provide valuable guidance on ethical design principles, emphasising the importance of embedding human values, rights, and well-being throughout the AI development process.[914]

Furthermore, international organisations like the OECD and the Council of Europe emphasise the importance of embedding human rights principles in AI development, deployment, and use, safeguarding fundamental freedoms, fairness, and privacy.[915] By integrating principles of human-centred design, regulations can promote transparency, explainability, and user control over AI-driven decision-making processes. Moving beyond simply avoiding harm, a human-centric approach actively promotes the development and deployment of AI systems that align with human values, ethical considerations, and user well-being.[916]

This necessitates integrating human-centric principles throughout the AI development lifecycle. Regulations should emphasise key aspects like transparency, explainability, and user control. Transparency plays a vital role in establishing trust in AI systems, necessitating the accessibility of AI models and algorithms to stakeholders.

911. *Ibid.*
912. Giulio Caviglia & Alessio Sammartano, *Syzygies in Hilbert Schemes of Complete Intersections*, 619 J. Algebra 538 (2023), https://arxiv.org/abs/1903.08770.
913. World Economic Forum, *Global Risks Report 2023* (11 Jan. 2023), https://www.weforum.org/reports/global-risks-report-2023.
914. IEEE SA, *IEEE Global Initiative on Ethics of Autonomous and Intelligent Systems* (April 2016), https://standards.ieee.org/initiatives/autonomous-intelligence-systems/.
915. OECD.AI, *OECD AI Principles: Human-Centred Values and Fairness* (May 2019), https://oecd.ai/en/dashboards/ai-principles/P6;https://www.coe.int/en/web/commissioner/-/ensure-human-rights-in-the-era-of-ai-and-unleash-its-potential-to-protect-rather-than-harm.
916. Future of Life Institute, *Artificial Intelligence, Future of Life Institute* (14 Nov. 2015), https://futureoflife.org/cause-area/artificial-intelligence/.

When AI solutions are transparent, stakeholders gain insight into decision-making processes, data utilisation, and the rationale behind decisions, enabling informed decision-making and mitigating the risk of errors and misuse.[917] Explainability ensures AI outputs are comprehensible, fostering trust and enabling human intervention when necessary.[918] Furthermore, user control empowers individuals to make choices about how AI interacts with their lives.[919] By embracing a human-centric approach informed by such initiatives, AI governance can foster trust, empower individuals, and ensure RAI development for the benefit of society.

In summary, a human-centric approach in AI governance goes beyond simply avoiding harm; it actively promotes the development and deployment of AI systems that align with our fundamental values, ethics, and well-being. This approach emphasises the importance of embedding human-centric principles throughout the entire AI development lifecycle, from initial design to deployment and ongoing usage. By embracing these principles, we can harness the transformative potential of AI technology while safeguarding against potential risks and ensuring that AI remains a force for good in our world. This comprehensive approach not only promotes transparency, explainability, and user control but also fosters trust, empowers individuals, and contributes to responsible and beneficial AI development for society.

11.4.3 Human Oversight and Accountability

In the ever-evolving landscape of AI governance, ensuring responsible development and deployment necessitates a crucial partnership: human oversight and accountability. Human oversight involves the participation of human individuals in the creation, implementation, and operation of AI systems to guarantee that they uphold human dignity, autonomy, and principles. The nature and extent of human oversight can vary, depending on the specific context and objectives of the AI system.[920] It is worth noting that the European Commission's AI Act 2024 places a strong emphasis on human oversight of AI. Article 14 specifically mandates that high-risk AI systems be designed and developed in a way that allows natural persons to effectively oversee them throughout their operational phase.[921] This highlights the growing recognition of human oversight as a critical component of RAI governance.

Effective human oversight can be achieved through various approaches. Regulatory frameworks can mandate different levels of human involvement depending on the risk profile of the AI system. Frameworks such as the 'HITL', 'Human-on-the-Loop'

917. Reid Blackman & Beena Ammanath, *Building Transparency into AI Projects*, Harv. Bus. Rev. (20 Jun. 2022), https://hbr.org/2022/06/building-transparency-into-ai-projects.
918. Rudresh Dwivedi et al., *Explainable AI (XAI): Core Ideas, Techniques, and Solutions*, 55 ACM Comput. Surv., Art. 194 (2023), https://doi.org/10.1145/3561048.
919. Ned Thornton, *Understanding the User Control: The Cornerstone of Online Privacy*, Privacy End (2 Apr. 2024), https://www.privacyend.com/user-control/.
920. Marco Repetto, *How Human Oversight and Transparency Can Ensure Trustworthy AI in the EU*, CertX, certx.com (3 Nov. 2023), https://certx.com/ai/how-human-oversight-and-transparency-can-ensure-trustworthy-ai-in-the-eu/.
921. *See supra* n. 853.

(HOTL), and 'Human-in-Command' (HIC) models represent varying levels of human oversight in automated systems. The HITL model necessitates the most frequent human intervention, particularly for critical decision-making scenarios like those involving autonomous weapons systems. In contrast, the HIC model provides a more supervisory role, typically applied to lower-risk tasks such as managing recommendation algorithms.[922] Additionally, establishing clear guidelines for data collection, training, and deployment practices can help mitigate potential biases and ensure fairness in AI decision-making. For instance, requiring developers to document data collection methods and potential biases within datasets can help ensure fairness and transparency throughout the AI lifecycle.

By implementing these measures, we can ensure that AI is held accountable for its actions and remains aligned with our values. Clear lines of responsibility for developers and operators established through regulatory frameworks ensure they are held accountable for any potential harm or negative outcomes arising from AI use.[923] Furthermore, fostering trust and promoting RAI development necessitates ongoing efforts to ensure AI serves as a tool for good, benefiting society while mitigating potential risks.

Accountability signifies the responsibilities of AI operations and their consequences. It compels AI developers and operators to explain the goals, motivations, and reasoning behind AI decisions to ensure they function ethically and responsibly.[924] Accountability in AI governance poses a complex challenge due to the opaque nature of some AI algorithms. Traditional models may not readily translate to these complexities. Nonetheless, establishing clear lines of accountability is essential for deterring misuse and ensuring responsible development.[925] Regulatory bodies can play a vital role in this regard by mandating transparency and explainability in AI decision-making processes.[926] This empowers stakeholders to understand how AI systems arrive at their outputs and identify potential biases or errors. Furthermore, fostering a culture of responsible innovation within AI development companies is crucial.[927] This includes establishing clear ethical guidelines for employees and holding them accountable for adhering to those principles.

By effectively combining human oversight and accountability, AI governance can navigate the complexities of this powerful technology and address the ethical challenges it presents. This collaborative approach ensures that AI remains a tool for good, serving humanity by enhancing productivity, efficiency, and innovation while also

922. Ashton DeKeyrel, *Managing AI Decision-Making Part 3: Human on the Loop,* Decision Management Solutions, https://decisionmanagementsolutions.com/human_on_the_loop/; https://www.deepscribe.ai/resources/optimizing-human-ai-collaboration-a-guide-to-hitl-hotl-and-hic-systems.
923. *See supra* n. 621.
924. *See* Claudio Novelli et al., *supra* n. 308.
925. European Commission, *High-Level Expert Group on Artificial Intelligence,* Ethics Guidelines for Trustworthy AI (2019), https://ec.europa.eu/digital-single-market/en/news/ethics-guidelines-trustworthy-ai.
926. *See supra* n. 621.
927. *See* Luciano Floridi et al., *supra* n. 716.

promoting societal well-being. Moreover, integrating robust oversight and accountability mechanisms fosters trust among stakeholders and helps mitigate risks associated with AI deployment, ensuring that AI technologies are developed and used responsibly. As AI continues to evolve, a balanced and proactive approach to governance, emphasising human values and ethical considerations, will be essential to harness its full potential for the betterment of society.

11.4.4 Risk-Based Framework

The ever-evolving landscape of AI necessitates a nuanced approach to governance. A one-size-fits-all regulatory framework may not be sufficient to address the diverse risks and applications of AI technologies. A risk-based framework may offer a more flexible and effective approach to AI governance, prioritising resources and regulations based on the potential risks posed by various AI systems. For example, facial recognition systems in public spaces raise different privacy concerns compared to recommendation algorithms on a music streaming platform. A risk-based framework can accommodate this diversity by tailoring regulations to the specific risks of each AI application. As AI capabilities expand and new use cases emerge, the risks associated with different applications may change. The framework can be updated to reflect these changes, ensuring that governance measures remain relevant and effective.[928]

A risk-based framework for AI governance provides a structured approach to identifying, assessing, and managing risks associated with AI systems. This framework involves evaluating the potential risks posed by AI technologies across various dimensions such as data privacy, security, fairness, transparency, and societal impacts. By prioritising risks based on their severity and likelihood of occurrence, organisations can allocate resources more effectively to mitigate high-risk areas and ensure RAI development and deployment.[929] For instance, high-risk AI systems, like those used in autonomous vehicles, might require stricter regulations and more rigorous testing procedures compared to lower-risk applications.

One of the key advantages of a risk-based framework is its adaptability to different AI applications and contexts. For instance, in healthcare AI systems, the focus might be on patient safety, data privacy, and ethical considerations, while in financial AI systems, the emphasis could be on data security, regulatory compliance, and algorithmic transparency.[930] This tailored approach enables organisations to address specific risks and challenges unique to each domain, thereby enhancing trust and accountability in AI technologies. Additionally, a risk-based framework fosters ongoing dialogue between developers, regulators, and the public. This collaborative approach ensures that AI governance reflects societal values and ethical considerations.

In conclusion, a risk-based framework is essential for effectively governing AI systems and managing the associated risks. By adopting a systematic approach to risk assessment and mitigation, policymakers can identify and address potential hazards,

928. *See supra* n. 916; *See* Luciano Floridi et al., *supra* n. 716.
929. *Ibid.*
930. *See supra* n. 621.

thereby ensuring the safe and responsible use of AI technologies. Moreover, integrating risk-based principles into AI governance frameworks helps promote transparency, accountability, and trust among stakeholders, ultimately contributing to the ethical and sustainable advancement of AI for societal benefits.

11.4.5 Algorithmic Impact Assessment

AIA is a crucial tool for AI governance, aimed at evaluating the potential impacts of AI systems on individuals, society, and the environment. As GAI continues to evolve and permeate various aspects of our lives, understanding and mitigating the risks associated with algorithmic decision-making becomes paramount. AIA involves a systematic and comprehensive evaluation of AI systems to identify potential biases, discriminatory outcomes, and ethical concerns.[931] By conducting AIAs, organisations and policymakers can proactively address issues concerning fairness, transparency, accountability, and societal impacts, promoting responsible and ethical AI development and deployment.

One of the key aspects of AIA is its focus on fairness and non-discrimination. AI systems can inadvertently perpetuate biases present in training data, leading to discriminatory outcomes. AIA methodologies, such as fairness audits and bias detection algorithms, help identify and mitigate biases in AI systems.[932] For example, in hiring algorithms, AIA can assess whether the AI system disproportionately favours certain demographic groups or exhibits discriminatory patterns, allowing organisations to rectify biases and ensure fair decision-making processes. AI bias occurs when the outcomes of AI systems are influenced by human biases present in the training data or algorithms, leading to distorted and potentially harmful results.[933] To mitigate discrimination and promote fairness, it is essential to prioritise the creation of unbiased algorithms while utilising diverse training datasets.

Effective AI governance necessitates fostering public trust and understanding. AIAs can play a vital role in achieving this by facilitating public participation in discussions surrounding AI development and deployment. Stakeholders can be involved in the AIA process, providing valuable insights into potential societal impacts and ethical considerations.[934] This collaborative approach promotes trust by demonstrating a commitment to the responsible development and use of AI. Furthermore, by incorporating public feedback into AI development and governance frameworks, AIAs contribute to a more inclusive and socially responsible approach to AI.

AIAs are not merely a one-time assessment tool; they can be integrated into the entire AI lifecycle, from development to deployment and ongoing monitoring.[935] By

931. *See supra* n. 328.
932. *See supra* n. 718.
933. IBM, *What Is AI Bias?* (22 Dec. 2023), https://www.ibm.com/policy/mitigating-ai-bias/.
934. Ayesha Gulley, *Here's Why Organizations Should Commit to Responsible AI*, World Economic Forum (22 Mar. 2023), https://www.weforum.org/agenda/2023/03/why-businesses-should-commit-to-responsible-ai/.
935. EqualAI, *EqualAI Algorithmic Impact Assessment (AIA) Tool* (22 May 2023), https://www.equalai.org/aia/.

continuously evaluating and refining AI systems based on AIA insights, developers can foster a culture of RAI development. This iterative process ensures that potential risks and biases are continuously identified and mitigated, promoting RAI practices throughout the entire development lifecycle. Moreover, integrating AIAs into the ongoing M&E phases allows organisations to adapt to evolving risks and challenges, staying proactive in addressing emerging issues in AI governance and ethics.

In conclusion, AIAs play a critical role in fostering RAI governance. Their ability to identify and mitigate risks, promote transparency and accountability, and build public trust makes them an essential tool for navigating the complexities of AI technology. By integrating AIAs effectively into governance frameworks, we can pave the way for a future, where AI benefits society, fostering innovation while safeguarding against potential harms. Moreover, AIAs can contribute to building a more inclusive and equitable AI ecosystem by addressing biases and ensuring fairness in AI systems, thereby enhancing trust among diverse stakeholders, and promoting social acceptance of AI technologies.

11.4.6 Sectoral Approach

The rapid development and deployment of AI across various sectors presents a unique challenge requiring a robust framework for governance. The sectoral approach has emerged as a promising strategy, advocating for tailored regulations and oversight mechanisms for specific industries where AI is being utilised. This approach recognises the inherent differences in risk profiles, societal impacts, and ethical considerations across different sectors.[936] By incorporating sectoral expertise into AI governance frameworks, policymakers can better navigate the complexities of AI technologies and ensure that regulations remain relevant and effective. Moreover, the sectoral approach encourages collaboration between regulatory authorities, industry stakeholders, and academic institutions to develop comprehensive guidelines and standards that promote RAI development and deployment in diverse sectors.

Proponents of the sectoral approach highlight its adaptability. Unlike a one-size-fits-all model, it allows regulatory bodies to leverage existing sectoral expertise within established agencies like healthcare or finance authorities. This fosters a nuanced understanding of the specific risks and opportunities associated with AI applications in each domain.[937] For instance, the healthcare sector might prioritise regulations on data privacy and algorithmic bias in AI-powered diagnostics, while the transportation sector might focus on safety and security standards for autonomous vehicles. The sectoral

936. European Commission, Directorate-General for Communications Networks, Content and Technology, *Sectoral Considerations on the Policy and Investment Recommendations for Trustworthy Artificial Intelligence* (2020), https://op.europa.eu/en/publication-detail/-/publication/6d266f0f-f7c3-11ea-991b-01aa75ed71a1/language-en.

937. Alex Engler, *A Comprehensive and Distributed Approach to AI Regulation*, Brookings (31 Aug. 2023), https://www.brookings.edu/articles/a-comprehensive-and-distributed-approach-to-ai-regulation/.

approach not only enhances regulatory compliance but also fosters trust and transparency among stakeholders, contributing to a more robust and sustainable AI ecosystem across sectors.

Examples of successful sectoral approaches can be found in the UK and Singapore. The UK released a white paper outlining a plan to empower existing regulators like the Equality and Human Rights Commission to develop sector-specific regulations for AI, guided by principles like fairness, transparency, and safety.[938] Similarly, Singapore's Personal Data Protection Commission (PDPC) established a Model AI Governance Framework that provides organisations with practical guidance on implementing RAI practices tailored to their industry.[939] By empowering existing regulatory bodies with the tools and resources to address AI challenges specific to their domains, both countries are paving the way for RAI adoption and sustainable technological development.

Nonetheless, the sectoral approach faces numerous challenges requiring collaborative approaches among diverse sectors and industries. Ensuring consistency and avoiding regulatory loopholes across sectors requires collaboration between different regulatory bodies. Additionally, rapid advancements in AI might necessitate revisions to existing sectoral regulations to keep pace with evolving technologies. Open communication and ongoing collaboration between stakeholders are crucial for the successful implementation of the sectoral approach in AI governance. Moreover, harmonising regulations, promoting knowledge-sharing platforms, and establishing regulatory sandboxes for testing AI applications can help overcome these challenges.[940]

11.4.7 Regulatory Sandboxes

The rapid progress of AI brings exciting opportunities and significant challenges for governance. While AI offers advancements across sectors, concerns arise regarding potential biases, discrimination, and lack of transparency in AI systems. Regulatory frameworks must navigate this complex landscape by fostering innovation while mitigating risks. Regulatory sandboxes emerge as a promising approach to achieving this delicate balance. A regulatory sandbox is a mechanism that enables companies to test new and innovative products, services, or business models under regulatory supervision. It offers innovators the opportunity to trial their ideas in a controlled setting, helps regulators gain insights into new technologies, and ultimately enhances consumer options.[941]

The UK FCA is credited with establishing the first official regulatory sandbox and propagating the concept globally. While there is no consensus on the sandbox

938. Industrial Strategy Council, *Effective Policy Approaches to Sectoral Issues*, https://industrialstrategycouncil.org/ (accessed 10 Aug. 2024).
939. Singapore Personal Data Protection Commission (PDPC), *Model Artificial Intelligence Governance Framework* (2020), https://www.pdpc.gov.sg/-/media/Files/PDPC/PDF-Files/Resource-for-Organisation/AI/SGModelAIGovFramework2.pdf.
940. Meredith Whittaker et al., *AI Now Report 2018*, https://ainowinstitute.org/wp-content/uploads/2023/04/AI_Now_2018_Report.pdf.
941. *See supra* n. 906.

definition, the FCA characterises it as 'a "safe space" in which businesses can test innovative products, services, business models and delivery mechanisms without immediately incurring all the normal regulatory consequences of engaging in the activity in question'.[942]

Following in the footsteps of the UK, many countries across the globe have established regulatory sandboxes, including Australia, Bahrain, Canada, Estonia, Europe,[943] Hong Kong, India, Indonesia, Jordan, Israel, Kazakhstan, Malaysia, Mauritius, Mozambique, Rwanda, Singapore, the UAE, and the US (specifically, Arizona, Florida, Kentucky, Nevada, South Dakota, Vermont, West Virginia, and Wyoming).[944] According to a World Bank report, globally, a total of 73 sandboxes have been adopted by 57 countries.[945] It is noteworthy that this is not an exhaustive list, but it highlights some of the leading countries that have adopted regulatory sandboxes.

In the face of rapid digitisation, regulators around the world are struggling to keep pace with evolving business technologies. Regulatory sandboxes offer a solution, providing a supervised environment for both regulators and businesses to experiment with innovative solutions. This approach offers a multitude of benefits. Sandboxes can:

- enhance the use of existing legislative frameworks;
- minimise risks associated with new technologies before legislative changes;
- reduce the regulatory burden on innovators;
- aid regulators in understanding the impact of new technologies;
- create opportunities for government development in integrating new technologies into traditional planning;
- help businesses test innovations with real customers;
- encourage regulatory learning to support business innovation;
- promote collaboration between businesses and regulators; and
- ensure consumer protection and prevent systemic risks due to close regulatory supervision.[946]

Nevertheless, regulatory sandboxes also have several drawbacks that warrant consideration. These tools often operate within a limited scope and duration, potentially hindering the full potential of complex technologies within the sandbox's

942. Financial Conduct Authority, *Regulatory Sandbox* (November 2015), https://www.fca.org.uk/publication/research/regulatory-sandbox.pdf.
943. European Commission, *Sandbox Project* (19 Jan. 2023), https://ec.europa.eu/digital-building-blocks/sites/display/EBSI/Sandbox + Project.
944. World Bank Group, *Key Data from Regulatory Sandboxes across the Globe*, World Bank (1 Nov. 2020), https://www.worldbank.org/en/topic/fintech/brief/key-data-from-regulatory-sandboxes-across-the-globe; Mondato, *Regulatory Sandboxes: Worthwhile in Developing Countries?*, Mondato Insight (9 Jun. 2019), https://blog.mondato.com/regulatory-sandboxes-worthwhile-developing-countries/; State Policy Network, *What Is a Regulatory Sandbox?*, SPN (12 Oct. 2021), https://spn.org/articles/what-is-a-regulatory-sandbox/.
945. *See* World Bank Group, *supra* n. 944.
946. Department for Transport, *Future of Transport Regulatory Review: Regulatory Sandboxes*, GOV.UK (4 Dec. 2023), https://www.gov.uk/government/consultations/future-of-transport-regulatory-review-regulatory-sandboxes/future-of-transport-regulatory-review-regulatory-sandboxes.

timeframe. Furthermore, some participants might exploit the environment for regulatory arbitrage, attempting to circumvent regulations entirely. Additionally, data privacy issues can arise due to reduced scrutiny, unproven technologies, or a lack of cybersecurity expertise among participants.[947] These limitations necessitate careful design and implementation of regulatory sandboxes to maximise their benefits while mitigating potential risks.

Despite their limitations, regulatory sandboxes play a crucial role in crafting adaptable and efficient regulatory structures for overseeing AI. They foster collaboration, promote cautious experimentation with risks, and facilitate learning, all of which are essential for creating a safer and more innovative AI landscape. By offering a space for experimentation and knowledge acquisition, regulatory sandboxes hold significant promise in establishing effective and flexible AI governance frameworks. Moreover, this approach has the potential to promote RAI development and deployment, benefiting society.[948]

11.4.8 Public Participation

Public participation is another essential measure for shaping effective regulatory frameworks for AI governance. Public participation in governance entails direct or indirect engagement of stakeholders in the decision-making process concerning policies, plans, or programs that pertain to their interests.[949] By involving diverse stakeholders in policymaking processes, regulatory frameworks can better address the intricate challenges and opportunities presented by AI. Multidisciplinary expertise and collaboration enhance the robustness and adaptability of regulatory frameworks, ensuring they remain relevant and effective amidst rapid technological advancements.[950] This section delves into the importance of public participation in AI governance, exploring strategies for fostering active engagement and collaboration among various stakeholders.

One approach to facilitate public participation in AI governance is to establish multi-stakeholder forums and consultations. These forums provide platforms for inclusive policymaking processes where different perspectives and interests can be voiced and considered. The European Commission's communication on AI highlights the need for open dialogue and collaboration between policymakers, regulators, researchers, industry leaders, and civil society organisations.[951] Such collaborative efforts can lead to more informed and balanced regulatory decisions that reflect the

---

947. Alyssa Abrams, *Regulatory Sandboxes: A Bridge Between Regulators and Business Innovation*, Sumsuber (10 Aug. 2024), https://sumsub.com/blog/regulatory-sandboxes/.
948. OECD.AI, *Regulatory Sandboxes in Artificial Intelligence*, https://oecd.ai/en/sandboxes (accessed 10 Aug. 2024).
949. Kathryn S. Quick & John M. Bryson, Public Participation, in *The Routledge Handbook of Public Participation in Planning* (1st edn, Edward Elgar Publishing 2020), https://doi.org/10.4337/9781800371972.00022.
950. *See supra* n. 860.
951. European Commission, *Artificial Intelligence in the European Commission (AI@EC) Communication*, COM (2024) 18 final (18 Jan. 2024), https://commission.europa.eu/publications/artificial-intelligence-european-commission-aiec-communication_en.

diverse needs and concerns of stakeholders. This inclusivity helps address potential biases, promote transparency, and build trust among stakeholders, contributing to the legitimacy and acceptance of AI regulations within society.

Moreover, multidisciplinary expertise plays a critical role in navigating the complexities of AI governance. By tapping into diverse knowledge domains such as ethics, law, technology, economics, sociology, and psychology, policymakers can develop nuanced and context-aware regulatory frameworks. Collaboration between academia, industry experts, policymakers, and civil society organisations can facilitate the integration of ethical principles, human rights considerations, and societal values into AI policies.[952] This interdisciplinary approach is in line with best practices advocated by organisations like the OECD, emphasising the need for holistic and inclusive approaches to AI governance.

In conclusion, public participation and stakeholder engagement are fundamental principles in shaping flexible, effective, and socially responsible regulatory frameworks for AI governance. These principles highlight the importance of engaging a wide range of stakeholders, promoting cooperation, and adopting inclusive approaches in policy-making.[953] By involving diverse stakeholders, fostering collaboration, and implementing inclusive policymaking processes, regulators can navigate the complexities of AI technologies while ensuring transparency, accountability, and societal benefits.[954] These approaches align with academic insights and policy recommendations aimed at promoting RAI development and deployment in the interest of broader society.

11.4.9 AI Education and Awareness

In response to complex AI challenges, fostering widespread education and awareness is crucial for effective AI governance. These contexts compel regulators and other relevant stakeholders to invest in comprehensive AI education programs targeting policymakers, regulators, businesses, and the general public. Initiatives such as those advocated by Artificial Intelligence for All (AI4ALL), and AI Ethics Lab offer valuable resources for developing educational content that addresses the complexities of AI technologies, associated risks, and potential opportunities.[955] By leveraging such resources, stakeholders can gain a deeper understanding of AI's implications, thereby facilitating informed decision-making in the realm of AI governance.

Capacity-building initiatives are essential components of efforts to enhance AI education and awareness. These initiatives should encompass a range of stakeholders, from government officials to industry leaders and members of civil society. Through targeted capacity-building programs, stakeholders can acquire the necessary knowledge and skills to navigate the evolving landscape of AI technologies and regulations.

952. *See* IBM, *supra* n. 776; *see also supra* n. 795.
953. Fernando Marmolejo-Ramos et al., *AI-Powered Narrative Building for Facilitating Public Participation and Engagement*, 2 Discov. Artif. Intell. 7 (2022), https://doi.org/10.1007/s44163-022-00023-7.
954. Christopher Wilson, *Public Engagement and AI: A Values Analysis of National Strategies*, 39 Gov't Info. Q. 101652 (2022), https://doi.org/10.1016/j.giq.2021.101652.
955. *See supra* n. 861.

Moreover, public awareness campaigns play a crucial role in engaging communities and fostering informed discourse about AI. These campaigns should emphasise not only the potential benefits of AI but also its inherent risks and the existing regulatory frameworks governing its use.[956]

Moreover, effective AI governance hinges on empowering public participation in discussions related to RAI development. By raising awareness about AI capabilities, limitations, and potential risks, we can build trust and encourage informed public discourse.[957] Such efforts enable individuals to engage meaningfully in debates about AI governance, contributing to the formulation of policies that prioritise ethical considerations and societal values. Ultimately, by investing in AI education and awareness initiatives, stakeholders can collectively work towards ensuring the responsible and equitable deployment of AI technologies in society.

In summary, education, awareness, and public engagement are crucial for RAI governance. By emphasising public participation, acknowledging AI's limitations, and utilising resources like AI4ALL's educational tools and public awareness campaigns, we can cultivate a more informed and ethical AI landscape. This collaborative approach not only fosters trust between developers and the public but also allows for the identification of potential biases and societal concerns early in the development process. Furthermore, ongoing public discourse can help shape regulations that are adaptable to the rapid evolution of AI technologies, ensuring they remain effective in safeguarding human values and promoting responsible innovation. It is therefore imperative to promote awareness and foster discussions that benefit society.

11.4.10 Agile Regulation

In the dynamic landscape of AI, traditional regulatory frameworks often struggle to keep pace with the rapid advancements in technology. To effectively govern AI systems and mitigate potential risks, there is a growing consensus on the need for agile regulation. Agile regulation is a framework aimed at crafting flexible and adaptable regulations capable of responding effectively to dynamic markets and a rapidly changing world.[958] It holds significant potential for regulating future goods, services, and activities. This approach focuses on prioritising end-user satisfaction, empowering teams, and utilising networks and innovation to address complex problems. Essentially, agile regulation seeks to achieve a balance between regulatory oversight and the necessity for adaptability in an ever-evolving landscape.

956. European Commission, *Communication on Artificial Intelligence for Europe*, COM (2018) 237 final (25 Apr. 2018), https://digital-strategy.ec.europa.eu/en/library/communication-artificial-intelligence-europe.
957. Lee Rainie et al., *Ethical AI Design*, Pew Research Center (16 Jun. 2021), https://www.pewresearch.org/internet/wp-content/uploads/sites/9/2021/06/PI_2021.06.16_Ethical-AI-Design_FINAL.pdf.
958. Ayo Aladesanmi, *Agile Regulation and the Future of Governance*, Penn Law (3 May 2023), https://www.law.upenn.edu/live/news/15808-agile-regulation-and-the-future-of-governance.

Another crucial element of agile regulation is its emphasis on continuous M&E of regulatory measures to ensure their effectiveness and relevance in addressing emerging challenges in AI development and deployment. By fostering collaboration between policymakers, industry stakeholders, and academic experts, agile regulation can harness collective intelligence to anticipate and mitigate potential risks associated with AI technologies. Additionally, agile regulation promotes transparency and accountability in the regulatory process by engaging the public in discussions and consultations on AI governance issues, thereby enhancing public trust and confidence in regulatory decision-making.[959]

Furthermore, agile regulation emphasises the adoption of risk-based approaches to AI governance. Rather than applying blanket regulations, risk-based approaches prioritise regulatory interventions based on the level of risk posed by AI systems.[960] This nuanced approach allows regulators to focus their resources on addressing high-risk AI applications while avoiding unnecessary burdens on low-risk ones. By encouraging AI developers and users to adopt proactive risk management strategies, risk-based approaches promote accountability and RAI deployment.[961]

Additionally, agile regulation encourages the establishment of mechanisms for international cooperation and information sharing to address cross-border challenges and promote regulatory harmonisation in the global AI landscape. Organisations such as the GPAI provide platforms for member countries to exchange ideas and create unified methods for governing AI.[962] This collaborative approach ensures consistency and coherence in regulatory standards while facilitating the responsible and ethical development and deployment of AI.

In essence, effective AI regulation requires more than existing structures; it demands continuous evaluation and adaptation. Agile regulation might offer one of the most viable alternative solutions to AI governance issues. It offers a promising approach to navigating the complex landscape of AI governance. Moreover, it allows for innovation while mitigating potential risks before broader deployment. Nonetheless, implementing agile regulation poses challenges, including the difficulty of developing clear and consistent regulatory principles while maintaining flexibility and ensuring adequate resources. By leveraging existing frameworks, fostering continuous evaluation and adaptation, and promoting international collaboration, we can build a robust governance ecosystem that fosters innovation while mitigating risks.

11.4.11 International Harmonisation

The global nature of AI development and deployment necessitates a coordinated approach to governance. Fragmentation in regulatory frameworks across different

959. OECD, *Practical Guidance on Agile Regulatory Governance to Harness Innovation*, OECD Legal Instruments, No. 669 (2024), https://legalinstruments.oecd.org/public/doc/669/9110a3d9-3bab-48ca-9f1f-4ab6f2201ad9.pdf.
960. Jon Truby et al., *A Sandbox Approach to Regulating High-Risk Artificial Intelligence Applications*, 13 Eur. J. Risk Reg. 270 (2022), https://doi.org/10.1017/err.2021.52.
961. *Ibid.*
962. *See supra* n. 758.

jurisdictions can hinder innovation, increase compliance costs for businesses and create uncertainty for stakeholders. To address these challenges, international harmonisation of AI regulations is crucial. By promoting collaboration among nations, harmonised standards can be developed, minimising regulatory fragmentation, and facilitating a more cohesive global AI ecosystem, as highlighted in the Montreal Declaration for a RAI.[963] This approach not only streamlines compliance for businesses operating across different jurisdictions but also enhances transparency and trust in AI technologies.

International collaboration fosters the responsible development and deployment of AI globally. Thus, efforts to promote international collaboration on harmonised regulatory frameworks for AI are gaining momentum. Organisations like the GPAI are leading initiatives to facilitate dialogue and cooperation among nations to address the complex ethical, legal, and social implications of AI technologies.[964] By fostering multilateral cooperation, GPAI aims to establish common standards that reflect diverse perspectives and values, thereby promoting RAI development and deployment worldwide.[965] These frameworks offer clear guidance to developers, businesses, and policymakers, helping them confidently navigate the intricate AI landscape.

Furthermore, international cooperation can help mitigate compliance burdens on businesses by establishing common standards for AI development and deployment. In an interconnected global economy, businesses often struggle to comply with a patchwork of regulatory requirements across different markets. Harmonised AI regulations can streamline compliance for businesses operating internationally. This not only benefits businesses directly but also contributes to fostering innovation and economic growth on a global scale. The OECD's work on AI, for instance, highlights the importance of international coordination between regulatory bodies.[966] By establishing common standards, businesses can avoid the administrative and financial costs associated with complying with diverse regulations in different countries.

In essence, the path towards international harmonisation of AI regulations is undeniably complex. National priorities, political landscapes, and cultural values can create significant obstacles to achieving a unified approach. Nonetheless, the potential benefits are equally undeniable. A harmonised framework could foster RAI development, accelerate innovation, and create a more cohesive global AI ecosystem. Through ongoing dialogue and collaboration, the international community can work towards a framework for AI governance that benefits all stakeholders. This collaborative effort will ensure that this powerful technology serves all of humanity, not just individual nations, or economic interests.

963. Université de Montréal, *Montreal Declaration for a Responsible AI,* https://recherche.umontreal.ca/english/strategic-initiatives/montreal-declaration-for-a-responsible-ai/.
964. *See supra* n. 758.
965. *Ibid.*
966. *See supra* n. 721.

11.4.12 Continuous M&E

The rapid evolution of AI demands a dynamic approach to regulation. Static frameworks risk obsolescence as technology advances. To address this challenge, continuous M&E are crucial. M&E processes assess the impact of existing regulations, identify gaps, and inform iterative improvements.[967] By engaging with diverse stakeholders and soliciting feedback from the broader community, regulators can address concerns and incorporate diverse perspectives into the decision-making process. This inclusivity not only strengthens the legitimacy of regulatory measures but also promotes accountability and responsiveness to societal needs and values.

Effective M&E necessitates collaboration between diverse stakeholders: regulatory agencies, industry, and academia. By pooling resources and expertise, stakeholders can enhance the comprehensiveness and accuracy of data collection and analysis. Furthermore, transparency throughout the process, through sharing findings with the public, fosters accountability and trust in AI governance efforts.[968] Additionally, establishing clear communication channels and regular meetings among stakeholders can facilitate the exchange of information and promote consensus-building on regulatory priorities and strategies. Moreover, involving civil society organisations and other non-governmental entities in M&E processes can provide valuable insights and perspectives, contributing to more comprehensive and inclusive decision-making in AI governance.

Regulatory impact assessment (RIA) serves as a vital instrument for policymakers to determine the necessity and manner of regulation in achieving public policy objectives. RIA aids policymakers in pinpointing the optimal and most impactful policy approach before decision-making. Over the last three decades, the adoption of RIA has grown significantly among EU Member States.[969] By collecting data and evaluating the impact of regulations, policymakers can identify gaps, measure effectiveness, and adapt as needed. Implementing relevant metrics and indicators aligned with regulatory objectives allows for objective evaluation. These indicators can track compliance, safety, fairness, and other critical aspects of AI deployment. Thus, resources from the National Academies of Sciences, Engineering, and Medicine (NASEM) offer guidance on developing effective metrics for AI governance.[970]

Finally, a key aspect of this approach is the incorporation of feedback loops. By encouraging ongoing dialogue with stakeholders such as industry, civil society, and the public, regulators can gather valuable insights to inform future iterations of the

967. National Artificial Intelligence Advisory Committee, *Rationales, Mechanisms, and Challenges to Regulating AI: A Concise Guide and Explanation* (2023), https://ai.gov/wp-content/uploads/2023/07/Rationales-Mechanisms-Challenges-Regulating-AI-NAIAC-Non-Decisional.pdf.
968. Wiley Rein LLP, *All Things AI*, https://www.wiley.law/practices-All-Things-AI (accessed 10 Aug. 2024).
969. OECD, *Regulatory Impact Assessment*, OECD iLibrary, https://www.oecd-ilibrary.org/sites/9b745623-en/index.html?itemId=/content/component/9b745623-en (accessed 10 Aug. 2024).
970. *See supra* n. 967.

framework.[971] Nevertheless, implementing a dynamic approach to AI governance presents challenges. Developing robust metrics and adapting regulations can be complex and time-consuming. Additionally, ensuring adequate resources for ongoing M&E is essential. Despite these challenges, the benefits of a living framework are clear. By continuously assessing and improving our regulatory frameworks, we can ensure AI governance keeps pace with the rapid evolution of this transformative technology.

11.4.13 Upskilling and Workforce Development

The rise of AI necessitates a paradigm shift in workforce development strategies. Effective AI governance, ensuring responsible and ethical use of this powerful technology, requires a skilled workforce equipped to navigate the complexities of AI systems. Traditional skillsets may no longer suffice in this new landscape. Upskilling and workforce development initiatives are crucial to ensure responsible and ethical AI development and deployment. Upskilling involves a long-term investment in enhancing the knowledge, skills, and competencies that assist employees in advancing their careers.[972] It includes the process of improving an employee's abilities to equip them for future challenges. Solutions must be developed locally, regionally, and nationally. Collaboration among stakeholders is crucial, including educators, government, and business leaders.[973] The development of the workforce involves ensuring that competent and efficient public employees are prepared to confront new policy challenges and increased uncertainty.[974]

To effectively upskill individuals for AI governance roles, comprehensive training programs must be established. These programs should cover a wide range of topics, including AI fundamentals, data ethics, regulatory compliance, risk management, and stakeholder engagement. Additionally, interdisciplinary approaches that integrate insights from fields such as law, philosophy, sociology, and computer science are essential for fostering a holistic understanding of AI governance challenges. For instance, the EU's Ethics Guidelines for Trustworthy AI emphasises the importance of interdisciplinary collaboration in developing AI governance frameworks that prioritise human rights, fairness, transparency, and accountability.[975]

Furthermore, partnerships between academic institutions, government agencies, industry stakeholders, and non-profit organisations play a crucial role in advancing workforce development for AI governance. Collaborative efforts can facilitate

971. OECD.AI, *Framework for Meaningful Engagement of External Stakeholders in AI Development*, OECD.AI (27 Mar. 2023), https://oecd.ai/en/catalogue/tools/framework-for-meaningful-engagement-of-external-stakeholders-in-ai-development.
972. Susan R. Vroman & Tiffany Danko, *How to Build a Successful Upskilling Program*, Harv. Bus. Rev. (18 Jan. 2022), https://hbr.org/2022/01/how-to-build-a-successful-upskilling-program.
973. Robert E. Moritz, *How Do We Upskill a Billion People by 2025?*, World Economic Forum (22 Jan. 2020), https://www.weforum.org/agenda/2020/01/2025-leadership-collaboration-skills-training/.
974. Organisation for Economic Co-operation and Development, *Public Employment and Management: Workforce Development*, https://www.oecd.org/gov/pem/public-sector-leadership-implementation/pem-workforce-development/ (accessed 11 Aug. 2024).
975. *See supra* n. 421.

knowledge-sharing, curriculum development, internship opportunities, and research initiatives aimed at addressing emerging issues in AI governance. For example, the Partnership on AI, a multi-stakeholder initiative, brings together leading companies, advocacy groups, and academic institutions to promote RAI development and deployment through research, best practice sharing, and policy engagement.[976]

Moreover, ongoing learning and professional development opportunities are essential for individuals working in AI governance roles to stay abreast of evolving technologies and regulatory landscapes. Continuous education programs, workshops, conferences, and online resources can provide practitioners with the latest insights, tools, and strategies for effectively managing AI-related risks and maximising societal benefits. By investing in upskilling and workforce development initiatives, stakeholders can build a skilled workforce capable of addressing the complex challenges and opportunities presented by AI governance in the digital age.[977]

In essence, effective AI governance requires a two-pronged upskilling approach. First, building technical proficiency through courses in data analysis, ML, and RAI development empowers professionals to understand AI fundamentals, core algorithms, and potential biases. Resources like online micro-credentials and specialised university programs can address this. Second, fostering a culture of critical thinking through training on algorithmic fairness, transparency, and accountability equips employees to identify and mitigate risks like privacy concerns and unintended consequences. Workshops on AI ethics and real-world case studies can be valuable tools in this process.[978] This continuous learning approach ensures a future-proof workforce capable of navigating the ever-evolving complexities of AI and promoting its responsible use.

11.4.14 Enforcement Mechanisms

Effective AI governance requires not only well-defined regulations but also robust enforcement mechanisms to ensure compliance. These mechanisms can encompass a range of tools and approaches, fostering responsible development and deployment of AI. While regulations and guidelines provide a foundation for RAI development and deployment, enforcement mechanisms are essential for holding stakeholders accountable and deterring non-compliance. One key aspect of enforcement mechanisms is the establishment of clear and enforceable legal frameworks that define rights, responsibilities, and liabilities related to AI technologies.[979] This includes laws and regulations that govern data privacy, algorithmic transparency, fairness, accountability, and ethical considerations in AI development and deployment.

976. Partnership on AI, *PAI Brings Together a Diverse Community to Address Important Questions about Our Future with AI* (2024), https://partnershiponai.org/.
977. World Economic Forum, *The Future of Jobs Report 2020* (2020), https://www.weforum.org/publications/the-future-of-jobs-report-2020/.
978. Deloitte Canada, *Omnia Upskilling Infographic*, Deloitte (2024), https://www2.deloitte.com/content/dam/Deloitte/ca/Documents/deloitte-analytics/ca-Omnia-Upskilling-Infographic-AODA-EN.pdf; *See supra* n. 279.
979. *See supra* n. 860.

In addition to legal frameworks, enforcement mechanisms should include robust oversight mechanisms to monitor compliance and address violations effectively. This may involve the creation of dedicated regulatory bodies or agencies tasked with overseeing AI-related activities and enforcing relevant regulations.[980] These oversight bodies should have the authority to investigate complaints, conduct audits, impose sanctions on non-compliant entities, and provide guidance on best practices for AI governance. Furthermore, these oversight bodies should be equipped with sufficient resources and expertise to navigate the rapidly evolving landscape of AI technologies and applications. Regular collaboration and information sharing among these bodies, both domestically and internationally, can enhance effectiveness in addressing cross-border challenges and ensuring consistent enforcement standards.

Moreover, enforcement mechanisms should leverage technology-driven solutions to enhance regulatory compliance and enforcement efforts. For instance, AI-powered tools can be employed for monitoring and auditing AI systems, detecting potential biases or ethical violations, and ensuring transparency and accountability throughout the AI lifecycle.[981] By harnessing the capabilities of AI technologies, regulators can enhance their capacity to enforce regulations effectively and address emerging challenges in AI governance. Collaboration between enforcement agencies and AI developers can lead to compliant AI systems, reducing the need for reactive enforcement. Continuous research in AI ethics should guide the ongoing refinement of enforcement for evolving needs.

Furthermore, international cooperation and coordination are crucial for ensuring the effective enforcement of AI in a globalised digital economy. Given the cross-border nature of AI innovation and deployment, harmonising enforcement efforts across jurisdictions is essential to prevent regulatory arbitrage and ensure a level playing field for businesses operating internationally.[982] This requires cooperation among regulatory authorities, law enforcement agencies, and international organisations to share information, coordinate enforcement actions, and develop common standards and practices for AI governance. By implementing robust enforcement mechanisms, policymakers can strengthen trust in AI technologies, protect individuals' rights and interests, and promote responsible and ethical AI development and deployment globally.

However, implementing effective enforcement mechanisms brings its own challenges. Determining the appropriate level of enforcement action, balancing innovation with risk mitigation, and ensuring fair and transparent enforcement processes are all crucial considerations.[983] Furthermore, the complexity of AI can make it difficult to

980. White & Case LLP, *AI Watch: Global Regulatory Tracker: OECD* (13 May 2024), https://www.whitecase.com/insight-our-thinking/ai-watch-global-regulatory-tracker-oecd.

981. World Economic Forum, *The Global Risks Report 2021* (2021), https://www.weforum.org/publications/the-global-risks-report-2021/.

982. European Parliament, *P9_TA (2022)0140, Artificial Intelligence in a Digital Age: European Parliament Resolution of 3 May 2022 on Artificial Intelligence in a Digital Age (2020/2266(INI))*, 2022 O.J. (C 465) 72, https://eur-lex.europa.eu/legal-content/EN/TXT/HTML/?uri=CELEX%3A52022IP0140.

983. Gina Cherelus, *Artificial Intelligence Regulation*, N.Y. Times (6 Dec. 2023), https://www.nytimes.com/2023/12/06/technology/artificial-intelligence-regulation.html.

identify and attribute responsibility for violations.[984] Additionally, ensuring resources and expertise within enforcement bodies is crucial.[985] Despite these hurdles, robust enforcement mechanisms are essential in building trust and ensuring that AI technologies are developed and deployed responsibly. By employing a range of enforcement tools, regulatory bodies can foster a culture of RAI development and deployment, ultimately protecting the public and promoting trust in this powerful technology.

11.4.15 Investment in R&D

Investment in R&D is fundamental to advancing AI governance by fostering innovation, addressing ethical concerns, and mitigating risks associated with AI technologies. Robust R&D efforts drive progress in understanding AI systems, developing new methodologies, and enhancing capabilities to ensure the responsible and ethical deployment of AI. Governments, industry players, and academic institutions must collaborate to allocate resources towards AI R&D initiatives that prioritise societal well-being, ethics, and safety.[986]

One crucial aspect of investing in AI R&D for governance purposes is the development of explainable and interpretable AI systems. XAI aims to enhance transparency and accountability in AI decision-making processes by enabling humans to understand how AI systems arrive at their conclusions.[987] By investing in XAI research, policymakers and regulators can ensure that AI systems are not only accurate and efficient but also interpretable, thus fostering trust and accountability in their use across various sectors, including healthcare, finance, and criminal justice. Investing in XAI facilitates the integration of human oversight, which is essential for identifying and addressing biases or errors in AI systems. Furthermore, widespread adoption of XAI can lead to increased public acceptance and confidence in AI technologies, paving the way for responsible and ethical deployment in critical domains.[988]

Furthermore, investment in AI R&D should prioritise efforts to address bias, fairness, and equity issues in AI algorithms and systems. Research initiatives focusing on algorithmic fairness and bias mitigation techniques are essential for ensuring that AI technologies do not perpetuate or exacerbate existing societal inequalities.[989] By developing fair and unbiased AI systems, policymakers can promote inclusive growth and reduce the risk of discrimination or harm resulting from AI deployment in critical domains such as hiring, lending, and law enforcement. Additionally, continuous M&E

---

984. International Association of Privacy Professionals, *AI Regulatory Enforcement Around the World*, IAPP (2 Aug. 2023), https://iapp.org/news/a/ai-regulatory-enforcement-around-the-world/.
985. *See supra* n. 732.
986. *See supra* n. 958.
987. Alejandro Barredo Arrieta et al., *Explainable Artificial Intelligence (XAI): Concepts, Taxonomies, Opportunities and Challenges Toward Responsible AI*, arXiv (22 Oct. 2019), https://arxiv.org/abs/1910.10045.
988. *Ibid.*
989. IBM, *IBM Research AI Fairness 360*, https://aif360.res.ibm.com/ (accessed 11 Aug. 2024).

of AI systems in real-world settings can help identify and rectify potential biases or inequities, ensuring that AI technologies contribute positively to societal well-being.

In conclusion, investment in AI R&D is essential for advancing AI governance by promoting transparency, fairness, accountability, and security in AI technologies. By prioritising research efforts in areas such as XAI, algorithmic fairness, and cybersecurity, policymakers can ensure that AI systems are developed and deployed responsibly to benefit society while minimising potential risks and harms. Collaborative efforts among governments, industry stakeholders, and academic institutions are essential to drive progress in AI R&D and establish effective governance frameworks that uphold ethical principles and protect the public interest.

11.5 CONCLUSION

The exponential rise of AI has become deeply integrated into various facets of society, ranging from healthcare diagnostics to financial algorithms. The transformative power of AI promises a future brimming with economic efficiency and improved quality of life. Nonetheless, this technological marvel is not without its potential pitfalls. Biases in algorithms can perpetuate social inequalities, while opaque decision-making processes raise concerns about accountability and transparency. Navigating this intricate interplay between AI and societal dynamics underscores the critical need for effective AI governance, requiring collaboration and coordination among policymakers, industry leaders, and civil society to address emerging challenges and safeguard collective well-being.

Understanding the multifaceted nature of AI governance is the first stitch in this intricate tapestry. Policymakers, regulators, and stakeholders must delve into the emerging trends and future challenges that define this ever-evolving landscape. Issues like algorithmic bias, privacy concerns, and the intricate dance between accountability and transparency necessitate a comprehensive and adaptable framework. Researchers across disciplines, from computer scientists to ethicists, must join forces to develop evidence-based solutions. Real-world case studies can provide valuable insights, informing policymakers as they craft regulations that strike a delicate balance, fostering innovation while mitigating risks.[990]

The journey towards effective AI governance requires a collaborative effort, a vibrant tapestry woven from the threads of diverse stakeholder engagement. Meaningful dialogue and partnerships between policymakers, industry leaders, academia, and civil society are essential for fostering consensus and driving change.[991] By harnessing the collective expertise of these stakeholders, we can develop robust and adaptable frameworks that not only address present concerns but also remain flexible enough to accommodate the rapid pace of technological advancement. Regular evaluations and

990. *See supra* n. 918.
991. Nicol Turner Lee & Samantha Lai, *The U.S. Can Improve Its AI Governance Strategy by Addressing Online Biases*, Brookings (17 May 2022), https://www.brookings.edu/articles/the-u-s-can-improve-its-ai-governance-strategy-by-addressing-online-biases/.

revisions are crucial, ensuring the frameworks stay relevant and effective in the face of continuous AI innovation.[992]

In conclusion, AI governance represents a pivotal frontier in our quest to leverage technology for the betterment of society. By embracing the challenges and opportunities presented by AI, we can pave the way for a future where innovation flourishes responsibly, risks are mitigated, and the benefits of AI are equitably distributed. Through collaborative efforts, informed policymaking, and a commitment to ethical principles, we can steer the course towards a more inclusive, transparent, and RAI ecosystem that serves the collective interests of humanity. We should acknowledge that the future of AI governance is not a pre-written narrative, but a tapestry yet to be woven. With collective action and a commitment to shared values, we can ensure AI serves as a force for positive societal transformation.

992. Partnership on AI, *White Paper: Engaging Stakeholders in AI/ML Development* (2024), https://partnershiponai.org/paper_page/1c5f463/.

Table of Cases

Index

C

D

F

www.ingramcontent.com/pod-product-compliance
Lightning Source LLC
Chambersburg PA
CBHW071242230926
51849CB00001B/194
* 9 7 8 9 4 0 3 5 3 3 4 7 6 *